BROWNFIELDS REDEVELOPMENT AND THE QUEST FOR SUSTAINABILITY

CURRENT RESEARCH IN URBAN AND REGIONAL STUDIES

Series Editor: **Steve Tiesdell**
University of Glasgow, UK
S.Tiesdell@socsci.gla.ac.uk

This new series of research monographs focuses on contemporary research in the fields of urban and regional studies and will present high-quality research monographs of particular interest to academics and policy-makers in the fields of Geography, Planning, Urban Studies, and Regional Studies. The series will especially focus on

- Economic development; communication technologies and their urban and regional impacts
- Regeneration
- Transport and travel; brownfield and contaminated land development
- Urban policy
- Urban form and morphology
- Urban governance and institutions
- Urban livability
- Urban cultural economics
- Land and property development
- Urban design
- Urban sustainability
- Globalization and its urban impacts.

Previous Volumes in the Series:

Institutions and Planning
VERMA

Bilbao: Basque Pathways to Globalization
SANTAMARÍA

Forthcoming Volumes:

Diverging Mobilities? Devolution, Transport and Policy Innovation
MacKINNON, SHAW, AND DOCHERTY

Related Elsevier Journals — sample copies available on request
Cities
Journal of Rural Studies
Landscape and Urban Planning
Land Use Policy
Progress in Planning

BROWNFIELDS REDEVELOPMENT AND THE QUEST FOR SUSTAINABILITY

BY

CHRISTOPHER A. DE SOUSA

Department of Geography, Brownfields Research Consortium, University of Wisconsin-Milwaukee, USA

ELSEVIER   Amsterdam • Boston • Heidelberg • London • New York • Oxford
Paris • San Diego • San Francisco • Singapore • Sydney • Tokyo

Elsevier
Linacre House, Jordan Hill, Oxford OX2 8DP, UK
Radarweg 29, PO Box 211, 1000 AE Amsterdam, The Netherlands

First edition 2008

British Library Cataloguing in Publication Data
A catalogue record for this book is available from the British Library

Library of Congress Cataloging-in-Publication Data
A catalog record for this book is available from the Library of Congress

ISBN: 978-0-08-045358-3
ISSN: 1745-9001

For information on all Elsevier publications
visit our website at books.elsevier.com

Printed and bound in The Netherlands

08 09 10 11 12   10 9 8 7 6 5 4 3 2 1

Working together to grow
libraries in developing countries
www.elsevier.com | www.bookaid.org | www.sabre.org
ELSEVIER   BOOK AID International   Sabre Foundation

Contents

Preface

Over the last two-and-a-half decades, policy-makers, planners, and urban researchers have been paying significantly more attention to measures designed to foster sustainable development and improve quality of life, particularly in urban areas where most of the earth's population now resides. Of the many issues that have received consideration of late, one that has gained widespread political support in the US, Canada, and other industrialized nations is the redevelopment of underused and potentially contaminated properties, commonly referred to as *brownfields*. Indeed, the hundreds of thousands of brownfields that dot the urban landscape represent the legacy of a careless past and point to a likely future unless a more sustainable approach is taken to developing our cities. That said, the plethora of brownfields also represent "opportunity spaces" for urban redevelopment and renewal. This book is about brownfields redevelopment in US and Canadian cities, and the role that such redevelopment is playing and can play in building a more sustainable urban future.

Simply put, the primary challenge faced by many policy-makers has been how to stimulate interest in, and find solutions to, the serious problem of brownfields given that such sites may contain hazardous materials (e.g., PCBs, benzene, lead, dioxins) that pose risks to human health and the environment. Interest on the part of developers and lending institutions in redeveloping potentially contaminated property tended to be minimal because they may involve high cleanup costs that limit their profit potential. Moreover, developers fear being held liable for any negative environmental effects that could be traced to the redeveloped site. However, these sites are potentially valuable because they are often located in the core sections of metropolitan areas and, as such, are prime candidates for urban redevelopment and renewal (Barnett, 1995; Bourne, 1996). It is obvious, therefore, that the brownfields issue is hardly a trivial one. Indeed, the problem it poses constitutes a major area of concern in the domain of urban and environmental planning today.

The realization that brownfields pose serious dangers came about in the late 1970s and early 1980s when pollution disasters such as Love Canal in the US and the Sydney Tar Ponds in Canada received widespread media coverage. The fact that toxic wastes were discovered in residential neighborhoods in Love Canal brought to people's attention the grave risks to human health and to the environmental integrity of a region that such sites pose; leading them to be known anecdotally, yet significantly, as "toxic time bombs" (Bullard, 1990). The public uproar over the disasters persuaded many governments to identify the nature of the risks posed by contaminated sites and then to act as quickly as possible to counteract them. Since then, the brownfields problem has become a highly visible one because of the increasing presence of numerous abandoned or underutilized industrial or commercial properties in urban areas that are suspected of being contaminated because of past activities (e.g., waste disposal, manufacturing, petroleum using services, etc.). In both countries, it has been estimated that as much as 25% of the land area in major urban centers may be potentially contaminated because of previous industrial, commercial, and transportation-oriented activities (Benazon, 1995, p. 18; Simons, 1998).

Just as important as their toxic risks is the simple fact that vacant and underutilized brownfields have become symbols of urban decay and blight that stigmatize many communities that have been left behind in a wake of deindustrialization and suburbanization. These sites often lie along waterfronts and riverfronts, and along busy highways and railways, serving as visible reminders of great pasts yet gloomy presents. Everyday, the weeds on these properties seem to grow higher, the garbage clinging to the fence accumulates, and the structures degrade as more windows are broken and more graffiti is drawn. This blight also begins to permeate into the surrounding neighborhoods, as places that once thrived on the very employment these sites provided now deteriorate under their shadow. It is little wonder then why the redevelopment of brownfields is becoming not just about managing contamination risks, but also about sparking community renewal and promoting more sustainable visions at the same time.

Understandably, policy-makers and planners are becoming increasingly anxious in getting brownfield sites redeveloped and back into productive use. In the US and Canada, this has led in the late 1990s and the early part of this century to a flurry of innovative policies and programs designed to lessen the cost and risk burdens associated with brownfields redevelopment, thus stimulating private investment in them. Such measures have met with success, as thousands of sites in both countries have been cleaned up and redeveloped over the past decade (Simons & El Jaouhari, 2001; US Conference of Mayors, 2006). However, the question remains of whether or not such redevelopment is contributing to a more sustainable future. This book synthesizes research on various aspects of brownfields redevelopment and argues that while progress has indeed been made, more still needs to be done to connect sustainability objectives and processes with public and private sector motivations to maximize sustainable development outcomes. Specifically, the book

- reviews the nature and character of the brownfields problem;
- puts brownfields redevelopment in the theoretical context of sustainable development;
- examines the public and private sector benefits and costs of urban brownfield versus traditional suburban greenfield development from a sustainability perspective; and
- examines an array of alternative end uses for brownfields, the opportunities and challenges facing the implementation of each, and the measures for overcoming these.

The research that is presented emerges largely from studies undertaken by the author over the last decade, but also incorporates research of other scholars and practitioners in the field. Given the size and complexity of the brownfields issue and the enormous amount of research and regulatory activity it has generated, it is evident that no single book on the subject can presume to be exhaustive and all encompassing. Suffice it to say that the present objective is to flesh out the link between brownfields redevelopment and its role in building a more sustainable urban future.

Structure of the Book

The book is divided into three parts. The first part is divided into three chapters that set the context and provide background information on brownfields and sustainable development.

The scope of the brownfields problem in the US and Canada, and the policies that govern redevelopment are examined in Chapter 1. This chapter defines brownfields, examines the scale of the problem in the US and Canada, briefly describes the risks to health, the environment, and to public welfare that make these sites unique in the urban landscape, and reviews several key issues, including regulatory procedures, cleanup standards, liability, and funding resources. These issues are covered in greater detail in later chapters of the book.

Chapter 2 puts brownfields redevelopment in the theoretical context of sustainable development. This chapter describes the social, economic, and environmental goals of brownfields redevelopment and outlines a broad array of indicators for guiding and tracking redevelopment from a sustainability perspective.

Chapter 3 examines the public and private sector benefits and costs of brownfield versus greenfield development in monetary terms. The chapter looks at brownfields redevelopment through the lens of the developer's pro forma (i.e., development appraisal) and discusses the quantifiable public benefits ensuing from it.

Part two examines alternative end uses for brownfields, including residential (live), green space (play), and industrial/commercial (work) redevelopment. Several chapters are devoted to each end use that set the policy, sustainability, and literature context, examine redevelopment trends and issues, and describe specific case studies in detail.

The final part consists of a single chapter summarizing the key ideas of the book and recommending ways to promote more sustainable brownfields redevelopment. Key challenges and opportunities are discussed more thoroughly, and areas for future research are highlighted.

Acknowledgments

I am deeply indebted to a number of individuals for their guidance and input on the research described in this book, as well as to several organizations that have provided research funding and the numerous public, private, and nonprofit sector stakeholders that have graciously shared their time, knowledge, and data with me over the years. The research on brownfields redevelopment in Canada was funded by various organizations, including the Consul General of Canada in Washington, DC, the Social Sciences and Humanities Research Council of Canada, the Ontario Ministry of Education and Training, and the University of Toronto. In addition to these organizations, I am truly grateful to Professors Virginia Maclaren, Larry Bourne, Sonia Labatt, Miriam Diamond, Meric Gertler, and Rodney White of the University of Toronto, and Professor G. William Page from SUNY-Buffalo, for their constructive comments and suggestions on my Canadian work.

Research on brownfields redevelopment in the US was also supported by various organizations, including the US Forest Service (North Central Research Station), the US Department of Housing and Urban Development (Urban Scholars Fellowship Program administered by the National Academies), the Sixteenth Street Community Health Center, the Greater Milwaukee Foundation, the Joyce Foundation, and the University of Wisconsin-Milwaukee's Graduate School, Center for Urban Initiatives and Research, Center for Nonprofit Management, and Consortium for Economic Opportunity.

Several colleagues have provided valuable assistance, including Marc Levine, Steve Percy, Peter McAvoy, Lynne Westphal, Dave Misky, and Laura Bray. In particular, I would like to thank Benjamin Gramling who co-directs the Menomonee Valley Benchmarking Initiative with me. I also appreciate the insights and support of many present and former students at UW-Milwaukee on various aspects of the book and research therein, including Will Sharkey, Deanna Benson, Josh Lang, Michelle Fontain, Carrie Check, Sandra Zupan, Wen Lin, Nelson Lopez, and Paul Scott. In particular, I would like to thank Lorne Platt and Kevin LeMoine for their assistance over the years. In addition, I would like to thank a number of reviewers that commented on peer-reviewed articles related to this project and the brownfields researchers in the US and UK that continue to inspire my work. The book would also not have been possible without Steven Tiesdell, the series editor, who encouraged me to put the manuscript together and offered numerous useful suggestions on how to improve it. Most of all, I would like to thank my family, particularly my wife and children, my parents and brother, and my in-laws, for all of their support and patience.

Chapter 1

Brownfields Background

In both the United States and Canada, there has been a growing interest in methods for revitalizing urban areas, improving the quality of city life, and promoting more sustainable development. In this regard, the redevelopment of the hundreds of thousands of potentially contaminated *brownfields* that blight the urban landscape has received particular attention from policy-makers, planners, and urban researchers because of the wide-ranging economic, social, and environmental benefits that such redevelopment can generate. Since the late 1970s, governments in both countries have sought to better understand the brownfields problem and develop a range of innovative policies and programs to foster redevelopment. This chapter sets the stage for the book by defining brownfields, discussing the scope of the problem, and describing how policy-making has evolved in the US and Canada to deal with the key obstacles to cleanup and redevelopment.

Defining Brownfields

To determine the scale of the problem and develop policies for managing it, a clear and unambiguous definition of the term "brownfields" is important (Alker, Roberts, & Smith, 2000; Yount, 2003). While the need for this would seem logical enough, the term brownfield has actually gone through numerous modifications as the issue has evolved. Looking back at government and media reports in the US, Canada, and Europe, the initial reference to these sites focused on the contamination issue. By definition, a *contaminated site* is generally one that has soil, groundwater, or surface water containing contaminants at levels that exceed those considered safe by regulators. The distinction was often made between *known* contaminated sites, which have undergone testing, and *potentially* contaminated sites, which are suspected of being contaminated because of their previous land use (i.e., waste disposal, manufacturing, military, petroleum-based activities, former dry cleaners, etc.) or an event that occurred at the site, such as a chemical or fuel spill. Despite this, efforts to move away from the negative connotations and liability implications associated with the label *contaminated* resulted in the use of alternative terms such as "derelict" in the UK and "brownfields" in the US.

In print, the earliest known use of the term brownfield was in the 1970s by the US steel industry, where the phrase "brownfield expansion" is employed to describe one type of process for modernizing existing steel plants (Yount, 2003). The term was generally used in economic development circles to refer to urban property, but did not specifically connote a potentially contaminated site. According to Yount (2003, p. 26), Charles Bartsch from the Northeast Midwest Institute employed the term "brownfield" during a conference on managing old industrial property, the name stuck and has been used thereafter in conferences and discussions in both public- and private sector circles throughout the United States.

The most commonly used definition of brownfield in both the US and Canada is the one posed by the federal US Environmental Protection Agency (EPA) when it formally launched its Brownfields Action Agenda (BAA) in 1995. Here, brownfields were originally defined as "abandoned, idled, or under-used industrial and commercial facilities where expansion or redevelopment is complicated by real or perceived environmental contamination." The more recent definition put forward in 2001 in the US *Small Business and Liability Relief and Brownfield Revitalization Act* (Public Law 107–118, H.R. 2869, p. 6) and signed into law in 2002 modifies the definition slightly:

> "Real property, the expansion, redevelopment, or reuse of which may be complicated by the presence or potential presence of a hazardous substance, pollutant, or contaminant."

Brownfields, therefore, refer to both *known* and *potentially* contaminated sites and, as Yount (2003, p. 32) cogently argues, the current definition employed by the federal government is "superior to others now in use in that it employs unambiguous terms and gives policymakers and practitioners flexibility to address brownfields as both environmental and economic problems."

Canada has also modified its definition over the years, from the rather expansive one put forward by the *National Round Table on the Environment and the Economy* in 1998a (NRTEE, 1998a, p. 4):

> Brownfield sites are abandoned or under-used properties where past actions have caused real or suspected environmental contamination. Although they are classified as a subset of contaminated sites, these sites exhibit good potential for other uses and usually provide economically viable business opportunities. They are mainly located in established urban areas, where existing municipal services are readily available, or along transportation corridors. They may include, but are not limited to decommissioned refineries, railway yards, dilapidated warehouses, abandoned gas stations, former dry cleaners, and other commercial properties where toxic substances may have been stored or used.

To one that is now in line with the US definition (NRTEE, 2003, p. ix):

> "Abandoned, idle or underutilized commercial or industrial properties where past actions have caused known or suspected environmental

contamination, but where there is an active potential for redevelopment."

While the term *contaminated land* continues to be used in legislative language in both Canada and the US, the brownfield term has become generally favored by both public- and private sector stakeholders because it avoids the negative connotations associated with the word *contaminated* and it constitutes a semantic counterpart to *greenfield*, the term used to refer to an agricultural or open space site located in the urban periphery. The brownfield term has been criticized for becoming too broad. Some complain that every property in an old industrial city could be considered a brownfield given that land filling, lead gasoline, waste disposal, and other human activities have likely polluted it in some way. Others also complain that there is too much emphasis on industrial and commercial land use when many residential properties can be contaminated due to leaking heating oil tanks and agricultural sites polluted by poor handling of pesticides and machinery. That said, getting a handle on the scope of the problem continues to be difficult and relies heavily on the definitions and methods used.

The Scope of the Problem

The brownfields problem is widespread in virtually every industrialized nation. Many countries have undertaken systematic, nation-wide efforts to collect, store, and disseminate information on both the whereabouts of brownfields and contaminated sites generally. Such information is useful for aiding in the identification of sites posing an unacceptable risk to human health and the environment, and for facilitating their cleanup and redevelopment. A multi-stakeholder forum that the author helped organize while with the Metropolitan Toronto Planning Department in 1997 identified the key functions of a brownfields inventory as follows:

- Lenders and insurers
  - To reduce the risk of personal liability;
  - To reduce the risk of a borrower being exposed to liability;
  - To assess the impact of sites on neighborhoods; and
  - To protect employee health and safety and protect banks from liability for their own property.
- Development review
  - To flag potentially and actually contaminated property;
  - To track cleanup approvals; and
  - To analyze data to help in economic development and project redevelopment.
- Regulatory
  - To fulfill regulatory responsibilities;
  - To prepare environmental reports; and
  - To manage government assets and avoid liability.

- Environment and health
  - To screen sites that are up for development, with an emphasis on directing public resources and protecting health and safety;
  - To allow for "informed participation" and "community awareness;"
  - To facilitate research projects examining the issue; and
  - To help promote brownfields redevelopment.

   In the US, a tiered system has come to exist over time whereby the different levels of government (federal, state, local) compile and manage different kinds of brownfields information in a complementary fashion allowing for some degree of coordination of information and management of such property. Sites that are deemed to pose the greatest risk to human health and the environment are placed on the EPA's computerized inventory system (Comprehensive Environmental Response, Compensation, and Liability Information System, CERCLIS), thus coming under the jurisdiction of the *Superfund* program (Hird, 1994). Of these, sites that exceed a designated hazardous ranking are put on the *National Priorities List*, while those that do not are assigned instead to state inventories. As of January 2007, 1,618 sites were listed on the National Priorities List (1,240 of these active, 61 proposed, 317 archived). The Resource Conservation and Recovery Act also created the RCRIS tracking system, now replaced by RCRAInfo, which tracks hazardous materials from cradle to grave and requires states to track underground storage tanks, solid waste facilities, and hazardous waste sites.

   Many states also maintain inventories of brownfield sites. The state of Wisconsin for instance, has developed the comprehensive Bureau for Remediation and Redevelopment Tracking System (BRRTS) database, which synthesizes information from an array of data sources and has been a useful tool in governmental efforts to protect public health and safety. The data collected on brownfield areas reveal whether the sites require management (open sites) or not (closed sites), the type of brownfield site (e.g., one where a spill has occurred, a leaking underground storage tank is located, etc.), whether they are considered a high, medium, or low priority, and whether land use limitations or conditions in place of deed restrictions have been placed on site following an environmental cleanup. Many states also maintain extensive records on projects involved in their voluntary cleanup programs (VCPs), although the specific data recorded often differs. A report by the US EPA (2006a) estimates that over 48,000 brownfields have already been completed under state VCPs.

   As for brownfield sites generally, the US EPA estimates that there are more than 450,000 brownfields across the country, while the US Government Accountability Office has estimated that there may be between 130,000 and 450,000 contaminated commercial and industrial brownfields. By another estimate, as many as 650,000 brownfield sites may be located throughout the country (Deason, Sherk, & Carrol, 2001). These figures typically include an array of former industrial properties, abandoned gas stations, dry cleaners, and commercial operations.

   In addition to federal and state inventories, numerous local governments have also developed their own brownfields inventories, many using funds provided in the 1990s through the BAA (Institute for Responsible Management, 1998). As with the federal and state registry programs, many local governments have developed their own approaches for classifying sites based on their hazard and/or economic development potential to better target technical assistance and government funds, as well as attract private investment. The US Conference of Mayors has surveyed munici-palities throughout the US in order to estimate the number of brownfield sites in urban areas throughout the country (2000, 2003, 2006). In 2006, 172 of the cities that responded estimated that there are as many as 23,810 extant urban brownfields, with an average size ranging from five to fifteen acres (2–6 ha) (see Fig. 1.1 for a comparison of several large US cities). Detailed research on 31 cities by Dr. Robert Simons from Cleveland State University estimates that brownfields occupy on an average 6% of a city's land area (Simons, 1998). As for the more hazardous properties on the National Priorities List, in 2002 most of the urbanized areas in the older industrial Frostbelt, for instance, had fewer than 20 such sites, except for the larger cities including Detroit, St. Louis, Chicago, and Philadelphia with 45–85 sites each.

In the early 1990s, the federal government of Canada also attempted to develop a national approach to inventorying brownfields, although the effort failed because provinces were unable to reach an agreement on the scope and potential use of a contaminated sites inventory (Auditor General of Canada, 1995). The federal government, therefore, set up a *Contaminated Sites Management Working Group* in 1995 with the mandate of gathering appropriate information only for federal lands. The Contaminated Sites Management Working Group (1997) has indicated that

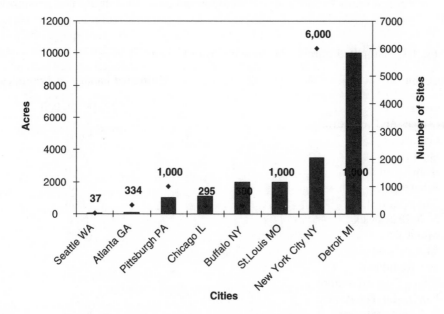

Figure 1.1: Brownfield sites in select US cities, 2006 (*Source*: data from US Conference of Mayors, 2006).

there are over 4,000 federal sites that have undergone some form of environmental site assessment. From those assessed, an estimated 2,680 contaminated sites have been identified and between 1,395 and 1,595 are suspect. Federal departments have also developed a consistent definition of contaminated sites and classify them based on the extent to which they require remedial action.

Except for the federal sites, only sporadic data can be found with regard to the situation in Canada. Estimates of potentially contaminated sites nationally range extensively from between 2,900 (NRTEE, 1996a) and 30,000 (Sisson, 1989). Tables 1.1 and 1.2 provide estimates of the number of suspected/known-contaminated sites in the different jurisdictions derived from a variety of published sources and surveys undertaken by the author.

Overall, brownfields in Canadian cities occupy an estimated 3% of urban land on average, which is less than the 6% estimated for US cities, but unsurprising given Canada's less intensive industrial history. While the overall percentage of brownfields may be small, these can still be problematic because they tend to be concentrated in specific locales within the urban core, such as former port lands or large industrial districts. Unfortunately, there does not exist a standard municipal approach for the making of brownfield inventories, with some cities reporting brownfield property only after it has "come to their attention" and been assessed and other cities basing their predictions on historic land use. The City of Montreal (Quebec), for instance, is developing a comprehensive brownfields inventory that is based on the potential risks posed by 155 former and/or current activities on properties throughout the city. As the brownfields issue begins to focus more on property redevelopment issues in addition to contamination risks, some municipal inventories

Table 1.1: Estimated number of brownfields in Canada.

Location	Estimated number of brownfields
Canada	20,000–30,000
Provinces and territories	
Ontario	3,900
Quebec	1,600
British Columbia	4,200
Alberta	10,000
Nova Scotia	1,000
New Brunswick	NA
Manitoba	1,500
Saskatchewan	71
Newfoundland	NA
Prince Edward Island	70
Northwest Territories	NA
Yukon Territories	40–50

Source: De Sousa (2001).

Table 1.2: Estimated number of brownfields in Canadian municipalities, 2004.

Municipality	Estimated number of brownfields	Estimate brownfield area (acres)	Brownfields as a % of urban area
Calgary (Alberta)	4	160	0.1
Vancouver (British Columbia)	500		5.0
Winnipeg (Manitoba)	6	500	0.5
Brantford (Ontario)	43	44	0.6
Burlington (Ontario)	1		
Cornwall (Ontario)	–	–	1.5
Hamilton (Ontario)	200		5.0
Innisfil (Ontario)	2	30	0.5
Oakville (Ontario)	20	30	0.1
Pickering (Ontario)	0	0	0.0
Toronto (Ontario)		860	0.6
Montreal (Quebec)	1,000	27,180	22.0
	1,942	28,804	3.3

Source: De Sousa (2006a).

are being maintained as property development portfolios similar to those held by real estate, rail, and other corporations to supply potential developers with relevant real estate information. That said, many local governments continue to ignore the issue and hope it goes away.

Brownfields Risks

The initial focus of policy-making efforts related to brownfields was on safeguarding public health and reducing environmental risks associated with contamination. People can be exposed to a wide range of contaminants through the ingestion of polluted soil directly or indirectly through food produced on these properties, the inhalation of airborne particulates that volatilize from the soil or abandoned chemicals, and from direct skin contact with contaminated water or airborne particulates. The contaminated soil and groundwater that may be contained in these properties can pose a wide variety of risks to human health and the environment depending on their toxic properties, and the route (mouth, lungs, or skin), duration, and quantity of exposure. Indeed, an extensive amount of research since the late 1970s has gone into studying these risks in detail, particularly those related to health given that without addressing these, redevelopment of brownfields cannot take place. According to Kolluru (1995, p. 45), the major types of health,

environmental, and public welfare risks associated with contaminated sites are as
follows:

- Health risks
  - High probability, low consequence, ongoing, chronic (human health focus)
  - *Effects/consequences*
    - Incremental cancer cases (all types of cancer)
    - Non-cancer hazards (e.g., respiratory, neurological, reproductive effects)
- Ecological/environmental risks
  - Subtle changes, complex interactions, long latency, macro-impacts (habitat/
    impact focus)
  - *Effects/consequences*
    - Species abundance and diversity
    - Habitat and ecosystem quality
    - Natural resource damage
- Public welfare/goodwill risks
  - Perceptions, property-value concerns, aesthetics (value focus)
  - *Effects/consequences*
    - Resource use restrictions (e.g., groundwater)
    - Nuisance odors, visibility impairment, aesthetics
    - Property values

Clearly, a broader sustainability approach requires addressing more than just the
health risks associated with these sites. However, our knowledge of the environmental and public welfare risks continues to evolve as research progresses.

Policy and Management

As a point-of-departure, it is important to review the policy-making measures that
have emerged in both the US and Canada since the late 1970s to deal with the key
obstacles affecting the remediation and redevelopment of brownfields. The primary
obstacles, which are also issues discussed in the European literature (European
Commission, 1996) include, the character and application of regulations, a lack of
standardized and practical cleanup criteria, uncertainties regarding liability ensuing
from environmental remediation, and funding resources available for remediation
and redevelopment. Indeed, I argue that brownfield policies and programs, both
within nations and internationally, are converging in style and content as
governments become more knowledgeable about the policies and programs best
able to deal with the primary obstacles associated with brownfields redevelopment.
This convergence has occurred with regard to dealing with contamination risks,
is now taking place in relation to promoting economic development, and must,
hopefully, converge towards more sustainable development.

United States.   The brownfields issue first came to the fore in the US in the late
1970s following such catastrophic events as Love Canal in Niagara Falls, New York

(see Box 1.1), Times Beach in Missouri, and the Valley of the Drums in Kentucky. In response, Washington passed the *Comprehensive Environmental Response and Liabilities Act* in 1980 (CERCLA, 42 U.S.C. § 9601–9675), commonly referred to as *Superfund* because the law made provisions for a specific remediation fund financed primarily by a tax on crude oil and certain chemicals for the EPA to use to cleanup property when the parties liable for contamination could not be found or were unable to pay for it. CERCLA gave the EPA and other federal agencies the regulatory authority to respond to a release or threat of a release of contamination into the environment that presented an immediate and substantial danger to public health and welfare. The legislation also enabled the federal government to recover the costs of cleanup actions from responsible parties or to cleanup sites at their own expense. In 1986, the *Superfund Amendments and Reauthorization Act* (SARA) was passed, broadening the federal EPA's mandate to include research and remediation activities and to increase state involvement in negotiating with responsible parties. The *Resource Conservation and Recovery Act* enacted in 1976 (RCRA 42 U.S.C. §§ 6901–6992k) and amended in 1986, which governs the management of non-hazardous (solid) waste, hazardous waste, and underground storage tanks, is another important federal act covering contaminated sites.

Box 1.1: Love Canal, Niagara Falls (New York)

Often considered the brownfield that started it all in the United States, the story of Love Canal actually began with the desire to create a model community. William T. Love, the namesake of Love Canal, felt that by digging a short canal between the upper and lower Niagara Rivers, power could be generated cheaply to fuel the industry and homes of his ideal community. However, fluctuations in the economy and advances in electricity transmission made his plan obsolete, and he failed in his original vision.

The site was abandoned and, eventually, the canal was turned into a municipal and industrial chemical dumpsite. While landfills can function as acceptable methods of hazardous waste disposal, they must be properly sited, managed, and regulated. Love Canal will always remain a perfect historical example of how not to run such an operation. In 1953, the Hooker Chemical Company, then the owners and operators of the property, covered the canal with earth and sold it to the city for one dollar. In the late 1950s, approximately 100 homes and a school were built on the site.

A record amount of rainfall led to the discovery that the landfill had not been properly maintained, and that concern for public health and welfare was not a priority for the chemical factory owners and operators. The lead paragraph of the headline story of the New York Times, August, 1 1978 (as referenced in Beck, 1979, p. 1) read as follows: "Twenty five years after the Hooker Chemical Company stopped using the Love Canal here as an industrial dump, 82 different compounds, eleven of them suspected carcinogens, have been percolating upward through the soil, their drum containers rotting and leaching their contents into the backyards and basements of 100 homes and a public school built on the banks of the canal".

The heavy rainfall had exposed corroded metal drums of toxic waste, buried in the backyards of homes and in the school play yard. This discovery led to then President Carter ordering a relocation of Love Canal residents in 1980. News accounts reported that President Carter declared an emergency to permit the federal government and the state of New York to undertake the temporary relocation of approximately 700 families from Love Canal. Faced with growing recognition of the cumulative evidence of exposure of Love Canal residents to toxic wastes from Hooker Chemical Company and mounting evidence of resulting health effects, the Federal government acted relatively quickly to address this public health crisis. A review by EPA's Hazardous Waste Enforcement Task Force indicated that a larger number of people in Love Canal were directly exposed to a broader range of toxic chemicals at high levels than at any other abandoned hazardous waste site in the country (US EPA, 1980). In addition, President Carter's declaration of an emergency at Love Canal was the only time this had been done for a hazardous waste site. This relocation was also made necessary by the filing of a federal lawsuit against Hooker Chemical for the damage done by the improper dumping of chemical waste.

The site was officially placed on EPA's list of hazardous waste sites needing cleanup in 1983. EPA worked with the state to cap the land to prevent rainwater from reaching the waste, built a system to clean water draining from the site, cleaned debris from the sewers and surrounding creeks, and removed polluted soil from nearby schools and residential properties. In 1984, the installation of an expanded 40-acre (16.2 ha) cap was completed. A long-term monitoring/perimeter study was implemented to evaluate the effectiveness of the leachate collection system and to assess the contaminant migration in the soil and groundwater at the site. Preliminary results indicated that pollutants have been confined to the site, while the amount of contaminated groundwater treated at the leachate treatment facility had decreased since the cap was extended. As a result of the cleanup, the site is considered safe and is being returned to productive use. The site was officially de-listed from the Superfund National Priorities List in 2004. Neighborhoods to the west and north of the canal have been revitalized, with more than 200 formerly boarded-up homes renovated and sold to new owners, and 10 apartment buildings have been newly constructed. The area east of the canal has also been sold for light industrial and commercial redevelopment (US EPA, 2004, 2006).

Within the CERCLA framework, individual state administrations are assigned responsibility for enacting and implementing their own contaminated site legislation. Minnesota was the first state to enact subsequent remediation legislation in 1989. By 1995, most of the other states had followed suit (Rogoff, 1997). The state governments have regulatory powers over remediation and redevelopment, but their regulatory practices must be consistent with federal CERCLA legislation, as well as other *Applicable, Relevant, and Appropriate Requirements* (ARARs) set out in federal law (e.g., soil, air, and water quality standards). Indeed, state cleanup activities must either *meet* or *exceed* the norms set by federal law.

Since the mid-1990s, there has been a reaction against the *Superfund* apparatus on the part of both state and federal policy-makers, because it had turned out to be cumbersome, inefficient, and costly (Stroup, 1997). Consequently, both the EPA and many state governments started addressing these inefficiencies in specific ways, which has led to a substantial increase in brownfield redevelopment throughout the US. It should also be noted that at this point both policy and discourse shifted from public health under the banner of contaminated property management to economic development and urban renewal under brownfields redevelopment.

The EPA introduced the BAA in 1995 to ignite interest in the redevelopment of brownfields. This *Agenda* contained four main components: (i) it provided funds for pilot programs to test redevelopment models and to facilitate stakeholder cooperation; (ii) it clarified the liability of prospective purchasers, lenders, property owners, and others regarding their association with a site; (iii) it fostered partnerships among the different levels of government and community representatives aimed at developing strategies for promoting public participation and community involvement in brownfields decision making; and (iv) it incorporated job development and training opportunities into brownfields efforts. In addition, the agenda put into place the administrative structures for linking brownfields redevelopment with other relevant socioeconomic issues and allowed the EPA to concentrate on the management of high-risk contaminated properties.

By June 2000, all 50 states had participated in the federal government's brownfield program. Over 45 individual states had also implemented the so-called *Voluntary Cleanup Programs*, up from 30 in 1997, to loosen the prescriptive structures that both federal and state Superfund-style legislation had imposed (Jenner, Block, Roy, & Weston Inc, 1997; Simons, 1998; Meyer & Lyons, 2000). These states have implemented policies offering more flexible cleanup options and affording the private sector more leeway to work on its own terms, while at the same time providing technical assistance, financial support, and protection from liability. However, some states, generally those with fewer sites, still maintain strict "State Superfund" programs that are more enforcement-driven and require more stringent cleanup standards to be implemented. Interestingly, the EPA remains involved in the development and operation of state VCPs, negotiating the content of VCPs with state governments, signing Memoranda of Agreement (MOA) or Memoranda of Understanding (MOU) with states to endorse many of them, and setting out basic criteria to evaluate them. Nationwide, the BAA and the VCP approach culminated in the 2002 passage of the federal *Small Business Liability Relief and Brownfields Revitalization Act* (Public Law 107–118, H.R. 2869, 2002). Unlike Superfund, which was a "top-down" regulatory program that was implemented and then revised in an iterative manner over time to address its problems, the Brownfields Revitalization Act evolved in a more "bottom-up" fashion whereby information on what worked and what did not at pilot programs implemented throughout the country trickled up and was then set into regulation.

Spurred on by the passage of the new brownfields law, EPA and many other federal partnering agencies renewed their commitment to work together in a timely manner to prevent, assess, safely cleanup, and "sustainably" reuse brownfields via the Brownfields Federal Partnership Action Agenda. The Action Agenda is a compilation of commitments, new initiatives, events, and activities that the participating federal agencies committed to undertake in partnership to help communities deal with brownfields and associated problems. Action Agenda commitments ranged from making funding and technical assistance available to brownfields communities, to changing policies to facilitate brownfields redevelopment, to launching a concerted effort to share program information with respective stakeholders (e.g., linking web sites). EPA continues to lead this effort by tracking the fulfillment of these commitments and by highlighting the progress that has been made. Over the past two years, the federal partners have made great strides toward fulfilling the commitments outlined in the Action Agenda. Successes range from the initiation of a Portfields Initiative to help cleanup and redevelop brownfields near harbors and ports, to the infusion of US$200 million in grant funds for brownfields assessment and cleanup, to holding workshops and creating websites to spread the word about brownfields redevelopment.

Overall, regulation has evolved considerably since the late 1970s to address several fundamental issues (cleanup levels, liability, and funding) and establish a stable and secure environment in which the private market can operate. Perhaps the most important issue from a health and environmental protection perspective has been the effectiveness and cost of cleanup procedures. When the contaminated sites problem first surfaced, the approaches to cleanup were as varied as they were largely ineffectual, often requiring sites to be cleaned up to "background or pristine conditions" (i.e., soil conditions that are similar to those found in remote locations or park lands) at a cost that was not feasible to investors. However, over the years, a consensus has emerged both intra-nationally and internationally that a more uniform approach to cleanup is highly desirable. Consequently, two types of criteria for evaluating the extent of soil pollution and formulating cleanup goals to protect public health and safety are currently being employed at an international scale:

(i) Generic numeric soil quality criteria: These are numerical indices that can be used for both assessment and cleanup activities derived from (eco)toxicological studies that identify levels according to a tolerable health risk. These indices can also vary according to the risks of contamination based on proposed land use (e.g., agricultural, residential/parkland, industrial).
(ii) Risk-based corrective action/site-specific risk assessment: These are procedures for developing soil and groundwater criteria that consider tolerance and risk levels associated with a specific site and/or land use to be implemented.

It is important to note that the improvement over the last two decades in both the understanding of risks posed by contaminated sites and the ability to manage those risks, has made it possible for governments and private sector stakeholders to pursue remediation and redevelopment with much more confidence and security. In the US, generic criteria and methods for risk assessment are more standardized among states because they have to be developed in a manner consistent with EPA policies and regulations. For example, the Risk-Based Corrective Action (RBCA) approach developed by the American Society for Testing and Materials (ASTM) is used by all states as a framework for developing risk-based cleanup criteria and methods. This is consistent with EPA regulations, and can be adapted to state and local legislative and regulatory practices. The review process for non-Superfund brownfields is under the jurisdiction of state governments and an important element of the Brownfields Act was the creation of the federal enforcement bar, which ensures that when a site goes through a state review program, the state becomes the primary regulator and the federal government cannot use Superfund enforcement authority over that site. Consequently, virtually all state agencies take a more active role in technical assistance and review activities; typically reviewing and approving work plans and remedial objectives put forward by the responsible party at the beginning of the remediation process and then reviewing its cleanup work for adequacy at the end. In the past, the US EPA has been reluctant to issue MOAs to states that give private parties too much control over these review functions (Simons, 1998).

Perhaps the most contentious of all brownfield issues has been liability; that is, who is liable for the cleanup of a site? How should liability be imposed/assigned? Should there be protection against liability after a site has been remediated to the standards of the day (i.e., future clause/prospective liability)? With regards to who should pay for cleanup, the debate centers around whether the polluter should pay for cleaning up old contamination, even if the release of those contaminants was legal at the time (i.e., retroactive liability), or whether the government should pay because it allowed the pollution to be released due to a lack of adequate legislation. As for imposing liability, the government typically employs two approaches. Under a *joint and several liability* system, one particular party can be held liable for the entire site cleanup, regardless of its contribution to the pollution of the site. It is then the responsibility of this party to seek recovery of funds from other responsible parties. Under an *allocated* or *apportioned liability* system, the different parties are held liable for cleanup in accordance with their individual contribution to the pollution problem. With regard to future clauses/prospective liability, the fear of those who have undertaken the cleanup task is that if standards change in the future, they will have to *reopen* the site and bear the responsibility of making the site conform to the new standards.

Under the *Superfund* legislation, the "polluter pays" principle is applied retro-actively, and the joint and several system is employed to charge those responsible for contamination. However, this system gave rise to a high amount of litigation. It has been estimated that between 30% and 70% of the US$40 billion spent on cleanup programs up to 1996 was spent on litigation (Chemistry and Industry News, 1996). Put simply, many felt that more money was being spent fighting over who should pay for cleanup than on cleanup itself. Under the BAA, the EPA has made a genuine effort to address the liability issue, even though the relevant legislation for most sites falls under the aegis of the individual states. Under the VCPs, individual states intervene only to compel parties to cleanup a site when it is deemed hazardous to public health and safety. Otherwise, cleanup activity is largely voluntary. If a cleanup is carried out properly via the state's voluntary program, the states provide *Certificates of Completion* and *No-Further Action* and/or *Covenants not to Sue* certificates that are designed to prevent future liability litigation (Bartsch, 1996; Simons, 1998). Although many states have powers to "reopen" a cleanup, a recent study by Simons, Pendergrass, and Winson-Geidman (2003) found, through a systematic inventory of VCP administrators in the US, that the incidence of reopeners was rather low. Among the 46 states with VCPs, only 12 cases were reopened out of 11,497 closed environmental cases, a reopener rate of between 0.1% and 0.2%. It should be noted, however, that "joint and several" and "strict" liability approach is still important because it sends a strong legal signal to those involved in the types of activities that may result in the creation of future brownfields to be wary of the activities taking place and perform their due diligence.

Dealing with the added cost associated with developing brownfields versus clean sites has also been a key focus of policy action. Today, all levels of government in the US offer a variety of funding sources and financial incentives to support remediation and redevelopment. From its outset, CERCLA created a trust fund to encourage the remediation of high-risk sites — initially set at US$1.6 billion dollars, it reached US$10 billion by 1990. Between 1999 and 2004, the US Congress appropriated an average of US$1.3 billion per year for the Superfund program, while the Department of Energy and the Department of Defense spent an average US$2.5 billion and US$2 billion, respectively for site remediation work (US EPA, 2004, p. 8).

EPA's Brownfields Program provides direct funding for brownfields assessment, cleanup, revolving loans, and environmental job training, awarding approximately US$150 million to communities and US$100 million to states and tribes in 2003. The EPA estimates that since its inception in 1995, investment in the Brownfields Program has leveraged more than US$6.5 billion in brownfields cleanup and redevelopment funding from the private and public sectors and created approximately 25,000 new jobs (US EPA, 2007). To facilitate the leveraging of public resources, EPA's Brownfields Program collaborates with other EPA programs and other federal partners, such as the Department of Housing and Urban Development, to identify and make available resources that can be used for brownfields activities. In addition to direct brownfields funding, EPA also provides technical information on brownfields financing matters. Virtually every state also offers a range of financial incentives for brownfields remediation and redevelopment including grants, bonds, loans, tax abatement, and/or tax credits. Many incentives are also available at the local level, including the increasingly popular Tax Increment Financing (TIF) approach whereby brownfield redevelopment projects capture the new taxes generated from the increased property value that results to repay expenses for environmental assessment, cleanup, and other eligible activities.

Canada.   Management of the environment in Canada is a shared responsibility among different levels of government. Although there is a federal *Canadian*

Environmental Protection Act, which covers most environmental issues and federal property, the ten provincial and three territorial governments were assigned primary legislative authority over the environment. Since these regional governments also have jurisdiction over property and civil right matters, it follows that contaminated sites fall largely under their legislative rubric.

In the mid-1980s, stakeholders in Canada decried the complexity, uncertainty, and variability of the regulatory systems in place to oversee remediation and redevelopment issues, favoring measures to simplify and standardize the ways in which environmental laws and standards are enacted throughout the country (NRTEE, 1996a, 1996b, 1997). Although provinces and territories are primarily responsible for environmental policy-making, they work cooperatively with the federal government via the Canadian Council of Ministers for the Environment (CCME), established in the 1980s as a coordination body in the area of policy-making. Indeed, it was through the CCME in 1989 that Canada took its first major step in dealing with the contaminated sites problem, namely, the National Contaminated Sites Remediation Program (NCSRP) — a program designed to provide both the human and financial resources to jurisdictions across the country for identifying and assessing contaminated sites, remediating high-risk "orphan sites" (i.e., abandoned sites without proprietors), and conducting research on issues such as cleanup technologies, liability policies, and remediation criteria. The CCME's Program allowed it to develop guidelines to deal with many of the latter issues. However, the regional governments have the option of *adopting, adopting and modifying*, or *not adopting* the recommendations contained in the guidelines. Encouraged by such an initiative, throughout the 1990s the provincial and territorial governments developed and/or updated their legislative apparatus pertaining to site remediation and redevelopment in a way tailored to meet their specific needs, while the federal government continued to provide sufficient resources and relevant information for policy formulation.

The cooperative relationship began to change, however, in the mid-1990s, as the federal government began downloading the responsibility for managing the environment to provincial governments (Harrison, 1996). They also allowed the NCSRP to end in 1995, despite the fact that there was still a demand for federal government assistance for dealing with contaminated sites (Auditor General of Canada, 1995). The federal government also did not pursue the development of comprehensive national legislation to deal with contaminated sites or soil management as had been done by the US and by many European countries. Rather than protest the added responsibility, most provincial governments began to take a more independent approach to developing legislation and management policies.

All the regional governments in Canada employ a regulatory approach that is generally similar to the one adopted in the US, whereby cleanup and redevelopment is held to be the responsibility of the private sector, with governments playing a regulatory role. However, the absence of federal leadership has made that role a highly variable one. For instance, in two regions — British Columbia and the Yukon Territory — a stronger regulatory approach to direct the remediation and redevelopment process was taken early on, whereby comprehensive legislation dealing with contaminated sites was developed and all aspects of the management of this process have been assigned to an overseeing environmental department. In contrast some other regions — Ontario, Alberta, Manitoba, Nova Scotia, New Brunswick, Prince Edward Island, and Quebec — initially adopted non-enforceable guidelines for cleanup and redevelopment activities, thus allowing the private sector greater leeway to regulate its own activities. Although a *Canada-Wide Accord on Environmental Harmonization*, formulated by the CCME, was ratified in 1998 by the federal government and all regions except Quebec, it has not had a major impact on the management of brownfields over and above what the CCME has already tried to achieve since 1989. Overall, however, many steps have been taken to deal with the fundamental issues related to brownfields redevelopment (cleanup levels, liability, and funding).

In Canada, the provinces and territories are responsible for developing both their own generic criteria and site-specific cleanup approach. There also exist national guidelines developed and updated by the CCME (1991, 1993, 1996, 1997) that contain both generic indices and suggestions for developing site-specific criteria. Only a few regions have adopted these outright, while most others have used these as a base towards developing criteria of their own. Cleanup criteria are in the form of legally binding standards in British Columbia and the Yukon Territory, while the other provinces initially employed more flexible guidelines that are not legally enforceable — however, not meeting or exceeding these guidelines may have liability implications for responsible parties. The variability in approaches has been a source of confusion among businesses operating in different regions and was the main factor leading some provinces, such as those in Atlantic Canada, to work together to develop a common set of generic criteria and site-specific risk assessment procedures. Interestingly, these regions based their cleanup approach on the RBCA model used in the US. Another aspect of cleanup that varies has to do with the degree of regulatory authority and mode of intervention assumed by provincial government agencies in terms of cleanup. In some provinces, an environmental agency works closely with the developer, providing technical guidance and supervision throughout the site assessment and remediation process and conducting a comprehensive review to ascertain whether the cleanup has been carried out properly. In other provinces, the environmental agencies focus mainly on the review of completed work, or the agency allows professionals to undertake remediation and to present evidence of the completed work to the agency, which may or may not review the cleanup. However, these do not protect parties undertaking remediation from future liability, thereby leaving open the prospect that they may be liable once again for cleanup if standards change.

In terms of liability, a CCME multi-stakeholder *Liability Task Group* recommended a series of legislative principles in 1993 governing contaminated sites in the hope of achieving regulatory consistency among the provinces. One of these was a version of the "polluter pays" principle, which stipulates that the person responsible for polluting the site pay to have it cleaned up. This principle was signaled out as being of paramount importance in framing contaminated site remediation policy and legislation, and has been embraced by all the provinces and territories. A second recommendation stipulated that provincial governments implement an allocated approach to imposing liability for cleanup, although only half have adopted this approach, while the other half continue to employ a joint and several approach instead. There is a general unwillingness across the country for governments to impose liability on those responsible for contamination and force a cleanup, except when the contamination at a site imposes a severe risk to human health or to the environment. Rather, governments have allowed responsible parties to cleanup sites *voluntarily* when they are transferring or developing them.

One of the primary differences between Canada and the US historically on this issue has been the limited amount of funding available for those developing brownfields. There was no formal Canadian federal government program for funding remediation or redevelopment projects until the Green Municipal Fund program administered by the Federation of Canadian Municipalities was established in 2000. This program has provided over CDN$550 million in grants and loans for various environmental initiatives including brownfields redevelopment, alternative energy, green infrastructure, and sustainability planning. In 2005, however, the federal government (Industry Canada, 2005; aboutremediation.com, 2006) announced several long-term commitments to funding brownfields redevelopment, including:

- a ten year, CDN$3.5 billion commitment to cleaning up federally owned contaminated sites;
- a ten year, CDN$500 million commitment to specific contaminated sites of concern across Canada for which it has shared responsibility (e.g., the Sydney Tar Ponds, see Box 1.2);
- CDN$550 million through Sustainable Technology Development Canada to support the development and demonstration of clean technologies for soil and water management; and
- a CDN$300 million allocation for the Green Municipal Funds, CDN$150 million of which is tagged for municipal cleanup and redevelopment of brownfields (the Green Municipal Funds have traditionally required a 50% + contribution from other project partners before funds are awarded).

Box 1.2: The Sydney Tar Ponds and Coke Ovens Site, Sydney (Nova Scotia)

Located on Cape Breton Island, Nova Scotia, the Sydney Tar Ponds and Coke Ovens site is considered to be one of the largest contaminated sites in North America. Beginning in 1901, industry brought economic opportunity to the region and steel company investors found that the Sydney property offered numerous advantages for their production needs. Local iron ore was mined to produce steel and the harbour provided a means to ship the finished product, as well as a source of water for cooling. Indeed, at one time, Sydney, Nova Scotia produced nearly half of Canada's steel (Sydney Tar Ponds Official Site of Clean Up Effort, 2006).

The factory had a variety of owners through the ensuing decades, but continued to produce steel until 2001. In 1967, a proposed plan to close the mill was met with a great deal of concern from the local government and the community due to the thousands of jobs that would be lost. Consequently, the government of Nova Scotia took over the mill and renamed it The Sydney Steel Corporation. The mining operation and coking ovens were also taken over by the government and production continued through the 1970s. It was during the 1970s that public concern intensified about environmental pollution coming from the site. Indeed, the prolonged steel production, coal mining, and coking activities had left more than a million tonnes of coal-based wastes to be cleaned up. In addition, an abandoned landfill also contributed to the toxic conditions found in the community.

The site is currently divided into several sub-areas. The Coke Ovens is a 68 ha former industrial property bounded by residential and former industrial lands. An estimated 560,000 tonnes (280,000 m^3) of soil on the Coke Ovens is contaminated with petroleum hydrocarbons, polycyclic aromatic hydrocarbons (PAHs), and metals. An additional 1,300 tonnes (1,000 m^3) of PAH contaminated sediment is present in the so-called Coke Ovens Brook, a 4.1 ha brook that runs from the Coke Ovens to the Tar Ponds, and 25,000 (12,500 m^3) tonnes of contaminated soil is also present in the in-ground tar cell. The Tar Ponds (consisting of a North Tar Pond and the South Tar Pond) is the common name for Muggah Creek, a tidal estuary that received industrial discharges from upstream industrial activities, including the Coke Ovens. The Tar Ponds cover 31 ha and contain more than 700,000 tonnes (550,000 m^3) of sediments contaminated with PAHs and metals. About 5% of the sediments (3.8 metric tonnes) also contain polychlorinated biphenyls (PCBs) in amounts greater than 50 ppm.

Progress toward cleaning up the site has been stymied over the past two decades. Plans to dredge the Tar Ponds and use a pipeline to transport the sludge to a temporary incinerator in 1986 had to be abandoned because the sludge was too thick to travel via the pipeline. A decade later, a plan to bury the Tar Ponds under slag produced from the steel mill was publicly criticized and also abandoned. In 1999, the federal government, along with provincial and municipal governments, funded an organization designed to allow for public input regarding the cleanup of the Tar Ponds. The Joint Action Group (JAG) was designed to gather information about public concerns related to cleanup, establish timelines for any plan to cleanup the site, as well as to undertake site assessments and carry out preliminary cleanup projects. This government organization has held in excess of 950 public meetings about the cleanup effort and has also commissioned more than 620 technical and scientific reports about site contamination and cleanup options, yet the site has still not been cleaned up.

In 2004, Canada and Nova Scotia signed a CDN$400 million agreement to clean the site over a ten-year-period. The plan consists of digging up and destroying the worst contaminants (PCBs and PAHs), then treating the remaining materials in place before containing them within an engineered containment system (AMEC Earth and Environmental, 2004). Environmental assessment and engineering design are expected to be accomplished by 2006, while incineration, cleanup, and capping activities are expected to last until 2013. There has been some controversy about the methods outlined in the plan for managing the site. For instance, the Sierra Club of Canada was against plans to incinerate PCB materials, while other residents want all contaminants removed from the soil and destroyed. However, the approach being taken seeks to manage contaminants in a cost effective manner.

As for the future, the Cape Breton Regional Municipality is responsible for planning land use. Preliminary visions see green space and light industrial use — however, no specific plans have been put forward.

While several provinces have a designated fund for orphan site cleanup, it is only used when high-risk sites pose a serious threat to human health and/or the environment. Most provinces also have programs directed to infrastructure, the environment, affordable housing and other issues that can provide funds for brownfields management generally. Quebec is the only province in Canada that has implemented a permanent funding program for brownfields, known as *Revi Sols*, which in its initial phase provided 50% of assessment and rehabilitation costs incurred by private developers or municipalities in Montreal and Quebec City (70% if contaminated materials were treated as opposed to landfilled). The Ontario provincial government also recently passed a measure to abate the province's share of property taxes to cover site remediation costs, as long as municipalities match the province's support. In Ontario, municipal governments are now permitted to use TIF to deal with brownfields related costs. Alberta has a program for remediating underground storage tanks and is also considering a TIF program for municipalities. In addition to having funded extensive brownfield projects on provincially owned land, British Columbia is also in the process of devising financial incentive programs for brownfields redevelopment. Overall, there are currently few incentive mechanisms in place in most provinces for attracting private investment on brownfield sites (e.g., tax incentives, revolving loan funds). Instead, local governments have been more active in providing grants, loans, and TIF programs to address brownfields costs, despite the limited funds at their disposal.

Brownfields Policy Convergence

Despite the intra-national differences in the way brownfields are managed in the US and Canada, it is clear that the degree of variability has started to diminish over the last few decades as comparable strategies are being implemented to deal with overcoming key obstacles to remediation and redevelopment. This "convergence" is due, in large part, to the fact that governments in both countries are implementing similar policies and programs to share a greater portion of the costs and risks involved in brownfields redevelopment and remediation with the private sector in an attempt to leverage investment. Indeed, this trend seems to be unfolding in predictable stages, as the policy-making efforts converge in both style and content.

The underlying factor steering the convergence of policies and programs is the realization that it is simply impossible for governments to remediate and redevelop the plethora of contaminated sites in their jurisdictions because the public will not bear all of those costs, and that this massive undertaking can only be performed and financed by the private sector in a sustainable manner over the long term. However, the remediation and redevelopment of brownfields is a costly and potentially risky proposition for the private sector, especially in North America where the availability of cheap and risk-free greenfield property is plentiful. To stimulate investment in these properties governments have, therefore, implemented policies and programs that reduce the costs and risks associated with remediation and redevelopment for the private sector.

The convergence of brownfields policies and programs has been ongoing for over two decades (see Table 1.3). It is proposed here that this trend can be characterized as unfolding in a *stage-like* fashion conceptualized as: *Cost/Risk Encounter* (stage one), *Cost/Risk Shuffling* (stage two), *Cost/Risk Awareness* (stage three), and *Cost/Risk Acceptance and Sharing* (stage four). During the *Cost/Risk Encounter* stage, governments become consciously aware for the first time of the health and environ-mental risks posed by contaminated sites and then start demanding scientific research to counteract them. In the US, this stage was set in motion by incidents such as the Love Canal in the late 1970s. Significantly, in Canada this stage occurred much later with the introduction of the NCSRP in 1989. Central governments typically take a leadership role by developing and implementing preliminary regulations designed to assess the scale of the problem, outlining cleanup goals, and funding the remediation of the most hazardous sites, while the rest of the sites are left for the private sector to deal with. The establishment of CERCLA in the US, with its extensive Superfund resources targeted to high-risk sites is a consequence of this initial stage.

In the subsequent *Cost/Risk Shuffling* stage, the different levels of government implement their own individual management approaches, with responsibility being "shuffled" among the governmental levels, on the one side, and between govern-ments and the private sector, on the other side, in an attempt to find the most workable balance between public and private costs/risks. However, it is this very shuffling that tends to cause an uneven approach to policy-making, leading to a "chill" in investment. In the US, this stage occurred in the early 1990s, as state and local governments began developing their own types of policies, criticizing federal efforts under *Superfund*. In Canada, this stage occurred, predictably, a little later in the mid-1990s as the CCME sought to develop national guidelines through the NCSRP, while at the same time provincial governments were developing their own idiosyncratic forms of policy-making.

In the following *Cost/Risk Awareness* stage, governments begin to understand and acknowledge the broader economic, environmental, and social risks associated with the problem. Scientists and policy-makers typically develop a better understanding of all the issues associated with contaminated sites and are more knowledgeable of how to devise scientific methods for remediating them in a reasonable and more affordable manner. Decades of work on the science of cleanup allows the focus to shift to economic development and the testing of alternative policies and programs by different

Table 1.3: A stage model of convergence in brownfields policy.

Policy drivers Cost/risk encounter	Cost/risk shuffling	Cost/risk awareness	Cost/risk acceptance/ sharing
– Initial encounter with the health and environmental risks posed by contaminated sites – Call for scientific investigation – Investment standstill – Central government takes on primary role	– Shifting of regulatory responsibility between different levels of government – Shifting of costs and risks among public and private sectors – Uncertainty = minimal investment	– Acknowledgment of the broader environmental, social and economic risks of inaction – Improved scientific understanding of risk – Testing of alternative policies and programs in different jurisdictions – Increased investment	– Government acceptance and sharing of financial and management risks – Harmonization of effective approaches and standards at all levels of government

jurisdictions follows in the light of the steadily growing knowledge of what works and what does not. Governments also allow private sector developers to cleanup sites voluntarily when economic conditions are suitable rather than put them in position of facing adversarial litigation. In the US, this stage coincided with the BAA in 1995 and the various state programs, which acknowledged the broader scope of the problem and sought to develop and test regulatory and economic tools capable of balancing public sector concerns with private sector needs (e.g., the implementation of VCPs by more and more states over the past few years). This stage is ongoing in most regions in Canada, with some regions (e.g., British Columbia and Quebec) experiencing greater progress than others are.

In the latter *Cost/Risk Acceptance and Sharing* stage, policy-makers and developers begin accepting and sharing the management and financial risks associated with remediation and redevelopment. With a better understanding of what works, policy-makers at all levels of government begin to actively harmonize cost/risk sharing approaches and policies that have proven to be effective at limiting costs and risks. The US has entered this stage, as federal, state, and local governments have started en masse accepting responsibility for more of the financial, legal, and management risks associated with brownfields. The harmonization process culminated in the passage of the *Small Business Liability Relief and Brownfields Revitalization Act* (Public Law 107–118, H.R. 2869, 2002). Canada as a nation is still working on this stage, but many provinces have moved to accept risks associated with cleanup by offering an array of what are now considered standard cleanup methods. Some are also assisting with financial risks as well.

Conclusions

Overall, the evolution of brownfields policy over the last 25 years has followed a typical "incrementalist" path. Put forward by Charles Lindblom (1959, 1980), the "disjointed incrementalism" theory maintains that policy-making occurs in brief stages through a process of mutual adjustment among a multiplicity of actors, each having different self-interests and divergent conceptions of the public interest (Hayes, 1992). Furthermore, because rational decisions are limited by a variety of factors, including different values, the lack of reliable information, time constraints, and the lack of consensus among stakeholders, it is proposed that changes will occur gradually through a process of feedback, or "successive approximations," as experience with minor policy changes gives rise to new demands for modification or expansion of existing policy. This demand then sets off another policy cycle that involves identifying a new problem, adopting policy and implementing it.

Using the US situation as a case-in-point it is possible to trace the incremental evolution of contaminated lands policy. The growing fear of hazardous waste and the lack of knowledge regarding the risks it posed in the 1970s led to increased calls for government action on the contaminated sites issue. Faced with massive remediation issues and costs, the US government proceeded to enact CERCLA legislation in 1980. In the late 1980s and early 1990s, information regarding cleanup and risk management improved and political attention turned toward economic development issues. As the values changed among the policy actors and information became more accurate on the risks associated with contaminated sites, CERCLA regulation was largely replaced by the BAA in 1995. The BAA was not actual legislation, but a program that was itself constantly evolving incrementally and producing multiple tools for dealing with the costs and risks associated with brownfield redevelopment, particularly those related to liability and funding. This ultimately led to the *Small Business Liability Relief and Brownfields Revitalization Act* (Public Law 107–118, H.R. 2869, 2002).

Given the rising interest in sustainable urban development in both the US and Canada, future policy will continue to move incrementally towards cost/risk sharing that seeks to address sustainability goals more broadly, as opposed to contamination issues and economic development ones specifically. While sustainability arguments already have been used to lend support to implementing policies for stimulating brownfields redevelopment, as will be discussed in greater depth in the following chapter, this next phase will "raise the bar" on brownfields redevelopment at both site-specific and regional scales by tying policy, programming, and funding more closely with marked sustainability objectives and outcomes. Indeed, future brownfields efforts will move forward in this direction by "riding" the success of previous efforts, building upon multi-stakeholder networks that have been established, and celebrating projects that are visible symbols of a more sustainable future. As a culture, we are fascinated by stories and TV shows where derelict homes and depressed lives have been transformed via renewal efforts — why should brownfields be any different.

While a more pessimistic view is that brownfields redevelopment will turn into just another real estate deal with a green twist, the policy evolution and convergence that has already been witnessed in the US and Canada leads one to be more optimistic that future brownfields efforts will not be stuck in a state of policy inertia. The network of shared common goals and values supporting more sustainable development have already lent their support to brownfields redevelopment and will continue to do so as more of these projects point the way to a more sustainable future. The next chapter goes into greater depth on this linkage between brownfields redevelopment and sustainability in terms of the barriers, opportunities, and parties involved.

Chapter 2

Brownfields and Sustainable Development

As discussed in the previous chapter, the overarching objectives associated with the management of brownfields and contaminated lands have evolved since the late 1970s, shifting from an initial focus on managing health and environmental risks to developing and implementing mechanisms for stimulating economic development and maximizing financial returns. As our ability to manage the risks and costs associated with brownfields improves and the perception of these sites improves among developers and consumers, more and more stakeholders are seeking to "raise the bar" on redevelopment in an effort to achieve a broader range of environmental, social, and economic objectives as specified under the rubric of sustainable development (SD). While many SD objectives can be realized through efforts to stimulate urban redevelopment and renewal generally, implementing policy to tie sustainability and brownfields redevelopment is of particular interest because of the fact that these sites have tended to be the least favored of urban lands due to their costs, risks, and blight effect. This chapter provides background on SD and then puts brownfields redevelopment into a sustainability context by outlining the barriers, opportunities, and stakeholders involved from a broader socio-economic and environmental point of view. An expansive set of criteria and benchmarks for tracking the link between brownfields and sustainability are then put forward and discussed, along with a case study of a benchmarking initiative being carried out to track the sustainable redevelopment of Wisconsin's largest brownfield district.

Sustainable Development

Since the mid-1980s, SD has become a widely embraced approach for integrating environmental needs with economic and social ones in human development. The World Commission on Environment and Development (1987, p. 3) characterizes the goal of SD as "development that meets the needs of the present without compromising the ability of future generations to meet their own needs." The crux of the SD approach is to be found in the concept that SD can be attained without compromising the environment, suggesting ways in which a balance and inter-connectedness can be maintained among the environmental, social, and economic requirements of human societies (Haughton & Hunter, 1994). In effect, SD entails that development must attempt to coordinate the protection of ecosystems with a guarantee of basic social rights (from health care to cultural expression) and with the provision of an economic system that will have a limited impact on the natural and social spheres. SD also works at multiple scales as evidenced by the wide range of indicators that have been devised to track progress at the global, national, regional, neighborhood, and site-specific levels.

It is at the urban level where the environmental, social, and economic dimensions of development often clash and vie for prominence. As more and more people live in cities and they continue to expand topographically, demographically, and economically, it is becoming clear that an SD approach is necessary to help guard against poverty, social inequality, and environmental degradation. Sustainable urban development (SUD) is a derivative of the more general SD approach that seeks to make urban development

- more productive, stable, innovative, and equitable economically;
- more capable of catering to social needs, especially in the areas of health services, and to preserving social values, traditions, heritage, and culture; and
- more sensitive to ecosystems and, thus, have minimal or at least controllable impacts on the natural environment.

The dominant finding of the SUD literature early on was that the proper management of the city's *urban form* and the preservation and reutilization of its built environment (i.e., its land, buildings, and infrastructure) is a necessary step toward achieving SD (Stren, White, & Whitney, 1992; Haughton & Hunter, 1994; Barnett, 1995). In the 1990s, policy-makers, planners, and environmentalists turned their attention in tandem to the role of *urban form* in breaking the destructive pattern of urban sprawl in North American cities, which had led to a serious underutilization of city lands, buildings, and infrastructures (e.g., Calthorpe, 1993; Haughton & Hunter, 1994; White, 1994; Bourne, 1996; Ewing, 1997). Burchell, Shad, Listoken, and Phillips (1998, pp. 6–8) put forward the characteristics of urban sprawl as follows:

- low density;
- unlimited and non-contiguous (leapfrog) outward extension of development;
- spatial segregation of different types of land uses;
- consumption of exurban agricultural and other frail lands in abundance;
- almost total reliance upon the private automobile as a means of assessing individual land uses; and
- a lack of integrated land use planning and fragmented governance authority and capacity.

The consequences attributed to urban sprawl have been extensive, ranging from the decay (and even demise) of the economy of the inner city, to the growing segregation of minorities, and to an increase in automobile-generated air pollution. To counteract sprawl, those seeking to attain SUD have advocated for more compact urban form with higher residential densities, enhanced employment opportunities, greater access to public transportation, and mixed land use activities. Such goals could be achieved by encouraging redevelopment in older and already built-up urban areas, whether through the intensification of existing land use activities or the redevelopment of vacant or underutilized brownfields (Great Lakes Commission, 2001).

In terms of the link between urban form and the economic integrity of urban areas, supporters of SUD call for an urban form that is more economically efficient to administer, and more able to provide adequate economic opportunities to its citizens. The main argument put forward in support of a more compact urban form is that it will increase the efficiency of existing services and reduce the need for expensive new ones, such as roads, sewers, water treatment and supply systems, public utilities, fire protection, and police. Empirical studies conducted in cities throughout the world have come forward to support more compact urban form, finding that the capital, operating, and indirect costs of both "hard" and "soft" services are correlated with population density and patterns of urban development (Blais & Berridge Lewinberg Dark Gabor Ltd, 1995; IBI Group, 1995a, 1995b; Persky & Wiewel, 1996; Ewing, 1997). Reviewing the data from nine major studies undertaken between 1950 and 1980, Frank (1989) argued that residential development costs related to sprawl were significantly more expensive (US\$35,000 per unit) than they were for compact development, and that these costs could be reduced primarily by locating near facilities and employment centers, by building various housing types, and by planning for contiguous development. Environmentalists are particularly interested in findings related to avoiding externality costs imposed by transportation (health effects, morbidity levels, etc.). In addition, compact urban form is often perceived to foster an increase in productivity and a reduction in the time costs of doing business by enhancing interaction among companies and facilitating the movement of goods. Relevant research has also found that compact urban form is also capable of stemming the outflow of wealth from the inner city to the urban fringe (Bourne, 1995) and allows for greater mixing of land uses, which helps promote social justice by giving all members of society better access to economic resources (Haughton & Hunter, 1994, p. 17).

As for social equity, there exists substantial data in the relevant literature to suggest that more compact urban form tends to promote greater diversification of land use and housing, which enhances social equity — thus ensuring safer and more economically flexible social ambiance (Isin & Tomalty, 1993). Cities that are more compact tend to promote a wider-mix of housing types, which in turn makes it more likely that the housing needs of a broad range of citizens (e.g., two-parent families, single parent families, singles, empty nesters) can be met and that housing can be made more affordable. The literature also suggests that more compact form makes accessibility to services and employment opportunities much more realizable, particularly for the young, elderly, and the poor (Ewing, 1997).

A focus of the research on the relation between SD and urban form has been motivated by environmental factors, such as the loss of open space and agricultural lands in the periphery, and the increase in energy costs and air pollution. Surveys of relevant studies reveal that over the last 30 years, urban development has tended to spread largely into prime agricultural land regions, and those places that have tried to grow more compactly have had some success in preserving such regions (from 15% to 60%) (Isin & Tomalty, 1993; Ewing, 1997). As for the link between form and energy consumption, the most frequently cited study is the one by Newman and Kenworthy (1989) that tested for the presence of causal relationships between levels of gasoline consumption and factors such as income, gas prices, car ownership, city size, and population density in a cross-section of 32 large cities — 13 in Europe, 10 in the US, 5 in Australia, 3 in Asia, and 1 in Canada. The authors compiled transportation data over a five-year period and found only a slight correlation between most of the above factors and fuel-consumption levels. The only exception was urban population density, explaining about 60% of the variability. The authors thus reach the following conclusion (Newman & Kenworthy, 1989, p. 29): "we would suggest that urban structure, directly under the control of physical planners, is central to explaining the patterns in gasoline use and automobile dependence." The data that the researchers compiled from New York City showing how fuel consumption declined as density increased (i.e., outer-area density 5.3 persons per acre and gasoline use 454 gallons per capita, versus inner area 43.3/153, and central city 101.6/90), lead them to recommend that to promote energy efficiency planners implement policies to

- increase urban density,
- strengthen the city center,
- extend the proportion of a city that has an inner-area land use,
- provide an efficient transit option,
- restrain the provision of automobile infrastructure, and
- improve pedestrian and cycling infrastructure (Newman & Kenworthy, 1989, p. 33).

The link between sustainability and urban form, however, is not without its critics. Gordon and Richardson (1996) for instance, found no significant statistical link between vehicular trip frequency and population density, while a study by Breheny, Gordon, and Archer found a weak link between density and transportation energy use (Neuman, 2005). In addition, May and Scheuernstuhl (1991) present data suggesting that a more transit-oriented urban form does not necessarily correlate with reduced levels of automobile use and energy consumption. As for health and well-being, many believe that high density causes emotional stress and other negative psychological conditions.

Overall, the study by Burchell et al. (1998), which constitutes by far the most comprehensive review of the ideas and arguments concerning sprawl in the US (approximately 475 citations are examined), provides a checklist of the alleged negative and positive impact areas associated with sprawl or with the specific characteristics thereof:

- public–private capital and operating costs (e.g., sprawl allegedly imposes higher infrastructure costs, higher public operating costs, etc.);
- transportation and travel costs (e.g., sprawl allegedly imposes more vehicle miles traveled, more automobile trips, etc.);

- land and natural habitat preservation (e.g., sprawl allegedly imposes loss of agricultural land, reduced farmland productivity, etc.);
- quality of life (e.g., sprawl allegedly imposes more air pollution, higher energy-consumption, etc.); and
- social issues (e.g., sprawl allegedly fosters spatial segregation, suburban exclusion, etc.).

Based on their synthesis, Burchell et al. then seek to determine (i) whether or not the impacts identified by the relevant literature actually emerge in a sprawl situation, (ii) if so, whether or not the sprawl is the generating factor of the impact, and (iii) to what extent there is consensus in the literature vis-à-vis (i) and (ii). The authors were able to determine that there were 27 negative impacts associated with sprawl, and only 14 positive ones. Overall, the value of the Burchell et al. study is that it established that there is generally more agreement in the literature with regard to the fact that sprawl is the source of increased public and private capital and operating expenditures, travel and transportation costs, and negative impacts on social issues. However, they found that there is less agreement that sprawl is a source of negative impacts on quality of life and on land/natural habitat conditions.

In a recent paper, Neuman (2005, p. 15) describes the basic paradox of the compact city as the "inverse relation of the sustainability of cities and their livability." That is, "for a city to be sustainable the argument goes; functions and population must be concentrated at higher densities. Yet for a city to be livable, functions and populations must be dispersed at lower densities." While many large cities in both the US and Canada are considered very livable and are growing in population (e.g., Vancouver, Chicago, Toronto, San Francisco), the move of wealth from many cities to the suburbs does lend some support to this paradox. Neuman goes on to argue that conceiving a city in terms of form is neither necessary nor sufficient to achieve the goals ascribed to the compact city. Instead, conceiving the city in terms of process holds more promise in attaining the elusive goals of a sustainable city. Indeed, this shift in focus from "form" to "process" has been emerging in the sustainability and brownfields arenas for several years now as seen, for instance, in the change in discourse from a focus on the "quantity" of redevelopment to the contribution of redevelopment to improving quality of life generally. More important than changing policy discourse is changing the fact that people often prefer lower density residential communities characterized by sprawl. As Williams (2004, p. 51) notes for the UK "big questions arise from evidence surrounding the extent to which mechanisms set out to achieve the urban renaissance match people's desires in terms of lifestyle, because there is undeniably a mismatch."

According to Adams and Watkins (2002), writing from a land use perspective, linking SD to broader quality of life objectives has several implications: (i) the presumption that SD can improve environmental quality and human welfare at the same time, which is in contrast to the doom-laden environmental discourse of the past; (ii) the contradictions at the local level between economic development and environmental protection; and (iii) the gross oversimplification that brownfield development is necessarily always sustainable and greenfield development is unsustainable. The authors go on to discuss the difference between strong definitions of sustainability, which call for more rigorous environmental protection via an ecosystem approach, versus weaker definitions, which allow more flexibility for linking various economic, social, and environmental interests. It should also be noted that to critical geographers, the term sustainability is simply a buzzword that allows us to paint a green face on gentrification and displacement-oriented processes. It is these implications that require greater attention from researchers — that is, can SD improve environmental quality and human welfare at the same time? What are the contradictions at the local level between economic development and environmental protection and can these be overcome? Is brownfield development more sustainable than greenfield development? How can brownfields redevelopment be made more sustainable?

While the debate over form has and will continue to rage for decades, the simple fact of the matter is that many urban areas in the United States, Canada, and in Europe have faced decades of deindustrialization and neglect, which requires us to consider redevelopment in terms of both form and process, as well as quantity and quality (Beatley, 2000). The brownfields left over from deindustrialization provide an opportunity to address these considerations under the auspices of sustainability.

Brownfield Redevelopment through the Lens of Sustainability

If SD is defined as development that meets the needs of the present without compromising the ability of future generations to meet their own needs, then the presence of contaminated land and brownfields represent a good example of how past activities have come to compromise this generation. Indeed, for many communities brownfields have become quite visible symbols of what happens when economic growth does not occur within a sustainability framework (Platt, 1998; Bjelland, 2004). Below, the challenges, objectives, and stakeholders associated with brownfields redevelopment are contextualized via the three-way lens of sustainability.

Brownfields and Sustainability: Challenges

The challenges associated with brownfields and their redevelopment, whether they are perceived or real, can be captured broadly through the three-way lens of sustainability. These challenges typically consider the negative impact of brownfields on community quality of life, the difficulties they pose as locations for new development (which ultimately influences the value of rent or sale price that can be attained) and the obstacles encountered during the redevelopment process (which influences the cost of redeveloping a particular site). From a general economic perspective, brownfields tend to suffer from high costs associated with assessment and cleanup and tend to generate lower returns in terms of rent or market value. As such, many sites generate little or no property tax revenue for local municipalities, which ultimately affects the municipality's ability to deal with them. While off-site infrastructure may be available, the on-site infrastructure present at many brownfields is often in poor condition. From an environmental perspective, the known or suspected presence of contamination continues to be the primary concern for developers, governments, and members of the community. For many, these sites are also perceived as being environmentally impaired areas where ecological renewal is futile. From a social perspective, brownfield sites, especially those clustered in industrial districts, are often perceived as pockets of high crime, poverty, and blight.

In the first chapter, three key challenges associated with redeveloping brownfield sites were examined (cleanup requirements, liability issues, and financial costs), but many studies have been carried out over the last decade to identify and prioritize the broader array of challenges imposed by brownfields and affecting their redevelopment from both a private and public perspective. One study carried out by the author in the late 1990s asked private sector stakeholders involved in brownfields redevelopment in Ontario, Canada to rank a list of obstacles according to a suggested scale — as *non-obstacle* (= 1 point), *moderate obstacle* (= 3 points), or *severe obstacle* (= 5 points) — with respect to how they are perceived to affect brownfield project costs and risks (see Table 2.1 for interviewee responses) (De Sousa, 2000). In that study, the liability issue was perceived as the most severe

Table 2.1: Private sector challenges associated with brownfield redevelopment.

Category	Potential obstacles	Average scaling
Moderate–severe obstacles (rounded off to 4)	Liability concerns	4.3
	High remediation costs	3.7
	Slow regulatory review process	3.7
	Complex municipal land use policies	3.6
Moderate obstacles (rounded off to 3)	Stringent remediation requirements	3.4
	Uncertainty related to the site-specific risk assessment	3.4
	Lack of government incentives	3.2
	Obtaining project financing	3.1
	Lack of knowledge/negative attitude on the part of the public	3.0
	Lack of knowledge/negative attitude on the part of stakeholders	3.0
Low–moderate obstacles (rounded off to 2)	More contamination than expected	2.4
	Potential impacts to adjacent properties	2.3
	High costs of insurance	2.2
	Lack of information on the history of sites	2.1
	Lack of remediation or disposal options	1.3

Source: De Sousa (2000).

obstacle, adding to project risks and costs, both directly (e.g., through higher legal fees) and indirectly (e.g., through reduced land values and time delays during the review process). Those interviewed also emphasized that, because they lengthen the redevelopment process, regulatory mechanisms continue to constitute serious obstacles to redevelopment projects, despite efforts to streamline them. The *moderate obstacles* identified and ranked by the private sector interviewees pertained mainly to policy (i.e., overly stringent remediation requirements, uncertainty regarding the application of RBCA), financing (i.e., lack of governmental incentives in Canada, difficulties obtaining financing), and property perception factors.

It should be noted that the challenges to redevelopment have changed over time as policies to manage them are introduced and as private sector stakeholders carry out more brownfield projects and become more familiar and comfortable with them. A good example of this is the downgrading of liability as a concern due to the implementation of better protection for those completing remediation.

In addition to the redevelopment challenges, many businesses also associate brownfields with various problems such as old infrastructure and buildings, high traffic, vandalism, pollution, litter, and other negative perceptions that reduce their attractiveness to customers. Table 2.2 lists the results of a business survey carried out in the Menomonee Valley, Wisconsin's largest brownfield district, in which respondents were asked about the disadvantages associated with the area.

The 2006 study of US cities carried out by the US Conference of Mayors identified similar impediments to brownfields redevelopment from a public sector government perspective. The most frequently identified impediment (156 cities/87%) was lack of cleanup funds, followed by the need for environmental assessments for brownfields sites (110 cities/61%) and liability issues (97 cities/54%). Indeed, these three areas of concern have been consistently identified in the last three surveys carried out by that organization (see Figure 2.1 for a list of impediments identified in the 2003 survey).

In a survey carried out by the author in 2003, over 400 people who were using and/ or residing near several brownfields-to-green space projects were asked what each site was like prior to redevelopment and what impact it had on the community (De Sousa, 2006c). Interestingly, most respondents (27.9%) said that they did not remember what had been there before the park was constructed, with some of those pointing out that they just did not go to the area until people told them about the "transformation" that had occurred. The next most frequent response was that the sites were "ugly, dirty, and dumpy" areas that were pretty much off limits. Homelessness, gangs, and crime were associated with all sites, but only by less than 10% of the sample. Interestingly, the brownfield site that did not contain derelict structures was remembered more positively as an unused empty area or as an unmaintained "natural wilderness" area, with fewer people having negative memories.

As for the perceived impact the site had on the community before the brownfield project was undertaken, one in four of those who responded, stated that they did not know. The most common problems put forward were that the site was not good for the community, it attracted crime and homelessness, constituted an eyesore, or was

Table 2.2: Challenges associated with underutilized brownfield locations for business.

Disadvantages	Frequency
Crime	9
Taxes too high	7
Poor access to business by customers	6
Parking	5
Traffic	5
Hard for customer to find	4
Retail/administrative changes in valley	4
Distance from customer base	3
Environmental hazards — poor water quality	3
City of Milwaukee restrictions	3
Vandalism/homelessness	3
State of disrepair	2
Foundation costs	2
Lack of expansion space	2
Aging buildings	2
Bad odor	2
Limited work force	1
Too much new reconstruction	1
Small city population	1
Lack of neighborhood	1
Seagulls	1
Access to freeways after reconstruction (13th St. exit)	1
Limited restaurants and shops	1
Flooding	1
Poor work force	1
Poor access to public transit	1

Source: Adapted from Menomonee Valley Benchmarking Initiative, Milwaukee, 2002.

perceived as dangerous and frightening. Interestingly, only two respondents mentioned concerns related to the cleanup of contaminated soil.

One brownfield challenge that has received more attention in the US of late is environmental justice. Environmental justice, by definition, calls for no community to be subject to a disproportionate amount of environmental hazards such as toxic emissions or excessive noise from factories, airports, highways, and other facilities. Various studies have noted that brownfield sites and other environmental hazards are indeed concentrated in communities of color and other low-income areas (Leigh & Coffin, 2000; Bullard, 1990; United Church of Christ, 1987; Agyeman, 2005, p. 1; NEJAC, 1996, p. 9; Jones & Rainey, 2006, p. 492; McCarthy, 2006).

In addition to the location of brownfields, issues related to their redevelopment are also becoming important because of the role they can play in reversing patterns of

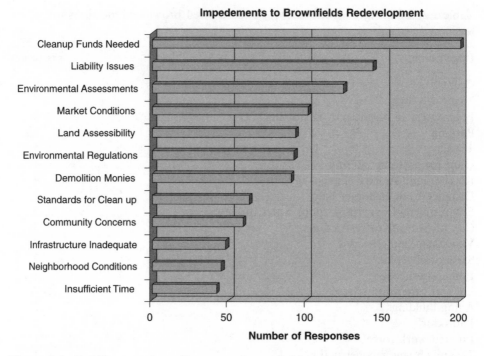

Figure 2.1: Public sector impediments to brownfields redevelopment. *Source*: Data
derived from US Conference of Mayors (2003).

neglect in inner-city neighborhoods. The question then becomes: Is brownfield
redevelopment being carried out in poor neighborhoods? And, if so, is government
funding for brownfield redevelopment going into poor neighborhoods? An
evaluation of the Environmental Protection Agency (EPA)'s Brownfields Assessment
Pilot Program found that the agency is working its way toward environmental justice
by disproportionately awarding grants to the most economically distressed cities with
a significantly higher rate of non-white populations, unemployment, infant death,
serious crime, etc. (Solitare & Greenberg, 2002). In a case study of Milwaukee,
Wisconsin, however, McCarthy identified that census tracts with above average
percentages of African Americans and Hispanics, although containing above average
numbers of brownfields per square mile and higher percentages of brownfields
compared to percentage of the city's area (2006), had below average city-assisted
redevelopments as a percentage of all brownfields (2007). Besides funding allocation,
the actual accomplishments of these programs in terms of achieving environmental
justice is difficult to assess given that, as Solitare (2001) notes, the concept of
environmental justice is not clear-cut, but multi-layered and requires addressing and
tracking outcomes on the basis of multiple environmental (i.e., a balance between
benefits and burdens, better environmental health/overall improvement in the quality
of life), economic (i.e., number and type of jobs, an increase in the tax base, an
improvement in infrastructure and education), and procedural factors (i.e., the

empowerment of the disenfranchised, the legitimatization of community perceptions, community-based planning, the increase of minority participation in decision-making). Indeed, the need to understand and track the capacity of brownfield redevelopment to achieve these factors is in line with the multiple lenses of sustainability.

Brownfields and Sustainability: Opportunities

For both public and private sector stakeholders, the decision to become involved in or to invest in brownfields is influenced by an array of economic, social, and environmental factors. While economic factors are often considered the primary motivation of private sector stakeholders, the author's study revealed a range of environmental and social factors motivates them as well (see Table 2.3).

As these results show, the decision by private sector stakeholders to invest in brownfield redevelopment is motivated primarily by economic factors, which were ranked as most important by the interviewees overall. Although the pattern of responses on the part of landowners was similar to that of developers, the

Table 2.3: Private sector motivating factors for brownfield redevelopment.

Motivating factors identified by interviewees	Frequency
Economic	
To maximize profit at the site by building a marketable new project or selling the property to yield a maximum return	15
To divest liability risks/costs	10
To act on the growing popularity of the downtown urban location	9
To take advantage of devalued brownfield property costs	6
To avoid high development charges levied by peripheral municipalities	6
To create jobs	3
To restore the tax base of government	3
Environmental	
To conform with environmental regulations	7
To protect public health and safety	6
To restore the environment	2
To reduce development pressure on greenfield sites	2
To protect soil and groundwater resources	2
Social	
To renew urban cores	4
To remove negative stigmas from affected communities	3

Source: De Sousa (2000).

landowners focused more attention on liability attenuation as the most important factor. The interviewees also identified and ranked five environmental factors, of which two turn out, in effect, to be economically motivated — namely: remediating the site to avoid any potential government intervention, and protection of public health and safety to limit liability risks.

The 2006 survey conducted by the US Conference of Mayors provides a picture of the potential benefits associated with brownfields redevelopment from a public sector perspective. Neighborhood revitalization was the most frequently cited benefit (140 cities/80%), followed by increasing the city's tax base (139 cities/79%), job creation (132 cities/75%), and environmental protection (109 cities/62%). While these are considered the top priorities, an examination of the brownfields literature reveals a much broader list of public benefits associated with brownfields redevelopment:

- Environmental benefits
  o Reduction of development pressure on greenfield sites
  o Protection of public health and safety
  o Protection of groundwater resources
  o Protection and recycling of soil resources
  o Restoration of former landscapes and establishment of new areas deemed to have ecological value.
- Social benefits
  o Renewal of urban cores, improving the quality of life in them
  o Elimination of the negative social stigmas associated with the affected communities by revitalizing them
  o Reduction of the fear of ill health, environmental deterioration, and shrinking property values in these communities.
- Economic benefits
  o Attraction of domestic and foreign investment
  o Restoration of the tax base of government, especially at the local level
  o Increased utilization of and reinvestment in existing municipal services
  o Development of remediation/decontamination technology.

A better understanding of the range and scope of these benefits is essential from a policy perspective because it helps justify the public administrative costs and the funding for brownfields policies and programs. Knowledge of monetary benefits is of particular interest and is examined in the next chapter.

Interestingly, little effort has gone into examining the perceived or realized benefits of brownfields redevelopment from the perspective of affected communities or those using these sites once they are redeveloped. As part of the author's brownfields-to-green space interviews, respondents were first asked about the *personal* impacts of these projects in an open-ended manner and then *community* impacts in a closed manner to more directly gauge their opinions on a list of 21 items adopted from the literature on quality of life and sustainable communities (Gobster, 1995; Gobster & Delgado, 1992; Maclaren, 1996, 2001; Tyler Norris Associates, 1997; Leitmann, 1999; Shafer, Lee, & Turner, 2000). The most noted *personal* benefits included physical activity (27.3%), children's play (20.4%), scenic beauty (19.7%), relaxation (17.6%), and access to nature (8.6%). Some also listed social interaction (6.1%) and providing "something to do" (6.1%) as key benefits. The majority of respondents pointed out personal benefits associated with aesthetics, physical fitness, and social interaction, as opposed to economic-oriented ones (e.g., economic stimulus 0.6%, higher real estate values 0.6%). As for community implications, the primary factors identified included scenic beauty, trails for walking, neighborhood appeal, natural areas, access to recreational areas, community pride, blight removal, and personal fitness (see Chapter 5 for a more comprehensive discussion of the results). Interestingly, those surveyed who never visited the parks (4% of respondents) but lived in the adjacent community also felt that it had a positive impact on many quality of life factors, particularly scenic beauty, trails for walking, neighborhood appeal, access to recreational areas, and property values.

Brownfields and Sustainability: Stakeholders

Stakeholders in the brownfields process are those directly or indirectly affected by a brownfield, have an interest in the actions taken therein, or see an opportunity presented by these sites. While some see these narrowly in terms of the typical parties involved in real estate development, a sustainable vision requires a broader perspective.

Typical "economic" stakeholders. *Landowners* The owners of brownfields property are faced with a number of issues. The primary one is liability for conditions on their property. Some brownfields owners are reluctant to have their properties assessed for fear of discovering environmental contamination or concern over quantifying contamination levels. Indeed, the owner will then be responsible for cleanup costs, whether by paying for them directly or by reducing land costs to cover the estimated remediation cost. Landowners also fear the stigmatization of their property, which can cause a reduction in land values even if contamination is minimal or non-existent. In a survey conducted by the author in Milwaukee, several interviewees complained that the tendency of many landowners to "stick their head in the sand" and ignore the problems at their site is a major impediment to redevelopment (De Sousa, 2005). There is also a fear that adjacent landowners might try to blame their own environmental problems on the property. At the same time, some landowners are holding on to their land while they wait for land values to increase. This is posing a particular challenge in many older industrial districts seeking to implement area-wide renewal strategies that are hindered by blighted properties that will not cooperate in the renewal process.

Developers The primary objective of developers is to make a profit and maximize their financial returns. All costs and risks must be considered in calculating a project's return. It is the aggregate cost of assessment, cleanup, demolition, legal advice, and interest from added time delays that must be offset by other reduced costs, as well as profits, if the private redevelopment effort is to succeed. While many developers tend to stick to a standard formula for making profits in the suburbs, more and more developers are "trying their hand" at brownfields redevelopment because they are interested in adding it to their portfolio of projects and many also see the market improving for such property.

Lenders   Lenders are primarily concerned with protecting their investment in a project and avoiding environmental liability. Lenders are particularly interested in making sure that brownfields are properly appraised to reflect the cost implications related to contamination so that these can be reflected in the lending package. In both Canada and the US, banks and lending organizations were at the forefront of the brownfields issue, and pushed to shift the focus from contamination and health to economic development. Indeed, some had come to own vast amounts of brownfield property, and most were seeking a more secure and less litigious regulatory system that could allow investment and redevelopment to take place. Lenders also play an important role in regulating redevelopment both directly and indirectly by scrutinizing the methods used and firms employed in the assessment and cleanup of brownfields.

Government agencies (economic development-oriented)   Many government agencies in the US and Canada promote brownfields redevelopment as a way to stimulate economic development and generate employment and tax growth. This includes economic development departments at the local level and departments of commerce, finance, and/or business development at the state level. While federal agencies tend to have broader mandates in terms of achieving environmental, social, and economic goals, many programs offered by key federal agencies are largely focused on economic development, such as the Brownfields Economic Development Initiative grant program administered by the US Department of Housing and Urban Development and many of the grant and loan programs administered by the EPA.

Typical "environmental" stakeholders.   *Government agencies (environment)*   Various government agencies are interested in brownfields redevelopment out of concern for managing risks to public health and the natural environment, as well as the opportunities these sites present for restoring ecosystem health and increasing opportunities for recreation space. Indeed, federal and state environmental or natural resource agencies are still primarily responsible for regulating brownfields given the initial focus on contamination issues. Locally, the departments that tend to be most engaged in brownfields with an eye toward the environment are public/environmental health departments interested in protecting citizens from brownfields risks, and parks departments that are interested in the opportunities brownfields present for restoring habitat and generating parks and open space.

Environmental consultants   They are responsible for assessing pollution levels and risks at brownfields and developing and overseeing cleanup strategies. In some locales, environmental professionals are also responsible for "signing off" on sites to guarantee that they are clean. Consultants can include a variety of professionals including environmental engineers or scientists, geologists, hydrologists, chemists, toxicologists, and public and occupational health professionals.

Typical "social" stakeholders. *Community members* Members of the local community, particularly those neighboring brownfields, are directly affected by the presence of these sites and by the redevelopment process. On the one hand, redevelopment results in the management of contamination and the regeneration of blighted property, while on the other, the local community is often concerned with how contaminants are managed during the construction process and what impact the project will have on their neighborhood. While some are interested in the opportunities presented by new development in terms of jobs, taxes, retail opportunities, others are concerned with gentrification, maintaining neighborhood character, traffic, parking, and other issues.

Community development corporations As Dewar and Deitrick (2004, p. 159) point out, "the mission of community development corporations is to rebuild low-income neighborhoods for the benefit of the residents." As such, they tend to be more concerned with the social implications of redevelopment projects and how such projects contribute to affordable housing and quality of life generally. These organizations are flexible and play multiple roles in brownfields redevelopment, including education and outreach aimed at building community awareness, as well as facilitation and advocacy for brownfields redevelopment and neighborhood renewal. Community development corporations (CDCs) can also act as intermediaries or pre-developers by assisting groups involved in brownfields redevelopment or actually assuming risk by acquiring brownfields, managing contamination issues, and then selling cleaned sites for redevelopment. More and more CDCs are taking a major stake in such projects by acting as their primary developers or financiers.

Other stakeholders. *Lawyers* They can work with various stakeholders to provide representation and advice to their clients with regard to actual and potential liability, remediation, reuse, financing, sale, lease, and the donation of brownfield properties. In addition to providing counsel on assessing liability, lawyers for the interested parties can offer representation in several areas, such as negotiating cleanup obligations, liability limitations, title and/or insurance acquisition, preparing land use controls (such as deed restrictions), and providing advice on funding and financing programs. Lawyers involved in brownfields activities generally have interdisciplinary experience and knowledge of several types of law, including environmental law, real estate, project finance, construction law, government contract law, commercial or corporate law, and international or trans-national law.

Brownfields associations and networks Groups such as the National Brownfield Association (NBA) established in 1999 in Chicago, about Remediation established in 2001 in Ontario, and the Canadian Brownfields Network established in 2004 in Ontario, are involved in education and advocacy aimed at stimulating the redevelopment of brownfields. Such organizations are typically involved in outreach and education-based initiatives aimed at raising awareness of brownfields redevelopment issues and policies. They also play an important role in creating linkages between private industry, government agencies, and non-governmental organizations and seek to influence policy-making as a group. Their vision also tends to be more progressive in terms of sustainability. For instance, the vision put forward by the Canadian Brownfields Network is "to advocate brownfields redevelopment as an essential component of sustainable communities and urban revitalization in Canada."

Nonprofits A nonprofit organization is one whose primary objective is to support some issue or matter of private interest or public concern for non-commercial purposes. Nonprofits can be involved in economic, social, and/or environmental aspects of brownfields redevelopment. Nonprofit developers are often community- or faith-based groups involved in building and rehabilitating for market and affordable housing in neighborhoods that are often shunned by the private market. Many environmental nonprofits, such as the Trust for Public Land and rails to trails, are involved in converting brownfields to parks and open space (see Chapter 5). Many brownfields nonprofits are also involved in social justice and community-based advocacy. The most influential nonprofit in the US in terms of promoting brownfields redevelopment has been the Northeast-Midwest Institute, which is a research organization that has generated numerous seminal publications on the issue.

Linking Brownfields Redevelopment and Sustainability via Benchmarking

Monitoring the scale of environmental problems and the effectiveness of policies and programs at managing them has become increasingly important as government budgets tighten and more effort is devoted to maximizing policy outcomes. The tracking of brownfields policy and practice has come under particularly close scrutiny in the US since the traditional top-down contaminated lands policy under Comprehensive Environmental Response and Liabilities Act (CERCLA) was effectively replaced by the more results-oriented bottom-up Brownfields Action Agenda (BBA). Indeed, the main component of the BAA was to provide funds for pilot programs to test redevelopment models and to facilitate stakeholder cooperation. The EPA and other researchers, including groups such as the Northeast-Midwest Institute and the Institute for Responsible Management, monitored the results of these pilot programs to determine what was working and what was not.

Early brownfields policy evaluation research concentrated on project-specific case studies (CUED, 1999; Pepper, 1997). As more projects have been developed, there has been a growing effort in recent years to track policy outcomes more broadly at the local and state levels. Simons and El Jaouhari (2001), for instance, surveyed brownfield program managers in 63 cities in 1997–1998, finding that local governmental policies sought primarily to encourage private sector-driven investment and redevelopment, making cleanup standards more flexible, and providing public funds and tax incentives to support redevelopment activities. Others, such as Bartsch and Deane (2002), have documented the implementation of policy-making approaches at the state level. Less attention has been devoted to tracking whether such approaches are achieving success at the local level. As Simons and El Jaouhari (2001, p. 18) aptly point out:

> Improvement is needed in the evaluation of local government intervention ... In the absence of an accurate tracking system, it is difficult for cities to achieve an efficient allocation of funds, quantify the cost/benefit ratio of public incentive programs, or determine the effectiveness of new initiatives ... It is also very difficult for policy makers to identify successful programs and recommend their implementation in other locales.

In 2002, the International City/County Management Association (ICMA, 2002b) joined the call for promoting the use of performance measures to monitor success in brownfields programs by publishing a report on the topic that discusses the basics of performance measurements, its application to brownfields programs, and the challenges associated with developing suitable measures. Some of the challenges to measuring success that the study puts forward that may keep people away include the multiplicity of stakeholders involved, the qualitative nature of many results, the inconsistency of time frames, the difficulty of selecting appropriate measures, and the individualized nature of measures.

The concern also exists among researchers and government officials that the policies being implemented and the outcomes examined are too narrow in scope, focusing only on economic development impacts and ignoring SD and other community goals altogether. A review by the EPA's Office of Program Evaluation in 2002 found, ironically, that its own brownfields performance measures were designed only to take into account development and economic outcomes, failing to contribute to the EPA's role in protecting human health and safeguarding the environment (US EPA, 2002). No wonder then that there is a growing call for governments to devise ways of tracking and assessing socio-economic and environmental consequences of brownfield policies (US EPA, 1998, 1999; CUED, 1999; US Conference of Mayors, 2000; Simons & El Jaouhari, 2001; Dair & Williams, 2001; US EPA, 2002).

Tracking progress toward achieving sustainability and improving the quality of urban life in a more holistic manner has become an important consideration for many communities in the US, Canada, and abroad (Maclaren, 1996, 2001; Tyler Norris Associates, 1997; Leitmann, 1999). Such tracking can take place at various scales including the global, (multi) national, state/provincial, city, community, and project-specific — with the city and community scale becoming increasingly popular. In the 1990s alone, 200 so-called "community indicator projects" were launched in the United States and at least 24 in Canada to provide a framework for assessing the "state of the community" (Maclaren, 2001). The framework is often a product of the collaboration of international organizations, various levels of government, business and community organizations, and academics. Typically, 20–35 indicators are examined in a single study. These indicators, also referred to as benchmarks or measures, are phenomenon that can be observed and measured to provide information on a particular aspect of quality of life (e.g., access to park space), health (e.g., infant mortality), development (e.g., new building activity), the environment (e.g., water quality), and a variety of other issues (Maclaren, 1996, 2001; Tyler Norris Associates, 1997; Besleme & Muffin, 1997; Leitmann, 1999) (for a comprehensive list of the hundreds of potential indicators see Sustainable Measures, 2006).

As in the case of the well-known Sustainable Seattle initiative, indicator projects employ benchmarks that aim to be integrating (i.e., take into account the links between the economy, the environment, and society), forward-looking (i.e., capable of measuring progress over time), distributional (i.e., take into account the distribution of conditions within a population or across geographic regions), and, most importantly, are developed with input from multiple stakeholders in the community (Maclaren, 1996). The indicator movement is motivated primarily by a need to educate the public, to gather background information for policy development, and to monitor and evaluate the performance of plans and programs (Tyler Norris Associates, 1997). This, in turn, reflects sensitivity to preserving the most cherished characteristics and priorities of a community, as opposed to the developer.

While some research has endeavored to measure the benefits and outcomes of brownfields redevelopment, it has done so primarily from the perspective of public officials and private stakeholders concerned largely with economic development outcomes, as opposed to a sustainability perspective that is also concerned with the broader socio-economic and environmental impacts these projects bring about. Research on the broader community impacts of brownfields has tended to focus on their negative implications from an environmental justice perspective, as these sites tend to be more concentrated in nonwhite neighborhoods (Leigh & Coffin, 2000), on their influence on local real estate values (Bond, 2001; Ihlanfeldt & Taylor, 2002), and on other economic issues related to employment, taxes, and property investment (CUED, 1999; Simons & El Jaouhari, 2001).

To identify and track sustainability-oriented impacts of brownfields redevelopment, a broader range of indicators is required to assess the merits of projects prior to development and track outcomes once they have been completed. Many relevant benchmarks for tracking the sustainability of brownfields redevelopment have been put forward by a variety of government and non-government sources in the United States (US EPA, 1999, 2002; CUED, 1999; US Conference of Mayors, 2000; Simons & El Jaouhari, 2001; Dair & Williams, 2001). In a study carried out by the author in Milwaukee, public and private sector stakeholders were presented with a list of these indicators and asked to rank them as not important (= 1), somewhat important (= 2), important (= 3), or very important (= 4) (De Sousa, 2005).

Both public and private sector interviewees viewed the economic outcome benchmarks as being the most important overall (score = 3.0 total, 3.03 public, 2.92 private), followed by environmental (score = 2.8 total, 2.8 public, 2.8 private) and social ones (score = 2.5 total, 2.5 public, 2.6 private). However, there was significant variation within individual outcome categories. Most viewed the increase in tax base, the influence on local property values, and the reduction of risks posed by contaminants as very important outcomes to track (see Table 2.4).

Table 2.4: Public and private stakeholder evaluation of potential brownfield performance/outcome measures.

Performance/outcome measure	Average		
	Overall	Public	Private
Economic			
Increases the local property tax base[c,e]	4.0	4.0	4.0
Influences local property values[b]	3.6	3.8	3.3
Public costs per private redevelopment dollars leveraged[a,d,g]	3.4	3.4	3.4
Influences local economic activity and income[b]	3.3	3.5	3.5
Land acres or building area developed[a,c–e,g]	3.1	3.2	3.0
Number of jobs created/retained[a,c–e,g]	3.0	3.0	2.9
Contributes to local business[f]	2.9	2.9	2.9
Number of "living-wage" jobs created[h]	2.9	2.9	2.8
Public costs per job created[a,d]	2.8	2.8	2.9
Impacts on local unemployment[a,c–e,g]	2.7	2.9	2.9
Puts new businesses on the site[a,b,d,e]	2.5	3.0	1.9
Draws on local enterprises for inputs[h]	2.4	2.6	2.6
Environment			
Reduces risks posed by contaminants[b,d,f]	3.6	3.6	3.7
Enhances the aesthetic image of the local community[b]	3.3	3.6	2.9
Improves regional environmental conditions by minimizing greenfield development[b,f]	2.9	3.1	2.5
Prevents pollution and reduces waste[b]	2.8	2.6	3.0
Provides infrastructure for public transit, walking, cycling[b,f]	2.7	2.6	2.9
Supports ecosystem functions[b]	2.7	2.6	2.8
Makes polluters pay for remediation costs[h]	2.7	2.7	2.6
Protects/preserves biodiversity[b,f]	2.6	2.5	2.8
Is energy efficient[b,f]	2.4	2.2	2.7
Involves "green" building features (renewable/recycled materials)[b,f]	2.4	2.3	2.4
Raises densities in comparison to typical development[f]	2.3	2.2	2.4
Social and community			
Allows for some level of local control over the project[b]	3.1	2.8	3.4
Enhances quality of life[b]	3.1	3.2	2.9
Improves the conditions of low-income population[b]	2.8	2.8	2.9
Fosters community cohesion[b]	2.8	3.0	2.6
Strengthens community capacity[b]	2.8	2.7	2.9
Physically conforms to community desires[b]	2.7	3.1	2.3
Involves coordination among multiple stakeholders[b,g]	2.5	2.5	2.6

Table 2.4: (*Continued*)

Performance/outcome measure	Average		
	Overall	Public	Private
Involves an open consultation process[b]	2.5	2.5	2.6
Permits equitable access to housing or employment[b,f]	2.4	2.6	2.1
Considers regional impact[b]	2.4	2.3	2.5
Reduces local crime rate[h]	2.3	2.3	2.4
Provides an opportunity for training[f]	2.0	1.7	2.5
Involves a mixture of land uses[b,f]	2.0	2.2	1.8

Source: De Sousa (2005).
[a]CUED (1999).
[b]US EPA (1999).
[c]US Conference of Mayors (2000).
[d]Simons and El Jaouhari (2001).
[e]Bartsch and Deane (2002).
[f]Dair and Williams (2001).
[g]US EPA (2002).
[h]Put forward by stakeholders.

Outcomes that were perceived as "important" (2.5–3.4 average) can be roughly classified as "standard ones" (e.g., public cost per private redevelopment dollars leveraged, land/building development, jobs), and those that focus on the community benefits related to renewal, blight removal, and improvement of community cohesion (enhancement of the community's image and quality of life, contribution to local business, fostering of community cohesion, and so on). Other than those used for employment outcomes, the interviewees were generally wary of measures that tracked the specific features of projects (factors and issues dealing with equal access to housing, local green building, density issues, end uses, etc.). Interestingly, while both public and private sector stakeholders revealed similar attitudes toward most of the outcomes, the private sector ones were more amenable to tracking the environmental features of their projects (such as access to alternative transportation, green building outcomes, energy efficiency), while the public stakeholders were more interested in community-directed outcomes (such as the enhancement of a community's image and overall cohesion).

Many comprehensive indicator-based approaches to track sustainability and urban regeneration of buildings, projects, and district-wide developments have also been developed and implemented over the last decade. The most popular approach in the US and Canada at the building level is the Leadership in Energy and Environmental Design (LEED) rating system introduced in the late 1990s by the US Green Building Council. LEED is a green rating program for designing, constructing, and certifying buildings. It is divided into five categories related to location, water conservation, energy, materials, and indoor environmental quality, plus an innovation and design category. Each category contains a specific number of credits and each credit carries one or more possible points. For instance, in the water efficiency category, points are given for reducing water consumption for irrigation by 50%; using only captured rain or gray water for irrigation, or not installing landscape irrigation systems at all; reducing the use of city water for sewage by 50% or treating 100% of wastewater on site to tertiary standards; etc. Brownfield redevelopment is allocated points within the sustainable sites category. A project that earns enough points (26) can become "LEED certified," on up the ladder to silver (33), gold (39), and platinum (52 +).

As of September 2003, 948 projects, representing nearly 140 million sq. ft. (13,000,000 m^2) of space, were registered in the program (US Green Building Council (USGBC), 2003). Unfortunately, a study of 38 first-generation LEED projects in the US found that only 3 of the 38 buildings were allocated points for brownfields redevelopment, including the well-known platinum-rated Center for Green Technology in Chicago (see Chapter 11). This is changing as many cities put pressure on developers receiving access to brownfields lands or funding for brownfields redevelopment to incorporate green elements into their projects. One notable example is the redevelopment of Southeast False Creek in Vancouver into a sustainable urban neighborhood in which all buildings will have to be rated at least LEED silver (see Chapter 6).

Indicator-based approaches for measuring sustainable urban regeneration have also been a subject of interest in Europe, particularly in the UK where measures are needed to track the outcomes of rather comprehensive nation-wide sustainability efforts. Sustainable urban regeneration evaluation frameworks typically follow an indicator-based approach by including contextual measures to identify the baseline conditions of projects or area-wide initiatives, the conditions within which the strategy is operating, and the effects of policy actions (Wong, 2000; Hemphill, Berry, & McGreal, 2004). Indicators can contribute to assessing the combined performance of individual agencies or interventions, the overall effectiveness of partnerships to improve well-being, or the cost-effectiveness of the main regeneration activities. Key indicators, such as those described in Table 2.4, need to be supplemented by qualitative and quantitative information on impact and performance from the perspectives of users and beneficiaries. In spite of the introduction of a "sustainability" strand to urban policy, however, there are few examples in the US, Canada, or Europe of evaluations examining the extent to which SD principles have been incorporated into brownfield efforts specifically, and urban regeneration policy and practice generally (DETR, 1998; OECD, 2000).

One study of note by Hemphill et al. (2004) recently put forward a comprehensive points-scoring framework for capturing sustainability performance of regeneration projects and applied it to various European projects. Expert opinion was employed to select and weigh indicators and to devise a point-scoring framework for assessing projects. Fifty-two indicators falling into the five areas of *Economy and Work, Resource Use, Buildings and Land Use, Transport and Mobility*, and *Community Benefit* were put forward, and data collection and scoring schemes established. This scheme was applied to both waterfront-led (Laganside Belfast, Dublin Docklands, Olympic Village Barcelona) and culture-led (Cathedral Quarter Belfast, Temple Bar

Belfast, Ciutat Vella Barcelona) regeneration efforts in three European cities to measure achievements in the delivery of SD projects. The study demonstrates that the more established and mature regeneration locations (Olympic Village, Ciutat Vella, and Temple Bar) deliver better sustainability performance than those areas that are less well developed, highlighting the importance of timing in regeneration areas. Methodologically, the model proved to be robust in terms of its application in different regeneration typologies and different urban contexts in terms of city characteristics, institutional structures, and policy frameworks. Indeed, such a model could be applied across regeneration areas and projects of differing size, scale, level of perceived success/delivery and at different phases of a particular initiative, including at the proposal stage to evaluate a project's contribution to achieving sustainability goals and throughout the development stage to keep it on course.

The selection of appropriate indicators for regeneration and brownfields projects is not without its problems. In a survey the author carried out in Milwaukee, the attitude of public and private sector groups of interviewees with regard to tracking other sustainability-oriented indicators was mixed. Public sector stakeholders felt that such indicators could help advertise the long-term benefits associated with brownfield redevelopment, which in turn would help justify short-term public expense and involvement. The main fear, however, was the difficulty of defining what constitutes a sustainable brownfield project, how its outcome would be measured, and who would do the measuring. The responses of the private sector interviewees were also mixed in this regard. Many felt that the desire to monitor and seek out broader outcomes was a valid objective given the level of public commitment and the need to obtain public support generally. Some also felt that a broader range of outcomes would take the focus away from job creation and tax base growth that, as one interviewee put it, has become the "fixation" of economically oriented agencies of government. Many of the private sector interviewees were also concerned that (i) small sites with less "social impact" would seem less attractive from a funding perspective, (ii) the outcomes would not only be used to measure performance, but be employed as specific criteria that developers would have to meet to attain funding, and (iii) that developers may not always be able to grasp the meaning of the outcomes themselves. Most importantly, almost half of the private sector interviewees felt that those redeveloping brownfields faced too many bureaucratic obstacles already, a fact that continues to make greenfield development more attractive. As such, it has proven particularly difficult to establish such frameworks, although their utility seems logical.

The Case of the Menomonee Valley Benchmarking Initiative (www.mvbi.org)

One effort to link and track brownfields redevelopment and sustainability via indicator reporting is the Menomonee Valley Benchmarking Initiative, which has been coordinated by the author and a member of the Sixteenth Street Community Health Center, a local non-profit, since 2001. The case study here summarizes the procedures employed for establishing the indicators, the approach taken for gathering and presenting data, key results from the benchmarking research, and the strengths and weaknesses of the initiative. The benchmarking initiative is useful because it provides a straightforward and cost-effective framework for developing an indicator program that can be applied to monitor brownfields redevelopment and urban renewal efforts in a manner that incorporates sustainability.

Milwaukee's Menomonee River Valley is Wisconsin's largest brownfields district covering roughly 1,400 acres (567 ha) in the heart of the city just southwest of the downtown core. Large industrial complexes, including tanneries, breweries, stock-yards, and railroad shops dotted the entire Valley in the late 1800s, and residential communities spread extensively along the Valley's bluffs, producing some of the most densely populated neighborhoods in Wisconsin.

In common with most of Milwaukee's central city communities, urban development patterns and economic disinvestment during the second half of the twentieth century hit the Valley hard, with many businesses closing their doors. What was once a jobsite for tens of thousands of people became an isolated, environmentally degraded industrial district. While sizeable tracts of vacant and underutilized properties are a testament to the Valley's past decline, there are more than 100 active businesses in the Valley ranging in size from a few employees to more than 1,000, and significant new investment is changing the face of the Valley for the benefit of Milwaukee's central city and the entire region.

Over the past decade, a significant amount of time and attention has been paid to positioning the Valley to serve as a driving force in Milwaukee's resurgence (see Chapter 11). A broad collection of partners from Milwaukee's public, private, and nonprofit sectors have worked together to develop a vision for the Valley that sees new businesses relocating to lands cleansed of past environmental contamination that provide family-supporting jobs to residents of nearby neighborhoods. At the same time, a new emphasis has been placed on the health of the Menomonee River and on creating new opportunities for recreation and community amenities to support Milwaukee's diverse residents. Together, this vision of economic development, environmental restoration, and community well-being forms the sustainable approach to redevelopment that is guiding new investment and the Valley's overall renewal.

The Menomonee Valley Benchmarking Initiative (MVBI) was established in 2001 to provide a systematic approach to gauge the impacts of redevelopment activities from a sustainability perspective and, just as importantly, to identify course corrections that may be necessary along the way. The MVBI was envisioned as an interdisciplinary, collaborative effort to systematically track and study the environmental, economic, and community changes taking place in and around the Valley. With the convening of "Indicator Work Group" meetings in 2001, issues and indicators were chosen and benchmark measurements were taken to identify then — current conditions in the Valley and its surrounding neighborhoods. The multi-stakeholder work groups identified 12 issues of concern and 51 indicators used to track the performance of those issues. For example, "water quality" is one issue identified by the work group, and "dissolved oxygen" is an indicator used to evaluate water quality. The number of indicators has since been expanded to 57.

In the most recent 2005 report, indicator analyses are sorted into three lenses (economy, environment, and community) of sustainability. The analysis of each indicator addresses three fundamental questions:

1. What has been measured? — describes the measures, sources of data, and methodological approach used for evaluating the indicator's performance.
2. Why is it important? — explains the indicator's role in achieving sustainability in the Valley community.
3. How are we doing? — describes the performance of each indicator within the study area by means of an examination of past trends and current conditions.

The highlights of the 2005 MVBI sections are presented and discussed briefly here because they illustrate one of the key benefits associated with taking a broader sustainability approach, which is to think about the area as not an agglomeration of derelict brownfield sites, but as part of a larger community (the complete report can be found at www.mvbi.org; De Sousa, Gramling, & Lemoine, 2006).

The main priority of policy-makers and economic development officials in charge of brownfields districts tends to be the state of the Valley economy. The economic highlights of the MVBI report include

• employment in the Valley and in the manufacturing sector declined slightly between 2002 and 2005, while service employment grew;
• job density, average reported salary, and total annual sales rose;
• one-fourth of Valley employees now live in closely surrounding areas;
• the assessed value of commercial property in the Valley has risen faster than the average city value; and
• businesses view its central location as the main advantage to locating in the Valley.

Information gathered for the 2005 report paints a less grim picture of the Valley's economic state than many Milwaukeeans perceive. While the survey found that employment declined (overall and in manufacturing), the decline was due primarily to the loss of a single large company that was forced to move out of the Valley due to a multi-million dollar highway project. Other key variables pointed in a more positive direction, including growth in job density, average salary, annual sales, commercial property values, commercial rental rates, health insurance to part-time employees, the number of access roads, and the number of businesses locally owned and headquartered in the Valley. There was also a slight increase in the proportion of Valley employees living in adjacent neighborhoods, which was considered a very important indicator according to stakeholders because it captures the link between job growth in the Valley and community benefits from that growth. One particular question from a business survey used to gather information from employers that captures the positive transformation of the Valley relates to the primary advantages and disadvantages of doing business there. In terms of advantages, employers like the Valley's central location, freeway access, proximity to downtown, and access to workforce, while the most common response for its disadvantages was "none" (other responses included traffic, crime, high taxes, and construction inconveniences). That said, a few economic indicators were less positive and require attention, including a slight decrease in the provision of health care to full time employees and a reduction in the number of transit routes servicing the Valley.

Typical to brownfields, the Menomonee Valley has suffered considerably from past environmental abuse and degradation stemming from poor land stewardship. Redevelopment activities in the Valley seek to ensure that environmental objectives (e.g., improved water quality) are taken into consideration. The MVBI developed air, water, ecosystem, and wildlife monitoring networks to assess the state of the Valley environment and to evaluate the impacts of redevelopment on the environmental issues identified by stakeholders. The highlights of the environmental section of the report include

- water-quality problems in the Menomonee River continue to be linked to stormwater management throughout the watershed;
- on average, 2004 atmospheric ozone concentrations were lower than 2003 concentrations, while some toxic air pollutants remain at unhealthy levels in and around the Valley;
- the quality of land cover and amount of habitat is limited due to the extent of impervious surfaces in the Valley (62% of all Valley land), and tree canopy coverage totaled a mere 3.4%; and
- the Valley is home to a surprising number of breeding bird species and a strong component of native tree and shrub species — perhaps due to recent ecosystem restoration efforts; but invasive species continue to threaten the Valley, and should be managed aggressively.

Overall, the study revealed that the Valley's environmental condition is generally poor, but that many opportunities for renewal exist. In terms of water quality, an index of biotic integrity (IBI) that examines aquatic ecosystem health on the basis of 10 individual metrics for the Menomonee river and the local canal received scores of poor and fair, and samples of temperature, conductivity, dissolved oxygen, pH, and turbidity also revealed many challenges associated with dealing with pollutants entering the Valley from throughout the watershed. Air quality benchmarks were also mixed, as ozone levels were generally safe, but four of the five air toxics examined (formaldehyde, acetaldehyde, benzene, 1,3-butadiene, and PCBs) remained above their respective risk factor thresholds (the atmospheric concentration at which there is a cancer risk to 1 in 1 million people exposed over a lifetime). While the data on bird diversity was a more positive sign, all environmental issues in the Valley were negatively affected overall by land coverage deficiencies; that is, tree canopy covers only 3.4% of the Valley and 62% of the Valley's surface is impervious.

A meaningful vision for a redeveloped Menomonee Valley must take into consideration ways of interconnecting new jobs and a restored environment with community life. Measuring and tracking the state of the Valley community involved gathering information on indicators related to such things as recreation, housing, health, and crime rates. The highlights from the 2005 report include

- housing values closest to the Valley have soared in the last five years, demonstrating that proximity to older industrial areas does not necessarily negatively impact residential real estate;
- childhood lead poisoning rates near the Valley continue to decline steadily;
- the neighborhoods surrounding the Menomonee Valley are highly ethnically diverse; and
- neighborhoods to the south of the Valley are strong in culture with numerous community recreation opportunities and public art installations.

Many of the community indicators painted a more positive picture of the state of the Valley. In terms of housing, owner occupancy rates rose, over 700 new housing units were constructed, and property values surrounding the industrial part of the Valley rose. Crime and lead poisoning rates witnessed a decline. Interestingly, many stakeholders wanted to know more about the availability of artistic installations and recreation venues in the Valley because they saw them as ways to revitalize its "blighted" image and draw people into the area. Fortunately, researchers found an increasing number of these sites throughout the Valley community. On the negative side, many of the neighborhoods surrounding the Valley continue to reveal a racial structure that is separated geographically — residents to the east and west of the Valley are predominantly white, African Americans live to the north, and Hispanic nationalities to the south. Many of those living in and around the Valley also live in relative poverty, as incomes are one-third less than the city average.

Overall, sustainability reporting activities aim to educate the public, inform policy-making efforts, and monitor the performance of policy-making and other renewal activities (Tyler Norris Associates, 1997). The MVBI has been attempting to achieve all three of these objectives by gathering analytical information reflective of overall redevelopment in an industrial brownfields district. While it is still too early to gauge fully the impact of the initiative, some benefits have already emerged. The MVBI has created an information clearinghouse on Valley data and generated a useful synthesis of raw data for the benefit of a wide variety of users. In addition, it has promoted the principles of sustainability in an urban brownfields context by linking the economic, social, and environmental issues that concern stakeholders. It has brought together, in a collaborative effort, disparate stakeholders, coordinators, data gatherers, and other participants to establish a human resources network. The report itself has been an important tool for presenting the Valley as a location and a community as opposed to an agglomeration of brownfields.

The MVBI has, however, encountered some problems consistent with the concerns of both public and private sector stakeholders described above. In particular, indicator reporting has proven to be time-consuming and difficult to coordinate given the extent and range of data and sources. The response from the economic development and business community has been lukewarm, which is discouraging given that they are largely in charge of coordinating and paying for redevelopment efforts in the Valley. The question then becomes whether such groups are truly that interested in having their activities tracked with such detail and via a framework that links environmental and social factors with traditional economic ones. In addition, are we at the point where government is willing to impose more sustainability-oriented demands on developers, or are we just happy to have them build whatever they can on whatever brownfield they choose?

Conclusions

As our ability to manage the risks and costs associated with brownfields gets better and the perception of these sites improves among developers and consumers, more and more stakeholders are seeking to "raise the bar" on brownfields redevelopment in an effort to link it more closely with SD objectives. SD generally, and SUD specifically, has become a widely embraced concept for integrating a broader array of environmental, economic, and social factors into urban development and growth. The proper management of the city's urban form and the preservation and reutilization of its built environment are integral steps toward achieving sustainability. Urban brownfields redevelopment, therefore, provides an opportunity to reuse and revitalize older urban areas in a manner that brings about the benefits inherent in compact form (e.g., lower capital and operating costs, reduced travel and transportation costs, benefits to social issues, preservation of greenfields), while at the same time incorporating environmental, social, and economic elements into project design.

Linking brownfields redevelopment and sustainability requires a more comprehensive understanding of the challenges, opportunities, and stakeholders involved. Challenges move beyond liability, cost, and contamination risks, to include crime, inner-city market conditions, poverty, ecological integrity, blight, and community quality of life issues. On the flipside, opportunities move beyond profit, jobs, and tax generation, to include public health improvement, aesthetics, social interaction, community pride, and the like. Raising the bar on brownfields also requires greater buy-in and involvement from traditional stakeholders, as well as a more extensive network of actors that includes community members, CDCs, brownfields associations, nonprofits, and government agencies.

Ultimately, a more sustainable approach to brownfields redevelopment will require the development and application of sustainability-oriented benchmarks to assess the merits of projects prior to development and to track outcomes once they have been completed. Many relevant benchmarks for tracking the sustainability of brownfields redevelopment have been put forward by a variety of government and non-government sources in both the United States and Canada, and a few efforts, such as the MVBI, are emerging to track how such projects are contributing to urban sustainability goals.

The next chapter examines the public and private sector benefits and costs of brownfield versus greenfield development in monetary terms in order to provide a more quantifiable perspective on the market barriers to redevelopment and the public benefits associated with it. Enhancing brownfields redevelopment activity and promoting a more sustainable approach requires a better understanding of these private costs and public benefits because developers are largely responsible for redevelopment as dictated by market forces, while the public sector is responsible for implementing programs and providing incentives to support such redevelopment. This public–private partnership model has been vital for moving brownfields redevelopment forward in the last decade and will continue to be the primary force moving us toward sustainability in the next.

Chapter 3

Costs, Risks, and Benefits of Brownfields

By the late 1980s, governments began to realize that the sheer magnitude of the brownfields problem and the costs associated with managing it were more than the public or private sectors were able to bear alone, and that the conflict-oriented approach that characterized public and private relations under Superfund was largely ineffective. To deal with this, a more market-driven, public–private partnership approach was pursued whereby developers were largely responsible for redevelopment as dictated by market forces, while the public sector would implement programs and provide incentives to minimize the costs and risks associated with such redevelopment. While some would point to this change in approach as just another example of privatization and neoliberalization, the more fundamental question is whether this approach has fostered redevelopment activity.

In order for a market-led approach to work, it is essential to understand what the market wants and know how it works. In an interview the author carried out over a decade ago, a developer summed up a typical developer's goal succinctly as: "some people pray to God, but many developers' pray to return on investment." That said, it is essential to understand brownfields redevelopment from a profit-based perspective in order to ascertain which cost and risk factors make such projects more difficult to realize and would improve the governments' ability to better target policies, programs, and incentives. Those interested in social and environmental aspects of brownfields redevelopment must also become familiar with understanding and calculating profits in order to understand the costs of their proposals and the impacts these have on project feasibility. Indeed, governments, particularly local ones, with a deep understanding of development economics, real estate conditions, prospective project returns, and developer expectations are the most capable of negotiating sustainability features with developers. Without this knowledge, those promoting sustainability features are simply unable to know how high they can raise the bar before it is impossible for developers to make it over, or how much they need to help developers to make it over the bar.

At the same time, governments at all levels are also under increasing pressure to minimize spending and to justify both spending and policy activities based on measurable outcomes, particularly those that can be put into monetary terms. Public support of private sector ventures is also under additional scrutiny, as taxpayers want to know whether their support is yielding public benefits or just enhancing private profits. It is for these reasons that many studies have sought to valuate the public benefits emanating from brownfields reuse from an economic development perspective, as well as from a broader sustainable development one. This chapter examines the public and private sector benefits and costs of brownfield versus greenfield development in monetary terms in order to provide a more quantifiable perspective on the market barriers to redevelopment and the fiscal opportunities associated with it.

A Private Sector Perspective

The shift in focus from engineering to economic development resulted in a flurry of research aimed at examining the relevant economic issues facing developers (Iannone, 1996; Bartsch, 1996; Simons, 1998; Center for Urban Economic Development (CUED), 1999; Meyer & Lyons, 2000). Research conducted by Bartsch and others from the Northeast-Midwest Institute (Bartsch, 1996; Bartsch, Collaton, & Pepper, 1997; Pepper, 1997), by Simons (1998), and by the former CUED (1999) shed important light on the costs and benefits involved in brownfield versus greenfield redevelopment in the US. These researchers found, largely through case study analysis, that brownfield property redevelopment for any use is hampered by a variety of additional direct costs (e.g., remediation, consulting) and by the prospect of low rental or sale revenues.

A few studies have looked at the issue by unpacking the developer's pro forma (development appraisal), which is the tool they employ to calculate Return on Investment/Equity. In a study conducted by the author, a financial pro forma analysis of hypothetical brownfield and greenfield scenarios was undertaken to sift through relevant cost and risk information and then examine the efficacy of different policies designed to encourage redevelopment (De Sousa, 2000). Several typical brownfield and greenfield development case study projects were used as models in the design of four hypothetical industrial and residential development scenarios, which included an eight-story residential condominium development constructed on a brownfield site with low-mid level contamination in the City of Toronto versus a greenfield site in Toronto's periphery; and a 26,136 sq ft ($=2,429\,m^2$) industrial facility constructed on a brownfield site with low mid-level contamination versus a greenfield site in Toronto's periphery.

Each analysis was based on four types of data: (i) property information; (ii) development cost information; (iii) development sales/lease information; and (iv) project returns. Regarding property information, the scenarios assume the same residential and industrial brownfield projects are undertaken on a small 1.5 acre (0.61 ha) parcel of land, even though the case study sites used to establish the scenarios varied with respect to both the characteristics of the buildings and the size of the site (ranging from 1 to 82 acres or 0.4 to 33.2 ha). The condominiums are eight stories and contain 97 units of 1,000 sq ft ($93\,m^2$) each. The industrial scenario concerns a smaller 26,136 sq ft ($2,429\,m^2$) building (40% coverage).

Overall, the development costs of the hypothetical development projects examined are higher for all the brownfield projects than they are for the greenfield ones (Tables 3.1 and 3.2 for a summary of pro forma results). Development costs in a pro forma analysis typically include: the land purchase price, land levies, and site

Table 3.1: Pro forma analysis of hypothetical residential scenarios, 2000.

Factor (costs Canadian $)	Brownfield		Greenfield	
Property information				
Lot size (acres/hectares)		1.5 acres/0.6 ha		
Number of units		97		
Building area		114,119 sq ft/10,606 m^2		
Development cost information	Cost ($)	Total (%)	Cost ($)	Total (%)
Land acquisition cost				
Land purchase price	1,500,000	7.5	600,000	3.3
Site costs				
Demolition	60,000	0.3	0	0.0
Site assessment	90,000	0.4	0	0.0
Remediation	375,000	1.9	0	0.0
Land levies	388,000	1.9	809,590	4.4
Construction costs				
Building hard costs ($100 psf)	11,421,478	56.7	11,712,369	63.8
Architectural/engineering/	690,000	3.4	690,000	3.8
consulting fees				
Soft costs				
Marketing and sales	1,255,000	6.2	1,255,000	6.8
Warranty and fees	209,000	1.0	209,000	1.1
Legal and admin fees	685,000	3.4	585,000	3.2
Realty taxes	250,000	1.2	200,000	1.1
Insurance and bonding	200,000	1.0	200,000	1.1
Development fees	580,059	2.9	585,695	3.2
Contingency	750,000	3.7	275,000	1.5
Construction loan/carrying costs	1,678,661	8.3	1,241,902	6.8
Total development costs	20,132,198	100.0	18,363,557	100.0
Development sales				
Number of units sold	97		97	
Unit sale price	$239		$191	
Revenue from sales	$23,183,275		$18,527,220	
Returns				
Revenues (based on average yield)	$23,183,275		$18,527,220	
Total development costs	$20,132,198		$18,363,557	
Project return (%)	15.2		1	
Revenue required for 10% return	$228 psf		$208 psf	
Revenue required for 15% return	$239 psf		$218 psf	
Site preparation time (months)	25		19	

Source: De Sousa (2000).

Table 3.2: Pro forma analysis of hypothetical industrial scenarios, 2000.

Factor (costs Canadian$)	Brownfield		Greenfield	
Property information				
Lot size (acres/hectares)		1.5 acres/0.6 ha		
Coverage (%)		40		
Building area		26,136 sq ft/2,42 m^2		
Development cost information	Cost ($)	Total (%)	Cost ($)	Total (%)
Land acquisition cost				
Land purchase price	102,000	5.8	360,000	21.8
Site costs				
Demolition	60,000	3.4	0	0.0
Site assessment	63,000	3.6	0	0.0
Remediation	225,000	12.9	0	0.0
Land levies	0	0.0	77,820	4.7
Construction costs				
Building hard costs ($40 psf)	1,063,894	60.8	1,061,587	64.2
Architectural/engineering/ consulting fees	21,693	1.2	21,693	1.3
Soft costs				
Leasing fees	35,284	2.0	35,284	2.1
Legal fees	13,000	0.7	6,500	0.4
Realty taxes	21,479	1.2	6,499	0.4
Insurance and bonding	2,500	0.1	2,500	0.2
Contingency	60,000	3.4	20,000	1.2
Construction loan/carrying costs	82,630	4.7	62,515	3.8
Total development costs	1,764,476	100.0	1,654,398	100.0
Operating cash flow				
Market rent	$5.35		$6.45	
Net operating income	$139,828		$168,577	
Financing and investment				
Levered yield				
Capitalized value (NOI/0.1)	$1,398,276		$1,685,772	
Loan amount (loan-to-value)	$978,793		$1,180,040	
Debt service (20 years at 9%)	$104,440		$125,914	
Cash flow before tax	$139,828		$168,577	
Equity requirement	$978,793		$474,357	
Return on equity (%)	4.6		9.0	
Unlevered yield				
Capitalized cost	$1,749,927		$1,654,398	
Cash flow before tax	$139,828		$168,577	
Yield (%)	8.0		10.2	
Rent required for 8% ROE	$6.60 psf net		$6.25 psf net	
Rent required for 12% ROE	$7.35 psf net		$6.95 psf net	
Site preparation time (months)	7		12	

Source: De Sousa (2000).

preparation costs (site assessment, remediation, and demolition). In brownfield transactions, developers and other land purchasers typically undertake the so-called "due-diligence" to determine whether a site is contaminated or not before purchasing it. If the land is contaminated, then the landowner is expected to reduce the price of the land from its "clean" value to cover the estimated cost of demolition, site assessment studies, and remediation, even if the landowner was not responsible for the contamination. Despite reductions, the land purchase price for a residential brownfield is higher than the greenfield price because of the high cost of residential land in Toronto and in the case study areas. Clearly, such high land prices are optimal for brownfield landowners because these allow them to cover the costs of assessment and remediation and still reap a profit from the sale of the land. The same cannot be said of some older industrial cities in Canada and the US where the value of the land is not enough to cover assessment and cleanup costs. This is often referred to as an "upside-down" site.

Industrial land in the inner city also faces many challenges that reduce its market value, including difficulties in site assembly and infrastructure, the perception of high crime, and labor force issues (Simons, 1999). Despite its relatively high value in Toronto, industrial land in the scenario would have to be discounted significantly to cover the cost of assessment and remediation. In this case, it is often in the best interest of the landowner to wait until industrial land prices rise, to seek a change in zoning to a more profitable use, or to abandon the site completely, especially if the site preparation costs exceed the value of the property. With regard to the total property costs, the price of brownfield sites for both residential and industrial scenarios balances with, or even becomes less than, greenfield sites because of the high land levies that peripheral municipalities in Ontario are required to charge for servicing related costs. This is not typically the case in the US where greenfield municipalities have substantial spending authority to minimize such costs in an effort to lure development.

Development cost information includes hard construction costs and other soft costs. Construction costs typically include those related to: the process of getting building permits, the construction of building structures and parking facilities, and architectural, engineering and consulting services. In the residential development scenarios, construction costs for a greenfield building of the same quality is assumed to be slightly higher because of the planning requirement that condominium properties built on greenfield sites contain more underground parking facilities than in urban areas. For the industrial scenarios, the permit-obtaining, and realty costs make the overall construction expenses for the brownfield redevelopments slightly higher than the greenfield ones.

With regard to soft development costs, discussions with those in charge of the projects used as the basis for the scenarios revealed that the legal costs associated with brownfield projects are generally double those associated with greenfield ones because of the need for additional legal services to cover costs related to, for instance, property review, consultation with government agencies, and communication with prospective purchasers. Brownfield projects may also entail higher contingency fees (reflecting the greater risks associated with such projects), higher realty taxes, higher development fees, and higher financing costs. It is to be noted that the financing costs involved in the different scenarios are typically higher for brownfield projects than for greenfield ones because the timelines for brownfield project completion are still considerably longer due to the compilation and review of soil research and remediation plans and to the remediation itself during the development process (25-month redevelopment period for residential brownfield redevelopment versus 19 months for a residential greenfield development; 12 months for industrial brownfield redevelopment versus 7 months for industrial greenfield development). Other soft costs, including condo marketing and sales expenses, industrial leasing fees, condo warranty fees, insurance/bonding fees, were taken as being the same for both brownfield and greenfield development projects.

Although the process of estimating project costs is straightforward and involves few assumptions, predicting revenues is uncertain because they fluctuate according to location, quality of product, zoning, and market variability. For the Toronto analysis, real estate values and market rents for spring 2000 were obtained from quarterly reports compiled by private industry research. To simplify the analysis, no vacancy was assumed for the newly developed buildings and the residential dwellings were assumed to be sold upon project completion. Fortunately, residential real estate values in Toronto, and in other large Canadian cities, have remained high in comparison to peripheral greenfield locations for all types of dwellings. According to the Greater Toronto Homebuilders Association, the high demand is being fuelled by changing demographics in support of urban living, favorable economic conditions, a growing supply of condominium buildings, and the presence of many approved left-over development sites from the 1980s (Wegler, 2000).

Over the last few years, there has also been a rise in the demand for industrial real estate in many urban areas throughout Canada and the US, which has led to an increase in both industrial rents and real estate values. Unlike the residential market in Toronto, however, the lease rates for urban locations of industrial sites in 2000 (averaging CDN\$4.35 psf net or CDN\$47/m^2 for buildings between 15,000 and 43,000 sq ft, and ranging between CDN\$3.75 and CDN\$5.50 psf or CDN\$40 and CDN\$59/m^2) were typically lower than for greenfield locations (averaging CDN\$5.45 psf net or CDN\$59/m^2 for buildings between 15,000 and 43,000 sq ft, and ranging between CDN\$4.50 and CDN\$7.35 psf or CDN\$48 and CDN\$79/m^2), while the property values were similar (Colliers International, 2000). For the hypothetical analysis, the lease rate for *new* industrial space was assumed to be CDN\$1 per square foot above the average.

The returns listed in Tables 3.1 and 3.2 are meant to reflect the returns predicted by each of the above development scenarios, according to revenue averages and the assumption that the buildings constructed are of the same quality. For the residential scenarios, those interviewed for that study pointed out that they expected a return of approximately 15% (ranging from 10% to 20%) for a residential project and between 8% and 12% (levered) for an industrial one. A study carried out for the Urban Land Institute (Shuman, 2002, p. 22) found developers of urban infill residential housing achieving returns in the 7%–21% range. In the present analysis, the residential brownfield projects will generate higher returns than greenfield ones due to the high sale price of residential property. The residential greenfield projects, however, would have to be built for less or sell for CDN$208 psf (CDN$2,239/m^2) to achieve the same yield, which is not outside the range for the periphery, but is above the average. The opposite is true for industrial projects, with only the greenfield development falling above the normal return expectancy (8%), despite the relatively high rents in the brownfield areas. The industrial returns include an estimate for unlevered yield, which assumes that the developer pays for the entire project at the end of the development period and then proceeds to lease it, and a levered one, which is more common in that it assumes that the developer will finance the project over time through a lender. While the returns for the brownfield project approach the 8% target for the unlevered yield, they are significantly lower for the levered one and would require a lease rate well above the city's average.

A similar analysis, carried out by Simons (1998) on retail, industrial, and residential projects in greater Cleveland, found that all types of brownfield projects were at a financial disadvantage to their greenfield counterparts, including the residential ones given the weaker market conditions in Cleveland's inner city. The lower rates of return for brownfields are caused not only by higher site development costs, but also by tougher financial terms. Simons adds that banks may require lower loan-to-value ratios to protect themselves from the possibility of having to own and manage stigmatized properties, which raises the requirements for equity well beyond what is reasonable and reduces potential returns. While lenders have become more familiar with brownfields situations over the last few years, many developers state that they are still more cautious, which raises costs. The pro formas discussed here are meant as cases in point. Indeed, each city will have slightly different costs and market characteristics that need to be considered. For instance, Howland (2003) found that in Baltimore, land contamination did not deter buyers from purchasing sites and that redevelopment occurred in a profitable manner via the market because sellers were willing to lower their price to compensate for the costs and risks associated with brownfields redevelopment.

Both studies provide a financial argument for the need for government subsidies to manage costs and risks. However, the Canadian case, whereby local governments rezone industrial land to residential use to raise its value, also helps explain why so much brownfields redevelopment in that country has been residential and why policies and incentives have lagged behind, particularly in provinces where large central cities with high residential property values dominate the political scene. For the Toronto study, the economic benefits of many policies and programs were assessed by applying them to the brownfield redevelopment scenario appraisals and calculating their impact on project returns. As it turns out, financial mechanisms, such as tax abatement, direct government-funding programs (through direct subsidies or Tax Increment Financing), could each improve the returns of the hypothetical brownfield scenarios. A reduction in municipal taxes charged to industrial operations in Toronto, to equal that charged in the periphery, would allow net rents to rise while not affecting gross rents, approaching the minimum 8% return target. Either a subsidy to offset the costs of site assessment and demolition, or site assessment and remediation, would also improve returns, although such cost reductions would likely benefit the landowner who is no longer required to reduce land price to pay the full cost of cleanup. The returns for industrial redevelopment, therefore, would only increase significantly if the landowner were still willing to reduce the land costs to cover extraneous costs related to brownfield development and to help offset the lower rental revenues.

Legal mechanisms to protect landowners and developers from future liability would also reduce cost and improve returns slightly for both residential and industrial redevelopments. More significantly, such mechanisms would reduce perceived future risks and limit the need for future liability insurance. Improving the regulatory environment by harmonizing policies and streamlining the approvals process for brownfield redevelopment, in line with the timelines associated with greenfield redevelopment, would significantly reduce the costs associated with the longer residential projects and more moderately reduce those associated with the industrial projects by bringing down financing costs. If the cleanup criteria were reduced or the application of the risk-based corrective action (or site-specific risk assessment) method were made to be less risky, as several of those interviewed for that study pointed out, then the developers would likely be able to save an additional 30% on cleanup costs. Overall, an examination of the workability of the mechanisms reveals that no single tool has the ability to improve returns enough for industrial brownfield projects to become feasible. Instead, a combination of tools is required to achieve parity with the greenfield returns.

The pro forma analysis highlights the following:

- Typical brownfield redevelopment is less cost-effective than greenfield development for developers, landowners, and other stakeholders involved due primarily to high costs associated with site preparation (demolition, site assessment, and remediation) and its risks (reflected here through higher contingency costs), complex regulatory mechanisms leading to time delays, low rents for industrial property in that city, and uncertain liability risks leading to higher legal costs.
- Industrial redevelopment projects on contaminated brownfield sites in that city are relatively unprofitable vis-à-vis their greenfield counterparts due to higher costs and lower lease rates, thus requiring assistance in order to make them more attractive to potential investors and developers and more marketable to landowners.
- Residential brownfield redevelopment projects in Toronto, and in a growing number of central cities in the US (e.g., Chicago), are just as or more profitable than their greenfield counterparts due to increasing real estate values in the city and inner suburbs. In the Toronto case however, the high costs associated with servicing greenfield municipalities born by developers and homebuyers, which is not the case in many US suburbs, played an important role in levelling the playing field. The growing popularity associated with living in urban areas has raised the value of residential real estate to a level that makes the more costly redevelopment of brownfield sites for residential dwellings potentially feasible, not only in fashionable lifestyle districts, such as the waterfront, but also in other (less trendy) urban areas.

• The implementation of cost/risk sharing mechanisms related to financing cleanup and redevelopment, reducing project timelines, and limiting liability would indeed improve the feasibility of brownfield projects overall according to the results of the pro forma analysis.

Another important observation that one can make from examining the pro forma is that developers are willing to take on brownfields projects provided the numbers work — and they are happy to avoid government involvement. For instance, as the City of Chicago's urban real estate market improves, more and more brownfield developers are *not* seeking brownfields funding support for their market-rate projects in an effort to minimize bureaucratic complications and time delays, which allows those funds to be put to more challenged parts of the city.

It is essential for those engaged in promoting more sustainable development of brownfields to know how to calculate such a pro forma and to assess how sustainability features might impact the costs (e.g., green infrastructure versus gray infrastructure), revenues to the developer (e.g., what is the market value of sustainable features), and projected returns. Table 3.3 outlines some of the benchmarks associated with sustainable brownfields and considers the perceived impacts of these on a developer's pro forma for an industrial project.

In addition to presenting the obvious problem associated with many sustainable features from a developer's perspective (i.e., that they are perceived as costing more in terms of consulting and development), there is general uncertainty on how these features will improve the bottom-line in terms of increasing returns. This uncertainty wreaks havoc on an orderly pro forma and often does not help when one goes to a lender to secure a loan for a project. In many interviews, developers have mentioned flat out that it makes no sense for them to change things when the current "development formula" is working and making them healthy profits. Consequently, there is a growing need for those promoting sustainable development on brownfields, and green building generally, to generate better data on the cost implications of their designs and their ideas, and on the potential profits these can bring in terms of higher sale or rents.

Furthermore, many of the benefits associated with brownfields redevelopment and sustainability do not go directly to the developer, but to the general public. This raises additional questions, such as: What are these benefits worth? Should developers pay to attain them? How can the public sector deliver these most efficiently (whether directly, or indirectly via developers)? The following section reviews some of the literature on the quantification of public benefits of brownfields, while the next chapters take a closer look at how brownfields redevelopment and sustainable redevelopment are being delivered.

Valuing the Public Benefits of Brownfields Redevelopment from a Public Perspective

An array of stakeholders interested in preserving the urban landscape and its economic traditions continue to seek government support for brownfield

Table 3.3: Developers' perceived impact of sustainability features on project viability.

Sustainability feature	Developer's perceived impact
Economic examples	
Number of jobs created; contributes to local business; draws on local enterprises for inputs; number of "living-wage" jobs created	• May limit the number of potential tenants • May raise marketing costs • May lengthen lease up time affecting revenues • Additional labor costs may get tenant to push for lower rent
Impacts on local unemployment	• Additional labor training costs may get tenant to push for lower rent
Environmental examples	
Reduces risks posed by contaminants	• Site assessment, cleanup, and related costs already discussed above
Enhances the aesthetic image of the local community	• Additional costs related to greenspace, public art, building façade enhancement required to compete with new industrial parks in greenfields • Impact on rents uncertain
Provides infrastructure for public transit, walking, cycling	• Costs for paths to "hook up" to municipal infrastructure • Impact on rents likely positive depending on workforce travel behavior
Supports ecosystem functions; protects/preserves biodiversity	• Additional consulting and landscaping costs • Impact on rents uncertain
Prevents pollution and reduces waste; is energy efficient; involves "green" building features (recycled materials)	• Adds to consulting and development costs • Likely to enhance rents and attract tenants • Will reduce long-term operating costs
Raises densities in comparison to typical development	• May be unattractive to tenants looking for a typical 1-story industrial parcel • May raise marketing costs • May lengthen lease up time affecting revenues

Table 3.3: (*Continued*)

Sustainability feature	Developer's perceived impact
Social and community	
Enhances quality of life; improves the conditions of low-income population; strengthens community capacity	• Assumed that remediating land, removing blight, and bringing employment back will do this • How do you define and track this?
Physically conforms to community desires; involves coordination among multiple stakeholders; involves an open consultation process	• Will add time delays and consulting costs to pro forma • May scare away potential tenants • May lengthen lease up time affecting revenues
Involves a mixture of land uses	• Additional planning and development costs • Developer may not be familiar with developing multiple land uses • May lower returns depending on the marketability of other uses • Industrial tenants may not like other users complaining about their practices

redevelopment programs, arguing that such redevelopment brings about a broad range of economic, social, and environmental benefits to everyone concerned. Public benefits can range from the increased wealth generated through greater compactness, to the immediate public savings from the more efficient use of infrastructure. Developers do not typically capture these benefits and brownfield projects whose redevelopment would add to the wealth of a city may not be redeveloped because the developers' pro forma does not show an adequate return. Thus, without intervention, the market fails to achieve the optimal redevelopment of brownfields.

Although there is little quantitative data to support the public benefits purported, available studies suggest their size is significant. Some of the literature focuses on the impact of derelict and contaminated brownfields on the value of surrounding property. Although the potential for increased property value captures only part of the potential increased public wealth and income generation, it does serve as a useful indication of the magnitude of third-party commercial benefits to brownfield redevelopment (Hara Associates, 2003). The literature on the impact of brownfields on property values considers commercial, industrial, and residential property types. Most of the literature focuses on the value of the brownfields themselves, and the recovery in property value after remediation and redevelopment. The public benefit associated with this is usually captured via increased taxes paid on that property due to its higher assessed value, or simply the fact that it has a tenant. However, there are also estimates of impacts on neighboring property values, most of which suggest there is a significant impact by brownfields on neighboring property values and that this value is recoverable upon redevelopment or remediation. For example:

- Page and Rabinowitz (1993) found that on-site groundwater contamination depressed commercial and industrial property values by 10%–50% in their six case study sites.
- Simons, Bowen, and Sementelli (1997) recorded an average 17% decrease in property values for unpolluted sites close to leaking underground storage sites in Cleveland.
- Ihlanfeldt and Taylor (2002) found that the value of commercial and industrial properties surrounding brownfields (within a 1.5-mile radius) were 10% lower on average after controlling for other location factors.
- Guntermann (1995) found that open solid waste landfills depressed surrounding commercial property values by as much as 45%, but that value was recovered when the landfills were properly closed.
- Longo and Alberini (2006) studied the impact of industrial and commercial brownfields on surrounding properties in Baltimore. They found that proximity to an industrial brownfield property that was either listed or delisted from a brownfields registry had no relationship on the value of surrounding industrial property, while proximity to a listed and delisted commercial brownfield did cause a negative externality on the value of commercial property. Specifically, the price of property increases in value as one moves from 500 m to 1 km away from a listed commercial brownfield by 6.98% and from a delisted commercial brownfield by 4.36%.

The impact of brownfields on residential property values is typically estimated to be larger than that for commercial land. However, there is significant debate in the literature on how much of this represents stigma rather than real risk, lost value of use, or the aesthetic impact of derelict structures (McCluskey & Rausser, 1999; Meyer & Reaves, 1998). This debate in turn affects the question of whether remediation can restore value, since pure stigma effects may perpetuate lower values. Nonetheless, a number of studies have shown that the presence of brownfields lowers the value of surrounding residential property:

- Jenkins-Smith, Silva, Berrens, and Bohara (2002), in a case study in Corpus Christi, Texas, found homes within 1.609 km of a lead smelter, where real estate agents were required to disclose the possible presence of contaminants and cleanup requirements, lost an average of 30.5% of their value.
- Bond (2001), in a case study of the Swan River, Perth, Australia, found that stigma effects in post-remediated residential sites causes a decrease of approximately 30% in the sale price of houses.
- Dale, Murdoch, Thayer, and Waddell (1999), in a case study in the Dallas area, found that prices do eventually rebound from stigma depression, though more slowly for sites closer to a contaminated site and in poorer neighborhoods.

- Ketkar (1992), in a study of 64 municipalities in New Jersey, found that the cleanup of one hazardous waste site in a municipality has the effect of increasing property values by US$1,500 on average.
- As for green space, some cursory research (their methodology is not explicitly outlined) conducted by the International Economic Development Council (IEDC, 2001) found the average increase in property values adjacent to seven brownfields-to-green space projects to be more than four times the increase witnessed in citywide property values.
- Kaufman and Cloutier (2006), in a study of the Lincoln Neighborhood in Kenosha, Wisconsin found that the remediation of a brownfield would raise property values for a representative house in the area by 1.7%–6.2%, while both remediation and conversion to green space would raise values by 3.4%–10%.

While most studies have focused on assessing a specific type of public benefit ensuing from brownfields remediation and/or redevelopment, a few studies have sought to examine the broader array of public benefits and to take a regional perspective by comparing the relative benefits of redeveloping brownfields in the city versus developing greenfields in the periphery. Indeed, these studies have many similarities to the costs of sprawl research undertaken in the US, such as the seminal Real Estate Research Corporation project in 1974 (see Burchell et al., 1998 for a comprehensive review of US costs of sprawl research). Persky and Wiewel (1996) carried out an early study comparing the costs and benefits associated with brownfield versus greenfield development scenarios for Chicago's Brownfields Forum, which, at the time, was one of the first citywide efforts to map out an urban brownfields strategy. Their main results are summarized in Table 3.4.

Such findings suggested strongly that locating an industrial facility in the urban core entails substantial benefits to society, whereas locating it in the outer periphery entails financial benefits only to the private developer, corroborating the pro forma results above. The Persky and Wiewel study is obviously useful for identifying and quantifying many of the purported qualitative costs and benefits associated with brownfield redevelopment.

More recently, similar studies have been carried out in the Canadian context by the author (De Sousa, 2002a, 2002b) and by Dan Hara, a senior economic consultant working for Canada's National Round Table on the Environment and the Economy. The author's study examined the potential economic, social, and environmental benefits ensuing to those in Toronto from brownfield versus greenfield development. To start with, by examining numerous "real-world" brownfield and greenfield projects, it was found that those who reside or work on redeveloped urban brownfields use up less space for living and working than those who reside or work on greenfield sites in the periphery (Tables 3.5 and 3.6). In effect, 1.75 acres (0.71 ha) of greenfield land was required to support the same population living on 1 acre (0.405 ha) of brownfield land; and that 1.25 acres (0.5 ha) of greenfield land was required to support the same number of industrial workers on 1 acre of urban brownfield land. An important and widely cited study in the US by

Table 3.4: Summary of social, public, and private benefits of brownfield versus greenfield industrial locations in Chicago.

Social and public benefits of brownfield location versus greenfield (1,000 employee facility) (US$)			Private benefits of greenfield location versus brownfield (1,000 employee facility)		
Area	Net benefits (employee/year)		Area	Net benefits (employee/year)	
	Low estimate	High estimate		Low estimate	High estimate
Savings from reduced automotive congestion	$150	$500	Increase in greenfield property values	$10	$250
Savings in social costs related to reduced auto accidents	$30	$650	Lower industrial wage costs	$2,300	$2,900
Savings in costs associated with reduced air pollution from automobiles	$10	$650	Lower land costs	10%	15%
Savings from access to open space	$2	$70	Lower taxes	$2,750	$3,700
Savings from lower rates of housing abandonment	$25	$300	—	—	—
Savings from reduced subsidies to infrastructure operation	$250	$1,350	—	—	—

Source: Based on Persky and Wiewel (1996).

Table 3.5: Characteristics of the residential brownfield and greenfield scenarios.

	Typical unit mix (by land area %)[a]	Net developed land area (ha)	Number of units	Market value (CDN$ per unit)	Persons/ unit	Population
Residential brownfield						
Single	9	0.727	25	392,197	3.5	88
Semi	20	1.621	76	309,492	3.4	257
Townhouses	33	2.639	157	238,300	2.9	456
Apartments	38	3.105	358	214,000	1.9	680
Total	100	8.094	616	—	—	1,481
Residential greenfield						
Single	62	8.900	182	267,209	3.5	636
Semi	12	1.722	72	177,849	3.4	244
Townhouses	26	3.732	207	171,910	2.9	601
Apartments	0	0	—	186,000	1.9	—
Total	100	14.36	461	—	—	1,481

Source: De Sousa (2002a, 2002b).
[a]Typical unit % calculated by averaging the % breakdown in the 8 Greater Toronto Area case studies examined; net developed land area is based on property sizes typical of the case studies; for market value, the brownfield estimate is based on the case studies, greenfield estimate is for 40–50 foot lots in Brampton based on Trimart-Trillion, *Trimart-Trillion Housing Report: GTA* (1999); Persons per new housing unit is a standard assumption based on Canada Mortgage and Housing Corporation, *Conventional and Alternative Development Patterns – Phase 1: Infrastructure Costs* (1997a). It is to be noted that the study is based on net developed land area (i.e., on land developed for the residential/industrial unit and its property), as opposed to gross developed land area (which includes net lands plus sidewalks, roads, laneways, public parks, etc.).

Table 3.6: Characteristics of the industrial brownfield and greenfield scenarios.

	Net developed land area (ha)[a]	GFA m^2 (1)	Employment (m^2/employee)	Employment total	Assessment estimate (CDN$/m^2)
Industrial brownfield	8.094	40,470	75	540	534.21
Industrial greenfield	10.118	40,470	75	540	702.88

Source: De Sousa (2002a, 2002b).
[a]Net developed land area and gross floor area (GFA) are based on an estimate of 50% coverage for the brownfield scenario and 40% coverage for the greenfield scenario; employment per square foot of industrial space based on Hemson Consulting, *The Need for New Residential Density and Mix Policies* (1998b); Assessment Estimate based on Royal Le Page Commercial Inc., *GTA Industrial Market Report, 3rd Quarter* (1999).

Deason et al. (2001) reached similar conclusions. It found that 4.5 acres (1.8 ha) of greenfield land were required to accommodate the same development as 1 acre (0.405 ha) of brownfield land; with a mean ratio of 1–6.24 acres (2.52 ha) (median = 1.33 acres) for industrial development, 1–2.4 acres (1 ha) (median = 1.74 acres) for commercial development, and 1–5.57 acres (2.25 ha) (median = 2.15) for residential development. The rather significant difference between Toronto values versus those put forward by Deason are largely due to the fact that building density of new industrial development in the city versus the suburbs is relatively similar (typically 50% coverage in the city and 40% in the suburbs) and that residential development in Toronto's suburbs is much more dense than in the US due to high land values and development permit costs that are more closely tied to the provision of off-site infrastructure.

Once the "typical" development scenarios, outlined in Tables 3.5 and 3.6, were established, a cost-benefit model was devised to calculate and compare their economic, environmental, and social costs and benefits to the public (the methodological approach and the assumptions made to calculate the individual public costs and benefits examined are described in detail in De Sousa, 2002a, 2002b). In that study, public sector economic costs and benefits (i.e., taxes and infrastructure) are calculated and compared using a fiscal impact assessment — a technique often used by cities to compare alternative land uses. Other costs and benefits associated with transportation, land preservation, quality of life, and various other areas of social concern were calculated based on information, including environmental values, obtained from a variety of relevant reports (Table 3.7).

The results in Table 3.8 show that when all of the public benefits and costs associated with redeveloping brownfields are tallied for the City of Toronto alone, the industrial redevelopment scenario would generate a moderate annual benefit while the residential one would entail, instead, a modest cost (Table 3.8). While residential redevelopment would bring about benefits to public finances, and improve health and neighborhood quality, it also generates high external costs related to transportation and air pollution effects. Both types of greenfield development (residential and industrial) also generate modest social costs. This finding supports the argument that, in general, the industrial reuse of brownfields generates greater public benefits for cities than residential reuse.

A comparison of the net benefits of redeveloping a brownfield site versus (instead of) a greenfield site revealed that both types of brownfield redevelopment scenarios result in significant net benefits to citizens of the Greater Toronto Area (Table 3.9). For residential redevelopment, the main net benefit comes from avoiding the high transportation costs incurred by people living in the peripheral greenfield areas who travel more by private automobile. For industrial redevelopment scenarios, the other benefits are just as substantial. By using estimates of the total amount of brownfield acreage in the City of Toronto, the total projected net benefits to citizens of the Greater Toronto Area of redeveloping all the brownfields in lieu of greenfield development would range from CDN$21.1 to CDN$31.7 million per year for industrial redevelopment and from CDN$15.6 to CDN$23.3 million per year for residential redevelopment. This is strong evidence for justifying the provision of

Table 3.7: Cost/benefit variables quantified and compared plus data sources.

Benefits associated with brownfield redevelopment in Canada	Data sources
Public/government fiscal benefits	
Restoration/enhancement of the tax base of government (property and income tax)	Fiscal impact analysis using municipal and regional property tax and operating budget information for 1998 (City of Toronto, 1999a; City of Brampton, 1999; Regional Municipality of Peel, 1999)
Increased utilization and efficiency of existing hard (infrastructure) and soft services	1999 development charges (City of Toronto, 1999b, 1999c), City of Brampton and Regional Municipality of Peel, personal communication) with typical greenfield capital emplacement costs (CMHC, 1997b)
Environmental benefits	
Protection of public health and safety	Site assessment and cleanup costs from case studies
Reduction of development pressure on greenfield (agricultural) sites	Agricultural productivity (Statistics Canada, 1996)
Reduction in externalities from transportation (air pollution, congestion, etc.) and industrial/residential activities	Urban automobile activity (Joint Program in Transportation, 1996)
	Truck freight activity (Metropolitan Toronto Roads and Traffic Department, 1987; Ontario Ministry of Transportation, 1995; NRTEE, 1998b)
	Emissions and rail freight data (IBI Group, 1995b)
	Point source emissions from residential and industrial activities (City of Toronto, 1993; Ontario Ministry of Transportation, 1995)
Protection of groundwater and soil resources	See protection of public health and safety above
Air pollution	Aggregate industrial and residential emissions (Ontario Ministry of Transportation, 1997; City of Toronto, 1993)
	External cost of controlling pollution emissions (IBI Group, 1995b)
Social benefits	
Maintenance of existing jobs and creation of new ones	Manufacturing activity (Hemson Consulting, 1998a and Case studies)
Renewal of urban cores/elimination of socioeconomic stigmas associated with living in the proximity of brownfield sites	Case studies: Estimated impact of redevelopment on the value of adjacent property

Source: De Sousa (2002a, 2002b).

Table 3.8: Total annual public benefits for the cities of Toronto and Brampton.

CDN$	Greenfield (Brampton/Peel)		Brownfield (City of Toronto)	
	Industrial ($)	Residential ($)	Industrial ($)	Residential ($)
Tax revenues	29,062	15,635	84,346	11,947
Development charges (annualized)	(16,569)	$3,600	$(2,578)	$7,733
Transportation externalities total	(40,679)	(62,149)	(31,679)	(43,614)
Land preservation (urban)	0	0	0	0
Reduced health risks	0	0	6,487	10,811
Air pollution	(20,845)	(5,313)	(26,056)	(8,867)
Property tax benefit of additional jobs	0	0	0	0
Neighborhood value benefit	0	0	5,138	5,246
Total annual benefits (costs) per hectare	(49,031)	(48,227)	35,658	(16,745)
Total annual benefits (costs) per development scenario	(496,075)	(692,363)	288,616	(135,535)

Source: De Sousa (2002a, 2002b).

government funds for promoting brownfield redevelopment through the implementation of appropriate cost/risk sharing policy instruments.

In a background study prepared for the 2003 Canadian National Round Table on the Environment and the Economy brownfields strategy report, Hara Associates (2003) updates, expands, and revises the Toronto calculations based on new research data and a few modified assumptions. Some of Hara's key changes include annualizing development charges at a 10% social discount rate instead of at 5%; adding the value of lives saved from reduced accident fatalities (8 cents per kilometer) to transportation externality costs; raising the neighborhood improvement benefit of redevelopment from a 5% increase in adjacent property value to a 10% increase on all property within 1.5 miles plus the inclusion of benefits to third-party neighborhood property owners, and new information on periodicity increases to non-property factors of production. In total, the expanded estimates provided by Hara increase the public benefits considerably for Toronto to CDN$1.2 billion–CDN$1.85 billion per year. Hara then projects his estimates to consider urban areas throughout Canada, estimating the overall value of brownfield redevelopment nationally at CDN$4.6 to CDN$7 billion dollars annually.

While there is significant anecdotal and qualitative evidence supporting the public benefits associated with brownfields, the application of an economic analysis to

Table 3.9: Total net public benefits for the greater Toronto area.

	Net brownfield benefits (City of Toronto) (CDN$)	
	Industrial ($)	Residential ($)
Tax revenues	48,019	15,785
Development charges	18,134	1,348
Transportation externalities	19,170	66,619
Agricultural land preservation	3,756	5,329
Reduced health risks	6,487	10,811
Air pollution	0	557
Jobs	0	0
Neighborhood improvement	5,138	5,246
Annual net benefit per hectare of brownfield versus greenfield development	100,703	74,124
Annual net benefit per scenario of brownfield versus greenfield development	815,089	599,962
Potential annual public benefits of redeveloping Toronto's brownfield inventory		
Low[a]	21,147,613	15,566,094
High	31,721,419	23,349,140

Source: De Sousa (2002a, 2002b).
[a]The low estimate assumes that of the 350 ha of brownfield space available for redevelopment, 60% of it is net developable (the other 40% is required for parks, public roads, sidewalks, etc.); the high estimate assumes 90%.

estimate these provides much needed quantitative support to these claims. Cost benefit analysis (CBA) approaches have been used extensively in the US, Canada, and other countries to assess the "social worth" of potential policies and activities based on the benefits they offer the public (Pearce, 2000; Turner, Pearce, & Bateman, 1993). This is especially true in the extensive urban sprawl literature. CBA allows these public benefits to be calculated in a systematic way that helps policymakers prioritize resource-use activities and allocate scarce resources. It also makes it possible to consider environmental values in the same analysis as the more typical development benefits, thus giving environmental impacts the same weight as other economic costs and benefits (Hanley & Spash, 1993).

There are several criticisms of CBA that need to be considered (Foster, 1997; Pearce, 2000). The first is the issue of public versus private benefits. Sagoff (1988) argues that environmental assets tend to be public goods, and therefore citizen preferences and not self-interest (private) preferences must be considered in the analysis. The current chapter separates private and public preferences, but the inherent problem relates to enabling public preferences to be considered in the private pro forma, whether through negotiation, direct legislation, or economic measures. A second criticism of the CBA approach that is well known in both the fields of environmental and urban economics relates to placing a value on environmental costs and benefits (the value of agricultural land, the value of limiting pollution, etc.) and allocating them realistically to different activities. There exist a wide range of approaches and assumptions that can be taken for determining the value of such externalities. Indeed, the extensive difference between the public benefit estimates of the author and those of Hara regarding brownfields versus greenfield development in Toronto show how incorporating updated research and slightly different assumptions can significantly change the calculated benefits.

In addition to the limitations of the CBA approach, a shortcoming of this type of research lies in the fact that averaging aggregate data to estimate the implications of the "typical" scenario may not be fully reflective of the actual costs and benefits of individual projects (for example, industrial emissions may be higher or lower depending on manufacturing activity). However, the use of case-specific data would make the results less generalizable. A second limitation that should be mentioned is that the results discussed here apply to Toronto, and are more relevant to those cities that are similar to Toronto (that is, cities with high property values that affect tax revenue estimates, cities that have extensive public transportation services, etc.). Clearly, these limitations and assumptions need to be considered when utilizing these values or applying them elsewhere. More research also needs to be conducted in order to inform the models and the assumptions made, as well as to make them as sensitive as possible to location.

This CBA approach does reveal a number of things — namely, (i) that "typical" urban brownfields redevelopment is inherently more sustainable than "typical" peripheral greenfields redevelopment and (ii) that some of these public benefits are associated with reusing brownfield land (i.e., minimizing health risks by cleaning soil, increasing the value of adjacent property by removing blight) and some are associated with just developing urban land versus greenfield land in the periphery (e.g., the transportation characteristics of those living on a former urban brownfield are likely to be exactly the same as those living on a clean parcel next door). That said, future CBA research needs to measure and compare the public benefits of typical/conventional urban brownfields redevelopment with those derived from projects that incorporate sustainability and green building features. Indeed, this type of analysis could also be carried out on clean land in suburban and urban areas.

In addition to CBA, other approaches have been used to value the economic impact of brownfields redevelopment. One study carried out for the Canadian National Round Table on the Environment and the Economy (2003) provides a macro-economic perspective. The goal of the study was to gain a better understanding of the economic impact of brownfields redevelopment in Canada resulting from its so-called "multiplier effect," which refers to how one dollar spent on an activity is re-spent (through several rounds) on further activities and commodities. The analysis involved devising a hypothetical brownfield redevelopment sector (or "cluster") within the Canadian economy in terms of its economic activities and commodities, modeling the cluster's income multiplier effects on the economy, and comparing the multiplier effects of brownfield redevelopment with those of other economic sectors. That is, one dollar spent by the cluster is allocated to all of those service sectors that provide it with initial inputs, such as environmental consulting firms, remediation contracting firms, engineering consulting firms, planning consulting firms, legal services, and insurance providers. Those initial sectors then use that income to make their purchases, and so on until the original dollar is fully consumed. The analysis concluded that Canada's brownfield redevelopment cluster has a very high multiplier effect (= 3.8 multiplier) compared with other sectors of the economy because of the high service content of the brownfield redevelopment cluster and the many interfirm linkages that typify brownfield redevelopment activity. In addition, the study also estimates the federal revenue implications from brownfield redevelopment activity, suggesting, for instance, that CDN$100 million a year in brownfield redevelopment activity generates an estimated CDN$21.6 million in federal revenues.

Conclusions

Brownfields are the result of economic decisions carried out in the past that were insensitive to sustainable development and ignored the broader array of social, economic, and environmental costs tied to those decisions. This trend will continue given that the private sector method for calculating return on investment does not incorporate these issues — that is, unless they are demanded by the consumer, imposed by government, or supported through government incentives. As it currently stands, urban brownfields redevelopment is typically less cost-effective and more risky than greenfield development for developers. The findings from private sector research suggest that they are motivated to undertake brownfield redevelopment only if it is economically profitable to do so, and that environmental and social motivations hold little sway with these stakeholders. In some cases, strong real estate values in the central city, whether for residential land in places like Toronto and Chicago or industrial land in Baltimore, can offset these costs and risks making the projects profitable. However, this may not be the case everywhere, and real estate in peripheral suburbs continues to be more valuable on average than in the central city. It is here where policy tools and other mechanisms have come into play to level the playing field. But why do this?

The chapter's central message is that typical urban brownfields redevelopment in Toronto and Chicago, and more compact urban redevelopment in general, is an economically viable undertaking for society at large, bringing about significant sustainability benefits in the areas of public capital and operating costs, transportation and travel costs, land and natural habitat preservation, quality of life (air pollution, energy-use, etc.), and a variety of social issues (employment, neighborhood improvement, etc.). Furthermore, the public benefits of brownfields versus green-fields development seem to be expanding as more research emerges on a broader array of socioeconomic and environmental benefits that such redevelopment brings about. The question that also needs to be addressed is whether or not we are satisfied with the outcomes of typical brownfields redevelopment (benefits by default) or whether we should raise the bar in terms of increasing sustainability components (benefits by default and design). That is, are the benefits derived from building a conventional project on a brownfield versus a greenfield enough, or should we be seeking to enhance them further by encouraging more innovative development through better design, green infrastructure, green building, and other progressive techniques. If so, how much will this cost and who will pay for it? The analysis of private sector costs and risks reveals that there is indeed a cost to most of these features in the pro forma, and very little evidence to provide certainty of the long-term benefits.

Given the importance of residential development to building more sustainable and vibrant communities the next three chapters focus on the conversion of brownfields-to-housing. Chapter 4 examines housing policy, outlines the components of sustainable housing, and then reviews literature on residential brownfields redevelopment. Chapter 5 takes a closer look at brownfields-to-housing trends in Chicago, Illinois and Milwaukee, Wisconsin, reporting on the scale and character of redevelopment activity and providing a developers' perspective on the barriers and opportunities to growth. Chapter 6 then reviews conventional and sustainability-oriented brownfields-to-housing case studies to draw out implications from them related to the factors contributing to project success.

Chapter 4

Brownfields, Housing, and Building Sustainable Communities: Housing Policies and Visions

A vibrant and viable city is one in which all types of people wish to live, work, and play at all stages of their lives. As such, housing is perhaps the most important element in the creation of such a city. This and the next two chapters examine the issue of redeveloping brownfields into housing, and how such redevelopment can contribute to the creation of more compact and sustainable residential environments. This chapter begins with an introduction to housing policy and objectives in both the US and Canada and an examination of how these have evolved over the last half century. The brownfields-to-housing issue is then examined in more detail, beginning with a look at current policy efforts and a review of the scholarly literature in the field. The components of sustainable housing are then reviewed in order to provide a framework for assessing the extent to which brownfields-to-housing efforts are contributing to achieving sustainability. Chapter 5 then takes a closer look at brownfields-to-housing trends in the cities of Chicago, Illinois and Milwaukee, Wisconsin to highlight the kinds of residential brownfield redevelopment activity taking place in terms of scale, character, value, and other key variables. The brownfields-to-housing issue is then examined from the perspective of developers, given that they are ultimately responsible for redevelopment, and the role of government in leveraging such development. Chapter 6 reviews brownfields-to-housing case studies in Milwaukee and Chicago in detail, and then chronicles the efforts taken in Vancouver, British Columbia to bring about a more sustainable residential vision along the shores of False Creek, a former industrial district dating back to the late 1800s.

Urban Housing Policy Change in Canada and the US

Housing policy in Canada has changed significantly in the post-war era, going through several distinct stages that have developed in response to different demographic and economic conditions, as well as ideological perspectives. Carroll and Jones (2000) outline these stages succinctly as follows:

- Economic development (1945–1968): focus on the development of a large-scale housing industry for building middle-income single-family dwellings, with some financial support coming from the federal government.

- Social development (1968–1978): focus on comprehensive planning, rational problem solving, and intergovernmental cooperation to deliver and sustain housing programs and manage related problems.
- Financial restraint (1978–1986): focus on reducing housing programs, minimizing federal government spending, and passing program delivery to provincial and municipal levels of government, but maintaining nonprofit and rehabilitation programs.
- Disentanglement (1986–1994): focus on gradually reducing the federal government presence in housing markets by partaking in cost-sharing, small-scale projects, and private sector partnerships.
- Disengagement and privatization (1994–present): focus on devolving housing responsibility and reducing government presence in markets, with a greater emphasis on partnerships, "third sector" programs, and transferring responsibility to local government for the delivery of housing programs.

The shift from federal government involvement in the support and provision of housing to the devolution of responsibility and market orientation in the mid-1990s has been dramatic. According to Hulchanski (2002), Canada now has the most private sector-dominated, market-based housing system of any Western nation (including the United States) and the smallest social housing sector of any major Western nation (except for the United States). Approximately 95% of Canadian households obtain their housing from the private market, close to two-thirds of all households own their own home, and only 5% of Canada's households are in non-market social housing (public housing, nonprofit housing, and nonprofit cooperatives). Furthermore, Canada spends only about 1% of its budget on programs and subsidies to support all the social housing units ever built across the country (about half a million units).

Overall, the role of Canada's national housing agency, the Canada Mortgage and Housing Corporation (CMHC) (established in 1946), has gone from establishing a housing community that included the private market and subsidies for social programs, to a more limited education and policy guidance role with some limited funding in place for social programs. In relation to sustainability goals, the federal government's primary focus has historically been on ensuring that the market provides adequate housing and that social housing opportunities exist to some extent. Currently, the CMHC has been promoting sustainability by encouraging neighborhood design and land use planning approaches that reduce costs and environmental impacts, while maintaining community livability. This has been achieved largely by providing examples of best practices in design and development, recommending tools for planners and designers, and publishing other research on sustainability.

The role of provincial and territorial governments in social housing and related urban renewal programs has declined concomitantly since the mid-1990s. Put simply, provinces have been reluctant to raise the capital required to make up for federal cuts in social housing for fear of annoying taxpayers. As such, all but two provinces, which spent little on social housing to begin with (Alberta and the Yukon Territory), drastically cut their social housing spending from 1995 to 1997. In the province of Ontario, for instance, funding for social housing activity declined from CDN$511 million in 1985 to CDN$29 million by 1997. While the Ontario Ministry for Municipal Affairs and Housing supports the creation of affordable housing and housing for the disabled in that province, its primary mandate is to foster private sector building.

Hulchanski (2002) notes that there has been nothing exceptional about the commitment of municipal government action on housing issues. This is due to several factors including low voter turnout (with homeowners voting in greater numbers and demanding proper attention from city government), extensive "not in my back yard" (NIMBY) pressures on municipal politicians to not locate housing or housing related services for low-income people in most municipalities, and the fact that municipalities typically have a limited tax base with which to fund such programs. Consequently, the devolution of housing to provincial and municipal levels of government has resulted in programs that are typically under-funded, varied, and "stand alone" (Carroll & Jones, 2000).

To many, this laissez-faire approach has led to a social housing crisis. While most Canadians have adequate housing, about 8% still live in dwellings requiring major repairs and about 5% live in housing considered to be overcrowded (Hulchanski, 2002). When this data is disaggregated, it reveals that renters bear the brunt of the problem with 20% living in housing considered either in need of major repairs or overcrowded. In addition, research has found that some property owners refuse to rent apartments to families with children, single mothers, or people on social assistance (Dion, 2001; Novac, Darden, Hulchanski, & Seguin, 2002). The most extreme manifestation of housing inequity in Canada has become homelessness, which is on the rise with families now the fastest-growing group among them. Race is also an issue as one quarter of the homeless people in some Canadian cities are Aboriginal and about 15% of Toronto's hostel users are immigrants and refugees (Toronto Mayor's Homelessness Action Task Force, 1999, p. 19).

Hulchanski (2002, p. 2) aptly sums up the implications of the current approach in terms of sustainable urban development as follows:

> If housing all Canadians adequately is a prerequisite for a sustainable social fabric, the toughest problem is how to house people with moderate and low incomes when the market mechanism is the main provider of housing. Although the problem of affordable housing and homelessness is not exclusively urban, in a nation that is 80 percent urbanized and in which half the population lives in the four largest metropolitan areas, housing need tends to be concentrated in expensive, big-city housing markets. "Affordable housing," as Tom Kent notes, "is the greatest of urban deficiencies" (Kent, 2002, p. 9). Housing is the most expensive item in the household budget, yet the wide gap between the highest and lowest income levels means that more and more people are excluded from the housing market — and some are left completely un-housed.

Both Canada and the US are very similar in the nature of their housing market and their approach to housing provision. Although incentives for home ownership are considered slightly more generous in the United States (i.e., the allowance of mortgage interest and property tax deductions), both countries retain about the same ownership levels (Wexler, 1996). Both countries also have about the same proportion of subsidized or social housing, although the delivery of such housing differs in that 54% of social housing in Canada is delivered by the so-called "third sector" (i.e., small, nonprofit, community-based groups, municipal nonprofit associations, and social housing cooperatives), 35% is public housing, and 11% is from the private sector. While in the US, 60% of federally assisted households are in the for-profit sector, 10% in the nonprofit sector and the remainder is public housing (Wexler, 1996).

The US federal government has played a much more direct and active role in the provision and funding of social housing, and programs in the US have been more closely tied to urban renewal efforts. Prior to the 1930s, the federal government had little involvement with the housing needs of citizens. The crash of the stock market in 1929, however, left many citizens crowded into housing units or homeless. Early federal initiatives in this period provided funds to finance low-cost and slum clearance housing. The end of World War II marked a turning point in US housing policy as the government became concerned with providing homes for service people returning from the war, as well as the worsening condition of many US cities (Colten, 2003). The Housing Act of 1949 declared that the general welfare and security of the nation required "a decent home and suitable living environment for every American family" and focused largely on providing funds for slum clearance and community development. Urban renewal programs were expanded significantly during this period to prevent the spread of slums, to rehabilitate blighted areas, and to work to create more public housing units.

The 1960s witnessed an upsurge in the number of federal assistance programs for housing and urban development, as well as an increase in federal funding. The Department of Housing and Urban Development (HUD) was established in 1965 in an effort to consolidate the numerous federal housing programs and to address housing policy concerns throughout the nation. Several programs were implemented during this decade to expand federal assistance to low- and moderate-income homeowners, including providing federally insured home mortgage loans to help low-income households purchase homes; offering a variable interest subsidy on down payment loans made by private institutions; and encouraging the construction of affordable rental housing by nonprofit or limited-dividend developers by providing an interest rate subsidy.

These policies were reassessed in the early 1970s and suspended in 1973 due to concerns over their budget implications and the negative image associated with public housing generally. In 1974, the Housing and Community Development Act contained two important components — Community Development Block Grants (CDBG) and Section 8. Instead of federal government defining specific categories of development required for funding local projects, CDBG offered 100% grants that allowed localities to create their own programs to meet local needs. Indeed, the

CDBG marked the start of a more decentralized (federalist) approach wherein responsibilities for making housing decisions and allocating funds were devolved to state and local governments. As for Section 8, it came in various forms, including programs to encourage the private sector to build or rehabilitate housing with the federal government subsidizing the rent of lower-income tenants, and a program that provided a housing allowance that tenants could use for any unit that conformed to a specified rent limit.

The increase in housing assistance in the 1970s was followed by a significant decrease in the early 1980s. As Colton (2003, p. 221) describes, the emphasis of government policy at the time made "it possible for low-income households to find housing in the existing stock, rather than have the federal government increase the housing supply." Although there was still some financial support for the development and rehabilitation of housing during this period, the small subsidies were not perceived as particularly effective. One important tax incentive for housing development introduced in this decade was the Low-Income Housing Tax Credit, which today represents the largest federal commitment to affordable housing construction and rehabilitation. This 10-year federal income tax credit is provided to private investors who provide the equity needed to build or rehabilitate housing. The credits are allocated to state and local housing agencies that then allocate them to developers with relevant projects, who in turn sell them to private investors to raise equity for the project.

Efforts in the 1990s emphasized the role of state and local governments in the creation of affordable housing and saw the introduction of the so-called HOME program, which was established to foster "public–private" partnerships to create affordable housing. The HOME program provides annual grants to larger communities and to states for a broad range of housing assistance efforts, including new construction, rehabilitation, and rental assistance. However, unlike previous programs, there are matching requirements for state and local governments interested in obtaining these funds. The HOPE program was also established to convert public housing units into units to be purchased by low-income residents, and to revive distressed public housing. In all, the budget for direct housing assistance has remained consistent in the latter part of the 1990s and the early part of this century.

Although the federal government continues to play a central role in housing policy and provision, there has been a growing emphasis on the role of state and local government since the introduction of CDBG in 1974. State and local governments are now given authority to devise local programs and are partially responsible for funding projects. They have created departments, housing authorities, and community partnerships to address local housing concerns and many have taken steps to acknowledge housing as a key element of their economies. Two key entities that have been created, and have expanded as a result, are state finance agencies and community development corporations (CDCs). State housing finance agencies have proven to be highly effective at delivering federal housing assistance to homebuyers, developers, and other groups. CDCs are more grass roots oriented networks that address a range of housing and neighborhood needs. These are typically considered more responsive to the need of local communities, particularly in low-income areas where they work closely with community groups and other nonprofits interested in neighborhood renewal. As in Canada, it is likely that housing programs in the US will continue to devolve, but with greater financial support from the federal level. As Colton (2003, p. 243) aptly puts it:

> In the final analysis, housing issues are generally local or, at times, state issues, and the needs of each community and state vary widely. The federal government can provide national programs and incentives, but the real solutions often come at the local level, community by community.

That said, the role of upper levels of government is to help set targets and ensure basic social and affordable housing needs are met locally, otherwise local communities may implement policies to limit or exclude such development since many of those governments have no incentives to change policies their voters want.

Housing and Sustainable Development

Linking housing and sustainable development requires us to consider the implications of residential location, the affect of development/renovation on the local community, and the broad range of environmental, social, and economic impacts of housing units themselves. Although there is no agreed upon definition of sustainable housing, the one put forward by Edwards (2000, p. 20) captures the essence of the definition put forward by the World Commission on Environment and Development:

> housing that meets the perceived and real needs of the present in a resource efficient fashion whilst providing attractive, safe and ecologically rich neighborhoods.

According to Edwards (2000, p. 20), assessing the sustainability of housing and its development requires addressing five distinct fields: (i) the conservation of natural resources (land, energy, and water); (ii) the sensible reuse of man-made resources; (iii) the maintenance of ecosystems and their regenerative potential; (iv) the equity between generations, peoples, and classes; and (v) the provision of health, safety, and security. It should be noted that while this book focuses on the impact of homes that are either newly developed on former brownfield sites or converted from industrial buildings, it is evident that the greatest sustainability impact would ultimately come from retrofitting the existing stock of houses. Despite this, residential brownfield projects could act as an example and a catalyst for such activity if the projects are tied into neighborhood renewal efforts more broadly.

Edwards' first field considers the environmental impacts of all stages of the housing life cycle, including construction, operation, maintenance, and demolition. Impacts include the use of non-renewable energy, land, and water; the generation of pollution involved in producing, transporting and disposing of materials, heating and cooling the building; and the use of lighting and appliances within the home. As discussed in Chapter 2, housing is a major consumer of land resources and contributor to urban sprawl on agricultural and pristine lands. Indeed, the US Department of Agriculture reports that the urban land area in the US has quadrupled from roughly 15 million acres in 1945 to an estimated 60 million acres in 2002, while the Census Bureau reports that the US population barely doubled over this same period (Lubowski, Vesterby, Bucholtz, Baez, & Roberts, 2006). Thus, urban land area has increased at about twice the rate of population growth and much of it has been due to expanding residential parcels. Growth in the periphery has been particularly rapid. Of the 2 million acres per year consumed by total urban growth, 1.72 million acres of this has been residential growth into rural areas. Evidence suggests the yearly rate of increase of residential land use may have been higher over shorter periods. For example, land used for all single-family housing, urban and rural, increased by about 2.3 million acres per year from 1994 to 1997 (Lubowski et al., 2006). It is little wonder then that the study by Deason et al. found that 5.57 (2.15 median) acres of greenfield land were required to accommodate the same residential development as one acre of brownfield land.

The energy requirements of residential buildings and the greenhouse gases emitted for supplying that energy are of particular interest given growing concern over global warming. It has been estimated that the residential sector accounts for close to 20% of the end-use energy consumed in Canada (Fung, Aydinalp, Ugursal, & Farahbakhsh, 1998). There are more than 76 million residential buildings and nearly 5 million commercial buildings in the United States today and collectively these buildings consume 65.2% of total US electricity and over 36% of total US primary energy. Those in single-family households, which make up 74% of total US households, also tend to consume more energy on average (115 million Btu) than those in mobile-homes (79 million Btu) and multi-family dwellings (60 million Btu). Electricity and natural gas use is highest for single-family detached dwellings and declines by almost half for attached and multi-family dwellings (RECS, 2001). While part of this difference is due to the size of the structure, much of it is simply because fewer walls are exposed to the elements in multi-unit dwellings.

Energy consumption related to travel is also an important consideration. Research by the Canadian Mortgage and Housing Corporation comparing different density neighborhoods in several cities finds that even though car ownership is relatively similar, driving distances and related greenhouse gas emissions range extensively between the central city and the outer suburbs. In Ottawa, Ontario, for example, even though car ownership is relatively similar in the central city, inner suburbs, and the outer suburbs (1.3, 1.5, versus 1.7 cars per household) the distance driven for weekday urban trips ranges considerably from 9,500 to 10,000 km per household in the central area (apartment versus mixed housing types), to 14,000 km/ household in the inner suburbs (similar for mixed and detached housing), to between 21,000 and 23,000 km/household in the outer suburbs (mixed housing versus detached). The estimated greenhouse gas emissions from those trips rises commensurately from 2,600 to 2,900 kg of greenhouse gas per household in the central area, to 4,000 kg/household in the inner suburbs, to 6,000–6,300 kg/household in the outer suburbs (CMHC, 2006).

Energy is not, however, the only resource to consider. Commercial and residential buildings also use 40% of the raw materials globally and 12% of the potable water in the United States. Building activity in the US also contributes over 136 million tons of construction and demolition waste (2.8 lbs/person/day), and produces 30% of US greenhouse gas emissions (US Green Building Council (USGBC), 2003).

The extensive use of raw materials and the disposal of demolition waste required for housing also affects Edwards' second field — the sensible reuse of man-made resources. Indeed, the reuse of buildings and infrastructure is a key aspect of brownfields redevelopment.

A topic of growing interest is the maintenance of ecosystems and their regenerative potential (Field 3) as part of the housing provision process. New developments are being asked, and in some cases required, to consider protecting sensitive areas, reducing impervious surfaces, and implementing Best Management Practices for managing stormwater, increasing tree canopy, and enhancing habitat. Issues related to ecological restoration of blighted landscapes, converting brownfields into parks, and incorporating green infrastructure into brownfields projects have received greater attention in the policy and scholarly literature (see Chapters 7, 8, and 9). This linking of housing and ecosystem management is also being promoted in suburban and rural residential development via the Conservation Subdivision design approach (Arendt, 1996), which has been presented as an alternative to conventional large lot residential development. A form of clustering, this planning approach emphasizes the quality as well as the quantity of land preserved (Austin, 2004). With open space conservation subdivisions, primary and secondary conservation areas are designated and set aside from development. Primary conservation areas are not buildable sections of land (e.g., steep slopes, wetlands), while secondary conservation areas include features such as wooded tracts, meadows, critical wildlife habitat, highly productive farmland, and areas with historic or cultural significance. Homes are then clustered on the remaining land and positioned such that homeowners have views and access to open space and natural areas. This format is considered to offer a means for local planning officials to accommodate residential growth while preserving natural areas, rural features, and wildlife habitat that is typically altered. Despite this, urban sprawl may still spread outward from urban centers and disrupt these areas. Furthermore, it does not address the loss of agricultural land and livelihood.

The social sustainability of housing takes into consideration Edwards' fourth and fifth fields (i.e., (iv) the equity between generations, peoples, and classes (v) the provision of health, safety, and security). Most of the government's efforts in housing and renewal have historically aimed at addressing these issues. Current interest in this domain lies in the mixing of housing types by size and affordability so that citizens do not need to move out of the community. Indeed, sustainable communities are considered lasting communities where people can invest long periods of time in their neighborhood. One problem, however, has been the tendency for the market to cluster housing in terms of class and race, particularly in suburbs, as opposed to promoting the development of mixed-income communities. Another problem relates to defining exactly what the optimal mix of housing type and housing prices/rents should be. There is also the issue of what approach is best for delivering public housing, or whether a mix of approaches is best. In addition to offering direct public funding for the provision of affordable housing, other basic approaches involve preventing localities from adopting specific rules inhibiting affordable housing, setting mandatory local or state targets for every community (e.g., 10% in Massachusetts), or forcing private housing developers to include affordable units in all projects they build.

While many residential development models have been put forward in an effort to limit disinvestment in central cities, the spread of sprawl, race and income segregation, and environmental deterioration, New Urbanism has become by far the most popular approach, boasting over 210 developments under construction or complete in the United States (Congress for the New Urbanism, 2006). According to the Congress for the New Urbanism, established in 1993 to promote such development, some key principles that guide the design of such neighborhoods include:

(i) Neighborhoods should be compact, pedestrian-friendly, and mixed-use;
(ii) Many activities of daily living should occur within walking distance;
(iii) Within neighborhoods, a broad range of housing types and price levels can bring people of diverse ages, races, and incomes into daily interaction;
(iv) Transit corridors, when properly planned and coordinated, can help organize metropolitan structure and revitalize urban centers;
(v) Appropriate building densities and land uses should be within walking distance of transit stops;
(vi) Concentrations of civic, institutional, and commercial activity should be embedded in neighborhoods and districts;
(vii) The economic health and harmonious evolution of neighborhoods, districts, and corridors can be improved through graphic urban design codes that serve as predictable guides for change; and
(viii) A range of parks should be distributed within neighborhoods.

Nevertheless, the approach has not been without its skeptics. As Richardson and Gordon (2004, p. 230) point out:

> a cynical view of New Urbanism might regard it as pie-in-the sky social engineering based on false diagnosis of society's problems, an excessive faith in the ability to change the world, and the prescription of policies that are difficult to implement.

Indeed, many researchers have criticized New Urbanism development for its failure to achieve equitability, transportation, and commercial-mix goals (Richardson & Gordon, 2004; Till, 2001; Zimmerman, 2001). On the other hand, one study that tested the environmental sustainability assertions of New Urbanism on the basis of 50 matched pairs of development projects in the US found that new urbanism does offer a greener and more compact alternative to traditional development as it is more likely to protect and restore sensitive areas, reduce impervious cover, and incorporate best management practices (e.g., tree planting, bioretention ponds, landscaping for infiltration). While New Urbanism developments in infill sites specifically are more likely to incorporate impervious surface reduction techniques and restore degraded stream environments than conventional projects, they were found to have equivalent levels of sensitive area protection and use of best management practices (Berke, MacDonald, White, & Holmes, 2003).

Ultimately, keeping track of whether or not housing efforts are addressing the sustainable housing fields put forward by Edwards requires the development and application of a broader array of sustainable housing indicators and targets that address those "fields." A look at some housing indicator lists taken from various sources finds that many address one or more of these fields, but that environmental, social, and economic variables still tend to be separated (adapted from Sustainable Measures, 2006; DETR, 1999a; Adams & Watkins, 2002):

- Housing availability indicators
  - House price to income ratio
  - Number of homeless people
  - Distribution of affordable housing throughout city
  - Home ownership rate
  - Share of new housing units going into incorporated parts of county
  - Waiting time for subsidized housing
  - Annual applicants for affordable housing
  - Single-family housing growth compared to population growth
  - Number of people using homeless shelters
  - Yearly percentage increase in number of dwelling units
  - Number of houses versus population
  - Average annual vacancy rate
  - New multi-family units as percent of total new residential units
  - Number of rehabilitated affordable housing units
  - New privately owned housing units
  - New housing starts.
- Housing condition indicators
  - Floor area per person in housing
  - Low-income housing with severe physical problems
  - Percent of dwellings in need of major repair
  - Housing that is inadequate, overcrowded, or costs over 30% of income.
- Housing cost indicators
  - Affordability of single-family home
  - Renters who cannot afford to live in the city
  - Low-income renters paying more than 30% of income on rent
  - Home ownership rate
  - Number of new homes that are energy-efficient
  - Housing affordability ratio-rent prices

○ Median family income as percent of median single-family house price
○ Median family income as percent of average rent on two-bedroom apartment
○ Median family income as percent of annual single-family house mortgage payment
○ Percent of households able to afford buying median single-family house
○ Median family income as a percent of average property tax.
• Sustainable residential development
○ Access to local green space
○ Community spirit
○ Energy efficiency of new domestic appliance
○ Energy use per household
○ Household waste and recycling
○ Household water use and peak demand
○ How children get to school
○ Noise levels
○ Quality of surroundings
○ Traffic congestion (adapted from DETR, 1999a and Adams & Watkins, 2002).

Clearly, a more holistic approach is required, particularly at the policy and project planning level. One decision-making matrix being developed to make housing more sustainable is the LEED for Homes Project Checklist developed by the USGBC (see Resource Categories and Credit types, adapted from Version 1.72 — August 18, USGBC, 2005b, 2005c), which touches on many of Edwards' fields except for those related to social sustainability:

• Location and linkages (LEED neighborhood, site selection, infrastructure, community resources, compact development)
• Sustainable sites (Site stewardship, landscaping, shading of hardscapes, non-toxic pest control)
• Water efficiency (Water reuse, irrigation system, indoor water use)
• Indoor environmental quality (ENERGY STAR, combustion venting, humidity control, outdoor air ventilation, local exhaust, supply air distribution, supply air filtering, contaminant control, radon protection, vehicle emissions protection)
• Materials and resources (home size, material efficient framing, local sources, durability plan, environmentally preferable products, waste management)
• Energy and atmosphere (ENERGY STAR home, insulation, air infiltration, windows, duct tightness, space heating and cooling, water heating, lighting, appliances, renewable energy, refrigerant management)
• Homeowner awareness (homeowner education)
• Innovation and design process (innovative design).

Efforts have also been made in the UK to develop an approach for assessing the quality of housing redevelopment projects, particularly when those projects request public funding (Department for Communities and Local Government, 2006). The feasibility of so-called Housing Quality Indicators (HQI) was assessed in 1996, followed by the development and testing of a more workable set of indicators. The HQI allows an assessment of the quality of key features of a housing project in three main categories: (i) location, (ii) design, and (iii) performance. These three categories produce the 10 "Quality Indicators" that make up the Housing Quality Indicator system. Indicators can be used to assess a wide range of housing including: general-purpose social housing; private housing; and new-build and refurbished properties. As with the US Green Building (USGB) indicators, the HQI consists of a number of indicators, each consisting of a number of topics covering the most important aspects of quality relevant to that indicator. The scoring maintains the concept of a range of quality rather than a single minimum standard in each aspect of quality like the USGBC checklist does. The main body of the HQI form contains information on the 10 indicators that measure quality. Each indicator contains a series of questions that are completed by the developer or client. The 10 indicators are (i) location, (ii) site — visual impact, layout, and landscaping, (iii) site — open space, (iv) site — routes and movement, (v) Unit — size, (vi) Unit — layout, (vii) Unit — noise, light, and services, (viii) Unit — accessibility, (ix) Unit — energy, green and sustainability issues, and (x) performance in use.

The second part of the HQI system is a scoring spreadsheet. Each indicator receives one-tenth of the total possible score, as they can all be viewed as equally, though differently, important in creating quality. Failure to meet suitable levels of, say, security or noise control may render a house so uninhabitable that other factors cannot compensate. However, this does not imply that these indicators should be more heavily weighted than other factors; merely that failure to meet a certain level is unacceptable for these indicators.

Although initially developed for use by registered social housing landlords, in the longer term, the aim is to develop the HQI system as a flexible measurement tool of housing quality used by consumers and developers alike for new and existing stock in both the public and private sectors. Despite this, neither scheme includes many social factors directly in the assessment framework, regardless of whether it relates to the housing project directly or to the project's impact on the neighborhood and environment more generally.

The Brownfields-to-Housing Literature

Even though the scholarly literature on the redevelopment of brownfields and contaminated lands has become rather extensive, the issue of housing has received relatively little attention. Only a handful of studies exist on the housing reuse issue in the United States. The work by Greenberg (1999) and his research team (Greenberg, Lowrie, Mayer, & Miller, 2001a) presents solid arguments both for reuse (since brownfields constitute an available supply of land for housing which can improve neighborhood quality) and against it (given that incompetence and greed are factors that might make such redevelopment risky on many counts). In an editorial, Greenberg (2002) comes out in favor of residential reuse because he sees it as the best strategy for revitalizing inner city communities, provided civic leaders and public health officials are involved in the process and developers are offered financial assistance to help attenuate costs. The basis for his assessment is a 2001-study (Greenberg, Craighill, Mayer, Zukin, & Wells, 2001b) in which Greenberg and his team interviewed 779 New Jersey residents to gauge their willingness to live on redeveloped brownfield lands. The team found 14% of respondents were willing to do so, most of whom were young and childless families, middle-class Latino and Asian-American families, and economically disadvantaged individuals living in apartments. The authors point out that a "critical challenge is to interest developers in building housing on brownfields," given that "developers have historically made large profits building in the suburbs;" and concluding that there is a need for "more data on what is needed to help developers" (Greenberg, et al., 2001a, 2001b, p. 534).

In a brief case study review, Kirkwood (2001a) argues that the redevelopment of brownfields for residential projects presents itself as a nation-wide opportunity for easing housing shortages, redirecting urban growth, and creating a more balanced regional diffusion of investment. These findings are echoed by Coffin (2002), who found that low-income households are already locating near brownfields, and a more formalized strategy would help provide solutions to both the brownfields and affordable housing dilemmas in low-income communities.

The International City/County Management Association (ICMA, 2003) has summarized the direct and indirect benefits to governments associated with residential brownfields redevelopment as follows: (i) it saves money through the use of existing infrastructure; (ii) it increases tax revenues; (iii) it promotes economic development; (iv) it helps cleanup the environment; and (v) it improves community morale by removing blight, reducing crime, preserving historic structures, protecting public health, revitalizing neighborhoods, curbing sprawl, and inspiring unique design. Perhaps the most commonly cited benefit associated with residential brown-fields redevelopment is that it will reduce redevelopment pressure on greenfields given that urban brownfields redevelopment is particularly denser.

The barriers facing residential brownfields redevelopment have received some attention in the professional literature. A survey of 44 state Voluntary Cleanup Programs by Bartsch and Dorfman (2000) found there was relatively little support for residential brownfields projects, with only 21 states providing suitable liability protection for them and only 8 making incentives available. A more recent study published by the National Center for Housing and the Environment (2003) discovered that funding and liability issues (in states that have not entered into an Memorandum of Agreement (MOA) with the Environmental Protection Agency (EPA)) continue to persist within the new framework of federal brownfields legislation. Examining residential brownfields redevelopment from the perspective of local government, ICMA (2003) found the key challenges to be the cost of remediation, protecting public health, the compatibility of surrounding land uses, preventing gentrification, preserving traditional neighborhood character and addressing specific community concerns. A recent report by the Northeast-Midwest Institute (Schopp, 2003) highlighted some additional concerns, including the presence of poor markets in some locales, higher cleanup costs for residential projects, and the impact of barriers imposed by the policies of the Federal Housing Authority (including remediation and technical constraints that have to be dealt with before a loan application can be considered).

Regarding policy for overcoming the challenges to redevelopment, a study of the US Department of Housing and Urban Development's site contamination policies carried out by ICF Consulting (2003) found many of its policies were not facilitating residential redevelopment and required upgrading. An early study by Pepper (1997) on the Circle F housing project in New Jersey found low-income housing tax credits, strong community involvement, and interagency coordination to be essential to project success. Studies by Meyer, Wernstedt, and Alberini (2004) and Wernstedt, Meyer, Alberini, and Heberle (2006) put a monetary value on some of the incentives that could be used to redevelop brownfields for residential use. From a survey of over 300 developers, the study found that eliminating third-party liability risk was the most valuable strategy, followed by the elimination of cleanup cost risks, and the elimination of a requirement of holding a public hearing. Indeed, the high value given to the desire to eliminate the requirement for a public meeting points to the disconnect between what is required by developers to make a profit and what is required to make a project sustainable. Beyond these studies, little work has been done to examine the application and effectiveness of alternative policies and programs to alleviate the barriers to residential brownfields reuse in particular.

In terms of redevelopment outcomes, the US Conference of Mayor's 2003 report estimates that residential reuse only accounts for 14% of brownfield projects. A study by the National Center for Housing and the Environment (2003, p. 3) points out that residential brownfields redevelopment is becoming a viable option in many states:

- California — developed 5,200 new housing units on brownfields sites;
- Colorado — developed 2,855 new units gaining approval through its voluntary cleanup program;
- Michigan — documented 1,400 new units at 11 different sites across the state;

As outlined in Chapter 2, research on the Canadian situation indicates that the housing option can result in a solid return-on-investment to private developers in strong residential markets such as the City of Toronto and that the attractiveness of residential brownfield projects can increase considerably with minor changes to existing land use policies and programs. The substantial public benefits of having people reside on urban brownfields, as opposed to suburban greenfields, are also extensive. Indeed, research by the author in Canada has found that residential redevelopment has played a much more important role in reusing brownfields than in the US. Based on information provided by seven Canadian cities, 47% of all brownfields redevelopment activity in Canada has been residential (De Sousa, 2006a, 2006b, 2006c). The survey also revealed that over 30,000 new residential dwelling units in 11 cities were constructed on brownfields. This trend is due to the relatively strong residential market near or within the cities and the tendency of most cities to rezone industrial lands in an effort to raise their value, which is historically one of the few tools available to them.

An earlier study (De Sousa, 2002a, 2002b) found that an extensive amount of brownfield redevelopment activity took place in the City of Toronto during the 1990s. In total, 358,192 m^2 of residential floor space (59% of total floor area for all uses) was developed and/or approved during that period. In fact, 300,000 m^2 of residential floor space was added from 1997 to 1999 alone, more than took place during 24 years of redevelopment activities on employment-oriented lands prior to that (Huther, 1997). Unlike other brownfield projects, residential ones also took place throughout the city, adjacent to the central business district and in the "inner ring suburbs." Case studies consulted for the project also revealed that a mix of new units was being provided — 10% of the construction consisted of single-family dwellings, 10% semi-detached dwellings, 35% town (row) houses, and 45% condo/loft units.

While scholarly research on brownfields-to-housing in Canada has been minimal, government efforts to study and promote such redevelopment through the CMHC have been growing. A recent review of the literature and key informant interviews carried out for the Canada Mortgage and Housing Corporation (CMHC) (2004, 2005) found that brownfield redevelopment for housing in Canada shares many of the same barriers as those experienced by brownfield redevelopment in general (i.e., liability, regulations, financing, technology, planning, stigma). However, the authors found that for brownfield redevelopment for housing, the liability and regulatory barriers are perceived as more significant because of the greater number of end users (homeowners and renters), which translates into a larger number of potential claimants, and potentially more expensive civil actions. Some of the suggestions put forward for reducing barriers for housing include:

- Eliminating/reducing the potential for regulatory and/or civil liability;
- Streamlining risk assessment procedures and increasing the reliance on qualified professionals for risk assessment/management;
- Providing more staffing and resources to government agencies to allow for the provision of expertise and timely review of projects;
- Introducing government funding programs to aid with up-front expenses for site assessment and remediation;
- Streamlining planning approvals and providing incentives for brownfields redevelopment (pre-zoning, density bonusing, streamlined approvals);
- Restricting greenfield development; and
- Publicizing successful projects and promoting outreach.

The study concludes that, while some progress has been made in most provinces on regulatory barriers, and progress has been achieved on financial barriers, more generally, the situation has not improved much in the last decade. Indeed, there is still a need in the Canadian context to better understand the relationship between these barriers in order to evaluate the impact of legislative, financial, and planning incentives and initiatives on overcoming these obstacles.

Issues related to residential brownfields redevelopment have received more attention in an international context, particularly in the UK where various levels of government have set an ambitious target of building 60% of new housing on brownfields (Fulford, 1998; Bibby & Shepherd, 1999; Box & Shirley, 1999; Cozens, Hillier, & Prescott, 1999; Walton, 2000; Adams, Hutchison, & Munjoma, 2001; Adams, 2004; Tiesdell & Adams, 2004, see Box 4.1 for more detail on UK brownfields-to-housing efforts). Examining the controversy related to the location of housing in the UK, and assessing the strategies and interests of diverse stakeholders, Adams and Watkins (2002) conclude that setting ambitious goals for residential brownfields redevelopment and pitting brownfields versus greenfields may not be productive ways to achieve sustainable housing. They suggest that more fundamental changes are needed in the institutional relationship between the public and private sectors and their respective modes of operation (see Box 4.1).

Box 4.1: Brownfields-to-Housing in the UK

Throughout the last century, the promotion of home ownership in British policy has resulted in many consequences, some of which have been intended, and others unintentional. Many new housing developments have been greenfield based, and therefore posed challenges to the goals of social and environmental sustainability (Adams & Watkins, 2002). During the 1990s, however, planning authorities restricted the availability of greenfield sites for development, in hopes of fostering brownfield redevelopment (Tiesdell & Adams, 2004). Recently, British policy has begun to focus on promoting sustainable housing programs that seek to reduce pressures on greenfields, while simultaneously addressing the social and economic concerns of the community.

Two key features of sustainable housing are technological advances aimed at alleviating energy use and cost, and residential design that minimizes its impact on the environment. There is a need, however, to consider other factors such as location of housing, (within urbanized area or along the periphery) and the previous land use upon which these developments are to be placed. Looking to continental Europe for inspiration, many arguments have recently surfaced that seek to alter the urban form of British cities, encouraging density and redevelopment in the already existing urban setting. Fostered by a strict regulatory environment, homebuilders must increasingly consider the challenges brought forth by redevelopment (Adams, 2004). Though not all commentators agree with this philosophy, the argument in favor of compaction necessarily involves the redevelopment of brownfields in British cities (Adams & Watkins, 2002).

Brownfield housing land use policy since 1990 has addressed several key concerns related to infill of existing urban areas. In 1995 for instance, the Department of the Environment aimed to build half of all new homes on reused sites in 10 years (by 2005). In the next few years, other agencies working toward sustainable goals increased that number to anywhere from 60% to 75%. The most recent plan put forward by the Labour government is to have 60% of new homes in England constructed on previously developed land or provided through existing conversions by 2008 (Adams & Watkins, 2002). Though the proportion of new dwellings built on previously developed land increased from 39% in 1985 to 48% in 2000, this type of housing development has been stagnant since 1992. The goal of 60% by 2008 could prove elusive, as issues with the homebuilding industry, existing contamination, and competition for other forms of reuse such as recreational, remain challenges. Although redeveloping brownfields does address some environmental concerns, some critics point to the need for increased awareness of design, green networks, and other such provisions to better foster a truly sustainable community.

The *Sustainable Communities Plan* was launched by the British government in 2003 to develop housing in both urban and rural markets. In addition to this plan, other documents such as the Office of the Deputy Prime Minister's (2005) (OPDM) *Homes for All* have been published in an attempt to address the concerns for sustainable housing into the near future. The *Sustainable Communities Plan* aims to address redevelopment in brownfields and other growth areas in an effort to bring social housing up to a decent standard by 2010 and improve "livability" while protecting the countryside from new development (OPDM, 2005). The recent government initiatives are driving policy that strives to reach the broad goals of sustainability through focused housing targets throughout England.

As part of the *Sustainable Communities Plan*, the government has established Planning Policy Statement 1 (PPS 1), which facilitates both urban and rural development that is implemented through regional and local plans. Recently, there has been an increase in the proportion of housing developed on brownfields in the UK. Unlike England, Scotland and Wales do not have official targets for brownfield redevelopment. However, planning policy is designed to encourage the reuse of vacant and derelict land to help achieve a sustainable environment (Adams, 2004). In 2003, 67% of new development in England took place on brownfields, as compared with 56% in 1997 (OPDM, 2005). The government monitors the progress closely through a national database, while simultaneously providing for economic incentives such as the Contaminated Land Tax Credit (CLTC) that helps developers to meet the costs associated with remediation. Other goals included in the *Sustainable Communities Plan* more broadly reflect the environmental benefits that can be achieved in the protection of open space/ biodiversity, as well as design of individual homes through environmentally sensitive construction techniques and architecture.

Conclusions

A sustainable city is one in which all types of people wish to live, work, and play at all stages of their lives. As such, the character, location, and accessibility of housing in urban areas is of the utmost importance. Housing policy in the US and Canada has changed considerably in the post-war era, with federal governments in both countries now taking a similar approach that involves the devolution of a significant amount of housing responsibility to markets and emphasizes partnerships, nonprofit programs, and more local government control. Both countries continue to support social housing and urban renewal efforts through a variety of funding incentives, education activities, and outreach schemes. Sustainable development is also starting to emerge in the housing policy discourse.

Linking housing and sustainable development requires us to consider the implications of residential location, the affect of development on the community, and the range of environmental, social, and economic impacts imposed by housing. Work by Edwards (2000) discussed in this chapter provides an overview of what issues need to be considered, while design approaches such as New Urbanism and scoring frameworks such as LEED for Homes and the Housing Quality Index point to what sustainability might look like on the ground.

In terms of brownfields, there has been little policy and research attention devoted to reuse for housing in the US and Canada; let along sustainable reuse. There is growing consensus, however, that the redevelopment of brownfields for residential use presents an opportunity for providing affordable housing, redirecting urban growth away from suburban greenfields, cleaning up the environment, and improving communities by removing blight, reducing crime, preserving historic structures, and revitalizing neighborhoods. In the way are many of the same barriers that face other forms of brownfields redevelopment, made even more complex by the greater number of homeowners and renters involved in transactions.

A positive sign overall has been the apparent growth in residential brownfields redevelopment in urban areas in both Canada and the US despite the obstacles. Little is known, however, about the scale and character of this growth, the barriers that continue to inhibit developers specifically, and the measures that can be implemented to overcome them. The next chapter addresses these issues by looking at brownfields redevelopment activity in Chicago, Illinois, and Milwaukee, Wisconsin in detail.

Chapter 5

From Brownfields-to-Housing: Redevelopment Activity in Milwaukee and Chicago

Many cities in the US and Canada have seen growth in housing development and revitalization over the last decade that has involved numerous multi-family condominium and lower-density housing projects. Historically, many cities in the Northeast and Midwest, where extensive tracts of brownfields are located, witnessed significant declines in their populations beginning in the early 1960s. Today, however, the urban housing market benefits from an array of factors including low interest rates, high consumer confidence, and low unemployment (Bayer, 2005). Furthermore, the easy commute to downtown is bringing many professionals to the area, as well as so-called "empty nesters" in their 50s and 60s who are looking to reside in a more socially active locale. The market for condominiums and loft properties in particular has been strong in downtown areas expanding into older brownfield districts, which presents an opportunity for residential reuse, urban infill, and the sustainability benefits inherent to compact form. However, the US Conference of Mayor's 2003 report estimates residential reuse accounts for only 14% of brownfield projects, despite the fact that investment in residential construction typically accounts for 60% of private investment and 50% of total investment in the US (United States Census Bureau, 2000).

This chapter, therefore, builds on the discussion in the previous chapter by taking a more detailed look at brownfields housing activity in the cities of Milwaukee and Chicago. Funded by the US Department of Housing and Urban Development through the Urban Scholars Postdoctoral Fellowship Program (administered by the National Academies), the research addresses four questions related to residential brownfields redevelopment:

(i) What kinds of residential brownfield redevelopment activities have been implemented in Milwaukee and Chicago in terms of scale, character, value and other key market variables?
(ii) Is brownfield redevelopment perceived as being less cost-effective and more risky than greenfield development for market rate and affordable housing?
(iii) Is government intervention important in this domain and, if so, to what extent and in what ways?

(iv) What implications does the project have for mapping out a strategy for future redevelopment issues in the cities of Milwaukee and Chicago specifically, and what broader implications does it have for redevelopment generally?

The City of Chicago (Illinois) was selected because it is a "rust-belt" city with a very strong residential market that has witnessed an increase in its urban population over the last decade, while the City of Milwaukee (Wisconsin) has also witnessed some residential redevelopment activity in certain areas, but it continues to lose population. Indeed, after decades of losing residents, many US cities are now experiencing gains in population — of the 20 largest cities (including census tracts within city limits), 16 gained population from 1990 to 2000 (Philadelphia, Detroit, Baltimore, and Milwaukee lost population during the period) (Urban Land Institute, 2001). Both cities are also in states with very good voluntary cleanup programs that offer a range of programs and incentives to promote brownfields redevelopment, including for residential use.

Brownfields Program Background

The state of Wisconsin has become a focus of brownfield researchers for the reason that it has over 10,000 brownfield sites and a progressive brownfields program (De Sousa, 2005; Wernstedt and Hersh, 2003; Wernstedt, Crooks, & Hersh, 2003). Redevelopment efforts got under way in 1994 with the passage of the state's *Land Recycling Law*, which provided financial and liability tools for redevelopment, as well as making available state-developed inventories for brownfield sites (Consumer Renaissance Development Corporation, 1998; US General Accounting Office, 2000; Wisconsin Brownfields Study Group, 2000). Many of the policy and funding initiatives can be traced to the efforts and suggestions of a multi-stakeholder Brownfields Study Group established in 1998 to advise the government. The state's brownfields program is administered by three agencies — the Department of Natural Resources (DNR), the Department of Commerce, and the Department of Revenue — that are responsible for administering many of the programs listed below. The DNR is primarily responsible for overseeing the state's Voluntary Party Liability Exemption program, which exempts any individual, business, or government agency that conducts an environmental investigation and cleanup of a contaminated property from future environmental liability provided the DNR's regulations are followed.

- Grant Programs
  - Brownfield Site Assessment Grant
  - Brownfields Green Space and Public Facilities Program
  - Community Development Block Grants (small cities)
  - Dry Cleaner Environmental Fund
  - Environmental Fund
  - Petroleum Environmental Cleanup Fund
  - Sustainable Urban Development Zone Program

- ○ Wisconsin Blight Elimination and Brownfields Redevelopment
- ○ Wisconsin Brownfields Grant Program
- Loan Programs
  - ○ Land Recycling Loan Program
  - ○ Industrial Revenue Bonds
- Tax Incentive Programs
  - ○ Business Improvement Districts
  - ○ Cancellation of Delinquent Taxes
  - ○ Environmental Remediation (TIF)
  - ○ Rehabilitation Income Tax Credits
  - ○ Tax Increment Financing (TIF)
  - ○ Wisconsin Community Development Zone Program
  - ○ Wisconsin Enterprise Development Zone Program

While the role of state governments in cleanup processes is undoubtedly important, the duty of attracting investors, guiding the redevelopment process, and managing most of the brownfield inventory ultimately falls on the shoulders of local governmental agencies. The present study looks at the kinds of strategies initiated by the City of Milwaukee (population 600,000) to encourage brownfields redevelopment generally, and housing projects on brownfields specifically. It is estimated that the City of Milwaukee has over 1,027 brownfield sites (McCarthy, 2006), making up 4% of its land area (Simons, 1998). The city's brownfields redevelopment program is carried out by a partnership between four city agencies — the Department of City Development (DCD), the Health Department, the City Redevelopment Authority (RACM), and the Milwaukee Economic Development Corporation (MEDC). Taking direction from the city's "Land Reuse Strategy," this partnership focuses its brownfields efforts on attracting private investment and creating jobs while restoring the environment.

Milwaukee's commitment to addressing the challenges of brownfields redevelopment is shown by it having budgeted for numerous staff positions, established various Tax Incremental Districts (directing cleanup), and the setting up of an environmental testing fund for tax delinquent properties. The city also supports the use of MEDC and RACM resources for redevelopment, as well as undertaking an extensive review of brownfield tax delinquent properties for development opportunities and approving a "Land Reuse Strategy" policy mechanism. City staff have participated in the city's task force to encourage flexible closure, clarify liability, streamline regulatory hurdles, allow new methods of cost recovery, and facilitate groundwater negotiated agreements. In addition, the city has taken a "one-stop" centralized approach for development permits in an effort to make the development process simpler, timelier, and more streamlined. As for sustainability, the city recently established an Office of Environmental Sustainability, which is charged with developing and implementing sustainability-oriented initiatives.

The Illinois Site Remediation Program (SRP) was created in 1995 to provide a mechanism for developers to receive guidance from the Illinois Environmental Protection Agency (IEPA) on site assessment, general technical issues, and "no further remediation" (NFR) determinations to facilitate cleanups. The program uses a Tiered Approach to Corrective Action (TACO) that permits the property to be remediated appropriately in line with its intended use, providing direction on issues related to contamination and site conditions. Those in the SRP must agree to conform to state regulations, allow their site to be evaluated by the IEPA, and prepare a remedial action plan approved by the program. Upon approval, the IEPA issues a clean site NFR letter certifying that the site does not pose a threat to human health or the environment. It also offers a variety of financial assistance programs for site assessment and remediation, including the Illinois Municipal Brownfields Redevelopment Grant Program, the Illinois Brownfields Redevelopment Loan Program, the Brownfields Cleanup and Revolving Loan Fund, the Underground Storage Tank Fund, and the Environmental Remediation Tax Credit.

Although the City of Chicago's Brownfields Initiative originally focused on industrial and economic redevelopment, job creation, and the provision of tax revenues, the city has expanded its purview to include the creation of green space, housing, parking, office space and other amenities. An interdepartmental team of project managers from the Mayor's Office and various City Departments guides the Initiative, which ultimately seeks to make brownfields redevelopment as attractive as any other type of development. Chicago began its brownfields program in the mid-1990s by investing US$2 million from General Obligation Bonds to redevelop five specific brownfield properties. This "Brownfields Pilot" was a resounding success, helping the city to subsequently secure US$74 million under Section 108 loan guarantees from the US Department of Housing and Urban Development (HUD). It was subsequently designated a Showcase Community by the US EPA. The funds allowed the city to engage in research, assessment, and redevelopment-oriented activities.

As part of the initiative, the city evaluated an initial sample of brownfields based on access and control, cleanup cost estimates, and developmental value. If a brownfield has industrial, commercial or residential development potential, the city can acquire the site through negotiated purchase, lien foreclosure, or tax reactivation on property that has been delinquent for two years or more. Once the nature of the site's contamination is assessed, the city may choose to add the property to its list of acquired sites. On occasion, the assessment is undertaken during the acquisition phase. After the initial assessment, a risk assessment is performed if needed and cleanup strategies and cost estimates are then determined. Remaining contaminants can be eliminated or reduced in various ways, depending on time, funding, and, primarily, on future development plans. The city enrolls nearly all its sites in the IEPA Site Remediation Program.

Housing Background

The City of Milwaukee has seen growth in housing development and revitalization over the last decade, involving numerous condominium and other specialty housing projects. Historically, the city underwent large growth from the turn of the century until the 1950s, when deindustrialization began to affect the need for more housing.

Of approximately 228,000 housing units, nearly 70% are single family, townhome, condominium, or duplex buildings, with the remaining 30% consisting of multi-family parcels (City of Milwaukee, 2002a).

The market for condominiums has been expanding throughout the downtown and east side areas. In 2001, there were 7,082 new units, of which 5,209 were in the downtown/east side area. Many of these were condominium, townhouse style, or loft, and the overall investment poured into this development activity (from 1997 to 2004) amounted to US$1.3 billion (City of Milwaukee DCD, 2004). According to the DCD, 1,210 new housing units are currently under construction or are being planned for the downtown core. The city's housing market is benefiting from the same factors that are enhancing housing projects throughout the nation: low interest rates, high consumer confidence, and low unemployment (Bayer, 2005). Furthermore, the easy commute to downtown is bringing many professionals to the area, as well as couples in their 50s and 60s who are looking to reside in a more socially active locale.

Condominium construction has contributed significantly to strong growth in Milwaukee, with specific neighborhoods getting a greater share of this type of housing market (Public Policy Forum, 2003). Although there is some increase in single-family housing on the city's north side, the properties lag behind in terms of average assessed property value. Conversely, the downtown area and east side have seen their value exceed those of neighboring communities.

Though Milwaukee's housing market is strong, there are several relevant issues in need of attention. On a larger societal scale, the issue of segregation remains a problematic one. The Mumford Index of dissimilarity ranks the Milwaukee-Waukesha PMSA third, behind Detroit, Michigan and Gary, Indiana (Public Policy Forum, 2003). The Milwaukee region is plagued by discrepancies in segregation patterns, with the outlying areas being comprised primarily of affluent and primarily white residents, whereas non-white residents largely inhabit the central city core. Other issues of concern include overcrowding and substandard housing, as well as boarded up homes and graffiti. Many of these problems are concentrated in the north/central part of Milwaukee, with issues of affordable housing related to the downtown and east side areas. Strategies being employed by the city to address such issues are (City of Milwaukee, 2002b):

- Strategy 1 — Increase new housing that contributes to Milwaukee's unique urban landscape;
- Strategy 2 — Promote preservation of existing housing;
- Strategy 3 — Provide public housing and community service programs that strengthen the social, economic, and physical environment;
- Strategy 4 — Maximize state, federal, and private dollars so as to help the city carry out its housing strategy;
- Strategy 5 — Market Milwaukee for in-fill and new housing development;
- Strategy 6 — Promote affordable home ownership and responsible rental property ownership; and
- Strategy 7 — Promote a range of housing opportunities with appropriate supportive services for the City's special needs population.

The City of Chicago (population 2,896,016) has seen significant housing growth since the 1990s, after a previous 40-year decline (Chicago Department of Housing, 2004). As a consequence, the city has added more jobs to its economic base, with the residential population growing commensurately. The city has maintained a good level of affordability, ranking as the third most affordable of the ten largest cities in the US. Despite the growth, the majority of housing stock is more than 30 years old, much of which is 60 years old or more. Although there has been an increase in the social diversity of homeowners, Chicago still faces segregation issues — especially given residents of African American origin continue to locate themselves in city's far west and far south sides (Leechman & Nyden, 2000).

As the city has become a much more desirable location for both business and residences over the last 10–15 years, distressed public housing sites have started to receive widespread development attention. The challenge for the city lies in developing these sites without further displacing its lower-income residents. Long established high-rise housing projects such as Cabrini Green are either being replaced or undergoing renewal. They are quickly becoming areas of interest for housing, posing a significant challenge in terms of accommodating real estate growth while simultaneously providing for the needs of lower-income residents. Essentially, the entire Chicago area is under a large "growth spell," with new condominium units or rehabilitated buildings sprouting up continuously throughout the city core.

However, this growth has not benefited all the residents. Gaps still exist — and in some cases are even widening — between what is available and what people can afford. Especially hard hit are lower-income residents, who tend to find themselves in economically depressed areas. This situation has come about, in part, by the resistance from suburban communities against affordable housing developments in their areas over the last three decades (Leechman & Nyden, 2000). In addition, many market rate units for sale have recently become far too expensive for the average resident in the city, thus prompting concerns along several lines.

The city is addressing the situation with strategies and goals through its Department of Housing:

- Build — Add to the stock of affordable housing, with expanded opportunities for low and moderate-income households and rental properties;
- Preserve — Protect federally assisted housing stock that is in danger of conversion to market-rate housing, employing tax relief, subsidies and various financing tools;
- Assist — Enhance affordability so as to help low-income and senior residents remain in their homes; and
- Lead — Work with other departments to seek funding and continue to strategize into the future.

The Department of Housing has recently devised other strategies to help alleviate the financial burden on homeowners. One of these is TaxSmart, which allows homeowners to subtract 20% of their mortgage interest payments from their federal tax liability. The so-called Housing Initiative also makes housing more affordable (State of Illinois 2003, p. 18). Other programs, such as the New Homes for Chicago and the Chicago Partnership for Affordable Neighborhoods (CPAN), provide incentives to developers to reduce development costs in order to provide new housing for moderate-income working families.

Research Method

The brownfields-to-housing study to be presented here was designed to be consistent with notions, approaches, and theoretical frameworks used by previous researchers in the field. Gathering the necessary information required a multi-method approach combining both qualitative and quantitative techniques. This made it possible to gather relevant information on both the attitudes of those directly involved in residential brownfield redevelopment and on the empirically quantifiable outcomes that such redevelopment entails. The multi-method approach involved:

  (i) gathering data on the location and characteristics of residential brownfield redevelopment activities in the cities of Milwaukee and Chicago from local and state government sources and databases;
 (ii) interviewing developers and other relevant stakeholders involved in the development of market-based and affordable residential development in order to assess their attitudes towards costs, risks, and measures for attenuating or overcoming them; and
(iii) reviewing residential redevelopment case studies so as to draw out implications from them related to the factors leading to project success from the perspective of the developer and the neighborhood.

In the first phase of research, general data on the location and character of residential brownfield activity in Milwaukee and Chicago was collected and classified from databases maintained by city and state governments. A different approach had to be taken for gathering data from the different cities because each state and city had its own distinct way of collecting and maintaining its information base.

For the City of Milwaukee, the Department of Community Development maintains a database with information about brownfields projects dating back to 1992. This database was cross-referenced, using address information, with their Master Property Record (MPROP) database that contains information on property characteristics (e.g., assessed value, residential type, etc.). Unfortunately, many projects were not completed or assessed, which necessitated gathering information on property characteristics directly from the developers. Project data was also cross-referenced with the Wisconsin DNR's remediation database (Bureau for Remediation and Redevelopment Tracking System, BRRTS), which contains information on remediation and regulatory issues. Census information was then gathered at the tract level. To identify brownfields projects that did not involve the city, a listing of all new development projects maintained by the City Assessors Office was cross-referenced with the BRRTS database to find matches. Relevant MPROP and Census data was then gathered from those sites.

For Chicago, the IEPA maintains a database with relevant information on site remediation and on the physical state of the brownfield sites enrolled in its SRP, including those that have already received a NFR letter. The NFR database from August 2004, which contains information on projects that received NFR letters between 1997 and 2004, was used for the study because the sites are now remediated and have been developed (or are in the latter stages of development). While the NFR database identifies whether a property was cleaned to a residential level, it does not explicitly state whether the resulting project is residential. For a few sites, IEPA records could be cross-referenced with property assessment information from the Cook County Assessors office to obtain property information. However, site visits and telephone calls to development companies were required to determine whether the final end-use was in fact residential and to gather project information (given that many sites were not assessed). Once the residential brownfields projects were identified, information on city funding and involvement was gathered from individual city departments given that a single department does not maintain such information as it does in Milwaukee.

While the merger of these databases helps establish a more comprehensive picture of residential brownfield redevelopment patterns and characteristics in these cities, several brownfield sites or residential projects may have been missed for several reasons. First, many new residential properties (with many new addresses) can be constructed on a brownfield property with a single address. Hence, the boundaries of the original sites had to be used to assess where the new development(s) took place. Second, the site address may change entirely if developers reorient projects on a corner lot from a main street to a side street or vice-versa. Moreover, address information may be maintained in a different manner depending on the database, which required the use of values and text in multiple searches. Ultimately, however, a field visit was made to each brownfield project to ensure that information in the databases was accurate.

The second phase of the research involved interviews with residential developers in the two cities. All but one interview was conducted on a face-to-face basis, which was useful because it helped garner both a higher response rate and more forthright answers. This also made it possible to double-check the accuracy of development information for some projects. Twenty-seven interviews (12 in Milwaukee and 15 in Chicago) were conducted. Interviewees were asked questions related to (i) the characteristics of the organizations they represent; (ii) their attitudes towards the costs, risks, and benefits associated with residential brownfields redevelopment; and (iii) the effectiveness of different policies and programs getting residential projects realized. Data from the survey is relevant for answering the second, third, and fourth research questions outlined above regarding developer perceptions and activities, as well as providing a basis for formulating recommendations for overcoming the barriers to residential redevelopment.

The third phase involved a more in-depth analysis of different types of residential brownfields projects, some of which are presented in Chapter 6. Information was gathered by means of interviews with developers and/or other stakeholders involved in the project, as well as by accessing project records, reports, and media reports to identify the types of development challenges encountered, how they were overcome, the benefits realized, and the lessons learned. The interviews were largely informal and open-ended. Data from this phase of the research inform all of the research questions by providing "real world" examples of the types of projects being developed (affordable/nonprofit, market), their challenges, and the approaches to overcoming them.

Given the complexity of brownfields redevelopment, the real estate market, and the enormous amount of stakeholders and regulatory activity involved in the redevelopment process, no single study and analysis can ever presume to be exhaustive and all encompassing. This chapter, therefore, seeks to flesh out general patterns in residential brownfields redevelopment.

Analysis of Development Activity: City of Milwaukee

Location and Characteristics of Redevelopment

In total, 32 residential brownfields projects have been developed or are in the latter stages of development in the City of Milwaukee. Twenty-one of these projects have received some public support for site assessment, remediation, and/or site preparation activities; these will be referred to as publicly assisted projects. Eleven projects have not received any public funding for brownfields management, but have been built on properties that had one or more records on the State of Wisconsin's BRRTS (brownfields) database. These will be referred to as private projects — however, it should be noted that a few of these did receive public funds for affordable housing or other infrastructure improvements. Of the 32 projects, 28 have already been constructed and four are either under construction or in the latter stages of planning.

Figure 5.1 shows the spatial clustering of these projects along both sides of the Milwaukee River in an area known as Beerline B and in close proximity to downtown (although several sites are scattered throughout the south and north sides of the city). In terms of size, the sites take up over 91.5 acres (37 ha) with publicly assisted sites using more than private sites in terms of total, average, and median size (71 versus 21 acres (29 versus 8 ha); 3.4 versus 1.9 acres (1.4 versus 0.8 ha); 1.0 versus 0.8 acres (0.4 versus 0.3 ha)) (see Table 5.1). Slightly less than half (43%) of the publicly assisted projects are less than 1 acre in size (0.405 ha), while 29% are between 1 and 3 acres (1.2 ha), or more than 3 acres in size. Most of the private sites (73%) are less than 1 acre, while 18% are in the 1–3 acre range, and 9% over 3 acres.

Projects have resulted in the development or planned development of 2,648 residential units, with a mean of 85 units per project and a median of 44. Over two-thirds of these units have already been fully developed (69%). On average, the private projects generated slightly more units per project, but there are twice as many publicly assisted projects and units.

The vast majority of units (83%) are multi-story (three floors and over) condominiums (for sale) and apartments (for rent). A higher proportion of private

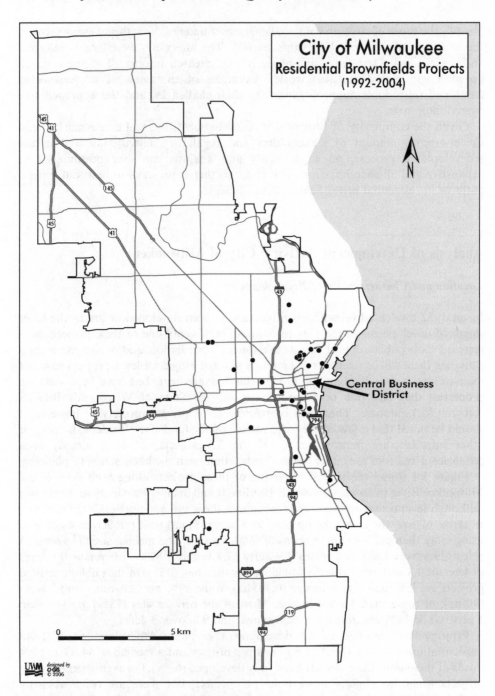

Figure 5.1: Residential brownfields projects, Milwaukee (1992–2004).

Table 5.1: Residential brownfields redevelopment data, Milwaukee.

Characteristics	Publicly assisted			Private			Total	
	Number units	% of Public	% of Total	Number units	% of Private	% of Total	Number units	%
Housing units	1,669		63	979		37	2,648	
Mean	79			89			85	
Housing type								
Condo apartments	573	34	22	442	45	17	1,015	38
Apartment	753	45	28	437	45	17	1,190	45
Townhouse/row	171	10	6	100	10	4	271	10
Duplex/two flat	18	1	1	0	0	0	18	1
Single family	154	9	6	0	0	0	154	6
New	1,609	96	61	538	55	20	2,147	81
Rehabilitated	60	4	2	441	45	17	501	19
Sale	830	50	31	542	55	20	1,372	52
Rent	839	50	32	437	45	17	1,276	48
Mixed sale/rent	606	36	23	428	44	16	1,034	39
Market rate	1,417	85	54	879	53	33	2,296	87
Affordable	252	15	10	100	6	4	352	13
Mixed	0	0	0	0	0	0	0	0
For-profit	1,417	85	54	551	33	21	1,968	74
Non-profit	209	13	8	0	0	0	209	8
For/non-profit				428	26	16	428	16
City	43	3	2				43	2

units are multi-story (90% versus 79%), which is likely due to their downtown location, the need to recover cleanup costs, and the desire to maximize profitability. In terms of lower-density housing, the publicly assisted projects are generating more low-density units than the private projects, particularly in terms of townhouse and single-family units.

To get a general idea of the proportion of all residential development in Milwaukee carried out on brownfields, the projects examined were cross-referenced with a list of developments maintained by the City of Milwaukee. Unfortunately, that list does not include single-family dwellings and is organized by project name, not address, so not all projects could be matched. On the basis of the 20 projects (10 of 21 public and 10 of 11 private) that were matched, residential brownfields redevelopment represents 18% of the projects built in the city between 1992 and 2004 and accounts for 37% percent of the total units (1,926) constructed.

The vast majority of publicly funded projects involve new construction versus rehabilitation of existing structures, while the private sector has been more involved in the conversion of industrial and warehouse properties into lofts. While twice as many brownfields projects generated sale versus rental housing, the split in terms of units was almost equal overall, and similar for publicly assisted and private projects.

It should be noted, however, that a large share of the rental units are part of three mixed (sale and rental) mega-projects in Milwaukee. The vast majority of the residential units on brownfields in Milwaukee are market rate (87%) rather than affordable (13%), and all but one of the eight affordable projects were carried out using public funding for brownfields related expenses. Interestingly, none of the projects combined market rate and affordable units as many projects in Chicago are seeking to do. As for the private projects, most are market rate except for those built by a company specializing in rental housing for the affordable market. With regard to who the developers are, most (14) are for-profit, followed by a group of nonprofit developers (6), one project was carried out collaboratively between a nonprofit and a for-profit entity, and one listed here as "city-based," given that the city was responsible for preparing land and making it ready for sale to individual property owners or builders (see City Homes case study in Chapter 6).

Cost Information

In total, the 32 residential brownfields redevelopment projects are valued at almost US$500 million dollars, or US$15.6 million per project. The publicly assisted projects are worth approximately US$329 million (US$15.7 million per project) and private projects approximately US$170 million (US$15.5 million per project) (see Table 5.2). Half of the projects range in value from US$5 million to US$25 million dollars, while 37.5% are valued at below US$5 million, and the remaining four are worth more than US$25 million. On the basis of the 2005 tax rate for Milwaukee County, the 32 projects will generate approximately US$13.5 million annually in gross taxes, with US$4.6 million of that going to the city. While home price data was not available for all individual units or on a per square foot basis, low/high sale prices gathered for over 20 projects in Milwaukee reveal an average range of $204,000 to $405,000 ($210,000–$320,000 median), with prices starting as low as $75,000 up to $1,000,000. While lower-income individuals may be expressing interest in living on these sites, the market is clearly producing for the middle and upper income buyers.

Table 5.2: Residential brownfields redevelopment dollars leveraged, Milwaukee.

Publicly assisted projects	21
Total redevelopment dollars	$ 329,580,000
Total redevelopment per project	$ 15,694,286
Private projects	11
Total redevelopment dollars	$ 169,952,208
Total redevelopment per project	$ 15,450,201
All projects	32
Total redevelopment dollars	$ 499,532,208
Total redevelopment per project	$ 15,610,382

Land Information

Information gathered on the former land use of the brownfield sites reveals that slightly over half (15) of the publicly assisted sites were vacant properties, many of which had been owned by the City of Milwaukee itself, which had acquired them because they were tax-delinquent or were to be used for transportation projects that never materialized. The other brownfield sites had been used for various industrial/warehouse (5), transportation (6), retail (5), residential (2), and commercial (1) uses. Eleven of the publicly assisted sites had multiple uses prior to redevelopment. Private sites, on the other hand, were primarily transportation (5), industrial (5), and retail (4) parcels, and the only vacant site happened to be a government-owned parcel that was initially intended for highway construction.

Data on the type of remediation activity undertaken at residential brownfields sites was obtained from the Wisconsin DNR's BRRTS database for 25 (15 public and 10 private) of the 32 projects. Many of the city sites without data were older files that had been "retired." The WDNR designates the types of remediation activity as follows: (i) leaking underground storage tank (LUST) sites; (ii) environmental repair program (ERP) sites, where the source of contamination was caused by something other than a LUST; (iii) sites contaminated by spills; (iv) general property sites where environmental conditions apply to the whole property, rather than to a specific source of contamination; and (v) No Action Sites where there was or may have been a discharge to the environment, but, based on the known information, the DNR does not require the responsible party to undertake an investigation or cleanup. Half the sites had multiple remediation activity designations, typically consisting of the removal of a LUST in addition to another designation. Most sites had a LUST or ERP activity code. The two properties that had no further action designations also had other designations, but these were considered to not pose a problem after a site assessment was conducted. Most of the private sites (80%) had a single remedial activity identified, typically a LUST (6 sites), an ERP (4), or a Spill (3). Sixty percent of the publicly assisted sites, on the other hand, had multiple activity designations, with a third of the sites having three or more activity records. Clearly, more complex cleanup requirements necessitated the need for public involvement and funding for site assessment and remediation.

Public Investment

As discussed above, public funding information retained for brownfield projects by the City of Milwaukee considers site assessment, remediation, demolition, and various related site preparation costs related to brownfields redevelopment. In entering this data, the city often rolls together funds with those from other levels of government. While it was possible to separate city funds from those provided by Milwaukee County, the state DNR, and the state Department of Commerce, federal funding could not be separated from the "amalgam." The City of Milwaukee draws on a range of financial support programs to support brownfields redevelopment. The most common source of funding for the residential brownfields redevelopment projects examined here was RACM (71% of projects), which consolidates funds from a variety of sources to support brownfield projects (including federal block grants and capital funds, and money retained from the sale of city-owned property). Other primary sources of funding administered by the city (in order of application) are the following: TIF funds (24% of projects), Community Development Block Grant funds (through HUD) (14% of projects), BGP funds (10%), general public funds (10%), resources from the MEDC (5%), and the Department of Public Works (5%). Money from upper levels of government was used for brownfields related activities at seven redevelopment projects, including the Department of Commerce Brownfields Grant (4 projects), DNR's Site Assessment Grant (2 projects), County funds (1 project) and Other (1 project).

In total, funding for brownfields management activities from public sources amounted to US$5.19 million dollars. Of this, 45% came from the city, 45% from Commerce, 7.7% from the County, 1.9% from the DNR, and 0.4% from other sources. City funds were used for all 21 "publicly assisted" projects, while other government funds were targeted at 7 of those projects. Overall, 1 public dollar of brownfields funding leveraged US$64 dollars in residential redevelopment (or 1.6% of total redevelopment leveraged), with one city dollar leveraging US$141 (or 0.7%). If one considers just the seven sites that received funding from multiple levels of government, then US$1 public dollar of brownfields funding leveraged US$79 in redevelopment. Furthermore, while those seven projects received 58% of public funds, they generated 70% of the redevelopment dollars leveraged and 65% of the units built or planned.

Several of the projects here, including a few of those designated as private, received government funding for non-brownfields-oriented costs such as the construction of affordable housing and, in a few cases, TIF funds that were employed in the upgrading of infrastructure (sidewalks, stairwells, streetlights, utilities, etc.). Many of the affordable housing projects received federal low-income housing tax credits, community development block grant funds, and low interest loans from the Wisconsin Housing and Economic Development Agency for housing construction. This funding occurs regardless of whether or not a project is constructed on a brownfield site. In terms of TIF funding for infrastructure, it is difficult to determine to what extent funding for infrastructure improvement, whether on or off site, directly affects a developer's willingness to develop a brownfield specifically. In fact, the projects where TIF was employed for infrastructure were large parcels owned by the government that had previously been cleared for transportation projects that never materialized and did not have severe brownfields issues.

Analysis of Development Activity: City of Chicago

Location and Characteristics of Redevelopment

Residential brownfield projects in Chicago were identified using the IEPA's NFR database. As of August 2004, 210 NFR letters had been granted to 159 projects by the IEPA for cleanup carried out to residential standards (some sites received multiple letters). Of these, 52 were determined to be residential projects based on site visits. Unlike the Milwaukee case, funding data maintained by the City of Chicago includes all project costs for site acquisition, construction, soft costs, and developers' fees. Brownfield assessment and remediation expenditures were not separated out for the vast majority of projects.

Of the 52 projects identified and according to information obtained from relevant city departments and developers, 25 received public assistance and 27 did not. Figure 5.2 shows that projects in Chicago are more scattered throughout the city. In total, residential redevelopment covered 133 acres (54 ha) of brownfields, with publicly assisted sites taking up more (78 acres, 31 ha) than private sites (55 acres, 22 ha). The average brownfield redeveloped was 2.5 acres (1 ha) (1 acre median) in size, with publicly assisted sites generally larger (3.1 acres mean; 1.5 median) than private sites (2 acres mean; 0.5 median). Almost half of the projects (46%) were less than 1 acre in size, while 44% were between 1 and 5 acres, and only 10% were over 5 acres. As in Milwaukee, the private sites are typically smaller than the publicly assisted sites.

Projects have resulted in the development or planned development of 7,362 residential units (based on 51 projects), with a mean of 144 units and a median of 82. Slightly less than two-thirds of these units are part of completed projects (57%). On average, the publicly assisted projects generated more units per project than the private projects (Table 5.3). The vast majority of units overall (83%) are multi-story condominiums (for sale 34%) and apartments (for rent 49%). A higher proportion of private projects are multi-story (93% versus 77%). In terms of lower-density product, the publicly assisted projects are generating more low-density units (14.2% of total) than the private projects (2% of total), particularly in terms of townhouse and single-family units (Figure 5.2).

Unlike Milwaukee, the vast majority of publicly assisted and private projects involve new construction rather than rehabilitation of existing structures, and the publicly assisted projects are rehabilitating slightly more units than in private ones. In a few cases, the rehabilitation project did not involve the conversion of an industrial or warehouse property into "lofts," but rather the sale and updating of existing residential buildings that triggered the need for an environmental action.

Most of the residential units constructed on brownfields are rentals (53%) versus sale properties (47%). The majority of publicly assisted projects are rentals, while slightly over half of the private units are sale (55%) versus rent (45%). Only three of the projects overall combine rent and sale units. These rather large projects represent 10% of the total units built on brownfields.

Overall, 2,653 "affordable" units were constructed on brownfields (or 36% of all units), which is significantly higher than in Milwaukee (13%). Although the specific affordability program is not always clearly outlined in the relevant reports or by the developers, it can be estimated that units consist of 1,244 Chicago Housing Authority units, 833 affordable units, and 576 affordable senior units. Of the 25 projects with

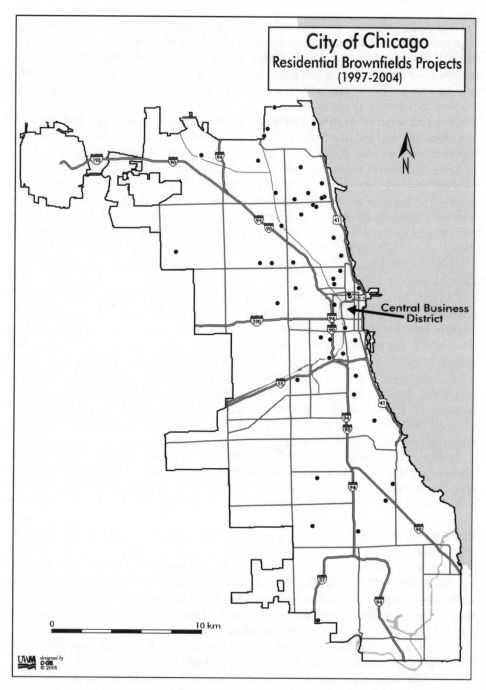

Figure 5.2: Residential brownfields projects, Chicago (1997–2004).

Table 5.3: Residential brownfields project data, Chicago.

Characteristics	Publicly assisted			Private			Total	
	Number units	% of Public	% of Total	Number units	% of Private	% of Total	Number units	%
Housing units	4,853		66	2,509		34	7,362	
Mean	194			105			144	
Housing type								
Condo apartments	1,279	26	17	1,202	48	16	2,481	34
Apartment	2,481	51	34	1,141	45	15	3,622	49
Townhouse/Row	603	12	8	34	1	0	637	9
Duplex/two flat	12	0	0	0	0	0	12	0
Single family	478	10	6	132	5	2	610	8
New	4,430	91	60	2,401	96	33	6,831	93
Rehabilitated	423	9	6	108	4	1	531	7
Sale	2098	43	26	1,368	55	17	3,466	47
Rent	2,755	57	34	1,141	45	14	3,896	53
Mixed sale/rent	549	10	7	173	6	2	722	9

assisted housing, 12 were solely assisted units, while 13 were in projects that mixed market rate units with assisted ones. These mixed developments generated 1,025 affordable units — 31% of the 3,337 units those projects generated overall. Information was also more difficult to obtain with regard to who the developers are given that a smaller percentage of Chicago developers were interviewed. Most are for-profit (41 projects), followed by a group of nonprofit developers (3 projects), one project that was carried collaboratively between a nonprofit and a for-profit entity, and seven were not determined.

Cost Information

In total, the 49 residential brownfields projects for which data was provided generated over US$2.17 billion in redevelopment (Table 5.4). Private projects were worth slightly more than publicly assisted ones, although the values were similar overall. While most projects were valued below 50 million dollars, the ten mega-projects valued at over 50 million dollars accounted for 79% of the total redevelopment dollars generated by all projects, as well as 60% of the total units. While home price data was not available for all individual units or on a per square foot basis, low/high sale prices gathered for over 22 projects in Chicago reveal an average range of $230,000 to $913,000 ($232,000 to $392,000 median), with prices starting as low as $133,000 up to $7,800,000.

Table 5.4: Residential brownfields redevelopment dollars leveraged, Chicago.

Public projects	24
Total	US$1,043,047,733
Total per project	$43,460,322
Less than $10 million	4
$10 million to $50 million	15
Over $50 million	5
Private projects	25
Total redevelopment $	$1,136,516,331
Total redevelopment $ per project	$45,460,653
Less than $10 million	8
$10 million to $50 million	12
Over $50 million	5
All projects	49
Total redevelopment dollars	$2,179,564,065
Total redevelopment per project	$44,480,899
Less than $10 million	12
$10 million to $50 million	27
Over $50 million	10

Land Information

Information gathered on the former land uses of the brownfield sites reveals that the majority of sites had previously been industrial or warehouse properties (23), followed by retail (11), residential (9), transportation (8), and commercial sites (6). Several had been vacant (6) before redevelopment. As in Milwaukee, many of the publicly assisted sites listed multiple previous uses. Interestingly, a few of the publicly assisted sites were former public housing properties that had been torn down or transferred to another owner. These may have required remediation due to LUST spills, leaks from adjacent land, or historically elevated levels of contamination that some developers claim affects the entire city and are tied to the Chicago fire of 1871 and historic filling practices. Private sites showed a similar previous-use typology, although few had been residential and outlined multiple uses.

In Illinois, the IEPA is authorized to issue an NFR letter to those who have successfully demonstrated that conditions at their sites do not present a significant risk to human health or the environment. Two types of letters are issued (i) a comprehensive letter, which is issued for the successful remediation of an entire site; and (ii) a focused letter, which is issued for the release or threatened release of specific contaminants. An equal number of residential developments examined in the present study were issued focused and comprehensive NFR letters (26 each), although publicly assisted projects were issued slightly more comprehensive letters (14 to 11) and private projects the focused letters (15 to 12).

The IEPA also records whether projects involve the use of institutional or engineering controls, an issue of interest to HUD in particular given its policy not to permit their use for multi-family projects. These typically reduce the cost of managing contaminated soils because, rather than treating or removing them, they allow certain contaminants to remain in place provided they are capped or there are policies ensuring that residents cannot be exposed to them. Many sites in the study (32) have an institutional control restricting the extraction of groundwater from the site. Slightly over half of the projects (27) also use an engineered barrier method to manage contaminants — for 15 of these projects multiple barriers are listed by the IEPA. The most common barrier is asphalt (e.g., to cap contamination under a parking lot), followed by clean soil, concrete, building foundations, clay, geomembranes, and geotextiles. Slightly more publicly assisted sites use these methods (15 public versus 12 private), which is probably due to the fact that they have more challenging financial and/or contamination issues that require more cost-effective management.

Public Investment

Unlike the data for the City of Milwaukee, public funding information for residential brownfield projects was not maintained by the City of Chicago in a methodical fashion for all projects, with funding allocated for several components of projects (e.g., infrastructure, public housing, cleanup, and assessment) rather than to brownfields related costs specifically. Information on funding was also retained by multiple departments, making it difficult to obtain a comprehensive picture of the amount of public subsidy provided. Despite this, data were obtained for 18 of the 25 projects that had received some form of public funding.

In total, the 18 projects with data received US$164 million dollars in TIFs, loans, bonds, grants and other forms of funding. Most of these projects (10 of 18) received support in the form of TIF, which was also the primary source of public funding overall (US$104 million). Projects also received funding directly from the EPA Showcase program (3 for US$13.2 thousand), Chicago's HOME program (2 for US$16 million), reduced land prices (2 for US$203 thousand), the Chicago Housing Authority (1 for US$1.7 million), and for infrastructure (1 for US$2 million). Tax Credits amounting to US$7.56 million were also provided by Chicago's Department of Housing (4 projects for US$1.95 million) and the State of Illinois (8 for US$5.6 million). Bond and loan programs were also employed, including City's HOME program (5 for US$21.3 million), Department of Environment (3 projects for US$5 million), Mortgage Revenue Bonds (1 for US$7.5 million), and Tax Exempt Bonds (3 for US$6.14 million). In total, the value of the 18 projects amounted to US$991 million dollars. TIF-funded projects generated over US$913 million dollars, with US$1 TIF dollar generating US$8.76 in investment. It should be noted that those receiving TIF funds for residential redevelopment in Chicago must include at least 20% affordable units.

Brownfields-to-Housings: Interviews with Developers

An important question for government officials seeking to attract brownfields redevelopment is what sort of development companies are willing to take on the challenge of such redevelopment. In Milwaukee, those interviewed have been involved in development for an average of 17 years and all have been involved in more than one brownfields project. The interviewees stated that they are involved on average in three brownfields projects in a given year, averaging about nine projects (5 median) since 1995, and only two are involved in more greenfield than brownfield projects. Developers interviewed in Chicago represent established companies that have been involved in development for an average of 23 years. They are involved in two residential brownfields projects per year on average, versus three greenfield (or clean site projects), with most having been involved in eight brownfields and 11 greenfield projects since 1995.

When asked to list and rank the factors/features that attracted them to a particular brownfield site, those that elicited three or more responses from Milwaukee interviewees included the property's proximity to the downtown core, access to services, good neighborhoods, proximity to natural amenities, the low price of land, and attractive views. In Chicago, the most common response was the property's proximity to public transit and the strength of the area's property market (six respondents each), while three or more interviewees also mentioned proximity to roadways and highways, good neighborhoods, and gentrifying/"yuppifying" neighborhoods on the cusp of renewal.

In terms of barriers to residential redevelopment, the most common response in both Milwaukee and Chicago was the cost (or amount) of cleanup required. In Milwaukee, two or more respondents also mentioned liability risks, longer project duration, and "unknown" or "surprise" costs. While in Chicago, at least a couple of interviewees also emphasized regulatory hurdles that added to project duration (at both the state and city government levels), unknown costs, the difficulty in obtaining financing, weak markets in some locales, and a lack of public funding for residential projects. A couple of interviewees also stated that the barriers to brownfields redevelopment were minimal nevertheless and, interestingly, no one mentioned liability risks.

In an effort to get a more detailed understanding of the barriers, interviewees were then asked to compare the difficulty of developing brownfields versus greenfields (or clean sites) in relation to specific stages of the development process, ranking the relative difficulty on a scale of 1 to 5 (with 1 = much less difficult, 2 = somewhat less difficult, 3 = same level of difficulty, 4 = somewhat more difficult, and 5 = much more difficult). Interviewees in Milwaukee noted that there is an equal level of difficulty in terms of project planning (3.1 mean, 3.0 mode) and profitability (3.4 mean, 3 mode), slightly more difficulty associated with acquiring brownfields (3.4 mean, 5 mode), stakeholder involvement (3.6 mean, 4.0 mode), and project financing (3.6 mean, 3.0 mode), and much more difficulty related to site preparation (4.5 mean, 5 mode). Interestingly, they also noted that it is slightly less difficult to market brownfield projects because of the current popularity of many downtown locations (2.6 mean, 3 mode).

Overall, most of those surveyed in Chicago found all aspects of brownfields redevelopment to be as difficult or more difficult than greenfield development. While profitability (3.1 mean, 3.0 mode) was considered virtually the same, site acquisition (3.6 mean, 3.0 mode), financing (3.9 mean, 3 mode), planning and development (3.5 mean, 3 mode), marketing (3.5 mean, 3 mode), and stakeholder involvement (3.5 mean, 3 mode) were considered slightly more challenging. Site preparation (4.4 mean, 5.0 mode) and project duration (4.1 mean, 4.0 mode) issues related to brownfields were both considered much more difficult issues to deal with by the private sector due to the need to obtain multiple approvals from regulatory agencies.

Lastly, when asked to point out measures for increasing residential development on brownfields, most of the public sector interventions perceived as necessary for increasing residential development on brownfields in Milwaukee related directly to improving the bottom-line of these projects, whether through some form of additional funding to help cover costs (i.e., 19 responses suggested funds for site

Table 5.5: Ranking of incentives for residential brownfields redevelopment, Milwaukee and Chicago.

	Milwaukee	Chicago
Tax increment financing	4.9	4.7
Site remediation and demolition grants	4.7	4.6
Federal/state tax credits	4.6	4.5
Community Development Block Grants	4.8	4.3
Fast tracking of approvals	4.2	4.8
Protection from future liability	4.7	4.1
Site assessment and remediation loans	4.3	4.5
Protection from third party liability	4.8	4.1
Property tax abatement	4.2	4.4
Government financing low interest loans	4.6	4.1
Loan guarantees	4.8	3.8
Site assessment grants	4.1	4.3
Public insurance (cost cap/future liability)	4.3	4.1
State housing finance assistance	4.2	4.1
Permitting the use of institutional controls	4.4	3.9
Rezoning property to residential use	4.1	4.1
Empowerment Zone loans	4.4	3.9
Density bonusing	3.9	4.2
Government performs assessment and cleanup	4.5	3.6
Coordination of project implementation and funding at the local level	4.3	3.7
Coordination of project implementation and funding at the state level	3.8	4.0
Government facilitates site acquisition	4.8	3.2
Public–private joint venture opportunities	3.9	3.4
Technical guidance manuals	3.4	3.1
Brownfields inventory	2.9	3.2
Government organizes public consultation	3.7	2.3

cleanup, residential reuse, site investigation; as well as tax credits, TIFs), relaxing regulatory requirements to minimize cleanup (3) and/or time-related (2) costs, or reducing land acquisition costs (3). Other suggestions included: assembling and remediating properties prior to redevelopment (by the city (3)), relaxing design guidelines (2), facilitating funding application procedures (1), and enhancing infrastructure (1). In Chicago, just over half (8) of those interviewed pointed out the need to streamline regulatory procedures in order to make them less time-consuming and onerous. Indeed, two of the interviewees pointed out that no more public involvement is required because, as they put it, "their involvement only complicates matters." Most other suggestions related to relevant costs (i.e., additional funding (5), TIF (4), funding for residential use specifically (3), and reducing land costs (2)), while the remainder related to regulation (i.e., loosening cleanup standards for urban sites (2), leveling the playing field in terms of access to brownfields (1), and developing a comprehensive brownfields plan (1)). Overall, the respondents revealed a similar outlook when they were asked to rank on a scale of 1 (not effective) to 5 (very effective) individual tools for facilitating redevelopment (see Table 5.5 sorted by whole interview sample score).

Discussion and Concluding Remarks

The results that have emerged from both the development data and the interviews reveal that despite the relatively limited attention paid to promoting residential brownfields reuse, such activity has been rather extensive. Developers are acquiring, planning, and building on brownfields in both cities and consumers at all income levels are buying and renting their products. While the patterns of redevelopment activity differ slightly in both cities, it would seem that Milwaukee is following a similar path to that of Chicago, but is at an earlier stage along that path. Thus far, brownfields redevelopment in Milwaukee consists largely of mid- to high-end, higher-density, market rate housing built by for-profit developers clustered in neighborhoods near the downtown core, while lower density and affordable units are constructed in other parts of the city mainly by nonprofits or the municipal government with greater public-assistance to cover environmental costs. In Chicago, market rate and affordable projects are increasingly scattered throughout the city, although proximity to the downtown core continues to attract much of the private development interest.

While developing on brownfields is indeed perceived as slightly more costly and risky than greenfields, such views are strongly tied to the experience of developers in managing them. The more experienced developers consider brownfields management as just another aspect of development, while those with less tend to react more cautiously, but are willing to "do it again." Projects, therefore, are occurring at an increasing rate driven by a small group of "veteran" urban developers, many of whom now concentrate on larger-scale mega-projects, and a cadre of new developers trying out the brownfields market typically on smaller properties. In both cities, the vast majority of developers feel that greater financial assistance is the key to increasing residential redevelopment. However, many are still willing to go about profitable projects on their own, particularly if it helps avoid bureaucratic entanglement and delays.

Government intervention is important for residential brownfields redevelopment on several counts. In areas with extensive cleanup problems, public funding is very important for managing costs. In areas with fewer cleanup challenges, the efficiency of government intervention is perceived as essential for managing time-related costs and attenuating developer frustration. Government planning is also important for shaping the scale, character, and location of residential redevelopment. The needs of both government and developers can be satisfied as far as the market allows it, even to the point of mixing affordable with market rate housing.

One concerns about residential development is that developers will build mainly mid- to high-end product to cover costs and maximize profits and, thus, contribute to the gentrification of neighborhoods. The data reveal that there is indeed some truth to this assumption, particularly in those areas close to the downtown core. However, in compensation, numerous affordable housing units are also being constructed, and in Chicago, efforts to mix affordable and market housing point to a more inclusive strategy overall.

Another area of concern is that residential development will take up the city's remaining industrial properties and push away industry. The data reveal, however, that these projects are taking place on brownfields that range extensively in size and previous use, and many sites have lain vacant for decades. Furthermore, both Chicago and Milwaukee have made efforts to clearly demarcate which industrial districts will remain "industrial" and which will not. Perhaps the attributes identified by developers here might help city governments better decide which industrial brownfields districts have the best potential for residential reuse.

As found in previous studies, the data here also reveal that many developers are willing to undertake residential projects on brownfields without government intervention and funding (De Sousa, 2000; Howland, 2000). The amount of contamination they are willing to cleanup is largely dependent on the strength of the market, although properties with more complex conditions still tend to require more government support from multiple sources. Governments, however, should not take this as an argument to continue to provide few resources to residential brownfields redevelopment. Indeed, the large-scale projects examined here that involve public–private partnerships generate an extensive number of units and redevelopment dollars, and, as a byproduct, increase taxes and erase large tracts of blight. Therefore, it is argued that greater financial support from government will not likely result in developers holding out their hands for projects they would have carried out anyway, but rather get them to take on more challenging brownfields properties.

The literature on brownfields has also raised concern regarding difficulties involved in acquiring financing for residential brownfields projects due to the lenders' aversion to risk and to policies developed by HUD and the Federal Housing Administration (FHA) that demand stringent cleanup standards. The development data and the interviews reveal that these concerns do not seem to be inhibiting redevelopment, but that stakeholders try to work through these constraints in order to realize the project. HUDs willingness to be flexible with its policies in Chicago also point to the success that other cities can achieve. Market and private lenders also seem to be willing to accept the use of both engineering and institutional controls as a way of managing contamination at residential projects. It is important therefore such policies be reevaluated. It should be noted, however, that both the public and private sectors must maintain more detailed and geographically accurate databases on the location of these sites and the controls employed.

In terms of incentives for generating affordable housing, which is a challenge for both cities, most developers believe that more funding is the best option, particularly for the non-profits and Community Development Corporations operating in more challenging markets. The data reveal that deciding when to "push" the affordability issue on the for-profit market can be tricky. In Milwaukee, many for-profit developers feel that they are already generating public benefits by remediating and redeveloping derelict and contaminated brownfields and that there is enough affordable housing in the city. The Chicago case reveals, however, that in a strong market, city-based programs and incentives can get developers to incorporate affordability, even in "higher-end" projects.

Overall, it is important at this stage for governments to take a closer look at the potential of residential redevelopment to help manage the brownfields problem and to harness its potential in a more strategic way. Cities must take a more comprehensive look at their brownfields inventories, develop portfolios of city and privately owned brownfields, and then devise site-specific or areawide strategies for renewal based on public and private interests. The market for residential redevelopment is strengthening in many cities across the US, and optimizing the environment for both for-profit and non-profit developers to work in, in terms of procedures and incentives, will allow them to better "ride" that market. Clearly, residential reuse is an important piece of the brownfields and urban revitalization puzzle that should no longer take a back seat to other uses.

But what about sustainability? The examination of redevelopment activity in these two cities reveals that many sustainability goals are being achieved, although they are not often considered explicit goals for these projects by developers or governments. Indeed, some of the key sustainability benefits that have been realized in both cities include:

- The redevelopment and management of real/perceived contamination on 224.5 acres (90.8 ha) of brownfields land, which, based on Deason et al's (2001) research, would have consumed approximately 1,250 acres (500 ha) of greenfield land;
- The energy savings related to high-density housing (over 90% multi-unit and 83% multi-story);
- The reuse of urban infrastructure to support all of the housing developed and the reuse and rehabilitation of building stock to produce over 1,000 units;
- The production of over 3,000 affordable housing units, as well as the introduction of middle- and upper-income units into communities allowing for class mix;

- The extensive removal of blight; and
- Government tax base growth to support local services.

The sustainability benefits listed here are extensive. The question remains as to whether the bar can be raised in terms of promoting green building, green infrastructure, better community participation, and more attention to social housing issues at these sites. The case studies in the next chapter present a more in-depth analysis of different types of residential brownfields projects being constructed, including a more sustainable effort that started in Vancouver, British Columbia, over two decades ago.

Chapter 6

Housing Case Studies

Building on the more general analysis presented in the previous chapter, this chapter provides a more in-depth description of brownfields-to-housing project case studies in order to draw out implications from them related to the factors contributing to project success. Information for these was gathered by means of informal interviews with the developers and/or other stakeholders involved in the projects, as well as by accessing project reports, media reports, and scholarly literature. The case studies offer "real world" examples of the types of projects being developed (affordable/ nonprofit, market), their challenges, and the approaches to overcoming them. In addition to projects in Milwaukee and Chicago, the chapter also reviews the redevelopment of False Creek in Vancouver, British Columbia, which has been touted as one of the most successful large-scale brownfields redevelopment projects anywhere in North America. This project provides perhaps the best example of planning that seeks to link sustainable development concepts with the construction of residential neighborhoods on formerly industrial brownfield sites.

As discussed in the previous two chapters, residential brownfields redevelopment faces a host of barriers, including high cleanup costs, liability risks, longer project duration, regulatory hurdles, "unknown" costs, and many other factors. While increasing demand for residential real estate in some urban neighborhoods provides an opportunity for brownfields reuse, poor market conditions in low-income neighborhoods continue to pose a challenge to sustainable development. The cases below outline a small sample of projects and partnerships that have succeeded in overcoming local obstacles to redevelopment.

Milwaukee, Wisconsin

While the conversion of brownfields into housing in Milwaukee has taken a back seat to efforts aimed at industrial and commercial redevelopment, nonprofit, public, and private sector stakeholders have made several notable efforts to support the development of both market and non-market homes throughout the city. Three catalytic projects are examined here:

- Milwaukee's CityHomes project, which took a vacant parcel in a blighted part of the central city with low real estate values and turned it into a thriving neighborhood and a model for surrounding redevelopment.

- The Parkwest project initiated by the New Covenant Housing Corporation (NCHC), in which a faith-based nonprofit development affiliate of New Covenant Missionary Baptist Church worked to bring affordable family housing to their community.
- The Trostel Square project and Beerline B neighborhood plan, which turned a former industrial corridor into a hip place to live.

CityHomes

> *Developer*: City of Milwaukee, Department of City Development and Independent Builders
> *Date completed*: Residential brownfields project completed in 1995, although the CityHomes program is ongoing
> *Site area*: Project: 6.6 acres (2.7 ha)
> *Number and type of units*: 43 single-family dwellings
> *Pre-development usage*: Vacant land
> *Sale price (2004)*: US$100,000–US$150,000.

CityHomes is a public–private partnership coordinated by the City of Milwaukee's Department of City Development aimed at revitalizing urban neighborhoods in decline. The original CityHomes project was initiated in the early 1990s on an area of highly concentrated vacant lots, many of which the city acquired because they were tax delinquent. The project is located in one of Milwaukee's most segregated and poverty-stricken neighborhoods in which over three quarters of the population is considered low income. In addition, the postal code district where CityHomes is located witnessed a 19% decline in the job market between 1994 and 2003 due to major layoffs and plant closings (Levine, 2006, p. 8) and the community had some of the lowest residential real estate values in the city in the early 1990s.

One of the first subdivision projects to be constructed in Milwaukee's central city in decades, the first CityHomes project consisted of 43 parcels that were prepared for development by the city and sold to prospective homebuyers and small builders for the construction of single-family dwellings. CityHomes is a new urbanist-style development reminiscent of early twentieth century homes that blend in with the surrounding neighborhood (Figure 6.1). While the neighborhood is located just two miles from downtown Milwaukee and has good access to public transportation and the interstate, it had suffered from decades of disinvestment that made it unattractive to private development. The success of the program's first phase has led to its expansion in the surrounding area, which includes new development, as well as city assistance for the rehabilitation of existing homes.

The original CityHomes project was constructed on cleared underutilized land. The property was designated by the Wisconsin DNR as an Environmental Repair

Figure 6.1: CityHomes Milwaukee, 2005.

Program site, but environmental assessment and management costs were relatively minor at just over US$72,000. Indeed, the main problem at the site, which had been primarily residential decades earlier, was the need to remove many old basements that had been buried.

To fund assessment, cleanup, and site preparation, the city established a tax incremental financing (TIF) district. Sites were graded and lots were sold to prospective homebuyers and builders for US$1. Initially, construction of the homes cost approximately US$110,000 and a TIF district helped to write down the purchase price. In addition, homebuyers were offered US$10,000 in the form of a forgivable second mortgage from the City of Milwaukee — an amount later paid off within a six-year period through property taxes. Fortunately, market interest rates were low at the time, which also helped foster the project's development.

Marketing of the project was aimed initially to those residing in the immediate area, but soon spread via lenders, buyers, and builders as they became aware of the initiative. By 2000, the city had a waiting list of 300 people for homes (Derus, 2000). Homes initially valued at US$70,000–US$80,000, in a community where the average house was US$10,000–US$15,000, now lie in the US$100,000–US$150,000 range. The project has also been a catalyst for sparking renewal in the surrounding neighborhoods, particularly Lindsey Heights — a 40 square block area that has also suffered from disinvestment.

The City of Milwaukee, along with area partners (i.e., the Wisconsin Housing and Economic Development Authority [WHEDA], the Neighborhood Improvement Development Corporation [NIDC], and the YMCA Community Development Corporation) are actively promoting restoration by employing similar tactics to those described above, as well as a host of home improvement loans and educational programs. Residents of the adjacent Walnut Way neighborhood are also in the process of reviewing various issues aimed at promoting rehabilitation, and Habitat for Humanity has been very active in helping redevelopment in the community as well. Furthermore, the Wisconsin Housing and Economic Development Authority recently awarded US$1.1 million to a developer for the expansion and renovation of 115 units for low-income renters, a rehabilitation that will be part of a larger effort to improve and redevelop the area in conjunction with the CityHomes and Lindsay Heights efforts.

The project has been well received locally because it has played a central role in breathing new life into the community. New families are interested in moving into the neighborhood, and existing residents feel more secure in investing and improving their properties. The city has also added new phases to the project and hopes to add 100 new homes in the neighborhood. Private investment is also entering the neighborhood in the form of new residential and retail development. The positive response has been a good thing for the city given its initial concern about whether anyone would buy the parcels that had been readied for housing. The lots turned out to be needed and in high demand due to several factors, including their attractive location, proximity to downtown, buyer's perception of investment in the community, the desire by many buyers who grew up in the neighborhood for new housing, and a sufficient concentration of land that could contribute to the formation of a new "neighborhood."

CityHomes is an example of a housing project that has converted a highly concentrated, vacant, city-owned brownfield into a thriving community. Despite uncertainty regarding interest in the project and the low value of property in the area, the city-led project turned into a significant success, exceeded expectations, and was soon replicated in the neighboring Lindsay Heights community. Indeed, the postal code district in which the project is located is one of the few in the inner-city area that has seen income growth in the last decade. The city intends to replicate its success in other parts of the city on other underused brownfields properties. At the time of writing, the city was in the process of completing a brownfields-to-housing project Josey Heights, a 53-unit house and condominium project built on land originally intended for a freeway.

Parkwest

Developer: New Covenant Housing Corporation
Date completed: Phase I — 1994; Phase II — 1999
Site area: 2.31 acres (0.93 ha)

Number and type of units: 72 residential (apartments and townhouses)
Pre-development usage: Vacant land
Rent: Affordable rental properties.

NCHC is a faith-based nonprofit development affiliate of New Covenant Missionary Baptist Church in Milwaukee. Its first project, Parkwest, was developed in two phases. The first phase completed in 1994 includes 16 apartment units in 4 buildings and 22 townhomes all for affordable rentals (Figure 6.2). The second phase completed in 1999 consists of 34 townhouse units. The developer constructed these homes to address the lack of affordable "family-sized" housing in this central Milwaukee neighborhood and to rebuild neighborhood confidence after decades of economic disinvestment. Rents for the mix of townhouses and apartments are affordable and targeted to low- and middle-income families. Project buildings are designed to complement the surrounding architecture and each unit has an attached garage. Many of the units have additional amenities such as partially finished basements, in-unit laundry facilities, and 1.5 bathrooms. Green space, play areas, a community building, and an on-site office are also part of the development.

The NCHC's mission is to provide residential, commercial and economic redevelopment opportunities to low-income and minority residents. Since 1989, it has played an important role in the revitalization and stabilization of one of Milwaukee's most disadvantaged areas (bounded by North 35th Street to North 43rd Street and West Center Street to West Brown Street). Within these boundaries, there are 6,146 people, 91% are African-American, with 94.2% of the population

Figure 6.2: New Covenant Housing, Milwaukee, 2005.

making less than 50% of the area median income. NCHC is guided under the belief that an individual's well-being is inextricably linked to the well-being of the community, and that people are personally responsible, self-reliant citizens, and not helpless victims.

The Parkwest project was developed on land cleared in the 1960s for a freeway that was never constructed. Although the freeway project was ultimately abandoned, numerous properties were knocked down in the process, blighting the community and accelerating disinvestment. Fortunately, the area cleared was primarily residential and contamination issues were minimal (under US$20,000), consisting of site assessment and the removal of a leaking underground storage tank. Milwaukee's redevelopment authority and community development block grant funds covered assessment and cleanup costs.

NCHC sponsored the US$8 million development and is currently responsible for its management. The Wisconsin Partnership for Housing Development, a nonprofit corporation that forms partnerships for affordable housing in Wisconsin, acted as a development consultant to help with project planning, feasibility analysis, and the coordination of the two-phase development plan. The Partnership also assembled the financing for both phases, which included federal low-income housing tax credits, public and private grant funds, and debt financing. A TIF district formed for the North Avenue district by the city also brought public improvements to the site.

Milwaukee's Department of City Development targeted North Avenue with a TIF district between N. 31st St. and N. Sherman Blvd. The US$1.5 million district provides slightly over US$1 million for streetlights, wider sidewalks, and an improved city-owned parking lot. The district also includes a US$400,000 business development fund, which provides building facade improvement grants and seed capital for new businesses. The higher property tax revenue generated by new development in the area will recover the funds invested. It has become a mantra among central city boosters in Milwaukee that the heavy population density in this part of the city creates a total purchasing power that is much higher on a per-square-mile basis than most suburbs, which are more affluent, but less densely populated. This means that clothing stores, shoe stores, hardware stores, super-markets, auto supply stores, restaurants, and other retailers should be interested in locating in the neighborhood.

The project has been extremely successful overall. The majority of neighborhood groups and community economic development leaders praise the new rental housing stock, although a few fear that the availability of new rental space may discourage investment in home ownership. Some would like to see the city expand its single-family housing plan and CityHomes into the area to encourage more home ownership. The project's success is reflected in the redevelopment it has sparked in the local community. In fact, Phase III of the Parkwest project could not move forward because a grocery chain snapped up the land to build a 57,000-square-foot supermarket and drugstore on the site. Seeing this as a positive sign for the community, NCHC is moving the area's revitalization ahead by developing several new projects. The Gateway I and II projects will convert two vacant buildings into 24 rental housing units and 10,500 sq ft (970 m^2) of commercial space. In addition,

NCHC is undertaking a US$6 million mixed-use development that will convert a former library into 14 rental units and 25,000 sq ft (2,322 m²) of retail. For-profit developers are also entering the market with plans to build residential and commercial space. Both the nonprofit and private sector efforts are receiving support from the City of Milwaukee, the Milwaukee Economic Development Corporation, several Milwaukee banks, local foundations, and other nonprofit groups such as LISC (Local Initiatives Support Corporation, the nation's largest community development support organization).

New Covenant's Parkwest project provides an example of how a faith-based nonprofit with no redevelopment experience, but high expectations, turned a vacant brownfield into a catalyst for inner-city renewal. The development not only provided needed housing for families in the community, but also caught the attention of public and private investors willing to be part of an up-and-coming neighborhood. New Covenant's leadership and success has also encouraged other faith-based institutions in Milwaukee to consider residential redevelopment of brownfields in their communities as a means of sparking neighborhood renewal.

Trostel Square

Developer: Mandel Group, Inc.
Date completed: 2004
Site area: 4.5 acres (1.8 ha)
Number and type of units: 126 residential units, 27 condominiums, and 99 apartments
Floor area: Apartments — from 772 to 1,346 sq ft (72–125 m²), Condos — from 1,100 to 2,500 sq ft (100–230 m²)
Pre-development usage: Tannery
Condominium sale price: US$260,000–US$480,000
Rental price: From US$1,040 to US$1,680.

Since the late 1990s, the City of Milwaukee and the private sector have also been involved in the renewal of a former industrial corridor known as the Beerline B (Figure 6.3). Dating from the early 1800s, the corridor received its name because of a railroad route that served various industrial facilities including the Schlitz and the Pabst breweries. The catalyst for this project is often considered to be the Trostel Square development. Trostel Square is a residential community located on the banks of the Milwaukee River in close proximity to the downtown core and to popular neighborhoods. Valued at approximately US$20 million, this 126-unit residential community consists of 99 apartments located in two three-story buildings along North Commerce Street, and 27 condominiums located in three clusters along the river. The development has added to the public Riverwalk and generated some open

Figure 6.3: The Beerline "B" (courtesy of Misky, 2005).

space for the neighborhood. It also includes a private clubhouse and boat slips for residents.

Mandel Group, Inc., a large residential multi-family developer operating primarily in the greater Milwaukee area, carried out the project. The Mandel Group is an integrated real estate services firm with operations in development, construction, and property management. Since its formation in 1991, it has developed and constructed over US$200 million in residential and retail developments, and has financed, acquired, and/or sold approximately US$300 million in developed units. Communities developed by the Mandel Group have received several awards for design excellence, including the prestigious Urban Land Institute 1999 Award for excellence for the East Pointe redevelopment project, and the National Association of Home Builders 2000 Award for Best Mid-Rise Apartment Community in the United States. Indeed, the company and its portfolio are regarded as one of the finest in metropolitan Milwaukee.

Trostel Square was built on land that housed the former Trostel Tannery, which was vacated in February 2000 when US Leather closed the Pfister and Vogel complex and other Milwaukee operations putting 525 employees out of work. The site was contaminated with heavy metals, volatile organic compounds, and sulfides that required cleanup to meet residential standards. Furthermore, the site's closure was dependent on all soils being managed on site. Site engineering included preparation of the site, grading and utility plans, and exhibits for the Department of Natural Resources. To build on the unstable soils, buildings had to be constructed on pilings sunk down as far as 50 ft (15 m) into glacial till. Developers also had to construct a new dock wall for the Riverwalk, at a cost of as much as US$1,500 a linear foot.

Funding to manage contamination at the former tannery came from several sources, including the Wisconsin Department of Commerce Brownfields Grant (US$700,000), tax increment financing, remediation tax credits, and other city sources. The Wisconsin Department of Natural Resources oversaw environmental remediation. Mandel Group has agreed to pay over US$3.4 million for the property, which is higher than the original assessed value of the tannery's main building (US$262,600) and land (US$948,700). The Trostel Square project produced a closure strategy that was cost effective and sensitive to development options. Condominiums sold quickly without environmental encumbrances, while apartments were financed with reasonable encumbrances. The developer financed all other development-oriented costs.

From a marketing perspective, Trostel Square's apartments and condominiums are luxurious residential units (Figure 6.4). According to the developer, residents are drawn to its convenient location that offers easy access to the downtown core, the interstate, and numerous other amenities and services. The project has also contributed to the community's renewal boom. Indeed, Milwaukee's Beerline "B" area has become a center of residential construction with more than US$120 million worth of private investment, including many of the brownfields projects examined in the previous chapter. Condominium prices range from the low US$200,000 to US$500,000 and up. While many factors have contributed to the area's remarkable

Figure 6.4: Trostel Square, Milwaukee, Wisconsin, 2005.

turnaround, developers and other key players attribute the boom to a combination of far-sighted planning and location: 20 riverfront acres (8.1 ha) that include bluffs with panoramic views, all within minutes of the downtown core. Developers especially liked the predictability offered by the City's Plan for the Beerline corridor, which many stated was a "huge" incentive in their long-range investment planning.

In 1999, in cooperation with residents, businesses, and stakeholders, the City completed the Beerline "B" Planning Study, which provided a blueprint for the area's redevelopment as a high-quality residential and commercial neighborhood. In addition to guidelines for private development, the Beerline "B" Plan includes strategies for improving public infrastructure, enhancing recreational space, increasing public access to the river, and connecting the area to the adjacent neighborhood. Indeed, many of these projects have been already carried out including the construction of several pedestrian bridges and stairwells to improve access to the site and the river.

Guided by the Plan, which many developers regarded as creating a more predictable setting for investment in the community, development in the area has occurred at a rapid pace and has received little negative reaction from the public. Some residents of nearby communities have been concerned about the loss of green space and about a growing gentrification problem. City officials, however, note that usable parkland in the area has actually increased, while developers argue that the surrounding neighborhoods are among the primary beneficiaries from the removal of blight that traditionally plagued the area. Another community concern relates to the high density of several new projects and the fear that some developers are placing too many units along the river.

The Beerline B Plan and the Trostel projects have acted as tremendous catalysts for redevelopment in the area. Indeed, seven other residential developments have been constructed within the Beerline B area in the last few years, adding over 300 units. Numerous projects have also been developed near to and across the river from Beerline B adding over 200 units, and several are currently under development. Beerline B's success is also moving down river toward downtown where in 2002 the city demolished the Park East freeway spur that had been part of a failed transportation plan dating back to the 1960s. Connecting the southern tip of the Beerline B neighborhood with the northeast part of the new Park East neighborhood will be an 8-acre (3 ha) project constructed by the Mandel Group to be known as The North End. Mandel purchased the former Pfister and Vogel tannery site for US$3.4 million in 2001, a year after it closed. The developers plan to build 395 condominiums, 88 apartments, and 20,000 sq ft (1,850 m^2) of street-level retail space on the site, valued at an estimated US$175 million. The development will also include one-quarter mile of public Riverwalk, two public squares, and the developers have discussed their intention to have the project meet some Leadership in Energy and Environmental Design (LEED) standard. To pay for the estimated US$5 million in demolition and environmental cleanup costs, Mandel has already received US$900,000 from the Wisconsin Department of Commerce and is seeking additional support from the city in the form of TIF funds. Those funds will also assist with public improvements, including construction of the Riverwalk and a new street that will be built running along the river.

Trostel Square is an example of a mid- to upper-range housing project that has successfully converted a vacant and unused tannery complex into what has become one of Milwaukee's most desirable urban neighborhoods. This brownfield site and others along the Beerline required some environmental remediation and government support from multiple levels to get off the ground, but its locational attributes and area-wide planned vision helped turn the area into a taxable asset for the government and a thriving neighborhood for Milwaukee. While issues of gentrification and access to green space have been a concern, there are ongoing attempts to address these on County-owned land in the adjacent Park East where, according to the Park East Redevelopment Compact, projects must have added benefits for the community (e.g., employing minority workers, providing prevailing wage jobs, and requiring green space).

Chicago, Illinois

As discussed in the previous chapter, Chicago has witnessed extensive residential brownfields redevelopment activity over the past decade for both market and non-market housing. The three projects described here — Columbia Pointe, University Village, and Lakeshore East — provide a snapshot of the redevelopment activity that has and is currently taking place. Indeed, it should be noted that the data for the Lakeshore East project was not included in the sample discussed in the previous chapter because although it was in the Illinois Site Remediation Program, it had not received a No Further Remediation (NFR) letter when the study commenced. Project information was, nonetheless, provided by the developer as an example of a for-profit, large-scale, residential brownfields project that did not receive public funding related to brownfields management. The Lakeshore East project is also significant because its value alone is estimated at US$2.5 billion, slightly higher than the US$2.2 billion value of all the brownfields-to-housing projects examined in that chapter.

Columbia Pointe

Development Team: Woodlawn Preservation and Investment Council, the Woodlawn Community Development Corporation, the Chicago Center for Community Development Enterprise, and the Neighborhood Rejuvenation Partners
Date completed: Phase I ongoing, Phases II and III currently under funding and planning
Site area: Phase I, 5.5 acres (2.2 ha)
Number and type of units: Phase I — 51 homes, Phases II and III initially planned for 89, however, 209 additional units now under consideration
Pre-development usage: Vacant commercial property
Price range: US$200,000–US$400,000, with 20% affordable.

The Columbia Pointe Housing project is the result of four neighborhood organizations — the Woodlawn Preservation and Investment Council (WPIC), the Woodlawn Community Development Corporation (WCDC), the Chicago Center for Community Development Enterprise, and the Neighborhood Rejuvenation Partners — coming together to build a place to live for community residents in need of housing. The project's first phase resulted in 51 single-family homes (Figure 6.5). The initial plan was to construct 89 additional homes, but recent changes have raised the figure to 209 additional units, of which 90% will be single-family units and 20% will be affordable. The Woodlawn community is located eight miles from Chicago's central business district near the University of Chicago campus. The community has lost almost half of its population since the 1960s and its racial makeup has changed little, remaining about 95% African-American. It is historically a rental community, although owner-occupied housing is up slightly (to 18%) due to the construction of new condominiums and single-family homes. Although poverty levels have decreased, 39% of residents continue to live below the poverty line and 16% receive some form of public assistance, while only 28% of households have annual incomes of more than US$35,000.

As mentioned, the project is being developed via a collaboration of four key partners. The WPIC is the lead agency for the New Communities Program, which in alliance with LISC, supports community development in 16 Chicago neighborhoods, including Woodlawn. The five-year program seeks to catalyze redevelopment and revitalization in Woodlawn and is committed to building housing "that poor people

Figure 6.5: Columbia Pointe (Phase I), Chicago, 2005.

can live in, not poor people's housing." WPIC is committed to increasing residential housing opportunities and supportive commercial uses to achieve an economically and racially integrated population in Woodlawn. The WCDC was founded in 1972 to serve as the umbrella for the Woodlawn Organization's real estate development and management activities. The Woodlawn Organization is a nonprofit community-based organization founded in 1960 that consists of an alliance of block clubs, churches, tenant councils, and other civic and institutional entities organized to build a viable and healthy Woodlawn community. The WCDC has developed more than 1,659 units of single family and senior housing in 14 different developments and is experienced in creating site, phasing and financial plans, determining unit mixes, and working extensively with government subsidy programs. The Chicago Center for Community Development Enterprise, operated through Citibank, provides financing packages to help bring community development projects to fruition. The program offers for-profit and nonprofit developers and businesses financing packages for projects in low- and moderate-income areas in cities across the United States. The fourth partner — Neighborhood Rejuvenation Partners — is a for-profit group limited liability company (LLC).

The Columbia Pointe site had previously been home to various commercial establishments, including a laundromat, hardware store, and a public library. The property was contaminated and, consisting of abandoned buildings and vacant lots, had become a visual blight on the community. Initial investigation indicated that the surface of the site consisted of fill material to depths ranging from 3 to 9 ft (2.7 m) containing polynuclear aromatic hydrocarbon compounds (PNAs), bis (2-*cloroethyl*) ether, and lead at concentrations exceeding the Illinois Environmental Protection Agency (IEPA)'s Tier 1 Soil Remediation Objectives for residential property. Benzo(*a*)pyrene and lead were also present at a level exceeding the objectives for construction worker exposure. In total, approximately 245 tons of lead-impacted soil, 2,000 tons of PNA-impacted soil, and a 1,500-gallon underground heating oil tank were removed from the property prior to development. Assessment and remediation were performed in accordance with the IEPA's Site Remediation Program and an "NFR" letter was obtained for the property.

The City of Chicago invested nearly US$480,000 to research and ultimately remedy the environmental damage at the site (for Phase I) via the Department of Environment. The Citibank Center for Community Economic Development (CCDE) provided two financing vehicles for the Columbia Pointe project — (i) a US$5 million revolving line-of-credit from Citibank to be used by the Woodlawn Park, LLC to redevelop the site and (ii) special "first-time" mortgages for qualified buyers. Similarly, the University of Chicago increased its involvement in the Woodlawn neighborhood with a US$399,999 grant awarded to the Office of Community Affairs by the US Department of Housing and Urban Development through its Community Outreach Partnership Center. For Phases II and III, LISC will be acting as the main equity member for the US$70 million project. This is the first time LISC, the nation's largest community development support organization, has acted in this capacity for a residential project, and the reason for the recent increase in the number of residential units planned.

In terms of marketing, Phase I of Columbia Pointe sold out within two weeks of opening to the public and, therefore, not much was required beyond advertising in small local and larger regional newspapers. The features and prices were attractive enough to potential buyers that essentially "word of mouth" was sufficient to fill the housing quickly. Columbia Pointe's proximity to Lake Michigan, the Loop, Hyde Park, and convenient transit (Metra), all in a project providing relatively ample lot sizes, supplied all the marketing necessary. Though no specific communities or groups were specifically targeted for sales, the intent of the development was to draw from a range of potential buyers. Within this goal of creating a diverse community, buyers came from a variety of racial and ethnic backgrounds including Asian, African-American, Caucasian, and others. The design, attributes, and marketing of Columbia Pointe all converged to help enhance an already vibrant neighborhood, and to foster future success through diversity in housing and community growth in general.

Located within the community of Woodlawn, Columbia Pointe is a part of the overall Quality of Life Plan completed in May 2005. This plan was devised under the leadership of the WPIC, combining the views of more than 300 neighborhood residents, business owners, institutional leaders, and community youth. Working in conjunction with the Woodlawn Organization and with technical guidance from the University of Chicago, the WPIC has provided a framework for pursuing eight strategies that can assist in the prosperity of the Woodlawn Community. The strategies focus on community-wide issues and concerns, including the expansion of new housing to provide for a mix of incomes and improve existing housing stock. Additional strategies seek to develop a mix of retail and business, while promoting economic opportunity for the community and its residents. Additionally, the plan seeks to help Woodlawn schools excel, expand activities and programs for youth, enhance recreational activities for all ages and support health and social service agencies within the neighborhood. Ultimately, the plan hopes to accomplish this by improving communication among organizations, residents, and institutions.

In response to local investments, many residents have joined together to create a more visually stimulating community. Along the streets are bike trails, alleys are well-lit and paved, and where there were once vacant lots, neighborhood gardens now provide residents with fresh fruits and vegetables. The private housing market is also returning with rehabilitated rental and condominium units. The Woodlawn neighborhood still faces numerous challenges however, after a long period of economic decline and population loss. Some of the key issues of concern for residents include the need for more affordable housing, better youth programs, enhanced retail options, activities for seniors, and the general sense that too many condominiums are replacing subsidized rental housing, which is pricing residents out of their own neighborhood. Fortunately, many of these issues are being addressed in a concrete way by the efforts of the community-based stakeholders involved in the process.

Much of Columbia Pointe's overall success derives from the joint efforts made by several neighborhood organizations, as well as public and private partnerships. Once a decaying, neglected commercial property, long vacant and an eyesore, Columbia Pointe has blossomed into a community with new single-family and duplex homes, of which approximately 20% are designated as affordable housing.

University Village

> *Developer*: South Campus Development Team
> *Date completed*: Ongoing
> *Site area*: 86-acre (35 ha) project, 25 acres (10 ha) of residential development
> *Number and type of units*: 930 units — 284 townhomes, 234 walkup condominiums, 226 condominiums, and 186 lofts. Constructed in three phases
> *Pre-development usage*: Railroad, industrial, and retail
> *Price range*: US$165,900–US$1,299,900.

University Village is part of a larger University of Illinois at Chicago's (UIC) South Campus redevelopment project that commenced in 1997 and is being carried out by the so-called South Campus Development Team. When completed, the US$650 million project will include more than 900 privately developed condominiums, townhomes, and lofts, in addition to student housing, academic buildings, parks, and a mixture of retail shops, restaurants, and increased parking. The private residential component of the project is valued at US$300 million and is being constructed in three phases on 25 acres (10 ha) of land located in the south end of campus. When completed, it will consist of 646 condominiums and lofts, 210 townhomes, and 31 single-family dwellings, with 185 affordable units. Over 75% of homes in the project overlook a park or open space. The homes also connect and ultimately lead to university athletic fields, which are also open to the public. Stores and restaurants have been located mainly in the middle of South Campus along Halsted and the historic Maxwell streets. The Metra station is located a block south of University Village, and it is a short drive to major expressways. Student apartments and other university-related components of the project are located in the northern part of the site. The new residences of University Village are constructed in a new urbanist-style. Preservationists fought to save the look of historic Maxwell Street, once a mixture of immigrant culture, as well as Chicago's theater of commerce and enterprise, with partial success. The facades of 21 old buildings have been incorporated into the new development, while 13 facades of vintage buildings in the area were deemed architecturally interesting and will be attached to the front of the new parking facility to be built on both sides of Maxwell Street (Figure 6.6).

The South Campus Development Team is a consortium of three development organizations in Chicago — Mesirow Stein Real Estate, Inc., the New Frontier Companies, and the Harlem Irving Companies — each with established track records in residential, retail, commercial and institutional development in Chicago. Mesirow Stein, the real estate arm of Mesirow financial, is one of the Midwest's largest development firms and carries out real estate development and consulting activities for the public sector, private corporations, and individuals. The New Frontiers Companies is a group of 11 firms with expertise in new construction, real estate development, and retail/residential management. The Harlem Irving Companies are

Figure 6.6: Historic Maxwell Street, University Village, Chicago.

involved in retail development, leasing, and management. Together, the consortium is responsible for developing the private housing component of the site and is the program manager for UIC's part of the development.

The developers and the university have worked extensively with the city to realize the project. A special Roosevelt-Union Tax Increment Financing District, covering one of the largest underutilized areas southwest of city, was established to help drive the project. The US$75 million TIF was allocated by the city to the university to help acquire land, develop infrastructure, and conduct environmental assessment and remediation activities. Historically, commercial and light industrial businesses occupied the property, including a gas station, auto repair facility, junkyard, warehouses, and a railroad trestle embankment. The remediation portion of the project proceeded in phases during the construction of University Village. The developers worked closely with the IEPA and requested NFR letters for each parcel as the construction work was completed and prior to the sale of individual units. An extensive remedial investigation identified the target areas of contamination at each parcel and cleanup included underground storage tank removals, contaminated soil removal, and railroad embankment removal. The developer described site assessment and remediation activities as being straightforward overall.

In terms of marketing the project, the initial push was to get faculty and staff from UIC to move in as part of a pre-construction program. Indeed, about a third of the 150 units initially offered were sold to UIC buyers. The developers have since implemented a more traditional marketing plan for the site, selling it as a master planned community, as opposed to an infill project. The developers attribute the high demand for the property to the project's innovative floor plans, great location, and the demand for the high-tech, energy-efficient new construction. In addition to attracting faculty and staff from the University, the development has also drawn homebuyers that work at nearby hospitals, city employees and suburbanites moving back to the city. An agreement with the city resulting from the provision of TIF funds calls for 21% of the units to be in the "affordable" range, meaning they are priced for buyers who make 80–120% of the median income for the metro area. Median income for a two-person household in Chicago, for example, is US$56,400 and for a four-person household, US$70,500. The affordable units are priced between US$143,000 and US$228,000.

University Village is part of the University's largest expansion since 1982. In 2000, several city coalitions, including the Coalition to Protect Public Housing, the Maxwell Street Historic Preservation Coalition, and the St. Francis of Assisi Preservation Committee, boycotted the project in an effort to get the developers to address issues related to affordable housing for the very poor and displaced residents, to give existing businesses an opportunity to remain in the area, and to preserve 60 historic buildings on Maxwell Street. Although few, if any, residents were physically displaced by the project, hundreds of vendors who had operated in the well-known "Maxwell Street Market" were displaced. Locals also fear that new residents will alter the fabric of surrounding neighborhoods and cause exclusionary displacement of residents and businesses. At the same time, many feel that this planned community has exceeded expectations, making it one of Chicago's most well-known and popular residential developments. Indeed, the project was awarded the City Development of the Year in 2001 by the Chicago Sun-Times and the redeveloped Maxwell Street Historic District won unanimous approval by the Illinois Historic Sites Advisory Council to go on the National Register for Historic Places.

University Village is located within the Chicago's Central Area Plan. This document establishes three themes in helping to facilitate future development and to act as a framework for making decisions. The first theme (Development Framework) seeks to create a dynamic Central Area with high-density, mixed-use corridors that extend beyond the Loop and link various neighborhoods through existing transit. In addition, the development framework aims to preserve the architectural and cultural heritage in downtown, while strengthening industrial corridors and the educational/cultural assets of Chicago. The second theme focuses on transportation, aiming to make transit the first choice for people coming to the Central Area. In concert with this, the plan aims to improve the quality of the pedestrian environment, manage traffic circulation, and parking while simultaneously encouraging alternative modes of transit. An increase in the capacity of the CTA and Metra would contribute to this overall vision. The expansion and connection of waterfronts and open spaces is the last theme in the framework for planning of this area. This plan strives to strengthen the lakefront and develop the Chicago River as not only a premier public space, but also as a continuous open space system. In order to support the growing population, the plan calls for new urban and neighborhood parks. The final element in this theme involves the expansion of landscaped streets and boulevards.

University Village is a large-scale project that has successfully taken a large blighted property and generated a highly diversified mixed-use neighborhood. Currently undergoing its third phase, after an extremely successful Phases I and II, this multi-million dollar development project will add over 900 units to the community. Built in a historic area adjacent to the UIC, the project has caused some controversy, which for the most part was settled through the partial historic preservation of the site.

Lakeshore East

> *Developer*: Magellan Development Group and Near North Properties Residential and Development
> *Date completed*: Expected 2,010
> *Site area*: 28 acres (11 ha)
> *Number and type of units*: 5,000+ condominiums and apartments
> *Pre-development usage*: Vacant shipyard/rail facility and an interim use golf course
> *Price range*: Sale: low US$200–US$3.5 million, Lease: US$1,000–US$2,300.

Lakeshore East spans 28 acres (11 ha) in the heart of downtown Chicago and is believed to be the largest parcel of downtown land under development in any major US city. The project is expected to take 12–15 years to complete, house an estimated 10,000–12,500 people, and cost US$2.5 billion. The mixed-use project will produce an entirely new urban neighborhood, which will include approximately 4,950 residences, 2.2 million gross square feet (200,000 m^2) of commercial space, 1,500 hotel rooms, a 6-acre (2 ha) public park, and a public school. Sub-neighborhoods are organized in a manner that is pedestrian friendly and transit oriented, with retail areas located along streets. The US$12 million School is designed for approximately 400 students on the first two floors, while the top floor will house Park District offices, a gymnasium, and a rooftop garden. As with University Village, Lakeshore East is located within the Chicago's Central Area Plan.

Two large companies, Magellan Development Group and Near North Properties (NNP) Residential and Development, have joined forces to create Lakeshore East. Magellan Development has built a number of significant residential high-rises since 1990 in the River North, Gold Coast, and West Loop areas, making it one of the city's most prolific development firms. NNP Residential and Development is a diversified real estate company responsible for many notable residential projects in Chicago, including several constructed on brownfields.

After the Great Chicago Fire of 1871, the property was filled with charred detritus from the conflagration. Added later were canal and harbor-mouth dredging from the expansion of the area east of Michigan Avenue. In the 1960s, urban planners decided it would serve as the site of a mega-development called Illinois Center, but the economic downturn of the 1970s caused the eastern half of this retail-and-office complex to be scaled down. Briefly considered as the location of a new Chicago Bears stadium in the 1980s, the site was later reborn as a nine-hole downtown golf course. The old docks and boat slips of the harbor, which were buried under the fill, presented some concerns during early work, while the site's problematic history was revealed further when early testing showed traces of thorium, which is a radioactive element, on a small part of the site. Between landfill operations and the construction of locks to reverse the river's flow at the beginning of the twentieth century, some of that thorium made its way into the ground. Thorium at the site was excavated as far down as 13 ft ($4\,m^2$) into the ground, and excavation throughout the site was done in 18-inch lifts so that the material could be scanned on an ongoing manner. Contaminated materials were transported to a facility near Moab, Utah for management. The US$4 million assessment and cleanup costs were borne by the developers and the only public assistance provided for this project was in the form of a public improvement bond for sewer and water infrastructure.

The Lakeshore East developers have recently refinanced the massive mixed-use project with a loan from an AFL-CIO pension fund. The transaction gives the Chicago-based developers fresh working capital for new buildings. The US$70 million loan underscores the rise in the value of downtown development sites amid the continued condominium building boom and the refinancing is considered a remarkable turn for the huge project, whose prospects seemed risky just seven years ago according to the Chicago Tribune (2005). Indeed, Magellan-NNP agreed to buy the site in 1998, but could not close on the purchase for four years, as the venture steered the massive project through zoning approval and financing. In 2002, financing was so difficult to obtain that Magellan-NNP had to borrow nearly US$24 million from the seller to buy the US$81 million site. The land cost was reduced by US$25.8 million when the developers sold part of the site to the city for streets and a park, though they contributed about US$11 million toward the 6-acre (2 ha) park, which opened in 2005.

Lakeshore East is being marketed in a traditional manner. It consists of both sale and rental units. Prices range considerably, with rentals starting at US$1,000 for a studio and some penthouses slated to be sold for prices of several million dollars. For buyers, this location enjoys some of the best lake, park, and skyline views in the city, and the commute times to offices in the Loop are minimal. The city's best cultural institutions and one of the nation's most prestigious retail districts, the Magnificent Mile, lie within walking distance.

The company took an integrated approach to planning this massive development, ensuring that new buildings in Lakeshore East came together with the area's existing properties to form a complete community. NNP Residential and Development achieved this vision by dedicating more than two years of time working with community associations, city officials, neighborhood organizations, condominium boards, and other groups interested in the well-being of the neighborhood. Before mapping out any plans for the 11-hectare parcel, NNP Residential and Development and its co-developers participated in more than 400 public meetings in the community to discuss the Lakeshore East project. In addition, instead of a forest of skyscrapers, Lakeshore East's plans call for a mix of mid-rises, high-rises, and low-rise Parkhomes, a modern twist on the traditional Chicago townhome. One of the condominiums is being constructed to meet the requirements for LEED certification in order to differentiate it from other buildings in the market. LEED points are being granted for its sustainable location, water efficient landscaping, reduced design energy costs, use of local materials and recycled content, management of construction waste, indoor air quality management, daylighting, innovative design, and various other factors.

Additionally, in one of the nation's most dense areas, the planning approval mandates 45% of site area to be retained as open space. With the 2-hectare park serving as the focal point of the neighborhood, NNP Residential and Development provided public space to serve as a catalyst for the community. According to many Lakeshore East proponents, the largest remaining vacant site in Downtown Chicago has been developed with sensitivity to views from existing towers and reducing building height toward the lakefront. According to others, however, Lakeshore East's architecture lacks character.

Lakeshore East's principal achievement is to have converted what used to be one of the largest vacant lots in the downtown of any major US city into one of Chicago's most prestigious mixed-use neighborhoods. The luxury neighborhood responds to a high demand for residential and retail space. By 2010, the development is expected to consist of 4,950 residences, 2.2 million gross square feet (200,000 m²) of commercial space, 1,500 hotel rooms, a public park, and a public school.

Vancouver, British Columbia

While not heavily industrialized, the City of Vancouver's (population 500,000) inner harbor was once home to extensive rail, manufacturing, and port facilities that began to move to surrounding communities up until the 1970s due to poor transportation access and high land costs. Fortunately, the high value of land in Vancouver has ensured that the market for brownfields remains relatively strong, particularly those near the downtown core. While the city does not maintain a formal brownfields inventory, over 500 sites have already been assessed, cleaned up, and/or redeveloped, with the brunt of activity in the form of large-scale projects in the False Creek area of downtown. This section presents the story of False Creek's redevelopment, including the initial redevelopment of False Creek South into a medium-density residential community, False Creek North into a high-density urban neighborhood, and the ongoing planning and development of South East False Creek (SEFC) into a model "sustainable community."

False Creek South

In the late 1960s, citizens of Vancouver began reacting against the scale, form, and quality of development in the city and particularly in the downtown core. In 1968, a political group with strong professional management and academic representation known as TEAM (The Electors Action Movement) became a powerful voice in efforts to change the nature of redevelopment. One of the major platforms of a key TEAM member, Alderman Walter Hardwick, a former university of British Columbia geography professor first elected in 1970, was "the promotion of a livable city through good planning practice" (Punter, 2003, p. 26). Hardwick had always been particularly interested in redeveloping and revitalizing the derelict False Creek industrial area. As Punter (2003, p. 34) notes:

> The False Creek South redevelopment project was the brainchild of TEAM Alderman Walter Hardwick. With fellow University of British Columbia Professor Wolfgang Garson (architecture), Hardwick had used the site for a major student project in 1965. The results showed how False Creek could be transformed from an obsolete industrial area around a largely polluted inlet to a high quality, mixed-use area.

The City of Vancouver acquired the industrial brownfield lands on the south shore of False Creek in 1968 as part of a land exchange with the provincial government and the Canadian Pacific Railway. Planning for the 30-hectare site began in earnest when TEAM took power in 1972 and, by 1973, the city had adopted a series of guidelines for the area's redevelopment. The planning process would ultimately lay the foundation for one of the largest works in the city's history, and a redevelopment approach to urban brownfields redevelopment that would ultimately come to be known as the Vancouver Model (Punter, 2003; Design Center for Sustainability at UBC, 2006).

Although the project predated the modern concept of sustainability, site planners sought to apply innovative ideas to its redevelopment. Indeed, efforts to link quality of life and the built environment were very explicit, and according to Cybriwsky, Ley, and Western (1986, p. 112), the design guidelines for False Creek South were "a quite deliberate and unusually direct transfer of prevalent social science theses concerning the built environment." As Punter (2003, p. 374) aptly points out, in addition to the work by noted architect Christopher Alexander (1977), "the guidelines also subsumed ideas from Gans (1962, 1968), Jacobs (1961), McHarg (1969), Lynch (1960), and Cullen (1961) to reflect the progressive — most utopian — urban design approaches that Hardwick and Gerson had advocated in their 1965 student project."

One of the primary objectives of the False Creek project was to create a community with a diverse social mix adjacent to the downtown core. The intent was to help balance the development of the West End, which had been predominantly for middle- to high-income earners. A target was set for one-third low-income housing, one-third middle-income housing, and one-third market rate housing. Housing forms were also to be mixed, comprising market units, townhouses and apartments for families, and non-market housing in the form of co-ops and nonprofit rentals (Figure 6.7). The city also wanted to provide housing and recreation amenities for families, with a specific goal of 25% of units being set aside for families with children (a set aside of 25% for couples, 15% elderly, 35% singles). In total, 2,977 residential units housing over 5,000 residents were constructed on the site and although the proportion of family housing has changed as the community has matured, it remains more socially diverse than surrounding neighborhoods (Design Center for Sustainability at UBC, 2006).

A second major project objective was the provision of parks and open space. This included developing a hierarchy of green space incorporating private yards, semi-private open areas, paths, and public parks. Also important was the opening up of the waterfront to the public, which had not been accessible for almost a century. Opening up the waterfront involved removing polluted soils for off-site disposal, opening up bays, and lining up the shore with an extension of Vancouver's seawall. In total, the site offers over 10.5 ha of open space.

A third objective was to encourage socialization amongst residents. The design of the housing units was mixed and enclaves of clustered homes were constructed to maximize the potential for social contact, particularly among families. The early phase included two areas of development: a low-rise family-housing neighborhood and a medium-rise mixed neighborhood, each subdivided into three or four distinct

Figure 6.7: False Creek South.

enclaves. These were all interconnected with multiple types of green space to achieve optimal social interaction.

The innovative approach to planning and development implemented in False Creek South was subject to professional and political debate at the time, including a post-occupancy evaluation conducted by the federal government. As Punter (2003, p. 40) notes:

> It revealed that the project was achieving the desired social mix but not always providing adequate visual and aural privacy. The study showed that the semi-private spaces, which were the focus for the enclaves, were differentially but generally under used, while the park and the seawall were very well used and widely enjoyed. The evaluation concluded that the close grained social mix did not enhance the residents' experience of environmental quality; that residents might prefer "less personal, more anonymous, possibly higher density site plan[s]" than that provided by the enclaves and that privacy was as important as community in the design of gradations of public space … . These important conclusions provided justification for much higher density housing development on the north side of False Creek in the 1990s.

False Creek North

While False Creek South was under development in the 1970s, a rather different future was being formulated for the north side of False Creek. The land there was entirely owned by Marathon, the property arm of the Canadian Pacific Railway. Negotiations between Marathon and the city ensued in the early 1970s, with the developer wanting high density and the city wanting one-third low-cost housing to be sold at non-market rates. In the mid-1970s, the land attracted the attention of the provincial government as a possible site for a world's fair, and in the late 1970s, the province acquired some 71 hectares of False Creek North, paying Marathon CDN\$30 million in cash and an equivalent sum in downtown properties, along with other undisclosed assets (Punter, 2003, p. 187). In 1980, the premier announced the construction of a new sports stadium known as BC Place and the decision to hold a World's Transportation Fair (Expo 1986) to celebrate the centennials of the city and of Canadian Pacific. Also revealed were plans to build 10,000 residential units and 700,000 m² of offices on the lands after the exposition.

The redevelopment project catapulted the provincial government into a situation of financing much of the brownfields cleanup. The site had been the industrial heart of Vancouver for over 100 years and included two coal gasification plants, a dozen saw mills and wood preserving operations, metal shops, and the Canadian Pacific Railway (CPR) rail yards. These activities left the soil and groundwater contaminated with a range of metal and organic contaminants (Figure 6.8). To manage this, the province devised a comprehensive approach for managing contamination

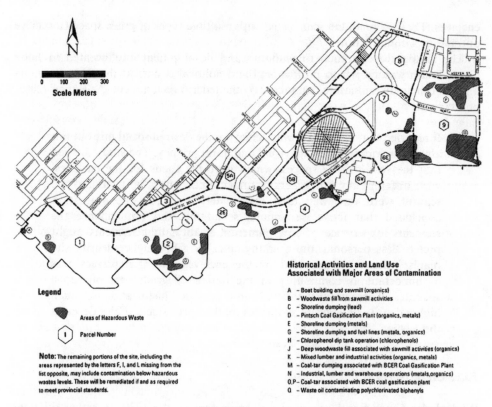

Figure 6.8: False Creek North, areas associated with contamination (reprinted with permission from the British Columbia Ministry of Agriculture and Lands, 2006).

that permitted the use of more cost-effective site-specific and risk-based approaches. Still the total price tag of the cleanup was over CDN$75 million paid for by the province.

The Expo was considered a significant success, raising the profile of the city and stimulating its economy. Just as important as the development that took place was, as Punter (2003, p. 192) notes, "the fact that it raised public expectations for street life, design quality, and amenities" and that it gave the public access to False Creek's entire northern waterfront. Shortly after the Expo, the province announced it would sell the site to Li-Ka-Shing, Hong Kong's wealthiest property tycoon. There was considerable controversy over the price paid for the site, reputedly CDN$320 million. While considerably more than the amount the province paid for the site less than a decade earlier, it was considerably less than the CDN$1 billion the land was alleged to be worth once the official development plan was approved in 1990. Critics also argued that taking account of government financing for remediation, the actual land price was closer to $125 million (Olds, 1995).

The planning process for False Creek North involved extensive public and private sector cooperation, another feature that would come to shape the nature of development in Vancouver and, in my opinion, is the primary factor in the city's ability to work with developers to maximize sustainability-oriented amenities. Indeed, the developer in this case paid for all of the costs related to the city's planning and regulatory work, which allowed for the creation of a dedicated staff team of city officers (planners, engineers, park board members, housing offers, social planners, and cultural affairs) to work across departments and alongside the developers and their designers (Punter, 2003). The project also involved extensive public consultation via meetings and workshops. Through this, seven key organizing principles emerged to guide the development's design:

1. *Integrate with the city*: False Creek North should not be a self-contained new town in the city, but an integral part of Vancouver.
2. *Build on the setting*: The special characteristics of this setting should be used as a basis for development (i.e., water-oriented land uses and activity settings, walking distance to employment, history of the place).
3. *Maintain the sense of a substantial water basin*: The False Creek water basin is an important geographical feature in the center of the city; adjacent development should enhance its presence.
4. *Use streets as an organizing device*: A pattern of streets and sidewalks, along which buildings can be constructed, should be used as a primary ordering device. Such a pattern will accommodate incremental development, provide flexibility, and integrate with the nearby development.
5. *Create lively places having strong "imageability"*: Open spaces, including streets, parks, plazas, and walkways should be planned and designed to be identifiable, memorable, and lively.
6. *Create neighborhoods*: The creation of neighborhoods should be a basis for organizing the area's development (i.e., neighborhoods should have distinctive identities, a diversity of people should be accommodated in each neighborhood).
7. *Plan for all age groups with a particular emphasis on children*: To achieve robust neighborhoods, which have flexibility to accommodate all residents and the needs of children should be emphasized.

The project involved high-density market and non-market residential units, extensive park space, a waterfront path, and an array of other public facilities (Figure 6.9). The official development plan for False Creek North was completed and approved in 1990 as a concept master plan accommodating up to 9,818 residential units (918,248 m^2) with floor-space maximums prescribed for each of 10 sub-areas, and a quarter of the units to be suitable for families with small children, and one-fifth to be non-market housing (City of Vancouver, 2004). The amount and mix of dwelling unit types was also relegated by sub-area, although there was some room for modification. Office uses of up to 145,872 m^2, retail and service uses of up to 55,948 m^2, and some warehouse uses were also allowed on specific parts of the site. In addition, community uses included two schools, a community center, eight daycare centers, a branch library, a field house, and eight separate pieces of parkland totaling 17.05 ha linked by a continuous walkway. Close attention was also taken in

Figure 6.9: Photo False Creek North (2004).

the official plan to ensure that new structures do not interfere with the downtown's view shed.

The False Creek North neighborhoods are virtually complete. While the trails and parklands create a seamless link between the new developments along the waterfront, the links between the waterfront sites and the established neighborhoods to the north have taken root as people move to and fro to enjoy the green space or just walk along the water.

South East False Creek: A Model Sustainable Community

In 1991, the City of Vancouver determined that SEFC be developed as a residential community that incorporated principles of energy efficient design in its area plan and enabled the area's development as a model "sustainable community." The SEFC study area comprises a total of approximately 80 acres (32 ha) of former industrial land near downtown Vancouver. The majority of the land is city-owned, although over 30 acres (12.1 ha) is privately owned. SEFC has been an industrial area since the late 1800s, with uses such as sawmills, foundries, shipbuilding, metalworking, salt distribution, warehousing, and the city's public works yard (Figure 6.10). The area north of the original shoreline was filled over time with materials from many sources, including a railway cut and ash from a former incinerator.

Despite the city's determination to build a sustainable community in the area, Punter (2003) points out that there were serious tensions between conventional and

Figure 6.10: Derelict buildings in South East False Creek lie in sharp contrast to the glittering Science World Sphere built for Expo 86 and the residential towers of CityGate across the water in False Creek North (2004).

sustainable development interests. Indeed, the city manager and real estate division funded an extensive master plan for the area in 1996 that did not include sustainable development in its terms of reference. The conventional master plan was carried out by the same individual responsible for the False Creek North plan and included a pro forma analysis to establish the project's profitability. In contrast to this elaborate plan, the city's planning department, which was responsible for helping define the sustainability vision, could only fund a summer student to research the policies and precedents for sustainability development (Punter, 2003). To break the tension, the Vancouver Planning Commission sponsored a two-day conference on urban sustainability that attracted city councilors and several hundred delegates. The traditional real estate development report was shelved, and several consulting studies were undertaken both to better understand sustainability indicators and performance targets, and to link these into a more traditional official development plan.

The site had been home to a city works yard and various industrial and storage uses including an incinerator, asphalt paving plant, storage of bulk construction materials, a machine shop, vehicle storage, repair and servicing, PCB transformer storage, explosives storage, underground fuel storage, steel fabrication activities, and brick and cement manufacturing. Consequently, various heavy metals, hydrocarbons, and some PCB wastes require remediation. A 1992 study put the costs of cleanup for redevelopment between CDN\$15 million and CDN\$150 million (Punter, 2003, p. 228). Cleanup estimates, however, continue to evolve as the site is planned and in early 2000s it was expected that much of the contaminated soils could be encapsulated on a raised site with an estimated cost of CDN\$18 million to CDN\$20 million.

SEFC is envisioned as a "community in which people live, work, play and learn in a neighborhood that has been designed to maintain and balance the highest possible levels of social equity, livability, ecological health and economic prosperity, so as to support their choices to live in a sustainable manner" (City of Vancouver, 2006). SEFC will be a mixed-use community with a focus on residential use, developed at the highest density possible while meeting livability and sustainability objectives. As with New Urbanism, this community will ensure goods and services within walking distance and housing that is linked by transit and in proximity to local jobs. The public realm, which includes open space, parks, streets, and pathways, will connect the entire site and link the adjacent neighborhoods. Movement within the site will be through a network of paths and streets designed for pedestrians, cyclists, and transit. The planning process for SEFC included 18 months of research and public consultation that resulted in a draft policy statement and comprehensive design guidelines (CMHC, 2001).

Housing will comprise of 2,353 units for 4,949 people, with family housing a priority. Housing may also be included for an additional 8,575 people on the private lands, with live-work space as a priority. Community amenities and commercial-industrial space will also be provided in an effort to allow residents opportunities to "live, work, play, learn, and interact with neighbors."

The built form will celebrate the heritage of the site through the revitalization of the Domtar Salt Building and its designation for public use. The buildings will be designed to be healthy, livable, and efficient in their use of energy resources and water. The neighborhood will provide a wide range of parks and recreational experiences along the waterfront, and will include shoreline improvements and completion of the seaside pedestrian–bicycle route. Parks and open space will be required to meet ecological objectives, including re-establishment of wildlife habitat, and private and community gardens will be encouraged. In some areas of the site, demonstration projects in advanced environmental technologies, such as renewable energy supplies, water management, green building design, and urban agriculture may be explored.

The Official Development Plan for SEFC (City of Vancouver, 2006) provides a comprehensive guide for the sites, which will be developed over the next decade. Some of the key sections of the development plan outlining urban design principles, sustainability principles, and sustainability strategies, are summarized below. Twelve principles govern design at the site:

1. *Overall basin form legibility*: Development is to create a legible overall form that reinforces the idea of the False Creek "basin" with lower buildings near the waterfront stepping up to higher buildings to the south.

2. *Distinct neighborhood precincts*: SEFC is to consist of three neighborhood precincts that derive their form from the historic patterns and uses of SEFC, adjacent communities, and False Creek.
3. *Integrated community*: Integration of all sub-areas is to occur through street pattern, ground plane design, and overall building form.
4. *Street hierarchy*: The street network is to provide access but discourage through traffic circulation.
5. *Connected public open spaces and parks*: Parks and public open spaces are to be central features in organizing the community, and open spaces are to connect with adjacent areas by foot and bicycle paths to create a walking and cycling friendly neighborhood.
6. *Integrated transit*: Development is to allow for an integrated public transit streetcar system to serve SEFC and adjacent neighborhoods with stops at community and commercial locations.
7. *Vibrant commercial heart*: A vibrant commercial focus is to act as a "heart" for the community.
8. *Waterfront animation development*: To engage and animate the public waterfront through the selection of land uses and design of shoreline features.
9. *Clustered community services development*: To include a centrally located broad range of community services and amenities with good access to parks and waterfront.
10. *Heritage recognition*: Preservation of buildings with heritage significance, and recognition of the historic patterns of former industrial uses, is important.
11. *Incremental varied development*: Development is to encourage land parceling and a coordinated parking strategy that allows for incremental development at a variety of scales.
12. *Demonstrated sustainability*: SEFC is to demonstrate a comprehensive approach to sustainability reflected in both open space and building design.

The Official Development Plan has also established a set of 14 sustainability principles, which in conjunction with the urban design principles, guide the development of a sustainable community:

1. *Implementation of sustainability*: SEFC is to promote the implementation of sustainable development principles in an urban setting, and thereby contribute to improving the mainstream practices of urban development throughout the region.
2. *Stewardship of ecosystem health*: A significant goal of changing the land use from industrial to mixed use is to improve the ecological health of the False Creek basin. A further goal is that the need to conserve, restore, and manage the local and regional ecosystems, including conserving resources and reducing waste, may help to satisfy the needs of present and future generations.
3. *Economic viability and vitality*: Development is to create a framework for economically viable projects, to enable the transfer of knowledge gained to other

developments, and to create opportunities for employment and investment to ensure long-term prosperity.

4. *Priorities*: Priorities include setting social and environmental performance targets at the beginning of the development process, with the intent of finding ways to meet such targets in an economically viable fashion.

5. *Cultural vitality*: Development is to encourage vitality, diversity, and cultural richness in a manner that respects the history and context of SEFC.

6. *Livability*: Development is to promote livability, and to enhance the social and natural environment by creating a walkable, safe, and green neighborhood that contributes to the well-being of residents and visitors.

7. *Housing diversity and equity*: Development is to promote opportunities for housing for a range of income groups along with social and physical infrastructure that is accessible to the whole community, especially children.

8. *Education*: SEFC is to encourage awareness and understanding of the principles of sustainability, and how their implementation can occur.

9. *Participation*: Development is to encourage public participation in decision-making.

10. *Accountability*: Development is to include implementing a process to promote accountability for decisions and actions by monitoring impacts and outcomes using post-occupancy studies and community consultation.

11. *Adaptability*: Development is to promote adaptability and diversity by ensuring that SEFC is a community that, as it grows and changes, can renew and adapt itself effectively to new social and economic conditions, policies, programs, legislation, and technology.

12. *Integration*: Development is to promote the integration of SEFC into the city through planning, urban design, community involvement, and the provision of public amenities.

13. *Spirit of the place*: Development is to include the promotion of planning and development guidelines that celebrate the unique natural, social, and historical context of SEFC.

14. *Complete community:* SEFC is to develop as a complete community that enables its residents to live, work, play, and learn within a convenient walking, cycling, or transit-riding distance.

Specific strategies and performance targets, summarized below, support these principles (many of these are further defined in a green building strategy):

Environmental Sustainability

- *Energy*: Energy efficiency is to be a key design consideration for all buildings. The goal is to establish an energy efficient greenhouse gas neutral neighborhood based on renewable resources. The basic strategy for meeting that goal is to consist of three interrelated design approaches including (i) conservation strategies such as efficient building envelope, green roofs, building orientation and configuration, unit energy metering, user controls, manual ventilation, and day-lighting; (ii) core system strategies such as heat pumps, green hydroelectric, hydronic slab heating systems, thermal storage, and building mass; and (iii) heat source and system strategies such as horizontal ground-source loop, district heating, sanitary sewer heat recovery, waste hot water heat recovery, solar hot water, and passive solar gain.

- *Water*: All water systems are to minimize the use of potable water from the municipal water system; to minimize irrigation, and, where necessary, provide irrigation through rainwater collection or high-efficiency drip systems.
- *Stormwater*: All development is to include provision for collection of stormwater from roofs, podiums, and other impervious surfaces, and retention of stormwater on-site for irrigation and landscaping, or for its transportation to False Creek along the surface in right of way bioswales.
- *Solid waste and recycling*: Each "CD-1" re-zoning is to include requirements regarding the separation, collection, and storage of garbage, organics, and recyclable materials; on-site organic composting for landscaping needs; and the management of construction and demolition waste to ensure a minimum of 50% landfill diversion.
- *Landscaping*: Aspects to consider include drought-tolerant landscaping, minimized irrigation requirements, edible landscapes, urban agriculture, and green roofs.
- *Urban agriculture*: SEFC is to include a community demonstration garden in the park and a site for a farmer's market. A goal with respect to urban agriculture is to encourage podiums and low- and mid-rise concrete developments to accommodate green roofs for urban agriculture in addition to stormwater management and to provide for on-site composting and rainwater collection. Further goals are to seek edible landscaping within public spaces in specified locations, and to explore other opportunities, through design guidelines, for garden plots.
- *Habitat and ecosystems*: The planning process is to support biodiversity and habitat corridors in parks, and to pay particular attention to integrating ecological needs into areas planned for recreation and amenity.
- *Movement*: Movement system planning is to support transportation alternatives to vehicles by requiring dedicated space for bicycle lanes, greenways, and tramways, and limited automobile ownership through parking demand management and the proactive application of neighborhood transportation demand management.
- *Green buildings*: The Green Building Strategy adopted for SEFC requires that all buildings on city lands be constructed to a minimum LEED Silver standard, with an objective of LEED Gold standard.

Social Sustainability

- *Meeting basic needs*: Appropriate, affordable housing: (i) Affordable housing is to comprise at least 20% of the housing areas; (ii) modest market housing is to comprise up to 33% of the housing in specific sub-areas. In order to achieve affordable accommodation for families, the further aim is to achieve a household mix of 25–35% for families within specified sub-areas. Provisions are also included to provide opportunities for health care, crime prevention, and Affordable Child Care.

- *Enhancing human capacity*: Creating local employment opportunities, opportunities for resident involvement in the selection and production of public art, and life-long learning, and recreation and cultural facilities.
- *Enhancing social capacity*: To provide a unique community identity; to establish a neighborhood association to promote public involvement and education; and to promote social interaction by developing numerous places throughout the community.

Economic Sustainability

- *A different financial approach in this community*: Development of a model that values social and environmental measures, and considers the long-term economic viability of the community, is to inform the financial approach that is to support economic sustainability.
- *Economic security*: Goals include promoting a range of job opportunities through the construction process, and through the operation of retail, service, and office uses in several locations throughout the community; providing quality, licensed child care to allow parents to participate in the labor force; and encouraging the construction process to promote equitable hiring practices, and to ensure the representation of unemployed members of low-income communities.
- *Local self-reliance*: Development is to encourage a complete community where residents may purchase items needed for daily life without use of an automobile.
- *An ecological economy*: Development is to support the introduction of businesses and technologies that build on practices, such as recycling, employed in the community.
- *An economic advantage*: Another goal of development is that the economic gains resulting from conserving energy, reducing waste, living close to work and play, building pride and identity in the community, and supporting local economic enterprise are to create an economic advantage in the community.
- *Maintaining the vision*: Creating a neighborhood association to provide community input during and after development is a priority. This association is to help with strategies for monitoring and fine-tuning the neighborhood's social, economic, and environmental performance.

The SEFC project was recently given a boost with the announcement in July 2003 that Vancouver would be home to the 2010 Olympic and Paralympic Winter Games, often billed as the sustainable Olympics, and that the SEFC development site will be the future site of the Vancouver Olympic Village. The Olympic Village in the heart of the site (approximately one-fifth of total site area) will be home to approximately 2,800 athletes and officials during the Winter Games. In terms of site remediation, the more extensive storage and logistical requirements of games have limited the amount of polluted soil that can be managed on site, raising the cost estimate to between CDN $27 million and CDN$30 million.

The Olympic Village will be turned over to Olympic organizing committee in early November 2009 for the final preparations and use during the 2010 Winter Games. The buildings will then be returned to the City of Vancouver in late March 2010. After the 2010 Winter Games, those buildings used by the athletes will provide approximately 1,000 residential units, including 250 affordable housing units, a community center, daycare, retail, and service space for the new residents of SEFC. Development of the remaining City Lands (approximately two-fifths of the total area) will continue to 2018. Development on some of the private sites (remaining two-fifths) may occur prior to the 2010 Winter Games and will likely continue beyond 2018.

The Vancouver Model as it has been applied to False Creek is often considered one of the most successful mega-projects in North America. The quality of life-oriented approach to the area first implemented in the development of False Creek South has indeed evolved, as more is known about the economic, social, and environmental factors that contribute to the quality of human life and natural systems. Although many have critiqued the approaches and outcomes taken to develop the area, it is clear that the public and private sectors have worked together to incorporate the interests of both in a framework that is open to the public and open to new ideas about methods for enhancing the urban environment. Upon speaking to planners, environmental managers, and various public and private stakeholders in Vancouver, it is clear that while they each have their own agendas, desires, and philosophies, they have shown themselves more than able to keep these in check and work together toward an approach that balances their needs. Indeed, I often joke to students about Vancouver being one of the only places where the environmentalists understand pro formas and the developers know about biodiversity. However, it is this cooperative planning model that ultimately leads to more sustainable urban development. Punter (2003, p. 238) describes the cooperative planning process that exists in Vancouver as follows:

> The cooperative planning process is characterized by a clear demarcation between political decision-making, which sets the overall parameters of the projects, and the technical resolution of development forms and designs that is delegated to city officials. The emphasis is on joint working by teams comprised of developer and city staff to prepare masterplans and convert them into official development plans and guidelines on their own. The developer pays for the creation of a dedicated planning team to work full time on the project's preparation, while the city works corporately, linking the planning function as necessary ... . The approach is complemented by sustained public participation at all stages of project development.

While this approach may seem onerous, it delivers a high level of certainty to developers once the official plan is in place, while delivering extensive public benefits to the public in terms of green space, affordable housing, and many other sustainable development factors. Most importantly, this approach allows the bar to be continually raised in a way that seeks to enhance economic, social, and environmental benefits. Efforts to monitor the achievement of such outcomes in previous phases of False Creek's redevelopment also ensure that approaches and strategies are not static cookie-cutter techniques, but dynamic ones that are continuously enhanced.

Conclusion

The brownfields-to-housing projects described in this chapter illustrate the range of projects being developed in an effort to supply the growing demand for urban homes, increase affordable housing opportunities, revitalize blighted neighborhoods, and bring about more compact and sustainable urban growth. Perhaps the most difficult projects from a market standpoint are those being carried out in low-income neighborhoods where the value of residential real estate is low, but the need for adequate housing, blight removal, and catalytic projects is high. The primary driver of these projects has been a less market-oriented stakeholder willing to take the lead, and risk, with financial and logistical support from other public, nonprofit, and private sector partners. In Milwaukee, the municipal government took the lead in the CityHomes project, while a faith-based nonprofit did the same through its NCHC. In Chicago, a consortium of four neighborhood organizations banded together to realize their vision. All of these projects have made considerable social, environmental, and economic contributions to neighborhoods that had suffered from decades of neglect and have since continued to expand into the surrounding community. These projects have also empowered other nonprofits to consider similar projects on brownfields and vacant lands in other parts of those cities.

For sites that are less challenged by weak market conditions, but where brownfields costs and risks still present an obstacle, public–private partnerships linking developers willing to take risks and government agencies willing to help them attenuate those risks is essential. Developers involved in the Trostel Square project, and others along the Milwaukee River, benefited from an area-wide plan and financial support for environmental remediation and infrastructure-related costs from several levels of government. University Village in Chicago required a strong partnership between an experienced development team, the university, and the city (TIF funding) to make the project a success. A very positive sign is that the regulatory and liability frameworks governing brownfields redevelopment in place now make it possible for private developers to move projects forward without public funding, and to bring compact and green development to the downtown core. One extremely positive note is that consumers of all types are purchasing units on these remediated sites.

If linking housing and sustainable development requires us to consider the implications of residential location, the affect of development on the community, and a host of environmental, social, and economic factors (Edwards, 2000), then the redevelopment of False Creek in Vancouver points in an optimal direction. The long-term and close collaboration among multiple actors has been vital for this project. Government intervention at the local and provincial levels has been essential for promoting and implementing a more sustainable vision in all three phases of False Creek's redevelopment, as well as for funding cleanup. Success in earlier phases of the project, as seen in the strong market for real estate and the public's support for it, have allowed the city government to continue to raise the sustainability-bar as seen in the planning for SEFC. The private sector has also worked collaboratively with the city on these projects, even funding their staff, and is currently reaping hefty profits from the extremely attractive community.

The goal of the last three chapters has been to examine the brownfields-to-housing issue and describe how such redevelopment is contributing to the creation of more vibrant, livable, compact, and sustainable residential environments. While the shift in federal housing policy in both countries to a less-regulated approach makes it more difficult to impose requirements for housing on brownfields and for sustainability features, the flexibility permits local governments, nonprofits, and private developers to determine what their communities need and to define what can be done. Fortunately, more and more stakeholders are looking to brownfield sites as opportunity-spaces for building new communities of varying types, while erasing blight at the same time. All of these projects generate the sustainability benefits inherent to brownfields redevelopment and more compact urban growth, and many are designing sustainability features directly into these projects to differentiate them from others on the market, as well as to meet requirements of local governments and growing demands from consumers and community members for more quality spaces. The next group of chapters focuses on the conversion of brownfields into parks and open space and its role in improving the state of the urban environment and enhancing urban livability.

Chapter 7

Work into Play — Turning Brownfields into Parks and Open Space: Policy and Vision

Since the mid-1990s, the focus of most cities has been on promoting and supporting brownfields redevelopment that generates new employment opportunities and allows municipalities to expand their tax base. More recently, however, a growing number of cities have started to convert brownfield sites into parks and open space as part of a more comprehensive strategy for improving the state of the urban environment and enhancing urban livability (Garvin & Berens, 1997; Harnik, 2000; US Conference of Mayors, 2003). In some European countries, greening has played a more central role in the renewal of urban communities. The most common type of redevelopment of derelict lands in England between 1988 and 1993, for instance, was targeted at sport and recreation uses (37%), followed by new industrial, commercial, agricultural, and forestry uses (DETR, 1999b). In Scotland, passive open space, recreation, and leisure space accounted for 21% of derelict and vacant land reuse between 1993 and 2002 (Scottish Executive, 2003), while the Netherlands estimates that 10–15% of their urban brownfields become green space (Netherlands Ministry of Housing, Spatial Planning and Environmental Affairs, 2004).

While similar greening projects have also been carried out in the US and Canada, they have generally tended to attract less attention from both the governmental and research sectors. Indeed, brownfields-to-green space projects only represent approximately 4% of brownfields projects in US cities. Recently, this situation has started to change, as both nonprofit (e.g., The Trust for Public Land, Rails to Trails, Groundwork USA, and the Conservation Fund) and government agencies (e.g., US EPA, 2000b, 2001, 2003; Pennsylvania DEP, 1999; Minnesota Pollution Control Agency, 2001; Wisconsin DNR, 2002) have come to realize that the greening of brownfields holds enormous potential for improving city environments, as well as for enhancing their recreational functions, ecological conditions, and aesthetic appearance (Garvin & Berens, 1997; Harnik, 2000). Also increasing are calls for greater incorporation of green features into the design of individual residential and commercial projects in order to increase urban vegetation and to replace gray infrastructure (storm sewers, cooling systems) with green infrastructure (storm water retention ponds, green roofs, tree shading).

This chapter and the next two chapters examine the implementation and impact of greening projects carried out on brownfields in US and Canadian cities. Chapter 7 sets the stage by describing urban open space policy and planning in both countries, discussing the link between green space and sustainability, and then reviewing current policy and scholarly literature on converting brownfields into green space. Chapter 8 looks specifically at the type of brownfields-to-green space projects that are being carried out, the planning processes involved in remediating brownfields and converting them into green spaces, the factors that motivate them, and the main obstacles to greening. Case studies in Chapter 9 show how specific projects have been implemented and offer lessons from "the field."

What is Greening?

The word "green" has often appeared in brownfields discourse, but usually refers to preserving greenfields in the periphery or as a synonym for money and cleanliness. In this section, greening is understood generally to mean the creation of open spaces within a city's built-up environment, which includes the production of parks, public spaces and gardens, outdoor sports facilities, natural habitats, greenways, and children's playgrounds through redevelopment (Garvin & Berens, 1997; Harnik, 2000; Bunster-Ossa, 2001). Interestingly, there is no internationally or even nationally recognized typology of green space. Francis (2003, pp. 2–3) provides a comprehensive typology of urban open space that contains various types of space, including parks, plazas, markets, streets, trails, wilderness areas, and the like. The following key types are considered in this chapter:

- *Public/City/Central Park*: publicly developed and managed open space as part of zoned open space system of a city, open space of citywide importance;
- *Downtown parks*: green parks with grass and trees located in downtown areas;
- *Neighborhood park*: open space developed in residential environments;
- *Pocket park/parkette*: small urban parks that offer passive recreation amenities (e.g., sitting areas, walking paths, etc.);
- *Squares and plazas*: formally planned areas in the city center;
- *Playground*: play area located in a neighborhood;
- *Community garden*: neighborhood spaces designed, developed, or managed by local residents on vacant land; may include viewing gardens, play areas, and community gardens;
- *Greenways*: interconnected recreational and natural areas connected by pedestrian and bicycle paths;
- *Urban wilderness/Natural heritage areas*: wild lands that contain historically significant and aesthetically important environmental features that require conservation and protection; and
- *Waterfronts:* open space along waterways in cities.

This chapter also discusses some of the green features designers are incorporating into individual projects in an effort to improve the function of buildings and the quality of the urban environment generally.

Urban Parks Policy in the US and Canada

Since the early nineteenth century, urban parks have played a key role in providing relief from an increasingly urban and industrial America. The rapid shift from a primarily agricultural to an urban/industrial economy brought tremendous growth in population, drawing workers from the rural country as well as large numbers of immigrants. Coinciding with this growth were the pollution and health problems of the city. Smoke and gases from the large factories as well as outbreaks of diseases such as cholera prompted the growing desire for an increased presence of nature in the city. Thus, the need for increased recreation, public health concerns, and relief from the toils of labor in the ever-industrializing city prompted the call for urban parks in the US.

At first, cemeteries were seen as potential remedies to the ills of this newly urbanized existence. Though they incorporated naturalistic scenery and curvilinear paths, they were fundamentally rural, difficult to access, and only semi-public (Schuyler, 1986). Beginning around 1850, civic advocates began addressing the need of the urban citizen by calling for urban parks to be built in cities throughout the country. Emulating European standards of art, beauty, and design, the urban park took on multiple meanings (Taylor, 1999). Not only would it serve to provide an element of country in the city, but these "Pleasure Grounds" would also elevate the moral and cultural value of the many workers (including immigrants) who would find respite within their confines.

The first notions of the urban park were to be realized in the largest American cities by a culturally elite group of designers and leaders. Influential in this project was Andrew Jackson Downing, who felt that "every laborer" was a "possible gentleman" if given the opportunity to unbend from the workaday life (Schuyler, 1986). Downing initiated the drive for what would become perhaps the most significant representation of country in the city, New York's Central Park. Following the ideals and virtues of Downing was Frederick Law Olmsted who firmly believed in creating a naturalistic park that would provide a much-needed juxtaposition to the urban grid of New York City. Working with Calvert Vaux, Olmsted would design a pastoral retreat from the city, incorporating both naturalistic features and structures such as carriage drives to afford access to the park. This model would be replicated in various American cities, including Philadelphia, Boston, Chicago, and San Francisco, throughout the second half of the nineteenth century.

As the urban park proliferated throughout the country, discussions about how it was designed and who it was to serve increased in the early years of the twentieth century. Parks were increasingly seen less as an elite cultural space for carriage drives and respite from the urban condition, and more as a service for families and children. The "Reform Park" movement (1900–1930) would contrast dramatically with the large Pleasure Ground in that organized activities centered around play and recreation could be provided in smaller, more accessible parks located throughout the city (Cranz, 1982). The era also saw an increasing role in the technical function of parks commissions and boards. Whereas discussions centered on ideal landscape design and natural features in the Pleasure Ground era, reform advocates concentrated on alleviating social ills by programming activities such as swimming, dancing, or athletics.

From the 1930s to the 1960s, parks evolved to merge within larger citywide projects, and were seen as part of the overall function of local government. Chicago, for example, encompassed park administration together with its many other bureaucratic divisions. San Francisco's City Planning Commission developed a master plan that included guidelines for park placement in concert with libraries and schools. Along with the increased management, parks were seen as a direct response to the overall condition of urban America. The societal Depression of the early 1930s had a significant impact on parks planning and public perception of leisure. Relief projects were intended to address these conditions throughout the 1930s and into the 1940s by providing activity, employment, and national renewal. As World War II occupied the thoughts and funds of America's cities, there was an increased need to justify the role of parks as vital to morale and national pride (Cranz, 1982).

Post-war America saw increasing distractions from urban life and a move towards suburbanization and the corresponding "white flight" that followed. With a diminishing tax base due to the increasing development in suburban neighborhoods, cities began cutting park funding. The emphasis on open space and recreation towards the periphery of American cities (1960s and 1970s) was both a response to increased suburban population and a commentary on the degraded and increasingly depopulated central cities. Federal programs such as the Urban Park and Recreation Recovery (UPARR) program in 1978 supplied some relief in the form of grant and technical assistance dollars. These funds were intended to encourage local planning for distressed urban communities and their recreation facilities. In the last few decades, however, much of this funding has been dramatically cut or stopped altogether, leading toward more non-governmental involvement and community-sponsored efforts at park advocacy.

Organizations such as the Trust for Public Land, Urban Land Institute and many more local "Friends" groups and park conservancies have emerged in the last decade or so to alleviate the funding problems inherent in urban parks. As discussed in more detail below, many contemporary arguments for parks are based on their role in achieving social, environmental, and economic objectives associated with sustainable urban development (Cranz & Boland, 2004). Additionally, parks can be presented as catalysts for urban revitalization and increased property values. Ultimately, America's urban parks are increasingly viewed as essential for many cities in their drive to market their quality of life, whether for urban neighborhoods, commercial developments, or the city as a whole.

In similar fashion to the United States, Canadian parks have developed in approximately the same period and with similar results. On the basis of the British example, Canadian parks began as attempts to incorporate elements of the rural within the rapidly industrializing urban areas of the cities. City dwellers separation from nature was seen as adding to the nation's physical, mental, and moral distress (Von Baeyer, 2006). Subsequent influence from the City Beautiful movement instilled a fondness for the idea of nature in the city in park design throughout Canadian cities.

Perhaps most influential in the development of Canadian parks was the design of Montreal's Mount Royal. Designed by Frederick Law Olmsted in 1874, Mount Royal incorporated the picturesque philosophy that permeated through much of his existing work in Central Park and other parts of the United States. The natural topography and location of Mount Royal (735 ft (224 m) in elevation, 1.5 miles long, 430 acres) presented both challenges and opportunities (Rybczynski, 1999). Olmsted broke slightly from his previous work, taking advantage of the intrinsic features of the mountain to allow for scenic vistas along the paths that curved amidst the wooded site.

Olmsted's involvement with Mount Royal signified not only the beginning of the Canadian urban parks movement, but simultaneously the development of his apprentice on the project, Frederick G. Todd. Though born in America in the late nineteenth century, Todd became involved in Mount Royal as an apprentice landscape architect and in later years saw through to completion many aspects of the project that Olmsted had originally called for in his design. Additionally, Todd was fundamental in designing a number of other parks, site plans, and public works throughout the early years of the twentieth century, including Winnipeg's Assiniboine Park and Regina's Wascana Park (Jacobs, 1983).

Parks became less of a priority during the depression years, and until the end of World War II, there was little development. In 1944, however, what would become the Canadian Parks and Recreation Association (CPRA) emerged. Originating from the Ontario Parks Association (OPA), the CPRA has advocated for the benefits of parks and recreation services on the local, provincial, and national levels for 60 years. Their latest vision paper, published in 2005, emphasizes the need for healthy communities that enhance social, environmental, and community development. Again, much like the current era in the US, Canadian parks have entered a sustainable era of park design, which strives to provide access to all, while fostering a sense of environmental stewardship and increased community health and vitality.

Urban parks and forestry initiatives are being embraced worldwide. In 2005, for instance, leaders from cities around the world signed a Green Cities Declaration charting a bold course for the urban environment. One of the actions put forward was to "ensure that there is an accessible public park or recreational open space within a half-kilometer of every city resident by 2015." Other actions related to urban nature included: conducting an inventory of existing canopy coverage in the city and then establishing a goal based on ecological and community considerations to plant and maintain canopy coverage in not less than 50% of all available sidewalk planting sites; and passing legislation that protects critical habitat corridors and other key habitat characteristics from unsustainable development.

Urban Parkland Inventory

Since 2001, the Trust for Public Land, a national nonprofit, has compiled comprehensive data on the quantity and management of urban green space in US cities through its Center for City Park Excellence. The most recent data show that green space represents 9.6% of city land area on average, with high density cities having a greater percentage of their land area devoted to green than low density ones (see Figure 7.1). In terms of population, this amounts to approximately 18 acres per 1000 people (Figure 7.2).

As one might expect, the Center for City Park Excellence (2006) finds that "some cities have plenty of parkland that is well distributed around town; others have enough land but an inequitable distribution; others are short of even a basic amount of park space for their citizens." Although there is no specific definition of what constitutes an excellent park system or an adequate supply of parks, some key factors put forward by park experts in the US include (Harnik, 2006):

(i) A clear expression of purpose (i.e., vision, mission);
(ii) An ongoing planning and community involvement process;

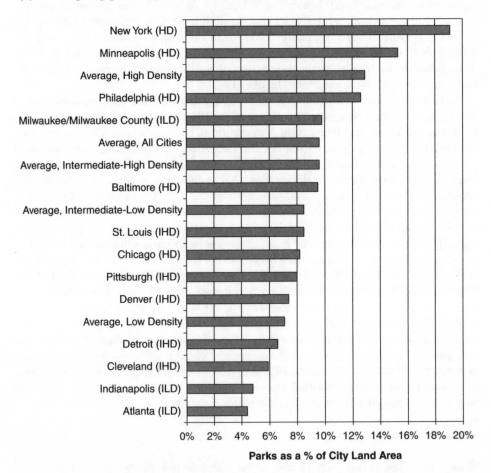

Figure 7.1: Parks as a percent of city land area, select US cities (Reproduced with permission from the Center for City Park Excellence, The Trust for Public Land (2006). *Note*: total park acres includes city, county, metro, state, and federal acres).

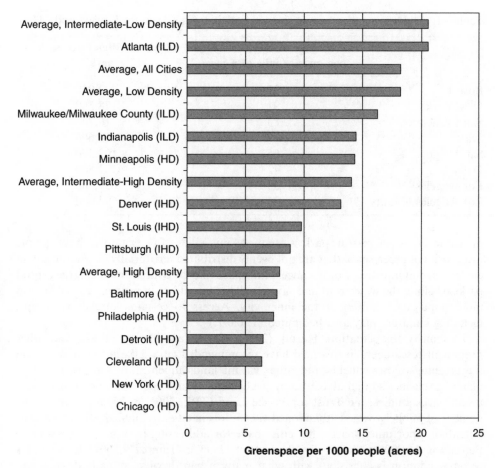

Figure 7.2: Parks per 1,000 residents (acres), US cities (Reproduced with permission from the Center for City Park Excellence, The Trust for Public Land (2006). *Note*: total park acres includes city, county, metro, state, and federal acres).

(iii) Sufficient assets in land (both for recreation and natural land), staffing, and equipment to meet the system's goals;
(iv) Equitable access (based on income and distance to park, that is 5 min by foot or one quarter mile);
(v) User satisfaction;
(vi) Safety from crime and physical hazards; and
(vii) Benefits for the city beyond the boundaries of the parks.

Those cities often considered to have excellent park systems, such as Minneapolis and San Francisco, usually have comprehensive and well-funded park programs, extensive park inventories with a mixture of green space types, and good access throughout the city. Merely considering the total quantity of green space is, therefore, not a good

Table 7.1: Children's park access in seven major cities (The Trust for Public Land, 2004).

	Percentage of children within one quarter mile of a park	**Children without access to a park**
Boston	97	2,900
New York	91	178,500
San Francisco	85	16,700
Seattle	79	18,600
San Diego	65	102,300
Dallas	42	182,800
Los Angeles	33	657,700
Los Angeles County	36	1,694,400

indicator of a successful park system. Many cities, for example, have ample inventories of green space that are not evenly distributed territorially — a source of an environmental injustice. For instance, park space may be concentrated in large central parks or along the waterfront and ravine valleys, instead of in proximity to older and more populous localities of the inner city. Access to certain population groups, including children, may also be limited (Table 7.1).

To remedy this situation, Harnik (2000), Garvin and Berens (1997), and other prominent researchers in this field have recommended cities take into consideration the greening of brownfields and other vacant lands much more seriously in their planning schemes so that all can enjoy the benefits of such space. In one of their early urban parks studies, the Trust for Public Land (TPL, 2001, p. 45) reported on the number of publicly owned, abandoned vacant lots in cities to highlight the number of potential opportunity spaces that cities have for addressing park access issues (e.g., Baltimore 14,000; Chicago 9,400; Detroit 26,800; Tampa 9,300). In fact, its recommendation is consistent with what many urban dwellers actually desire — in a survey of over 200 New Jersey residents by Greenberg and Lewis in 2000, 90% of their informants identified parks and play areas as an optimal end-use for brownfield sites.

Data on the Canadian situation have been compiled by Evergreen, a national nonprofit supporting urban greening. The organization found that gathering accurate and comparable data on urban green space was difficult given variation in the definition of "green space" from municipality to municipality, as well as differences in record keeping. Despite this, a data snapshot using information compiled in 2002 (Evergreen Foundation, 2004) showed that mid-sized cities (e.g., Edmonton, Ottawa, and Winnipeg) were among those with the highest green space to population ratios, while the populous urban areas of Toronto, Montreal, and Vancouver were among those with the lowest rates. One key finding from this study was that municipalities expressed a need for more and better green space in urban areas, particularly large cities where population growth outpaces the creation of new parks due to problems related to land availability and high real estate values. The study also found that even those mid-sized cities that seem to be achieving very high green space provision rates expressed a need for more support, improved acquisition tools, and new stewardship strategies (Figure 7.3).

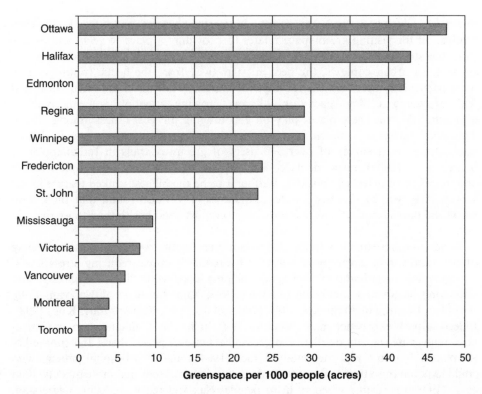

Figure 7.3: Parks per 1,000 residents (acres), Canadian Cities (Reproduced with permission from Evergreen Foundation (2004). *Note*: the amount of park land considered here only refers to that owned by the local municipality and does not take into account land owned by other agencies. Furthermore, there is variability in what constitutes green space, so readers should take these factors into consideration when reviewing this data).

Greening and Sustainability

Widespread interest in urban revitalization, sustainable development, and enhancing the quality of urban life has led, in turn, to greater interest in greening the city (Garvin & Berens, 1997; Harnik, 2000; Bunster-Ossa, 2001). But does greening make a city more sustainable? Empirical evidence is increasingly showing that the presence of such space contributes to urban quality of life in many ways adding to the social, economic, and environmental objectives of sustainable urban development.

Historically, the social role of parks and open space — recreation, aesthetics, relaxation, and socialization — has received significant attention from parks designers, planners, researchers, and proponents. To most, the main function of urban green space is considered to be for recreation, which deals with the refreshment of both the body via physical exercise and the mind via affording a place for relaxation, diversion, and enjoyment. Numerous studies have found the key motivation for visiting green space relates to providing a place to relax and escape from the stresses of everyday life (Chiesura, 2004). The results should come as no surprise. In urban contexts, the need to step away from the hectic routine of city life is particularly necessary. As for physical exercise, while parks are often associated with providing a play space for children, growing attention is being paid to examining the role these places play on encouraging physical fitness among adults. This is of particular concern in the US given rising obesity levels and its health implications. In a survey of over 500 users of greenway trails in Indianapolis by Shafer et al. (2000), respondents considered the trail's impact on people's health and fitness to be extremely positive, leading it to be the highest ranked feature in the survey. A survey by Godbey, Grafe, and James (1992) also found that those who used local parks frequently were more likely to report good health than those that did not.

In addition, research has found that urban greening improves the social well-being of city residents in a variety of ways — by reducing crime, reducing stress levels, strengthening neighborhood social ties, helping cope with "life's demands," and improving health and well-being (Kaplan, 1993; Kuo, Bacaicoa, & Sullivan, 1998; American Institute of Architects, 1999; Shafer et al., 2000; Kaplan, 2001; Kuo, 1998). Indeed, a park experience may reduce stress (Ulrich, 1981), enhance contemplative-ness, rejuvenate the city dweller, and provide a sense of peacefulness and tranquility (Kaplan, 1983). In a well-cited study, Urlich (1984) found that hospital patients who could look out onto trees and nature from their windows recovered more quickly. Kuo et al. (1998) found that greenery helps people relax and renew, reducing aggression. Another study by Kuo and Sullivan (2001) found that residents living in "greener" surroundings report a lower level of fear, fewer incivilities, and less aggressive and violent behavior. From a broader community perspective, studies have also shown that nature can encourage the use of outdoor spaces, increasing social integration, and interaction among neighbors (Coley, Kuo, & Sullivan, 1997). The presence of trees and grass in outdoor common spaces also promotes the development of social ties (Kuo et al., 1998). Additional health studies have found that contact with nature is associated with fewer sick call visits among prisoners (Moore, 1981); improved attention among children with attention deficit disorder (Faber, Kuo, & Sullivan, 2001); improved self-discipline among inner-city girls (Faber, Kuo, & Sullivan, 2002); decreased mortality amongst senior citizens (Takano, Nakamura, & Watanabe, 2002); and enhanced emotional, cognitive, and values-related development in children (Kellert, 2002).

Perhaps the most important benefit associated with greening the city is simply its aesthetic value. Landscape architects and designers, for example, have focused on the aesthetic benefits that green space-oriented redevelopment can bestow on urban areas and have begun tying them into other benefits such as improving environmental quality, restoring natural habitats, and enhancing recreational activities (Hough, 1994; Hough, Benson, & Evenson, 1997; Thompson & Sorvig, 2000). In a study of greenway-based trails in and around Chicago, Gobster (1995) found that more than anything else, people liked the trails for their scenic beauty.

The cost of developing and managing parks and open space in urban areas has also raised questions about the economic benefits associated with such space. Indeed, as early as the 1850s, landscape architect Frederick Law Olmsted justified the purchase of land for New York's Central Park on the basis of the rising value of adjacent property producing enough in taxes to pay for the park. By 1864, Olmsted could document a US$55,880 net return in annual taxes over what the city was paying in interest for land and improvements. By 1873, the park — which until then had cost approximately US$14 million — was responsible for an extra US$5.24 million in taxes each year (Lerner & Poole, 1999). In a comprehensive review of 25 studies that investigate whether parks and open space contribute to increasing property values nearby, Crompton (2001) found that in 20 of them, parks and open space did contribute positively. This effect is greatest for parks that are natural or serve a passive recreation role versus an active one. As for the magnitude of this effect, Crompton (2001, p. 62) suggests that:

> A positive impact of twenty percent on property value abutting or fronting a passive park area is a reasonable starting point guideline. If the park is large (say over 25 acres), well maintained, attractive, and its use is mainly passive, then this figure is likely to be low. If it is small and embraces some active use, then this guideline is likely to be high. If it is a heavily used park incorporating such recreational facilities as athletic fields or a swimming pool, then the proximate value increment may be minimal on abutting properties but may reach ten percent on properties two or three blocks away.

There is also some agreement that in addition to abutting property, parks have a substantial impact on property values up to 500 ft (150 m) away and in case of community parks of 40 acres or more, this impact can extend for 2000 ft (610 m) (Crompton, 2001).

The role of parks in enhancing the quality of urban life, and the importance of urban quality of life in making business location decisions, has also received attention from researchers. In many studies, the presence of recreation space and natural space is considered an important factor influencing the location decisions of business (Scanlon, 1984; Galbraith & DeNoble, 1988; Snepenger, Johnson, & Rasker, 1995). A study by Crompton, Love, and Moore (1997) found that decision makers in small companies (fewer than eight full time personnel) in particular ranked "recreation/ parks/open space" as their highest priority when asked to identify the quality-of-life elements influencing their business location decisions.

Similar kinds of positive findings are continuously emerging from research conducted by environmental economists (Lerner & Poole, 1999; Bolitzer & Netusil, 2000; Tyrvainen, 2001). Summarizing the main implications, Lerner and Poole (1999) contend that in addition to raising property values and attracting investment, greening projects in the US tend to reduce costs related to urban sprawl and infrastructure, invigorate local economies, boost tourism, preserve farmland, prevent flood damage, and safeguard environmental quality generally.

In addition to the social and economic benefits accruing primarily to humans, we are becoming more aware of the important ecological and environmental role urban green space plays in terms of enhancing biological diversity, improving water quality, cleansing air, recharging aquifers, and controlling floods. Indeed, open land provides the space for nature to perform life-sustaining services that would otherwise have to be provided technologically at great expense, such as breaking down organic wastes, filtering pollutants from soil and water, managing air pollutants, moderating urban climate, preserving genetic diversity, and pollinating plants.

Proponents of green infrastructure argue that urban trees, forested open space, and wetlands are particularly valuable. A significant amount of research has examined the benefits of urban trees and has placed monetary values on many of them. Trees control erosion, help clean the air of pollutants, mitigate global warming by absorbing carbon dioxide and other greenhouse gasses, and help shelter and cool our homes. The forestry organization American Forests, for example, estimates that trees in the nation's metropolitan areas contribute US$400 billion in storm water retention by eliminating the need for expensive facilities (in Lerner & Poole, 1999, p. 125). In addition, approximately 800 million tons of carbon is stored in US urban forests with a US$22 billion equivalent in control costs (Coder, 1996). Projections suggest that 100 million additional mature trees in US cities (three trees for every un-shaded single family home) could save over US$2 billion in energy costs per year (McAliney, 1993). Clearly, in addition to increasing urban open space, trees can be incorporated into the design of residential, commercial, and other brownfields projects, as well as urban lands generally.

Overall, the identification of such benefits is essential for countering the barriers, real or perceived, that are often associated with urban open space, including the high maintenance costs often associated with parks, the safety concerns it may raise, and poor accessibility it may create (Garvin & Berens, 1997). This is often a particular concern in the case of greening of brownfields, which are associated with a host of additional socioeconomic and environmental costs and risks.

Brownfields-to-Green space

Research on the greening option for brownfields has traditionally been minuscule in comparison with other end-uses, with most of it focusing on design and planning aspects (e.g., Braswell, 1999; Kirkwood, 2001b; Lowrie, Greenberg, & Knee, 2002; De Sousa, 2003). A study by Braswell (1999) traced the implementation of the Woonasquatucket River Greenway project in Rhode Island, outlining matters related to planning, financing, and community involvement. Kirkwood (2001b) and other contributors in their volume discussed novel approaches to the design and remediation of contaminated lands for public park and commercial uses in the US and abroad. While most of the studies focus primarily on single flagship projects, a study by Lowrie et al. (2002), provided an overview of the opportunities that greening brownfields in New Jersey can bestow on inner-city neighborhoods, but contended that the costs associated with building and maintaining these spaces are perceived by many government officials as a "sensible" investment only if other job/tax creating and housing options are precluded.

The International Economic Development Council (IEDC, 2001) and the International City/County Management Association (ICMA, 2002a) are two professional agencies that have gathered useful information on the greening of brownfields from an economic development perspective. While the ICMA study looks at the greening option from a general standpoint of its overall potential, the IEDC study examines the actual outcomes of multiple greening projects, providing useful data on project funding, development costs, and other relevant aspects. Some important findings emerging from the IEDC study are that even though the public sector is largely responsible for funding these projects (67% of funding in the 25 projects examined, with state and local funding making up 90% of that amount), the value of property adjacent to several of these projects increased substantially after greening took place. Indeed, the assessed value of property located adjacent to seven of the brownfield-to-green space projects examined rose by an average of 106% (median 86%), while citywide property values only increased by 25% (14% median) during the same period. It also contends that the keys to success for these projects include the involvement of diverse stakeholders, a creative mix of funding, a role for state standards and assistance, and partnerships to carry them through.

The environmental dimension of the greening option for urban brownfields has only recently become a topic of interest on the part of ecologists (e.g., Burger, 2000; Harrison & Davies, 2002). The ecological studies have generally aimed to investigate methods for achieving the successful recovery of natural systems by identifying native ecosystem conditions on brownfield sites and by assessing the types of ecological risks that these present. Such ecological restoration is considered a vital factor in terms of repairing the human relationship with the natural environment. As Cairns (1995, p. 6) notes:

> If society's goal is to maximize the total number of humans inhabiting the planet over the next million years, shifting to a sustainable-use strategy is essential. Humans are clearly a part of ecosystems, not apart from them; therefore, changing attitude toward natural systems will be just as important as changing behaviors.

Cairns goes on to define *ecological restoration* as "the return of an ecosystem to as close an approximation of its condition prior to disturbance." In restoration, ecological damage to a resource is repaired and the structure and function of the ecosystem are recreated. Thus, natural resource restoration often requires the reconstruction of antecedent physical, hydrologic, and morphological conditions; chemical cleanup or adjustment of the environment; and biological manipulation, including revegetation and reintroduction of absent or now non-viable native species. Complete ecological restoration requires self-maintenance and/or self-perpetuation over the long term (Sharkey, 2005). In general, restorers are looking to recreate functioning ecosystems that have high levels of biodiversity and are maintained at a certain secessional state to retain that biodiversity (Burger, 2000).

Despite this, while most research supports the idea of cleaning up brownfields and restoring pre-development ecological function, some studies propose that, because of the high levels of biodiversity often found within them, many brownfields should be left "as is" (Pearce, 1998; Harrison & Davies, 2002). Studying sites in England, these researchers claim that many brownfields display a higher rate of diversity than is found in the countryside and that many of the species found are rare in other parts of the country. In a handful of situations, industrial processes have created distinctive landscapes that have resulted in unique plant communities (Sharkey, 2005). Some examples include alkali waste heaps left behind from the nineteenth century Leblanc process of manufacturing soda from common salt, which has bequeathed "vast swamps of orchids" at Nob End in Bolton, and rare meadow grasses that inhabit the limestone slag heaps left by early blast furnaces in the West Midlands (Pearce, 1998). Harrison and Davies even advocate the preservation of the non-native species found in London's brownfields, arguing that the plants add to the biodiversity of the sites, have integrated into functioning ecosystems, and may cause more harm to the ecosystem if removed. But, as Sharkey (2005, p. 30) points out, "to protect non-native plants and animals that could negatively impact the larger environment around them seems to only add to an already extensive problem associated with the negative impacts from invasive species in native ecosystems."

Some of the brownfields literature has examined other aspects of "greening," including the use of natural systems to remove contaminants and improving design through green building and technology. A growing amount of studies are looking at the role ecological elements can play in cleaning up sites, while also adding to habitat. Such ecological restoration can be as simple as planting trees or other plants to improve unattractive views of industrial or brownfield sites. These are often called screens, as they do little to clean anything and are simply intended to improve a site's visual quality (Greenberg, Schneider, & Martell, 1994). Other more involved processes include phytoremediation and bioremediation.

Phytoremediation is defined by the Environmental Protection Agency (US EPA, 2000a) as, a set of emerging technologies that use various plants to degrade, extract, contain, or immobilize contaminants from soil and water. It is claimed that the technique enhances the degradation of organic contaminants, cleans ground and surface water, breaks down pesticides, adds vegetation cover, and extracts and stabilizes many other contaminants. Phytoremediation practices most often use trees, though grasses and other plants can be used depending on the contaminants, which are planted in areas contaminated with heavy metals, organic solids like oil and gas, and a host of other contaminants. The cheapest option, more suited to organics than to heavy metals, is simply to allow natural attenuation through biodegradation, dispersion, dilution, absorption, or volatilization (Dickinson, 2000). The trees absorb the problem components and lock it into their wooden core. After several years, the trees are harvested and disposed of as hazardous waste, taking the pollution with them. This process takes time, but is very effective at removing pollutants in the top and subsoils of contaminated brownfields, along with the added benefit of providing green space during the growing process (GWRTAC, 2005; Sprigg, 2003; Abercrombie, 2003). Although concerns related to the bioaccumulation

Figure 7.4: Signs describe a phytoremediation project along the Lachine Canal in Montreal, but the reader seems to prefer her book.

and biomagnification of contaminants entering the ecosystem via these trees continue to be expressed by some (Figure 7.4).

Bioremediation, on the other hand, uses microorganisms to degrade organic contaminants in soil, sludge, and solids that are on site or have been excavated from a site. Put simply, the microorganisms break down contaminants by using them as a food source. Aerobic processes require an oxygen source, and the end products are typically carbon dioxide and water. Anaerobic processes are conducted in the absence of oxygen, and the end products can include methane, hydrogen gas, sulfide, elemental sulfur, and dinitrogen gas (US EPA, 2006b). On-site techniques stimulate and create a favorable environment for microorganisms to grow and use contaminants as a food and energy source. Biosolids and fungal spores are some of the newer examples of these revolutionary technologies being used to clean brownfields to ever-higher standards, with ever-increasing speed (Abercrombie, 2003). Biosolids are used as a growing medium that absorbs certain contaminants and holds them for plant uptake. Fungal elements are used much like plants, they are injected into a contamination zone where they consume pollutants and break them down into less harmful components (Abercrombie, Abercrombie, Dees, Ford, & Runnells, 2003).

Although these green techniques have only recently been considered for use in urban contexts, they have been used more extensively in decommissioned mining areas. Prior to 1977, little or no effort was made by coal companies even simply to infill their holes when they were done, let alone reforest or remediate mined sites (United States Department of the Interior, Office of Surface Mining, 2003). The US

Surface Mining Law now requires mining companies to restore the environment to set government standards. The law requires that refuse piles be infilled into the mining pits and that top soil be laid and native plants and trees planted (Sharkey, 2005). The idea is to make the landscape as similar to pre-disturbance as possible. Consequently, many restored sites are beginning to draw wildlife back to these areas, while water quality in lakes and streams has greatly improved and local erosion from waste piles into the watersheds has dramatically slowed or stopped (United States Department of the Interior, Office of Surface Mining, 2003; Wali, 1999; Bradshaw, 2000).

Research has also explored the use of greening as a way to deal with brownfields owned by agencies such as the United States Department of Energy (DOE) and the Department of Defense (DOD). A half-century of developing, testing, and managing weaponry and nuclear products at these sites has resulted in massive areas of radioactive contamination, chemical spills of toxic and explosive elements, and unexploded ordinance areas across the US (Burger, Carletta, Lowrie, Miller, & Greenberg, 2004a; Burger, Powers, Greenberg, & Gochfeld, 2004b; Burger, 2000; Greenberg et al., 1997). Although rarely located in urban areas, the knowledge gained at these sites regarding the use of environmental remediation technologies can be useful for greening urban sites (Garczynski, 2000). Research on these sites has also highlighted how many of them have pristine ecological conditions possessing high biodiversity of native flora and fauna not seen in the surrounding areas because they have been closed off for decades. Indeed, the preservation of "native" species in large-scale industrial brownfields districts located in urbanized areas, such as the Calumet region in Illinois and Indiana, is an issue that requires additional research. Another question then becomes whether it is necessary to destroy these sites in order to clean them up or whether it is possible to use less invasive environmental technologies and to maintain the integrity of their ecosystems (see Burger, 2000).

Another shade of greening that has entered the brownfields literature deals with growing interest in eco-friendly green development and design. As Lange and McNeil (2004) note, there is a market sector that is drawn to efforts of restoration, of which redevelopers are well aware. These projects may combine green building technology, landscape architecture, and even green remediation techniques in an effort to improve the sustainability of a project, raise public interest and create a market niche (Abercrombie et al., 2003; Bunster-Ossa, 2001). Over the last few years, the US Green Building Council (USGBC) has become the most widely recognized green building promoter in the US and Canada. Its Leadership in Energies and Environmental Design (LEED) rating system, the first to assess the sustainability of new commercial construction and renovation projects, has grown to include various other programs such as existing building operations and maintenance, commercial interiors projects, core and shell development projects, homes, and neighborhood development. The USGBC is also developing LEED for Schools, LEED Retail for New Construction, LEED Retail for Commercial Interiors and LEED for Healthcare. Promoters of green building and design highlight the myriad of benefits that can ensue, ranging from higher worker productivity, lower life-cycle costs, reduced energy consumption, heat island mitigation, and the like (Bunster-Ossa, 2001). Currently, the LEED program provides points for reusing a brownfield site. Despite this, many US and

Canadian communities are beginning to push for green building on brownfields and some, such as Kingston, Ontario, even provide funds to support green building planning and certification as part of its brownfields funding.

Interest in green infrastructure and using brownfields land to enhance it has also been expanding. In fact, when the President's Council on Sustainable Development initiated efforts to apply the concept of sustainable development in the United States, it identified "Green Infrastructure" as one of several key strategies for achieving sustainability in its May 1999 report, *Towards a Sustainable America – Advancing Prosperity, Opportunity and a Healthy Environment for the 21st Century*. Green infrastructure is defined by Williamson (2003, p. 4) as "an interconnected network of protected land and water that supports native species, maintains natural ecological processes, sustains air and water resources and contributes to the health and quality of life for America's communities and people." Early work to incorporate green infrastructure on brownfields as a means of replacing traditional infrastructure and improving the urban environment was carried out by Michael Hough, who, in addition to his seminal book *Cities and Natural Process* (1995), helped lay out a green restoration strategy for the Don River and Toronto's port lands with the Waterfront Regeneration Trust in the early 1990s. Discussions of green infrastructure took place at many scales, including the construction of a 325 km linear corridor along the north shore of Lake Ontario, the linking of brownfields along Toronto's heavily urbanized Don River, and the greening of Toronto's port lands, which included numerous site-specific strategies for managing storm water and enhancing ecosystem viability (see case study in Chapter 9) (Hough et al., 1997).

Conclusion

While the focus of most cities has been on supporting brownfields redevelopment that generates jobs and taxes, a growing number of cities have started to convert brownfields into parks in an effort to improve the state of the urban environment and enhance their recreational opportunities, ecological conditions, and aesthetic appearance. In the early nineteenth century, the call for parks was prompted by the need to increase recreation, address public health concerns, and provide relief from the toils of labor in ever-industrializing cities. Contemporary arguments for parks are based on their role in achieving an array of social, environmental, and economic objectives associated with sustainable urban development, as well as catalysts for urban revitalization and increased property values. Indeed, an extensive body of empirical evidence is also emerging to back up these benefits.

While some cities in both the US and Canada have established considerable park inventories, many continue to fall short of even a basic amount of park space for their citizens. Considering the total quantity of green space is also not sufficient because a successful park systems requires equitable distribution throughout the city. It is here where brownfields provide an opportunity space for new parks. A handful of studies have examined the planning and implementation of such projects in North America and Europe. While others have delved deeper into the ecological implications, investigating methods for achieving the successful recovery of natural systems by identifying native ecosystem conditions on brownfield sites and by assessing the types of ecological risks that these present. Some of the brownfields literature has also examined greening as it relates to the use of natural systems to remove contaminants and to improving design through green building and technology. Several cities have sought to achieve one or more of these many shades of green through their brownfields-to-green space efforts. The following chapter examines the implementation and outcomes of a set of greening projects carried out in US and Canadian cities, and also considers the growing role of nonprofits in this domain of planning.

Chapter 8

The Nature of Brownfield-to-Green Space Projects

Despite the focus of brownfields efforts on industrial, commercial, and residential redevelopment, several cities have been involved in the greening of brownfield sites. This chapter examines the implementation and outcomes of a set of greening projects carried out in different US and Canadian cities. Several issues are examined, including the type of greening projects being developed on brownfield sites, the planning processes involved in cleaning up brownfields and converting them into green space, the benefits associated with greening, and the obstacles hindering its implementation. The chapter also considers the growing role that nonprofit organizations in the United States are playing in facilitating the conversion of brownfields-to-green space. The chapter concludes by looking at research on the benefits such greening projects have had on personal and community quality of life. This chapter synthesizes the results of several research projects carried out by the author since 2001 and funded by the US Forest Service, Northern Research Station, and the University of Wisconsin-Milwaukee. The chapter also draws on surveys completed by public and nonprofit stakeholders involved in 20 greening projects from throughout the US (Table 8.1) and a further 10 in the City of Toronto (Table 8.2). The discussion is also based on observations made from numerous site visits throughout the US and Canada.

Brownfield-to-Green Space Project Types

The greening of urban brownfields in both the US and Canada has lead to the creation of a variety of green spaces and a significant addition to urban park inventories. In aggregate, the 20 greening projects examined in US cities generated approximately 1,144 new acres of green space (463 ha) and range in size from 2 to 400 acres (0.81–162 ha). The mean size of the projects was 57 acres (23.1 ha) and the median size 14 acres (5.7 ha), with most (13) of the projects in the 2–20 acre range (0.81–8 ha). The brownfields were developed into various types of parks and open space projects. Seven were converted into linear parks or greenways (mainly on previous railway corridors); six involved the creation of large-scale parks intended

Table 8.1: Brownfield-to-green space project sample in US cities.

Sites	Greenspace only acres (ha)	Former uses and potential contaminants	Proposed greenspace and other uses
Aberdeen Brownfield, City of Aberdeen, WA	400 (161)	Sawmill, truck maintenance, landfill, residences, and wetlands Metals, petroleum hydrocarbons	Natural habitat, trails, and active recreation space Light industrial redevelopment
B.F. Nelson, Minneapolis, MN	18 (7.3)	19th-century paper and sawmills Petroleum hydrocarbons and asbestos	Passive recreation space, trails, and natural habitat
Beacon Landing, City of Beacon, NY	13 (5.3)	Rail yard, coal and oil storage facility, and salvage yard Petroleum, PCBs, metals	Natural habitat, trails, and passive recreation space Mixed-use development
Burnham Greenway (Park 499), Chicago, IL	7.1 (2.9)	Railroad line Fly ash	Greenway trail
Depot District Project, Salt Lake City, UT	8 (3.2)	Railroad corridor Creosote, gas, oil	Passive recreational space Mixed-use redevelopment project
Doyle Street Greenway, Emeryville, CA	2.6 (1.1)	Rail spur Metals, arsenic, PCBs	Greenway trails Part of a broader renewal effort
Floral Farms and Dallas Eco-Business Park, Dallas, TX	45 (18.2)	Abandoned residential area used for illegal dumping "Junk" and general waste	Natural habitat and flood control Business park and educational facility
Hank Aaron State Trail, Milwaukee, WI	50 (20.2)	Industry, transportation, and fuel storage Diesel organics, metals	Greenway trail
Long Beach Hilltop Sports Park, Long Beach, CA	56 (22.7)	Oil/gas production, vehicle repair, sandblasting, recycling, and earthquake debris VOCs, metals, methane	Active-recreation space, community center, natural habitat
Mill Ruins Park, Minneapolis, MN	12.75 (5.2)	Mills, canals, and tailraces PAH, Diesel Range Organics	Greenway trail, archaeological education and preservation
Nine Mile Run, Pittsburgh, PA	106 (42.9)	17 million cubic yards of slag dumped from 1920–1970 Metals, organics	Active and passive recreation, trail, and natural habitat Mixed-residential
Origin Site, Chicago, IL	2 (0.8)	Grain storage, passenger terminal, locks, gas station, and truck storage PNAs	Passive recreation and natural habitat

Table 8.1: (*Continued*)

Sites	Greenspace only acres (ha)	Former uses and potential contaminants	Proposed greenspace and other uses
Phillips to the Falls, Sioux City, SD	18 (7.3)	Scrap metal recycler, railroad roundhouse and a brick/tile company Petroleum, metals	Greenway trails, natural habitat Possible retail and office development
Riverview Supper Club site, Minneapolis, MN	5 (2)	Industrial, restaurant/club	Greenway trail Adjacent residential development
Scripto Factory Property/ Martin Luther King Jr. National Historic Site, Atlanta, GA	2 (0.8)	Pen and ink factory abandoned in the 1960s Petroleum hydrocarbons, metals, PCE, TCE, cyanides, methelyne chloride	Greenway trail Parking area
Springdale Park, Austin, TX	14 (5.7)	Former city landfill TBD	Active and passive recreation
USX South Side Park, Chicago, IL	123 (49.8)	Manufacturing steel mill closed in 1992 Contaminants remediated to residential standards by landowner	Active and passive recreation, and natural habitat Industrial, commercial, residential, and entertainment redevelopment
Venice Beach Skate Park, Venice, CA	2 (0.8)	Oil storage Petroleum hydrocarbons	Active recreation and greenway trail Commercial and recreational revitalization along the boardwalk
Washington's Landing/ Herr's Island, Pittsburgh, PA	10 (4.1)	Meat packing plants, scrap yards and a rendering plant PCBs, PAHs, organics, TCE	Active and passive recreation, trails, and natural habitat Commercial, industrial, retail, housing
Wilmington Riverfront, City of Wilmington, DE	250 (101.2)	Warehouses, fuel storage tanks, industry, and a train station Metals	Passive recreation, greenway trails, and natural habitat Some residential redevelopment

Source: Adapted from De Sousa (2004).

for multiple recreation uses; four smaller spaces for neighborhood recreation, and three for habitat restoration. Thirteen of the projects involved both recreation and habitat creation/restoration, and 11 the creation of educational amenities (i.e., markers, signs, site tours, visitors/education centers). Eight of the sites also involved the preservation of historically significant structures and areas (buildings, bulkheads, rail cars, machinery, etc.).

Table 8.2: Brownfield-to-green space project sample in Toronto.

Sites	Size	Former use	Current/proposed use(s)
Village of Yorkville Park	0.36 ha 0.9 acres	Houses were demolished in the 1950s to make way for a subway line that lies under the site. A parking lot then occupied the site	Upper-scale parkette with "artistic" design theme
Parliament Square	0.5 ha 1.25 acres	Rail corridor situated just south of a former coal gasification plant and north of a former roofing and tar paper-dipping facility	Active and passive recreation space
The Music Garden	0.8 ha 2 acres	Industrial area with uses ranging from machine shops to warehouses and ship building	Upper-scale parkette with a waterfront garden named with classical music terms
Domtar Polyresins	2.2 ha 5.5 acres	Facility for testing and manufacturing of polyresins	Ecological habitat
Sorauren Park	2.3 ha 5.8 acres	Industrial uses including an armaments manufacturing facility and a transit maintenance and garage establishment	Active recreation, ecological habitat
Chester Springs Marsh	3 ha 7.4 acres	Ravine partially filled with municipal ash, rubbish, and cinders	Reconstructed wetland
Woodbine Park	12 ha 30 acres	Racetrack and stables, contaminated by incinerator ash and leaking underground storage tanks	Ecological habitat, active and passive recreation space (includes amphitheater)
Don Valley Brickworks	16.6 ha 41 acres	Brick-manufacturing facility	Ecological habitat
Toronto Port Lands	Green space planned for 25% of Port (101 ha/250 acres)	Industrial/commercial/park space containing industrial and petroleum refining industries	Active and passive recreation site and ecological habitat
Leslie Street Spit (Tommy Thomson Park)	471 ha 1,164 acres	"Lakefill" consisting of earth, brick, asphalt, concrete, and rubble; disposal cells storing several hundred thousand cubic meters of dredge spoil	Ecological habitat and passive recreation

Source: Adapted from De Sousa (2003).

The City of Toronto provides a good case of a single city using brownfields as an opportunity space for several greening projects. The 10 greening projects studied generated 614 ha (1,520 acres) of new green space, and ranged in size from just under half a hectare (1 acre) to 471 ha (1,164 acres), with a median of 2.7 ha (6.7 acres). Most of the larger greening projects involved redeveloping sites near or within existing parklands (e.g., the waterfront, existing parks, greenway corridors, etc.), while the smaller ones, instead, involved adding parks to more densely-populated areas of the inner city that were "parks poor." Four of the parks were redeveloped primarily for ecological restoration purposes; two for local active and passive recreation purposes; two for "pocket parks" or "parkettes"; and two for multiple uses to serve both local and city residents.

One particularly popular type of greening in US and Canadian cities has been the construction of greenways and linear trails. These projects are either constructed on railway lines that are no longer in use or on industrial and commercial properties, located along waterways that often have to be painstakingly pieced together (Otto, McCormick, & Leccese, 2004). Interest in greenways is widespread because it serves multiple functions and offers multiple benefits. In addition to providing parks and open space for active and passive recreation, greenways provide an aesthetically pleasant transportation route for cyclists and pedestrians. They usually involve the enhancement and connection of habitat along corridors that allow for species migration, and are usually tied to a broader economic development oriented strategy that sees residential and commercial development springing up along the greenway (see Minneapolis Case in Chapter 9). The importance of linking green space development with additional benefits beyond those associated with recreation and nature provision is particularly important in the US context. Indeed, while all the US projects examined were free-standing ones, almost three quarters were redeveloped in conjunction with other land uses or as part of a broader redevelopment scheme.

Smaller neighborhood projects in both countries aimed at providing a wide range of active and passive recreation activities and are typically constructed in mid-density older neighborhoods lacking green space. Senka Park in Chicago, for example, has a baseball diamond, a soccer field, volleyball courts, a children's playground, a rollerblade hockey rink, basketball hoops, a trail, a water play area, a few "habitat" areas, and several tables for playing chess and other games. The decision to construct such parks is often reactive, with parks departments under severe pressure from community residents to increase park space in these park poor areas. Sometimes, as in the cases of Senka park in Chicago and Sorauren park in Toronto, the community comes together to support the need for green space when another use is proposed for the local brownfield.

Many cities are also constructing smaller pocket parks or "parkettes" in high-density parts of the city to serve an array of residential, commercial, and retail users. These typically involve more elaborate design schemes, such as the Yorkville and Music Garden sites in downtown Toronto. The former was designed to simulate Canadian landscapes (i.e., pine grove, prairie, marsh, orchard, and rock out-cropping) and the latter was designed to represent the six movements of Johan Sebastian Bach's "Suites for Unaccompanied Cello."

A further park type is the multiple-use parks — large areas planned to offer a wide range of passive and active uses to both local and city residents. Woodbine Park in Toronto, for example, contains a festival green band shell that can serve over 20,000 people, garden gateway entrances, trails, a promenade, 15 acres (6 ha) of native plantings, an ornamental fountain, a children's storybook place, a memorial for the raceway formerly at the site, a storm-water retention pond, and a children's soccer field and playground. Washington's Landing/Herr's Island, Pittsburgh, PA offers a marina, tennis courts, walking and nature trails, and many grassy spots for leisurely recreation.

In addition to the diversity of parks created on brownfields, one of the benefits of green space is its flexibility in terms of the types of brownfields that can be used and their size. For instance, of the 20 US projects, 11 involved the greening of former industrial lands, 9 former railway corridors or other transportation-based sites, 6 previous landfill and waste disposal areas, and 3 fuel storage properties. Half of all the sites in question were likely contaminated by a combination of such activities.

It should also be noted that while many cities have shown an interest in the greening of brownfields, those carrying out such projects have traditionally given parks and open space planning a higher priority. Indeed, of the 20 US greening projects, more than half were carried out by cities that had a percentage of park and open space area greater than or equal to the US average (De Sousa, 2004). This is likely due to a higher level of government commitment aimed at supporting new park projects and to more public interest in open space conservation and funding.

Planning Processes

The planning and implementation processes used for greening projects are typically more complex than for other land uses and require the interaction of various levels of government, private sector participants, non-governmental organizations, and community-based groups. In both countries, a local governmental agency is typically responsible for taking the lead in coordinating the greening process. This is usually a parks planning department, in those cities large enough to have one (i.e., Chicago, Minneapolis, Toronto), or may include planning, community development, and economic development agencies. Upper levels of government also play an important role in terms of providing land, funding, technical expertise, and assistance with project coordination. In the US, the federal EPA, the Army Corps of Engineers and the National Parks Service were active during the initial planning stages for many of the projects examined. In Toronto, and in other communities in Ontario, regional conservation authorities are very involved in planning and development activities, particularly if the projects involve lands within floodplains and the construction of riparian habitat.

As for the private sector, developers, landowners, and other private sector participants were involved in slightly over half of the US projects, both directly (site construction or property donation) and indirectly (coordination of projects). This was not the case in Toronto, probably because many of these projects were solely park projects and not directly tied to a broader economic development scheme. Nonprofits — land trusts, community groups, and environmental associations — are also playing a more active role in raising awareness of the need for the greening projects and in helping to push them forward in the US and Canada, as will be discussed in more detail later in this chapter. All in all, the diverse array of partners and their efforts to achieve broad economic, social, and environmental goals demonstrate that greening projects are particularly challenging, requiring collaboration among various, and often adversarial, stakeholders. For this reason, such projects take a long time to bring to fruition, requiring from two to thirteen years to complete for the US projects, and three to five years in the Toronto case.

As with any brownfield project, greening also involves additional costs associated with site assessment and remediation. Using data on the cost of site assessment and remediation available for 19 of the 30 projects, the average cost for site assessment and remediation was approximately US$1.2 million a project or US$128,000 per acre, with costs for the US projects being slightly higher than those in Toronto due to the redevelopment of more large-scale properties in heavily impacted industrial areas. It should be noted, however, that cleanup costs ranged extensively from US$40,000 to US$13 million per project. In the US cities, site preparation and remediation costs represented approximately 19% of the total project costs (based on estimates from 14 projects), but about 25% of total costs in the Toronto case. This is on the upper end, but roughly in line with the 10%–20% rule of thumb for the proportion of total brownfield project costs attributed to remediation.

As with all brownfield projects, a primary objective is to keep cleanup costs down. This is particularly true for green space development because it often brings about fewer economic returns than other uses. Consequently, several projects (10) involved the use of capping, landscape features, or other engineered barrier methods to secure contaminants and minimize exposure. Indeed, there is a close link between park design and the management of contaminated soils. More traditional approaches, such as off-site disposal (i.e., dig-and-dump) and pump-and-treat technologies, were also used. Although they are becoming more prevalent, phytoremediation, bioremediation, and natural attenuation were only used in a few instances. Multiple methods were employed at 10 of the 11 US sites where data was available. This often involved the use of capping and barrier methods in tandem with off-site disposal or on-site remediation techniques. Soil is often shifted throughout the site and managed depending on its contamination levels and risk. Indeed, while early efforts promoted the removal of contaminated soil and its replacement with clean fill, a more cost effective and sustainable approach involves the management of soils on site, which maximizes the reuse of soil resources and does not just transfer the problem elsewhere. This makes it somewhat difficult to specify cleanup costs because a cap can serve other functions in addition to contamination management (e.g., a road or parking lot for automobiles, soil for grading and planting, a tennis court, etc.).

Although a common fear traditionally associated with planning for and redeveloping brownfields, as reported by the literature, is exposure to contamination (US EPA, 1999; Eisen, 1999; De Sousa, 2000; Greenberg et al., 2001a, 2001b; Greenberg, 2002), coordinators on both sides of the border indicated this issue received "little" or "no" concern on the part of their communities. This finding was supported in a recent study carried out by the author in which only 2 of the 476 park users and community residents surveyed at 3 brownfields-to-green space projects mentioned contamination as an issue of concern (De Sousa, 2006c). The reasons often given for this are that people spend relatively little time at these sites; that the sites are publicly owned and managed; and the fact that the sites are safer and cleaner than they would otherwise be. In fact, some vacant brownfield sites already serve recreational or habitat functions, such as for hiking, dog walking, mountain biking, and riparian habitat.

Another issue standing in contrast to other kinds of market-oriented brownfield redevelopment initiatives is the very important role communities play in greening projects (Eisen, 1999). Pressure for greening and decisions related to all aspects of the redevelopment projects examined were strongly influenced by community involvement and input. Such involvement came about through various structures and in diverse contexts, including, for example, consultation forums, design charrettes, working groups, committees, site visitations, and educational tours. In only a few of the cases were there any differences of opinion on the type of redevelopment appropriate for a site. In the Toronto case, support for ecological restoration projects typically came from established environmental groups, while support for green space in under-serviced neighborhoods typically came from smaller, ad hoc groups united by a community leader (or leaders). Community members there pushed hard for participation beyond project planning and visioning. Many called for park design conducive to public participation in the site's long-term management and maintenance (e.g., planting events, walking tours, educational programs, monitoring of habitat, coordination of cleanup activities, etc.). One of the downsides of this extensive community involvement at many sites, however, was the emergence of a debate over what type of green space was to be created. The debate over providing more active sports and recreation facilities versus more passive recreation and habitat-oriented sites is a common one facing parks planners in both US and Canadian cities.

As projects have a real cost, a significant amount of research has gone into valuing the benefits associated with parks and open space. The average total cost for a greening project in the US cities was US$6.05 million based on 18 projects (= US$3.99 million median cost, or US$750,000 per acre/US$1.85 million per hectare). For those in Toronto it was CDN$1.8 million per hectare (CDN$660,000 per acre), while the median cost was CDN$580,000 per hectare (CDN$211,000 per acre). The discrepancy between the mean and the median values is no doubt due to the high costs tied to projects involving constructing or rehabilitating buildings/facilities for recreation-oriented purposes versus those involving ecological restoration or passive recreation. Although the US projects were typically grander in scale, many cities — such as Chicago, Minneapolis, New York, and Los Angeles — have since expanded the types of green space being built on brownfields in a similar vein to Toronto.

What is similar in all cities is that government is responsible for covering virtually all of the costs involved in the greening projects. Unlike other types of brownfield redevelopment, where government funding is provided mainly to help with the assessment and remediation of sites, in the case of greening projects it is typically the only source of funding. The city government typically pays for neighborhood parks built for recreation purposes, while various levels of government sponsor many of the larger parks and may assist with assessment and remediation costs. That said, local governments are also responsible for the long-term management and maintenance of these properties.

Benefits of Brownfields-to-Green Space Projects

Achieving the multiple benefits associated with greening is a key objective for many cities. Research by the author sought to identify the benefits of greening brownfields specifically, from the perspective of those implementing these projects and, more importantly, from those using them or living in the communities in which they are located. In terms of the implementers, those interviewed in the US tended to highlight as primary benefits (in decreasing order of frequency) the provision of new open spaces and recreational sites, economic benefits, aesthetic benefits (especially blight elimination), and the conservation and restoration of habitat. Other benefits identified included the interconnection of the newly formed green spaces to other parts of the city, the creation of new trails, new access venues to water, flood control, infrastructure improvement, enhancement of cohesion among the residents of a neighborhood, historical restoration, and direction for future greening efforts. Most of the benefits identified can be characterized as "human-oriented," in that they involve an increase in recreational places, pleasant and economically viable neighborhoods, environmental services (e.g., flood control), and community cohesion. While many respondents mentioned economic stimulation as a key benefit of turning brownfields into green spaces, few considered it the most important benefit.

Interestingly, those in the Toronto case identified the creation of new ecological habitat as a primary benefit associated with greening brownfields. This was closely followed by the context of collaboration these projects created among disparate groups — from community groups to governmental agencies, the provision of recreational places, and the opportunity for educating central city residents about restoration and habitat. While the perceived benefits put forward by those in the US differed from those in Toronto this is less due to a difference in worldview and more a consequence of those in Toronto representing parks and conservation interests, while those in the US represent a broader mix of backgrounds tied to urban renewal interests (i.e., parks, economic development, planning). As in the US, the other key benefits identified in Toronto were human-oriented — that is, they were seen as motivating stakeholder collaboration and involvement, providing more recreational spaces, offering models for future redevelopment, enhancing educational opportunities, controlling floods, improving of neighborhood aesthetics, preserving historical significance, and the like.

Although not initially considered as a primary goal of the Toronto projects, many stakeholders praised the social networks that emerged and the long-term interaction that was evident (often leading to new greening projects). Even a private developer pointed out that initial apprehension quickly dissolved as site development progressed. Stakeholder interaction and capacity building are perceived as central to the process of creating social capital — an increasingly sought after objective of community economic development initiatives. The social capital tied to greening brownfields has formed in Toronto over time and over many projects, and is forming at a rapid pace in cities like Minneapolis, Pittsburgh, and Chicago, where early successes are fueling continued efforts.

The development of brownfields to enhance alternative types of green space in the central city is also viewed as important for achieving parkland objectives, both in terms of the number of such sites and their accessibility. Another noteworthy offshoot benefit is that greening projects act as "flagship" or "marquee" demonstration "experiments" serving as models for future greening endeavors. As one interviewee put it: "these projects advertise the potential that greening has to heal brownfields and improve inner-city communities." Overall, it is evident how the success of these projects has made park planners and other stakeholders more confident in pursuing, supporting, and acquiring other brownfield sites throughout the city for greening purposes.

An additional social benefit that many implementers commented on was the marked improvement in neighborhood image resulting from the removal of abandoned industrial buildings. A few others identified the flood-control infra-structure benefits that such projects brought about. Some projects also provided new technological opportunities. The Domtar Polyresins and the Woodbine Park projects, for example, involved the use of innovative remediation technologies that have since been used in other brownfield redevelopment projects within Toronto. Many projects have also been able to preserve historic buildings, landscapes and other features that add character to their neighborhoods and preserve the history of the city's urban environment.

But this is what implementers say. Are these benefits really experienced by those who use these sites and reside in surrounding communities? In the summer of 2003, in order to gather information on park uses and community quality of life impacts, the author conducted a study at three brownfield-to-green space sites in the mid-west–Ping Tom Memorial Park and Senka Park in Chicago, Illinois and Mill Ruins Park/Stone Arch Bridge in Minneapolis, Minnesota. Based on a 20-question survey, the study was conducted on three consecutive days (Thursday through Saturday) during three consecutive weeks in July and August 2003. While several researchers were on site, respondents were given the option of completing the survey as an informal interview, filling it out independently at the park and returning it to a member of the research team, or taking the survey with them and mailing it back in a pre-paid return envelope. In total, 476 surveys were completed — 139 at Ping Tom Park, 151 at Senka Park, and 186 at Mill Ruins Park.

In terms of the quality of life impacts of the projects, respondents were first asked about personal impacts in an open-ended manner and then community impacts in a close-ended manner to more directly gauge their opinions on a list of 21 factors adopted from the literature on quality of life and sustainable communities (Gobster, 1992, 1995; Maclaren, 1996, 2001; Tyler Norris Associates, 1997; Leitmann, 1999; Shafer et al., 2000). The most noted *personal* benefits included physical activity (27.3%), children's play (20.4%), scenic beauty (19.7%), relaxation (17.6%), and access to nature (8.6%). Almost half of those at the neighborhood parks (Senka Park, and to a lesser extent Ping Tom Park), described the site as a good place for children (47.7% and 17.3%, respectively) and for families (15.9% and 10.1%). Some also listed social interaction (6.1%) and providing "something to do" (6.1%) as key benefits. Highlighting the neighborhood's history was also considered an important personal benefit at Mill Ruins Park (10.8%), adding to community pride. The majority of respondents pointed out personal benefits associated with aesthetics, physical fitness, and social interaction, as opposed to economic-oriented ones (e.g., economic stimulus 0.6%, higher real estate values 0.6%).

As for community implications, respondents were presented with a list of quality of life impacts and asked to point out whether the greening project had a major negative, minor negative, no impact, minor positive, or major positive impact (values range from 1 to 5). Table 8.3 shows that the projects were considered to have a positive impact on all quality of life factors. The primary factors, in order, are scenic beauty, trails for walking, neighborhood appeal, natural areas, access to recreational areas, community pride, blight removal, and personal fitness. Those at Mill Ruins Park, an architecturally significant project and historically the most blighted, had higher positive opinions overall, highlighting community pride, neighborhood appeal, and blight removal benefits. The presence of playgrounds for children was also judged to have a major positive impact at Ping Tom and Senka Park. The perceived economic impacts were similar for all parks, with property value impacts rated highest at Ping Tom and Mill Ruins given that a significant amount of new residential and commercial redevelopment ensued after park development. Interestingly, those who never used the parks (4% of respondents) also felt that it had a positive impact on all quality of life factors, particularly scenic beauty (mean score 4.75), trails for walking (4.69), neighborhood appeal (4.67), access to recreational areas (4.47), and property values (4.43).

As a brownfields researcher, undertaking interviews in the field was truly inspiring and revealing. Indeed, the desire of the vast majority of those asked to simply participate in the survey because they "just loved the place" was a sufficiently positive sign. Perhaps the most unexpected result to the aesthetically challenged author, was that most people were most impressed by the scenic beauty brought about by these projects and their ability to erase blight in the community. As scientists we often focus on measuring neatly defined ecological, social, or economic benchmarks, when in essence, people really appreciate attractive places and good design, including distinctive and sensitive design that brings out a brownfields industrial history as in the case of Mill Ruins Park.

In addition to the responses related to quality of life impacts associated with these projects, there were several other results of interest:

• Although the overall sample showed the typical park user traveled to the site from home (75%), 85% of respondents from Mill Ruins Park went there from work.
• Most respondents (77%) traveled a distance of one mile or less to get to the park, although 11% at Ping Tom Park and 22% at Mill Ruins Park traveled over four miles.
• Overall, 72% of respondents visited the greened brownfields at least once per week during the summer, with 25% of these visiting every day.
• For all parks, both the cumulative results and the individual park results identify walking/hiking as the most popular activity.

Table 8.3: Community quality of life impacts of brownfield-to-green space projects.

Community quality of life impacts	Ping Tom mean score[a]	Rank	Senka mean score[a]	Rank	Mill Ruins mean score[a]	Rank	All sample mean score[a]	Rank
Scenic beauty	4.61	1	4.73	3	4.84	1	4.74	1
Trails for walking, hiking, and biking	4.42	8	4.65	6	4.83	2	4.66	2
Neighborhood appeal	4.53	3	4.63	7	4.76	4	4.66	3
Having natural areas present	4.46	6	4.77	2	4.66	6	4.63	4
Access to recreational areas	4.46	5	4.79	1	4.58	7	4.61	5
Community pride	4.36	11	4.58	9	4.76	3	4.59	6
Blight removal	4.44	7	4.31	17	4.69	5	4.51	7
Personal fitness	4.35	12	4.54	10	4.55	8	4.49	8
Property values	4.34	13	4.52	12	4.51	9	4.46	9
Access to quiet area	4.47	4	4.46	13	4.45	11	4.46	10
Social interaction among residents	4.37	10	4.61	8	4.42	12	4.46	11
Personal health	4.37	9	4.52	11	4.45	10	4.44	12
Access to children's playgrounds	4.60	2	4.70	4	3.84	21	4.31	13
Planned activities for children	4.13	15	4.65	5	4.07	18	4.30	14
Having wildlife present	4.02	16	4.41	15	4.41	13	4.30	15
Access to picnicking areas	4.32	14	4.43	14	4.19	16	4.29	16
Access to educational displays/ programs	3.78	18	4.37	16	4.38	14	4.22	17

Table 8.3: (*Continued*)

Community quality of life impacts	Ping Tom mean score[a]	Rank	Senka mean score[a]	Rank	Mill Ruins mean score[a]	Rank	All sample mean score[a]	Rank
Economic/ business activity	3.81	17	4.07	19	4.27	15	4.09	18
Public facilities (restroom, water fountain)	3.59	19	4.08	18	4.03	19	3.93	19
Crime levels	3.36	20	3.66	20	4.18	17	3.78	20
Drug problems	3.35	21	3.56	21	3.93	20	3.65	21

Source: Adapted from De Sousa (2006c).
[a]Mean scores were calculated based on a five-point scale where 1 = major negative impact, 2 = minor negative impact, 3 = no impact, 4 = minor positive impact, 5 = major positive impact.

- Enjoying the scenery and relaxing/resting/hanging-out make up the top three activities overall, with each of these being among the top five for the individual parks.
- Most respondents (27.9%) said that they did not remember what had been there before the park, pointing out that they just did not go to the area until people told them about the new park or the "transformation" that had occurred. The next most frequent response from Ping Tom Park (15.1%) and Mill Ruins Park (24.2%) was that the sites were "ugly, dirty and dumpy" areas that were pretty much off limits.
- As for the perceived impact the site had on the community before the green space was constructed, of those who provided a written opinion, one in four stated that they did not know (24.6%), while some stated that the brownfield was not good for the community (12.2%) or had no impact (11.8%); Mill Ruins Park respondents had the most negative recollections that it was not good for the community (18.3%), attracting crime and homelessness (8.6%), constituting an eyesore (5.9%), or was perceived as being dangerous and frightening (4.3%).

The most telling result from the survey was that 90% of respondents felt the green spaces were a good use for the brownfield sites. Only 1% felt that it was not a good use for the site, while the remainder (9%) did not know. It is also noteworthy that 89% of those respondents that never used the parks also stated that they were a good use for the brownfields.

Project Obstacles

Despite these benefits, the greening of brownfields has also been hindered by a variety of real and perceived obstacles according to implementers. The single most challenging barrier is a lack of financial resources for planning, coordinating, and undertaking remediation and redevelopment for green space. One problem is that the front-end costs associated with purchasing land and preparing brownfield sites for parks and open spaces are often perceived as too costly. Another relates to the difficulty associated with accessing brownfields funding because it typically targets land uses that generate employment or direct tax benefits. While the EPA has been contributing up to US$50,000 in funding to cities that include a greening component in their Brownfields Showcase proposal since 2001, that amount is a drop in the bucket given the costs involved. Funding for greening brownfields is also not a priority for most states. In fact, Wisconsin's Green Space and Public Facilities Grant, which was first introduced in 2004 and has designated US$1 million to help local governments cleanup brownfield sites for parks, recreational areas, libraries, and municipal garages, continues to be the only program of its kind in the country.

Another related obstacle often mentioned by those involved in greening is the perception that the economic benefits of such projects (and in some cases its environmental benefits) were debatable. Despite the many studies revealing the benefits, many government officials see open space as a frivolous amenity that is too expensive to service.

A third common problem involves the acquisition of land, particularly when piecing together multiple parcels to create a linear greenway. Often, cities will commence a trail system using the land they already have, and the success of this system leads to desires to expand it. These desires hit a roadblock when landowners continue to want their access to water or rail unimpeded, do not want their land tested, or are simply unwilling to provide even a sliver of land for trail access because of operational concerns. While many systems try to go around these sites, their large size can make this a difficult prospect.

Other factors impeding the conversion of brownfields-to-green space mentioned by implementers included:

- concerns about the impacts of soil contamination on human health and the environment and of the appropriate scientific methods for dealing with such contamination;
- a lack of government leadership and poor coordination among governmental agencies;
- a lack of staff expertise with respect to green space planning;
- a lack of trust within governments and between them and other stakeholders to work together;
- alternative redevelopment priorities;
- limited examples of similar projects to provide guidance; and
- the long-term maintenance of the green space once it is developed.

Given that many of the parks and recreation departments in cities throughout the US and Canada are facing budget cuts, overcoming these challenges will continue to be difficult. Indeed, most of those interviewed that were involved in greening projects called for more support and funding from the federal government and community organizations, and for an increase in public/private partnerships to support greening. They also called for a general change in attitude on the value of open space within cities. A site's location was considered extremely important to the potential success of a project, especially in areas where the project would enhance its economic potential (e.g., along waterfronts or riverways), its aesthetic appeal, or service a community that lacked green space. Other strategies for overcoming barriers and facilitating greening projects include establishing specific planning mechanisms, streamlining the regulatory process, and encouraging greater involvement and support from both private sector and nonprofit organizations. Many of these proposals are similar to those suggested for facilitating brownfield redevelopment generally. It is important to note, however, that many of those interviewed during the site visits stressed that turning brownfields into green spaces is still a relatively new option in the domain of brownfield redevelopment. In many ways, people are still learning from these early projects about the benefits greening can bring about and how they can be carried out.

Nonprofit Organizations and the Greening of Urban Brownfields

Greening brownfields has largely been public sector driven. But given cutbacks and alternative priorities, the public sector is looking to nonprofit entities to become more actively involved in the greening of brownfields in an effort to realize broader social and environmental goals. Four national nonprofit organizations in particular (i.e., Groundwork USA, Rails-to-Trails, the Trust for Public Land, and the Wildlife Habitat Council) have thus come to play a greater role in developing and conserving urban land, including brownfields, for public parks and open space in the US.

While the outcomes achieved by these groups are somewhat similar — namely, converting land into recreation and green space — their mission statements and stated objectives differ rather extensively. Two of the groups (The Trust for Public Land and Groundwork USA) have broadly defined mission statements, while the other two Rails-to-Trails Conservancy (RTC) and Wildlife Habitat Council) are narrower in terms of what types of green space they develop:

- The mission of the Groundwork USA network is to bring about the sustained regeneration, improvement and management of the physical environment by developing community-based partnerships which empower people, businesses, and organizations to promote environmental, economic, and social well-being.
- The Wildlife Habitat Council's land restoration mission is to demonstrate the methods and means by which state and local governments, industry, and community groups can use ecological enhancements to increase the rate at which contaminated

lands, both private and public (state, tribal, local), can be restored for a variety of reuses, including wildlife enhancement as part of restoration designs.
- The Trust for Public Land (TPL) conserves land for people to enjoy as parks, gardens, and other natural places, ensuring livable communities for generations to come.
- RTC aims to enrich America's communities and countryside by creating a nationwide network of public trails from former rail lines and connecting corridors.

National nonprofits aim to carve out a niche in green space planning by either offering a service not performed by the public sector or not seen as viable to the private one. Both RTC and the Wildlife Habitat Council outline their specific niche product in their mission statements. RTC offers a service somewhere between that of a Department of Transportation (i.e., the provision of a route for walking and cycling) and a Parks Department (i.e., the provision of recreation space). The Wildlife Habitat Council seeks to link the provision of wildlife habitat (something local governments typically have little expertise in) with a new remediation technology that may lower cleanup and land-holding costs of large public and private companies (e.g., petrochemical companies, the Department of Energy, etc.). The TPL and Groundwork USA have a slightly broader mission — Groundwork USA undertakes regeneration projects that may involve many types of greening, economic development, and/or job training, while the TPL conserves land in both cities and rural areas. Groundwork USA's forte tends to be in working in impoverished parts of inner cities, while the Trust for Public Land's strength lies in its real estate and financing expertise.

Each of these nonprofits is organized in a broadly similar manner and all have experienced rapid growth over the last decade. The TPL, RTC, and the Wildlife Habitat Council expand in those communities that have embraced their services or where opportunities abound. TPL and RTC, the oldest organizations, each have a head office, a Washington office, and numerous field offices throughout the US. The field offices are responsible for setting their own priorities, becoming engaged in relevant local projects, and identifying new projects, while the head office and Washington office are responsible for project-specific activities in its own region, as well as overall management, research, and lobbying activities. Groundwork USA is the only nonprofit here that operates more as a franchise in which independent local "trusts" are opened in places where community groups, government agencies, and other organizations have made an effort to obtain them. The affiliation is much looser, tied together largely by a common mission and a website, but the renewal focus of each individual trust can be radically different.

Discussions with stakeholders from these groups in 2004 identified their key roles in terms of redeveloping of brownfields into green space:

- Raising awareness about the need for parks and open space in urban areas, while acting as educators and cheerleaders. As mentioned, the TPL has published numerous reports on the availability of parks in US cities and the economic benefits of parks and open space.

- Advertising successful projects through various media and forums, including conference presentations, websites, meetings, etc.
- Providing technical expertise regarding a specific type of green space (e.g., Rails-to-Trails) or a component of the greening process (e.g., financing, community involvement).
- Using their nonprofit status to the advantage of both public and private sector stakeholders when planning and financing projects. For instance, the private sector receives tax breaks for selling or donating land to a nonprofit and the public sector can get nonprofits to raise private funds for projects.
- Bringing together public and private stakeholders and the local community to participate in projects.
- Allowing governments and nonprofits to take a hands-off approach. Groundwork USA, for example, is sponsored by the USDA, which sees it as an organization for addressing severely blighted inner city areas. The WHC has a cooperative agreement with the US EPA and works with large private companies and other government agencies to implement and study the feasibility of converting brownfields into wildlife habitat using the so-called "ecological enhancements."

As with public agencies, nonprofits face various challenges affecting their capacity to carry out greening projects. First and foremost is the need for revenue generation. Because the greening of brownfields is costly to undertake, but does not generate revenue, the nonprofits have to generate their own funds for these projects via fund raising, grants, consulting activities, fees associated with land transactions, etc. While they have flexibility in terms of how they raise funds, sustaining those funds is a noted problem. As with the public sector, another challenge for nonprofits is raising awareness and interest related to greening. Undertaking greening activities in urban areas also poses many challenges. In poorer parts of cities where the market is weaker, there is often less community involvement, and there are greater concerns regarding safety and long-term maintenance. In wealthier parts of cities and in downtown cores, greening involves higher costs because real estate values are high. This in addition to the many costs and risks typical of assessing, remediating, and redeveloping potentially contaminated brownfield sites, particularly those associated with liability and high cleanup costs.

Despite these challenges, these groups are achieving marked success. Indeed, by 2005 they reported the following outcomes in terms of creating green space:

- The TPL has been involved in 2,708 land conservation projects since 1972 that have conserved 1.92 million acres (78 million hectares) of land valued at US$3.5 billion dollars. In US cities, TPL has created, protected, or designed more than 500 parks.
- RTC has assisted hundreds of communities and rail-trail advocates in building 12,650 miles of rail-trails throughout the US and the organization has over 100,000 members and supporters.
- The Wildlife Habitat Council manages or assists in the management of over 2 million acres (809,000 ha) of land in 48 states, Puerto Rico, and 15 other countries.

Over 120 companies are Wildlife Habitat Council members, as are two dozen conservation organizations, plus many supporters and contributors.

- While still relatively new, Groundwork USA is involved in dozens of brownfield projects throughout the country.

In all, the national nonprofits are playing a very active role in greening brownfields in the US and have found themselves at the forefront of this initiative in many respects (i.e., raising awareness, remediation, financing, planning and implementation, post-development promotion). Nonprofits can play an important role in this type of urban renewal in many ways. Most notably, nonprofits "fill-in a gap" or "act as a bridge" between the public sector, the private sector, and the local community (act as a trusted intermediary). Many are more experienced in dealing with risk (whether it is legal, financial, technological) and more creative in their ability to raise project funds from a variety of public and private sources. Unlike the private sector, nonprofits can engage in projects that do not bring about direct monetary benefits, but garner significant public benefits. They can also lobby government and businesses to force them to keep funding or delivering public benefits with less fear of retribution. Nonprofits also have many technical skills (fundraising, lobbying, etc.) that local governments, private companies, and the community may lack. For these reasons, their role will need to expand if governments wish to shift their brownfields efforts from an economic development focus to a broader urban renewal one that incorporates green space.

Conclusion

While tax dollars and jobs are integral to the economic sustainability of cities, there is a growing sense among researchers, government officials, and urban residents that a broader revitalization focus be considered so as to bring a higher quality of life back to the city, which, in turn, will lure back investors and residents (Platt, 2006). The greening experiences examined show how brownfield sites can constitute valuable opportunity spaces for developing various types of park and open space in urban areas and, thus, to contribute to this broader focus. Given that it is neither simple nor inexpensive to carry out, however, the greening of urban brownfields requires extensive stakeholder involvement and government commitment. Indeed, the financial challenges involved in cleaning up, constructing, and even justifying the expenditure of funds for greening projects is very difficult given the budgetary predicaments of many cities and states.

Based on the projects in this chapter and the related discussion, a number of key implications that need to be considered for enhancing the viability of the greening option can therefore be identified:

- The greening of brownfields seems to be most feasible when tied to other forms of redevelopment, regardless of type, and when it is justified on the basis of human uses and benefits.

- Greening is particularly effective when all parties can link green space needs with brownfield site availability as part of a comprehensive revitalization planning strategy.
- The involvement of communities in the whole redevelopment process is crucial, in both the short and long term.
- Potential funding sources must be identified and/or created through the involvement of public, private, and nonprofit interest groups.
- Municipal departments involved in the administration of parklands should be consulted and involved directly in all greening projects.
- Greening projects should be encouraged because they tend to revitalize "blighted" neighborhoods, with an eye toward enhancing their economic and social appeal.
- An appropriate risk-based corrective action method that integrates elements of landscape design with available and emerging site remediation technology should be used, since this will enhance the feasibility of greening projects.
- Greening projects present greater challenges than other forms of redevelopment in justifying end-use and project funding, but are more easily accepted by affected communities.

The next chapter reviews several cities that are at the forefront of greening brownfields in an effort to create more sustainable cities and improve the state of the urban environment.

Chapter 9

Brownfields-to-Green Space Case Studies

Once viewed as symbols of urban economic power, older brownfields are now perceived as little more than prime examples of urban decay (De Sousa, 2006b). The list of socioeconomic and environmental ills associated with these sites, and sometimes their surrounding neighborhoods, is an extensive one and includes such "blights" as high levels of crime, crumbling infrastructure, contaminated soils, vacant buildings, wasted space, poverty, and the like. While planners, community and business leaders discuss what can be done to revitalize these districts, one proposal that comes commonly out of the debate is the increasing role that the so-called "greening" must play in cleaning up such areas, enhancing their attractiveness for business and growth, as well as improving urban ecological health. This chapter examines efforts being undertaken in three cities — Pittsburgh, Pennsylvania; Minneapolis, Minnesota; and Toronto, Ontario — to utilize brownfields-to-green space as a key tool in the regeneration, revitalization, and restructuring of their brownfields. These case studies build on the previous two chapters by telling the story of several cities using greening as an overall strategy for revitalization, and how challenges were overcome and visions realized.

Pittsburgh, Pennsylvania

Due to the high number of brownfields that the city has and the large-scale nature of the brownfields-to-green space projects that have been undertaken there, Pittsburgh's greening efforts have received considerable attention from researchers, particularly those collaborating via the Brownfields Research Center and the Studio for Creative Enquiry based at Carnegie Mellon University. Two projects that are of particular interest from a greening perspective are Washington's Landing and the Nine-Mile Run discussed below.

Washington's Landing

The city's first major greening and mixed-use brownfields project — and one of the earliest successful brownfields projects in the US as evidenced by its 1997 Phoenix

Award — involved a 42-acre (17 ha) island on the Allegheny River adjacent to the downtown core known as Herr's Island. The island was later renamed Washington's Landing in 1987, because George Washington reputedly slept there in 1753 after his raft capsized in the Allegheny River. Although initially used for farming, the flow of industry to the island commenced in the early 1900s when the Pennsylvania Railroad bought a portion of it for use as a stopover for its Chicago to New York route. This purchase was in response to a Federal law requiring livestock to have rest, food, and water after every 36 h of travel. As well as livestock, meatpacking and rendering facilities soon followed and eventually covered the island, which became best known for its foul smell (Putaro & Weisbrod, 1999). As O'Neill (1996, from Putaro & Weisbrod, 1999) notes: "Odors from the island's animal rendering plant were foul enough to make a fellow just about swear off breathing." Over time, the island was used extensively for various industrial purposes, including oil refining and storage, tube works, soap works, stockyards and rendering, scrap metal recycling, and worker lodging (Figure 9.1). The trend of suburbanization and the traumatic decline of the American steel industry in the 1970s and 1980s, however, hit Pittsburgh particularly hard, leading to a loss of population and jobs that rippled through the area.

Visioning for the redevelopment project began in earnest in the mid-1980s. An initial environmental investigation revealed that the island's central and northern portion did not contain harmful contaminants, except for waste materials produced

Figure 9.1: Historic photo of Washington's Landing/Herr's Island (Reprinted with permission from URA, 2006a).

by rendering operations that gave off noxious odors. The site's southern portion, however, contained contaminants (polycyclic aromatic hydrocarbons (PAHs), polychlorinated biphenyls (PCBs), and total petroleum hydrocarbons (TPHs)) above standard safety levels, which would have to be dealt with by either excavation/off-site disposal or by excavation/on-site encapsulation. The encapsulation option was chosen because it was more cost effective (US$3.5 million) and could be incorporated into the park amenity (the tennis courts form the top of the containment cell for PCB contaminated soil). As they were clearing the northern tip to build the containment cell, project coordinators discovered 10,000 tons of organic wastes from previous meat packing activities and from animal carcasses dumped there by the Pittsburgh Zoo. Cleaning up this problem added US$750,000 to the project. In all, the remediation strategy included encapsulation of PCB contaminated soil (tennis courts), deodorization and off-site disposal of "special wastes" causing odors, UST removal, and on-site treatment of heavy metals with paved capping (boat storage/parking lot).

Before reconstruction of Washington's Landing began, the only infrastructure on the island consisted of old warehouses, abandoned railroad tracks, deteriorating railroad bridges, and the 31st Street Bridge that crossed it. Some early infrastructure projects performed by Pittsburgh's Urban Redevelopment Authority aimed to neaten up and reconnect the site to its surroundings. The necessary infrastructure works included, for example, US$150,000 in 1979 for designing roads, bridge connections, and water and sewer lines, US$1,235,607 (from 1978 to 1985) for demolishing cattle pens and a meatpacking plant, building utility lines and roads, and US$4 million for the construction of a new bridge to the site (Putaro & Weisbrod, 1999).

The project's green elements, for both the park site on the island's north end and the redevelopment as a whole, also received considerable attention. The park project contains five tennis courts, an outdoor amphitheater, several grassy play areas, a woodlot with native trees, a natural prairie, several lookout points, and a walking trail that meanders throughout the park site (Figure 9.2). A jogging and bike trail also encircles the entire island. Views of the city from the northern and southern tip of the site are excellent and have been augmented by a number of new overlooks. In addition to these public spaces, the marina and facilities for the Three Rivers Rowing Association also provide opportunities for more active recreation in the city. As for greening the rest of the site, developers were required by the masterplan to plant specific types of trees and bushes to enhance the beauty of the island. Comprehensive design standards for lighting, building materials, paths, landscaping, and other features are detailed in the masterplan to ensure consistency and high quality design.

The project also involved the development of commercial space in the middle of the island and residential space on the south end. The first site to open was the Three Rivers Rowing Association in September 1989. A flurry of office, research and development, and light industrial buildings soon followed, including the regional office for Pennsylvania's Department of Environmental Protection. Today, the site contains over 200,000 sq ft (18,500 m^2) of such space. In the early 1990s, the Rubinoff Company (also involved in the Nine Mile Run project below) began constructing 88 luxury townhouses on the site. Initially selling for US$140,000, they had virtually doubled in value by 2002.

Figure 9.2: Washington's Landing Lookout 2002.

Pittsburgh's Urban Redevelopment Authority (URA) and the city itself were responsible for the implementation of the project's redevelopment plan. The URA was responsible for land assembly, demolition, and site improvement activities, including public infrastructure, parks, and development of other public spaces pursuant to the plan. Extensive public investment was required to prepare Washington's Landing for private development — project funding totaling in excess of US$26 million was pieced together from a dozen local, regional (e.g., Appalachian Regional Commission), state, and federal sources (URA, 2006b).

The resulting mixed-use recreational, residential, commercial, and light-industrial redevelopment project was completed in 2000 at a total cost of US$71 million (URA, 2006b). The 8-acre (3.2 ha) park site now has tennis courts, trails, and a restored riparian habitat. It cost an estimated US$4 million dollars, US$1 million of which was spent on site assessment and remediation. Overall, this case study shows how greening can play an important role in brownfield remediation and in the management of soil contamination. It also demonstrates how unexpected costs can emerge during the redevelopment process.

Nine-Mile Run

Pittsburgh's Nine-Mile Run project is one of the most remarkable greening and residential mixed-use projects in the US. Plans in the early 1900s sought to turn the site into a majestic green space — but these fell through and about half of the 244-acre (99 ha) stream valley was purchased by the Duquesne Slag Products Company, which was established in 1906 to dispose of slag from various iron and steel mills along the Monongahela River. Slag is the industrial by-product of smelting metals and ores and at the time, more than a half-ton of blast furnace slag was produced for every ton of iron produced.

Duquesne purchased the rest of the land in the Nine Mile Run Valley slowly over 40 years, which helped it avoid attention and controversy (McElwaine, 2003). Dumping, according to the Company, began in 1922. The slag pile grew quickly. Aerial photographs of Nine Mile Run show a slag pile some 20–25 ft (7 m) in height by 1937, covering the northern and western portions of the property (McElwaine, 2003). When dumping ceased in the early 1970s, two large slag piles, almost 200 ft (60 m) high, rose up sharply from the Valley. Under and between them ran the heavily polluted Nine Mile Run stream. Initial plans to bury the entire stream valley with the slag and construct homes on top were very strongly opposed by the surrounding neighborhoods. After extensive public consultation, it was agreed that the Nine Mile Run stream should be restored and that residential redevelopment could take place on top of the existing slag piles (Figure 9.3).

In 1995, Pittsburgh's URA purchased the site for US$3.8 million dollars — at the time, it was the largest piece of undeveloped property in the city (McNeil & Lange, 2001). Site assessments showed that the slag was of relatively uniform composition with no evidence of serious industrial waste in it. Chromium and manganese levels posed some concern, but steps taken to keep down dust and the topsoil used for

Figure 9.3: Slag heap at Nine Mile Run (2001).

vegetation growth eliminated this concern since it essentially buried the metals in an effective manner. Indeed, in 2002, the top of the slag pile looked like a giant honeycomb because the slag for roads was at grade while slag for the housing properties had been dug a meter deep.

The degree of citizen participation in the project was extensive with over 400 public meetings having been carried out by 2002. A neighborhood group called Citizens for the Responsible Development of Nine Mile Run scrutinized every aspect of the development, sending out regular reports called Slag Bulletins. Much of the fear related to hazardous materials and dust released into the air from grading and construction activities. Indeed, as Ermann (2003) points out: "While chipping away at the slopes, workers did uncover abandoned cars, part of a freeway and some drums of petroleum, which they piled at the corner of the site." Concerned residents were, however, satisfied with the measures taken to deal with potential hazards.

The project's residential component, known as Summerset at Frick Park, is a 109-acre (44 ha) development being constructed in three phases. It includes 710 homes priced at US$200,000 to US$700,000, as well as separate green spaces to be constructed by the developer Rubinoff. Each project phase includes pocket parks, trails connecting to Frick Park, and access to the Nine Mile Run stream. Phase I encompasses 27 acres (11 ha) to be developed in two stages with a mix of home types and sizes. Phase IA includes 98 homes varying from the so-called Mansion

Apartments to large Estate Homes, and Phase IB include 113 homes. The Phase II and III neighborhoods will add 270 homes on 42 acres (17 ha) and 213 homes on 40 acres, respectively. Interestingly, the early phase of the site sold via lottery in a matter of hours, even though, at the time, the site was little more than a slag heap and a development plan.

Original plans for the green space saw the remaining 135 acres (55 ha) being redeveloped into neighborhood parks (8-acres/3.2 ha) and into a greenway that will contain wooded areas, playing fields, and trails. The greenway project has since evolved into a multi-phase aquatic ecosystem restoration, which includes channel reconfiguration, wetland reconstruction, and native plantings. Indeed, the Nine Mile Run Aquatic Ecosystem Restoration, sponsored by the Army Corps of Engineers and the City of Pittsburgh's Department of City Planning, is the largest project of its kind to be undertaken in a major metropolitan area in the US by the Army Corps of Engineers and involved the restoration of approximately 2 miles of stream. The stream restoration proceeded in three phases largely for financial reasons. Phase 1A (completed in 2002) included initial stream rechanneling and infrastructure improvements, such as reducing the impervious surface in the lower Frick Park parking lot and construction of a soccer field. Phase 1B (completed in the fall 2005) consisted of stream channel modifications and improvements. Phase two (completed in June 2006) extended the stream channel modifications and improvements.

Supervised by the Army Corps of Engineers in partnership with the City of Pittsburgh, a contractor was hired to complete the construction. Maintenance for the restored stream is the responsibility lies with the City of Pittsburgh's Department of Public Works, which manages all major city parks. In addition, support for the project came from local groups such as the Nine Mile Run Watershed Association.

Restoration cost a total of US$7.7 million, with the US$5 million federal contribution to the project being paid through Army Corps of Engineers Section 206 funding. The non-federal matching funds of US$2.7 million came from the City of Pittsburgh and Three Rivers Wet Weather Demonstration Program. Overall, the total development costs for the first two phases of the residential/park project are estimated at US$48 million dollars, with grading costs for site assessment, soil management, and site preparation estimated at US$33.7 million. The Studio for Creative Inquiry predicts the final phase will incur costs of approximately US$45 million for infrastructure, bringing a total of approximately US$185 million worth of public/private investment (McNeil & Lange, 2001).

This project offers a couple of very important lessons. First, it shows the shear scale of what can be envisioned for greening projects. From a planning perspective, the initial conflict over the site's end-use between the private developer and local economic development agency on the one side, and the neighboring communities on the other provides another good example of what can happen to a project when the public is not consulted early on in the planning process. Second, the project provides an excellent example of planning brownfields for multiple purposes (ecosystem health, quality of life, aesthetic enhancement, residential reuse, etc.).

Minneapolis, Minnesota

The Minneapolis Park and Recreation Board and the State of Minnesota are actively involved in promoting the conversion of brownfields-to-green spaces. Indeed, a multi-stakeholder group comprised of representatives from state, city, and non-governmental organizations has been pursuing the greening of over 30 brownfield sites in the Twin Cities region and throughout the state for a number of years. While planning for most of these sites is in its early stages, particular emphasis has been placed on projects along the Mississippi that cut through the heart of Minneapolis. The Park and Recreation Board's vision is to have a continuous, publicly owned riverfront park corridor on both banks that improves water quality and habitat, is connected to the city's neighborhoods, acts as a catalyst for economic development, and celebrates the city's history.

Nearly 12 miles of river flows through Minneapolis. Much of the lower portion of the river corridor was acquired in the early twentieth century and safeguarded for public use. The central and northern portions, however, are experiencing a green transformation. The Mill Ruins Park and Stone Arch Bridge project has become the centerpiece of this transformation in the central portion of the river system. In its heyday, mills, canals, tailraces (channels that carry water away from a mill) and other historic resources in the area comprised the largest direct-drive water powered facility in the world. Starting with a single sawmill in 1821, industry quickly developed along the St. Anthony Falls in order to harness its waterpower. Growth reached its peak in the late nineteenth and early twentieth century, and many of the great names in Minneapolis and American Industry (e.g., Pillsbury, General Mills) got their start there.

The Stone Arch Bridge was constructed to serve freight and passenger trains in 1882. Taking 20 months and requiring extensive inputs of human and animal labor, the construction of this majestic project was intense. A passage from the *Daily Minnesota Tribune* (November 23, 1883) posted at the site reads as follows:

> This viaduct ... is the only one of its kind that spans the Father of Waters, and is one of the largest and most noteworthy in the United States. Firmer than the earth which supports it, it is constructed to stand the test of time.

Registered as a National Historic Civil Engineering Landmark in 1975, the bridge's work supporting rail ended when the last train crossed it in 1978. After sitting vacant for over a decade, the Hennepin County Regional Railroad Authority purchased it in 1989 and transferred authority to the Minnesota DOT, which began transforming it into a pedestrian and bicycle trail in the early 1990s. According to the US Department of Transportation (1995), total funding for the project was US$2.8 million (US$2.184 million federal and US$616,000 local).

The park's redevelopment was planned in four phases, each of which would produce a park site on its own before the other phases were completed. The first phase began in the fall 2001, and involved the reopening of the historic canal, the uncovering of portions of the mill foundation walls, and the addition of bicycle and pedestrian path links to the adjacent Stone Arch Bridge and the river parkway. The second phase started in 2002 consisted of stabilizing and restoring the historic features uncovered during the first phase of construction. The third phase started in 2003, involved the reconstruction of a 650-foot wood plank that once capped the canal, and the construction of a bike/pedestrian trail connecting the downstream end of the plank to the river parkway trail system. The final phase involved the construction of pedestrian paths flanking the canal, additional excavation of mill foundations, and the introduction of additional interpretive features (Figure 9.4). For this redevelopment to occur, a variety of contaminants (PAH, Diesel Range Organics) required management and legal arrangements to ensure that certain portions of the site will not be disturbed in the future. Management costs of contamination issues for phases one and two are estimated at US$165,000.

The Mill Ruins Park and Stone Arch Bridge site was one of the projects surveyed by the author in 2003 to examine project use and its impact on quality of life (De Sousa, 2006c). General observations taken at the park found that a large number of employees descended upon it weekdays between 11:30 a.m. and 1:30 p.m., while many local residents and commuters frequented the site before and after work, and

Figure 9.4: Mill Ruins Park and Stone Arch Bridge.

on weekends. A number of interesting results came from the 186 surveys completed at the site and the surrounding neighborhood:

- Asked how often they visit the park during the summer, 39.2% of respondents visit a few times per week; 19.4% visit every day; 13.4% once a week; 10.8% once or twice during the summer; 8.1% a few times per month; 4.8% once a month; while 4.3% of the respondents stated that they never visit the park.
- Asked about the number of people a respondent typically visited the park with, in addition to themselves, the responses ranged from zero (34.5%) to ten other people (0.6%) visiting together. 38.5% of the survey respondents visit the park with one additional visitor, 14.9% with two, 6.3% with three, 2.3% with four, 2.3% with five, and 0.6% with eight other people.
- Presented with a list of activities and asked whether they partake in them "often," "sometimes," or "never," the top five uses were walking/hiking (96%); enjoying the scenery (77%); enjoying historic or interpretive signs/information (62%); relaxing, resting, or hanging-out (58%); and visiting or meeting friends (55%).
- Asked to describe the site before the park was built, 26% did not know/remember, 24% described it as an ugly dirty dump, 15% as industrial area, 11% as unused empty area, 5% described it as dangerous, 5% as railroad, 4% as an unmaintained natural wilderness, 3% as inaccessible, while 20% described it as other (i.e., homeless/gangs/crime 11.3%, rundown 4.3%, informal play/use 1.6%, positive, discovery, better 0.5%, trees/jungle 0.5%, etc.), while 9% had not been there prior to the park.
- Asked in an open-ended manner to describe the main personal benefits of the park, the main responses were physical activity/exercise (39.2%); beauty, scenery (36.0%); relaxation, quiet time, quiet activities (16.7%); history (10.8%); nature, flowers (9.7%); and social interaction, meeting friends, gathering (6.5%).
- Asked whether the park was a good use for the site or, if not, what it should have been, 91% of respondents considered that it was a good use.
- Presented with a list of quality of life factors, the top ranked factors included scenic beauty 4.84; trails for walking, hiking, and biking 4.83; neighborhood appeal 4.76; community pride 4.76; blight removal 4.69; having natural areas present 4.66; and access to recreational areas 4.58.

The results above reveal that people appreciate the wide-range of environmental, social, and economic benefits that emerge from more sustainable brownfields redevelopment that revitalizes historic infrastructure, incorporates open space, and removes blight. Indeed, many cast a regular vote for the project "with their feet" by visiting from work on a frequent basis "to find respite from the toils of everyday life." By showing that a recreational amenity in the urban core can be built on a site that exists on many feet of buried sand and gravel and that its historical legacy can be unearthed and revealed in the process, the Mill Ruins project constitutes an important case of redevelopment. The park project has also been a primary catalyst for extensive redevelopment of residential, commercial and other private and public uses in the surrounding area. The Minneapolis Park and Recreation Board (2004) estimates, for instance, that the US$205 million dollars invested in parks (public US$55 million) and public improvements (US$150 million) along the central riverfront (of which Mill Ruins is the centerpiece project) has already helped generate over US$1.2 billion dollars in private investment in the surrounding area and has stimulated the construction of more than 3,000 new residential dwellings (Figure 9.5). The project's incremental phasing is also a practical way to ensure a project moves forward, while funds are being raised.

Success at Mill Ruins has also led to work on various other projects in the central and upper river. For example, the 18-acre (7.3 ha) BF Nelson site, formerly home to paper and saw mills, is being remediated of petroleum products and asbestos and

Figure 9.5: Residential and commercial buildings sprout along the park.

developed into passive green space with a restored prairie, wetland and riparian slope areas, trails, and environmental and historical interpretive features. The 5-acre (2 ha) Riverview Supper Club site, in the upper river, is a mixed use project involving the development of townhomes by a private developer and the creation of a greenway trail in what still remains a largely commercial and industrial area.

Toronto, Canada

As discussed in the Chapter 8, one city that has been very proactive at converting brownfields into green space over the last decade is Toronto. The Planning and Parks departments of that city have used greening in an effort to increase the parks inventory and overall quality of urban life in the city (Toronto Planning, 2000). Indeed, the City of Toronto has been described as a "city within a park." With more than 1,500 parks (covering over 8,000 ha), Toronto's green space inventory is extensive (City of Toronto, 1999). Over 12% of its urban area is comprised of green space managed by the City of Toronto and the Toronto Region Conservation Authority, with 71% classified as natural heritage land (valley lands, ravines, woodlots, trails along the waterfront, etc.).

Historically, Toronto's green space planning and development activities gained momentum after 1954, when Hurricane Hazel ravaged the city. Following the hurricane, the city started acquiring "flood lands" in an effort to protect its residents from future natural disasters, while also enhancing recreational opportunities and protecting the natural environment generally. From an inventory of 67 ha in 1953, green space development spread rapidly, becoming more than 8,000 ha by 1999 (Metropolitan Toronto Planning, 1988; City of Toronto, 1999). In general, the City of Toronto generates funds for green space projects from development activities. A construction project is required by law to apportion 5% of its site to the city or pay the city a 5% tax on construction costs, or else to provide a combination of these. Fortunately, an extensive amount of redevelopment has taken place in Toronto, especially in the area of residential redevelopment, helping both to generate funds and to substantiate the need for additional green space.

Toronto's recent "greening experience" has resulted in the creation of many different types of open space on brownfields land. As discussed in the previous chapter, the ten greening projects studied in 2002 generated 614 ha (1,520 acres) of new green space and included two pocket parks, two neighborhood parks, and two large district parks to serve both local and city residents, and four ecological restoration projects. These ranged in size from just under half a ha (1 acre) to 471 ha (1,164 acre), with a median project size of 2.7 ha (6.7 acres).

The Music Garden

An example of a pocket park project is the Music Garden located on the central waterfront along Lake Ontario, just south of the Central Business District (CBD).

Once an industrial area with uses ranging from machine shops, warehouses, and ship building industries, the 2-acre site has been converted into a magnificent parkette that adds to a continuous green promenade that the city is creating along the water's edge. The project lies in an area of downtown that has seen extensive high-rise condominium development over the last decade and a half.

Designed to represent the six movements of Johan Sebastian Bach's "Suites for Unaccompanied Cello," the Music Garden project was originally intended for Boston's City Hall Plaza, but was lured to Toronto while Boston politicians debated its economic efficacy. The design is elaborate, consisting of forested paths, wildflower gardens, and a small performance area at the center of the site that is programmed with dance, classical music, and other performances throughout the summer.

The project was promoted by internationally renowned cellist Yo-Yo Ma and local philanthropist and President of the Art Gallery of Ontario, James Flick. Unlike most other park projects in Toronto, the Music Garden was a public–private partnership in which Flick and Yo-Yo Ma raised CDN$1.5 million to go with a contribution from the city of CDN$1 million. Using a risk-based corrective action approach (or Site Specific Risk Assessment as it is referred to in Ontario), heavy metals and PAHs at the site were used as roadbed and integrated into the park's design via landscape surfacing and a clean soil cap. Completed in 1999, the park has become a stunning addition to the waterfront and a good example of a public–private partnership that incorporates green space and art (Figure 9.6).

Sorauren Park

A good example of a brownfields to neighborhood park project in Toronto is Sorauren Park. It is located in an older, working class inner suburb, consisting largely of single- and multi-family homes. In 1986, the City of Toronto purchased a 5.6-acre (2.3 ha) parcel of land from the Toronto Transit Authority to use as a works yard. Despite the city's plans, a municipal councilor along with the community and several local schools came together with the aim of converting the site into a neighborhood park. After extensive consultation, the park was designed for an array of active and passive recreation activities to serve the community and the local schools. Completed in 1995, the site now consist of tennis courts, a baseball diamond, a small soccer field, a few "habitat" areas, a swale to manage surface runoff, and several grass play spaces surrounded by residential and industrial buildings (Figure 9.7).

The Sorauren site had been formerly occupied by a series of industrial uses, including an armaments manufacturing facility and a garage and maintenance yard. These former uses had left the property contaminated with heavy metals, fuels, and chlorinated solvents. Adopting a conventional approach to cleanup was estimated to cost over CDN$2 million, which made the project unviable (City of Toronto, 1998). Alternatively, a risk-based approach was taken that allowed certain affected soils to be left on site. An existing concrete slab and an integrated surfacing/cleanup soil cap using berms were applied to eliminate exposure risks over the bulk of the site.

Figure 9.6: Music garden prelude — an undulating riverscape with curves and bends.

Figure 9.7: Sorauren Park Toronto.

Approximately 25,000 m^3 of clean fill was imported to construct the required soil cap, railway berm, and for storm water grading, as well as for general park design. To eliminate a source of on-site groundwater contamination, a groundwater remediation plan was also established. Institutional controls are also in place to ensure the land is governed according to its management plan. Ultimately, the risk-based approach combined with capping via park design reduced pollution management costs to CDN$300,000, which allowed the project to be realized.

Woodbine Park and The Beach

Woodbine Park and the Beach project in Toronto's east end near the lakeshore provide an excellent example of a development partnership that has transformed a brownfield into a vibrant district park and residential community. The 90-acre (36 ha) site was once the north shore of the vast Ashbridges Bay marsh system, and was extensively filled in the early 1900s with sand, silt and an estimated 20,000 m^3 of coal and clinker ash (City of Toronto, 1998). Prior to redevelopment, the site was home to a large horse racing facility, grandstand, horse barns, utility buildings, and 16 acres of asphalt surface parking lots. Today, 60 acres (24 ha) consist of largely residential mixed-use development and the remaining 30 acres (12 ha) of parkland. The mixed-use development will contain over 500 single-family, duplex, and town homes, as well as several multi-story commercial and residential buildings.

Initially, more of the site was to be taken for development, but the local community pushed for less density and more community amenities on the site. Once the division of private and public space was agreed upon, much of the debate revolved around what type of green space was to be implemented. Several groups pressured the city to turn the site into an ecological habitat, while others lobbied for soccer fields, baseball diamonds, a marina, and other recreational uses. In the end, the completed park contains a festival green band shell that can serve 22,000 people, garden gateway entrances, trails, a promenade, 15 acres (6 ha) of native plantings, an ornamental fountain, a children's storybook place, a memorial for the raceway formerly at the site, a storm water retention pond, and a children's soccer field and playground.

The soil at the site was primarily contaminated with heavy metals and a few localized areas contained hydrocarbon contamination from underground storage tanks used by the racetrack operation. In addition, much of the site lay below the level of the lake and had to be raised significantly, making soil an extremely valuable commodity. A bio-pad treatment was used to treat petroleum contamination, and a novel X-ray fluorescent technology was used to reduce the amount of non-contaminated fill being removed from the site by carefully identifying only the contaminated soils that required treatment on an ongoing basis. Nonetheless, a further 500,000 m^3 of engineered fill had to be brought in to raise the site to grade. A full cleanup of the soils and groundwater was performed on the residential and commercial portions of the site, as well as at the southeast portion of the park where the storm water management facility was constructed. A risk-based approach integrating landscape surfacing and soil capping was used at other portions of the park site. Site preparation also included demolition of approximately 50,000 sq ft (4,650 m^2) of racetrack structures and the stripping of the asphalt parking lots, much of which was crushed on site and recycled for public roads. Interestingly, the developer of the residential project carried out remediation at the Woodbine Park. This made cleanup more cost effective for the city and, according to the developer, sped up the greening process so that the site would act as an aesthetic benefit for their project, as opposed to an unsightly liability. In all, the park site cost CDN$3 million, with approximately one-third spent on assessment and remediation.

The Don River

For over two decades, one of the key goals of the city, the Toronto Region Conservation Authority, nonprofits (e.g., the Waterfront Trust, the Task Force to Bring Back the Don), and other local stakeholders has been the restoration of the Don River to enhance the greenway and to restore its ecological functionality. The many brownfields-to-green space projects carried out along the Don have each envisaged an extensive reintroduction of native trees, shrubs, wildflowers, and herbaceous plants to enhance the ecological integrity of the wider area, as well as to improve water quality, increase access to recreation, preserve the river's heritage, and improve the corridor for cyclists and pedestrians.

Domtar polyresins.   About 4 km north of Lake Ontario is the 5.5-acre (2.2 ha) Domtar Polyresins site, once used for testing and manufacturing polyresins. The site was contaminated with extensive amounts of ethyl benzene, toluene, styrene, and PAHs. A risk-based approach was employed to deal with the site and an experimental bioremediation approach applied to clean it. The CDN$1.3 million dollar cleanup cost was split between the federal government, the Toronto Conservation Authority, and the company undertaking the remediation. Management of the site was undertaken in multiple steps that included site assessment, facility removal and demolition, grading, production and implementation of the bioremediation treatment approach, and planting. The bioremediation approach consisted of excavating the soil and placing it into a large treatment reactor where the soil was treated in batches over a period of 18 months. In the reactor, nutrients, indigenous microorganisms, and groundwater were applied to the soil. Clean soil was then removed from the reactor and spread onto the site. The City of Toronto then paid the remaining CDN$300,000 to develop the green space, which consisted of a reestablished Carolinian lowland forest, wildflowers, wet meadow and woody plant species, and a natural barrier created to protect the ecologically sensitive climax beech and maple forest connected to the site.

Don valley brick works.   About 2.5 km from the lake along the Don River lays the Don Valley Brick Works site, which operated as a brick making facility between 1890 and 1989 and provided materials for many significant structures in Toronto, as well as other North American cities. When the site went up for sale in 1984, the Conservation Authority could not afford the CDN$4 million asking price. A residential developer purchased the site and immediately began seeking approval to rezone the land to residential use. The developer began filling parts of the site for construction, but also leased it to a brick making company that continued to use it until 1989, by which time it had become the oldest brick facility in Ontario. Pressure from the surrounding neighborhoods, some of the wealthiest in Canada, as well as interest in conservation and flood-related issues, eventually led the provincial government to stop the residential project and permit the conservation authority to expropriate the land in 1987, for which it later paid CDN$21 million.

A masterplan commissioned for the site was completed in 1990. It proposed the revegetation of the land, public uses and facilities, and interpretive programming (Hough, Stansbury, & Woodland, 1990). In addition, plans were laid out for the preservation of the site's north end, which contains an 80-foot cliff designated a Provincially Significant Area of Natural and Scientific interest because it contains exposed geological site deposits and fossils from the two most recent ice ages. The masterplan sought a budget of more than CDN$25 million for various recreation oriented structures and green infrastructure. However, the revised and approved plan only provided CDN$5 million and was split between the city and the conservation authority.

Work on the project's greening components started in the summer of 1995, with the first phase being opened to the public in October 1997. The park consists of an open wetland area, a Carolinian lowland forest, a wildflower meadow, and walking paths. Many of the buildings are being restored for office and recreational use (Figure 9.8). Continued support for the site is coming from the city, the conservation authority, and a national nonprofit known as Evergreen, whose mandate is to bring nature to cities through naturalization projects. Central to Evergreen's proposed vision for the site are a series of demonstration gardens, the development of a native plant nursery, environmental education facilities, outdoor and wilderness experiences for youth, an art reuse center, ceramic programs, art demonstrations, and an organic-themed restaurant. Evergreen also plans to relocate its national office to the Brick Works site. Evergreen has put together a fundraising strategy to raise CDN$10–13 million for site renovations and CDN$4–5 million for community programming from various levels of government, businesses, foundations, and individuals. In December of 2006, the federal government also announced that it would provide CDN$20 million for the project, which hopes to achieve Leadership in Energy and Environmental Design (LEED) platinum status for the restored buildings.

Chester springs march. Just downriver from the Brick Works lies 7.4 acre (3 ha) Chester Springs Marsh. In 1992, a community Task Force proposed reconstructing a wetland on the site in order to restore habitat, enhance its water quality, and promote public awareness of wetlands. Covered by 7–10 ft (3 m) of landfill dumped in the

Figure 9.8: The Don Valley Brickworks.

early 1900s, a site assessment sponsored by the Task Force to "Bring Back the Don" found cinder, rubble, and some heavy metal contamination. These were not considered a health risk and their monitoring became part of the site's ongoing monitoring program. Wetland reconstruction and planting began in 1996 and the vegetation quickly took hold. The wetland has become a very successful project and provides an important educational resource for local residents.

In terms of funding, the Task Force provided the original CDN$40,000 required for site assessment and planning related costs, while the remaining CDN$400,000 came from federal, provincial, and municipal government sources. To deal with the cost issues, project managers and other interested parties sought funds from a wide variety of organizations for different aspects of a project (site assessment, design, construction, etc.). Ultimately, site acquisition was sponsored by public funds, site assessment by private funds, and design and implementation by public funds provided by five different agencies from the three levels of government. The city, the Conservation Authority, and various private sources currently fund plantings, maintenance, monitoring, and education activities. An interesting story related to funding the project in its early stages was the generous offer from a member of the community to help pay for the project by selling antique bottles he excavated from the site for fun. Needless to say, he had not anticipated the CDN$440,000 cost, figuring, as many do, that all that is needed to recreate a wetland is whip some seeds at the site for it to reappear.

Given that the creation of new habitat and the ecological viability of the Don Greenway have been of central importance, the city and local community groups continue to monitor the ecological outcomes of these brownfield projects and the state of the Don generally (TRCA State of the Don). The Chester Springs Marsh Monitoring Program (Task Force to Bring Back the Don, 2004, p. 2), for instance, established an environmental audit of the site through a combination of professional and community-based monitoring techniques that check for biological responses to the restoration project over time (recolonization and natural succession). So far, a considerable increase in the number and diversity of plant, bird, mammal, amphibian and insect species has been documented. In addition to the creation of habitat, the extensive use of interpretive signs at these sites has helped educate the public about the viability and importance of habitat in urban areas.

Port lands.   Perhaps the most ambitious project that is currently ongoing is the restoration of the mouth of the Don River, which spills right along Toronto's Industrial Port Lands before it hits Lake Ontario. It is here where the two sites and the two stories merge. The revitalization of Toronto's Port Lands has been the subject of intense debate for more than two decades. Located southeast of the CBD, the 1,000-acre (405 ha) property was created largely by fill from dredging, demolition, and other such activities in the city. Currently, there are a range of industrial, commercial, and recreational uses on the Port Lands, including Toronto's port facilities. Historically, the energy companies occupied a large portion of the area, with oil tank farms making up almost half of the total area (Hemson Consulting, 2000). The energy crises of the 1970s and the subsequent switchover to natural gas for residential energy led to a decline in the need for oil and, in turn, to the migration of oil companies away from the port area. While over 3,000 people still work for businesses located in the Port Lands, the site is gradually becoming abandoned and is extensively contaminated, containing over 100 individual brownfield sites (Hemson Consulting, 2000; Groeneveld, 2002).

The debate over the future of the Port Lands has always been heated. Some interests believe that it is best suited for residential redevelopment, bringing the district in line with other successful residential communities along the waterfront (Warson, 1998). Others envision the area as a continuation of the larger green space renewal efforts that have been taking place in contiguous areas to the Port — that is, the Don River to the north and the Leslie Street Spit to the south. The first comprehensive attempt at developing a greening plan for the Port Lands was undertaken by the Waterfront Regeneration Trust, an agency that grew out of a Royal Commission established in 1988 to study the future of the Toronto waterfront. More recently, greening of the Port Lands was used as a stratagem by the city of Toronto in its bid for the 2008 Olympics. Although the bid failed, a Waterfront Revitalization Corporation (WRC) was established to move redevelopment and renewal activity forward.

Thus far, the three levels of government have pledged CDN$1.5 billion dollars of initial funding for a variety of so-called Priority Projects, including the cleanup of contamination estimated to cost, depending on the approach taken, between

CDN$60 million and CDN$500 million dollars. One priority project is "restoring" the mouth of the Don River. According to the Toronto Waterfront Revitalization Corporation (2002, p. 1), "the green corridor is intended to serve as a welcoming entrance to the Port Lands and encourage private sector investment and future development." The project will connect Toronto's Waterfront to green space in the Don River Valley, transforming vacant lots and concrete into 52 acres (21 ha) of new parkland, wetland, and marsh areas. Fulfilling this vision will require extensive soil and groundwater remediation, removal of current infrastructure, and the reconfiguration of the mouth of the Don River. Two million dollars (CDN) have already been set aside for the assessment, design, and planning process itself (Toronto Waterfront Revitalization Corporation, 2002). Indeed, the project is envisioned as being another successful chapter in Toronto's greening story.

Conclusions

A land-use that is often favored by community residents, but less so by the economic development officials often in charge of brownfields projects, Chapters 7–9 have focused specifically on green space. The case studies discussed in this chapter suggest that greening brownfields plays an important role in bringing people together, providing recreational opportunities, promoting health and wellness, and enjoying scenic beauty in a way that draws on the area's historical significance. The new developments are quickly embraced and become important "connecting places," connecting people with each other, connecting locations, and connecting people to their natural environment.

Early calls for parks, as described in Chapter 7, were prompted by the need to address public health concerns, increase recreation, and provide relief from the toils of labor. These desires continue to ring-true today and the capacity of green space to address these, and other issues, is supported by a growing body of empirical research. While some cities in both the US and Canada have already established considerable park inventories, many older industrial districts and neighborhoods in need of renewal often suffer from a shortage of green space and a surplus of brownfields. The functioning of ecosystems in these areas has also been impaired by decades and even centuries of human activity. It is here where brownfields provide opportunity spaces for constructing restorative green space and green infrastructure. Although some policy initiatives and research studies have begun to address this issue, it has been a relative drop-in-the-bucket compared with the policy, research, and funding efforts addressing other forms of brownfields redevelopment.

The greening experiences examined in Chapter 8 show how brownfields of many shapes, sizes, and former uses in urban areas have been redeveloped into various types of open space, but that these projects are neither simple nor inexpensive to carry out. As such, many strategies for moving these projects forward were outlined, including tying greening to other forms of redevelopment, planning for green space and brownfields redevelopment in a more comprehensive manner that involves parks planning departments, involving a broader range of stakeholders and local citizens in visioning, planning, and fund raising, and managing costs through risk-based approaches and creative design.

In addition to revealing the sheer scale of the greening projects that have been envisioned, the case studies discussed in this chapter reinforce lessons learned in the previous chapter, while supplying additional ones. As with other forms of brownfields redevelopment, some of the cases demonstrate the benefits of consulting the public early and the potential for unexpected costs to emerge during the redevelopment process to make challenging projects even more challenging. Greening projects also benefit from a multi-use and multi-benefit perspective (ecosystem health, quality of life, aesthetic enhancement, residential reuse, economic development, etc.) that is consistent with sustainability thinking. Not only do governments enjoy the multiple benefits, but the general public also appreciates the wide-range of environmental, social, and economic benefits that emerge from more sustainable brownfields redevelopment that revitalizes historic infrastructure, incorporates open space, and removes blight. Another lesson is that working with the development community to plan for and even construct green space is a strategy for speeding up the greening process and reducing costs. A further lesson is that it is important to measure on an ongoing basis the economic, social, and environmental benefits of greening projects in particular to see if goals are being met, so as to help justify their existence and support future projects.

People choose to live and businesses choose to invest in attractive communities that are perceived to have a high quality of life. They want neighborhoods that are safe, abound in cultural amenities, support family life, celebrate the past, nurture creativity and an entrepreneurial spirit, and bring people together in a pleasant environment. Given that many of these considerations are typically associated with suburban life, those redeveloping urban brownfields must think beyond narrow site-specific and economic-oriented goals and integrate them with community revitalization and sustainability-oriented features. While these do broaden the land-uses to be considered and may require an additional layer of planning, the result will be worthwhile. The conversion of urban brownfields into green space is, therefore, a step towards a broader community revitalization approach, which, arguably, also paves the way for highly desired economic development activities that are discussed in the next two chapters.

Chapter 10

Back-to-Work-Brownfields Redevelopment for Industrial and Employment-Oriented Reuse: Policies and Visions

One of the most troublesome economic developments in American and Canadian cities since World War II has been the exodus of industrial firms from urban areas and the impact that this has had on the structure and evolution of the inner cities. Until the mid-twentieth century, manufacturing was the lifeblood of cities, providing life-sustaining jobs for large numbers of city residents and representing a substantial portion of city tax revenues. Since the 1960s, however, manufacturers have fled central cities in droves, moving to the suburbs, exurbs, and even to developing countries. Manufacturing reached its greatest share of total employment in the US in 1968, and has been undergoing a steady decline ever since with a concomitant rise in service-based employment (Chapman & Walker, 1991). The same trend has been witnessed by many Canadian cities where the pace of deindustrialization accelerated when branch plants of US firms moved to the US soon after the North American Free Trade Agreement was signed in 1994.

Despite this situation, the perception persists among many scholars and politicians that manufacturing is still the hub of a basically industrial economy and that a significant proportion of service-employment growth is actually intertwined with the manufacturing sector. In addition to its importance from an economic development perspective, urban industrial decline is also considered to be a principal cause of chronic unemployment and related social problems among inner-city minorities, as well as constituting the primary source of brownfields. It is for these reasons that policy-makers have focused much of their efforts on putting brownfields into productive use, so as to bring employment and taxes back to the city (Rast, 2005). This and the next chapter look at bringing "work" back to brownfields. The primary focus is on discussing reindustrialization efforts, although office and retail development are also examined.

Manufacturing, Deindustrialization, and Decentralization in the US and Canada

The role of the manufacturing sector in developed countries and its decline have been the focus of considerable debate. Manufacturing reached its greatest share of total employment in the United Kingdom in 1955, in the US in 1968, in Italy in 1969, in West Germany in 1970, and in Japan in 1971 (Chapman & Walker, 1991). In these, and other industrialized economies, the sector has been undergoing a steady decline ever since. The province of Ontario, for example, witnessed a decrease in manufacturing employment from 24.8% of total employment in 1981 to 17.5% in 1993, as service employment increased in the same time-span from 65.1% to 74%. In the Toronto Census Metropolitan Area, manufacturing employment dropped from 28% in 1976 to 17% in 1993, while service employment rose from 28% to 38% in the same period (Gertler & Berridge Lewinberg Greenberg Dark Gabor Ltd, 1995, pp. 23–24). The socioeconomic impact of this decline has been felt mainly in the urban core, where manufacturing activities had been concentrated since the latter part of the nineteenth century.

Many still argue, however, that manufacturing is still the nucleus of the economy. Fitzgerald and Leigh (2002, p. 103) point out that in the US manufacturing still accounts for 15.8% of the nation's employment and is still an important component of many urban economies. Indeed, even though the employment share of manufacturing has decreased in Ontario, its contribution to the production capacity and the export base of the economy continued to remain stable — in 1993, manufacturing still accounted for 23.4% of Ontario's GDP (Gertler & Berridge Lewinberg Greenberg Dark Gabor Ltd, 1995, p. 25) and over 60% of the Greater Toronto Area's traded economy (GTA Task Force, 1996, p. 51). Scott (1980), Chapman and Walker (1991), and Gertler and Berridge Lewinberg Greenberg Dark Gabor Ltd (1995) point out, moreover, that a significant proportion of service-employment growth is actually intertwined with the manufacturing sector, since many of the service functions once performed "in-house" by firms (e.g., accounting services, legal consultation, product design, etc.), and classified as "manufacturing" jobs, are now being contracted out to service providers and reclassified as "service" jobs.

The outflow of manufacturing industries from urban cores to peripheral areas seemed to reach its peak in the 1970s throughout the industrialized world. As Chapman and Walker (1991, p. 241) aptly phrase it, "this so-called urban-rural shift of manufacturing seems to have been a feature of virtually all developed economies and was clearly the geographic manifestation of an almost universal process." The shift brought about a concomitant transformation of the workplace, whereby only a portion of previous blue-collar workers were able to move over directly to the service sector, leaving many others to become chronically unemployed or else in search of retraining in some other occupation. Unfortunately, the lost manufacturing jobs tended to pay higher wages overall than service industries for people with comparable skills (Fitzgerald & Leigh, 2002). The decline also left behind large tracts of derelict industrial brownfield lands in the urban core. To understand the causes of this shift and the implications it might have on reindustrialization efforts, it is instructive to unravel the historical reasons for the tendency of manufacturing industries to locate initially within urban cores and then to move out.

The emergence of both large- and small-scale manufacturing activities in the central city is a consequence of the Industrial Revolution and nineteenth-century policies that encouraged industries to locate in urban cores. Location within the city also gave plants easy access to the waterfront and to an affordable railway infrastructure. This allowed them to import new supplies of raw materials and to get their products out to the marketplace cheaply and efficiently. This explanation, however, makes light of the role that accessibility to a bountiful labor force also played, over and above the one played by transportation infrastructure, which also helps explain why such a large number of small-scale labor-intensive firms chose to locate in city cores as well. For Scott (1980), who takes a broader structuralist approach to industrial location (IL), the attraction in locating within city cores on the part of smaller-scale firms lay precisely in the maximum accessibility to the cheap and plentiful labor supply that the cores offered. He also argues that the city provided an efficient network for production units that allowed for a higher degree of interconnectivity among them.

Gertler and Berridge Lewinberg Greenberg Dark Gabor Ltd (1995) stress the importance of both the accessibility to an affordable transportation infrastructure and to a large workforce. The unprecedented growth of manufacturing industries in post-industrial societies led smaller industries to amalgamate into larger establishments, which required access to a plentiful labor force, to transportation facilities, to large markets, and proximity to related industries. City cores satisfied all these requirements perfectly. Indeed, the location of manufacturing plants in city cores underlay the urbanization process that became widespread throughout the twentieth century.

In most US and Canadian cities, the pattern of location within the core continued right through the 1950s. However, it was in that decade that decentralization into suburban and fringe areas started to take place. Not only was space within the city becoming sparse due to population growth, but for the first time in the history of urbanization, many new industries were choosing to locate in the suburbs rather than in the city because the enormous growth in automobile traffic led to the construction of a convenient highway infrastructure that liberated them from previous dependence upon the railway and waterfront infrastructure of the core. Between 1971 and 1985, the number of people involved in the manufacturing sector within the emerging core of Toronto declined from 82,000 (26.5%) to 66,000 (18.2%), while it increased from 156,000 to 182,000 in the suburbs and from 71,000 to 116,000 in the fringe. In the US, the level of suburban manufacturing began exceeding that of cities in the 1940s, and by the 1960s more high value-added manufacturing was taking place in suburbs (Fitzgerald & Leigh, 2002). By the late 1980s, the location quotient (a common measure of economic concentration) for manufacturing in many US suburbs was higher than it was in corresponding central cities (Fitzgerald & Leigh, 2002). From 1967 to 1992, employment in manufacturing declined significantly in most US cities in the Frostbelt, although several of their suburban areas witnessed an increase (Levine & Callaghan, 1998) (Figures 10.1 and 10.2).

The debate surrounding industrial decentralization has been extensive, but it is valuable to review in order to assess brownfields reindustrialization and re-employment efforts. According to Scott (1980), the tendency for small labor-intensive firms to cluster together in urban cores versus the tendency for large capital-intensive firms to locate in cheaper peripheral locations has been the pattern for a large portion

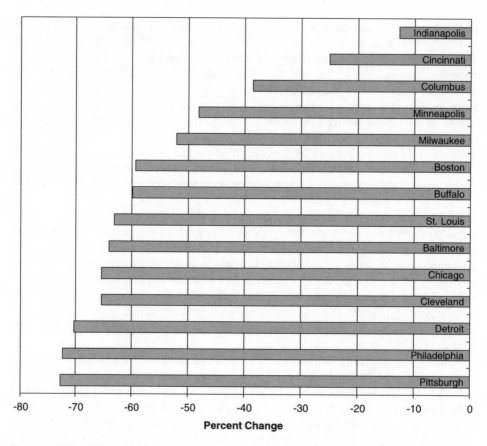

Figure 10.1: Urban manufacturing employment, 1967–1992 (Reproduced with permission from Levine & Callaghan, 1998).

of the twentieth century. The former type is attracted to an urban core because it purportedly requires both the city's larger population density for its labor input and proximity to related industries. Small industries require greater labor inputs because they produce non-standardized items and need to renew their production processes frequently. So, they tend to cluster together because the kinds of specialized products they manufacture requires the participation of kindred industries to provide the materials or parts necessary to make specialized items in a cost-effective way. Reducing transportation and communication costs between firms is therefore vital to these industries.

Peripheral areas have become attractive for capital-intensive operations because of their availability and due to lower location and construction costs. With the rise of vertical integration in the industrial sector throughout the century, the production capacity of firms has increased considerably as material inputs and outputs have become more and more standardized. The result has been a gradual replacement of human labor by technological processes, thus reducing the need for firms to stay

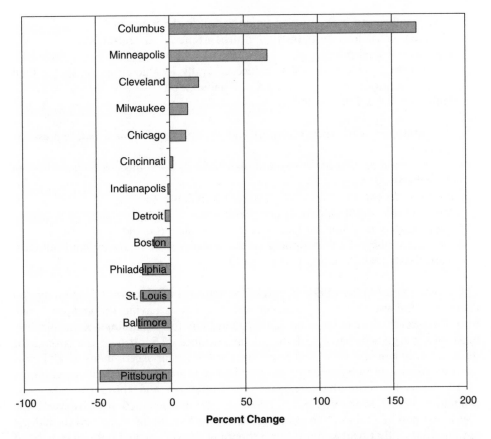

Figure 10.2: Suburban manufacturing employment, 1967–1992 (Reproduced with permission from Levine & Callaghan, 1998).

close to a large labor force in city cores. According to Scott (1980, p. 45), the phenomenon of decentralization, therefore, can be seen "as a fundamental long-run process involving changes in differential location costs as intermediated by a series of changes in capitalist production from labor to capital intensive." Chapman and Walker (1991) adopt Scott's dichotomy to explain decentralization, connecting their argument to the "push and pull" factors that the previous literature had identified as pivotal decentralizing forces.

- Push
  - the growth of firms and the lack of space for expansion at inner-city sites between 1971 and 1985,
  - obsolete central plant and equipment,
  - traffic congestion,
  - high central wages,
  - central labor shortages,

- ○ labor conflict and high levels of unionization in the inner city,
- ○ planning restrictions on industry and urban renewal in central areas,
- ○ high central land prices,
- ○ cost-benefit calculations which induce centrally located firms to vacate their present locations so as to capitalize site values, and
- ○ high central tax rates on industry.
- Pull
  - ○ the development of truck transport and the spread of intra-urban expressway systems,
  - ○ the invention of efficient horizontal plant layouts combined with cheap land in the suburbs,
  - ○ the prior decentralization of the working population,
  - ○ the favorable social climate of peripheral areas,
  - ○ the proximity of suburban locations to major airports, and
  - ○ the accessibility of the periphery to the residences of managers and administrative staff (based on Scott, 1980, p. 29).

Chapman and Walker (1991) highlight the shortage of space in the inner city and restrictive land use planning policies in urban areas as having the greatest "push force." However, their reliance on Scott's dichotomy for explaining decentralization makes their argument susceptible to similar critiques of Scott (i.e., the criteria for differentiating between small and large firms are not established, many small labor-intensive firms tend to be decentralizing, and some firms do not fit Scott's dichotomy at all, especially those that are small labor-intensive and those that are large capital-intensive). Moreover, Scott (1980, p. 29) himself actually dismissed the "push and pull" factors as "an eclectic collection of essentially static and formalistic explanations ... that read as much like a shopping list as they do a body of structured scientific investigation."

Gertler and Berridge Lewinberg Greenberg Dark Gabor Ltd (1995) explain the decline of industry in Toronto as a result of restructuring to adapt both to a globalized marketplace and to new techniques of industrial organization and production. As barriers to trade have fallen over the last two decades, the international flow of commodities has increased, leading to a globalized economic infrastructure. The ensuing liberalization of financial markets has also facilitated the exchange of capital across and between countries, inducing national markets to integrate with each other. Thus, Gertler and Berridge Lewinberg Greenberg Dark Gabor Ltd (1995) see the decline in manufacturing activity as a byproduct of globalization, whereby companies are forced to seek markets and production processes in more profitable locations. This has resulted, for example, in many US-based multinationals closing down their older Canadian branches and deciding to serve the Canadian market from their larger US-based plants. As a consequence, plant shutdowns, which tended to be located in the older industrialized areas of the core, have "contributed to what some have called the 'de-industrialization of the city,' creating extensive areas of underutilized or vacant industrial land in inner city locations" (Gertler & Berridge Lewinberg Greenberg Dark Gabor Ltd, 1995, p. 16).

Indeed, the trend today seems to be that industries will locate in any area of the globe that is advantageous economically, socially, and politically to their particular exigencies (Harrison, 1992; Maillat, Lecoq, Nemeti, & Pfister, 1995).

Gertler and Berridge Lewinberg Greenberg Dark Gabor Ltd (1995) also see enormous changes in technology and industrial organization as other significant factors in decentralization. The authors' claim that in the transition to a "post-Fordist" (non-mass-production) economy, manufacturing firms have started to vertically disintegrate into smaller and more specialized production units. This has entailed (i) the use of advanced computerized production processes in place of large-scale processes, (ii) the formation of specialized worker "cells" or partnerships, and (iii) the creation of regional industrial networks so that related industries can be in close proximity to each other. Overall, such changes have led to an industrial production system that is more "contracted" (i.e., more streamlined, more efficient in the use of factory space, and more reliant on inter-industry networking). According to Gertler and Berridge Lewinberg Greenberg Dark Gabor Ltd (1995), however, this contraction process has run its course and a new form of expansion is imminent. The main conceptual difficulty with accepting such a post-Fordist explanation of decentralization is that it does not spell out how globalization in itself would lead to the decline of industry in one location — the city core — but not in another — the suburbs and the fringe.

The different frameworks devised to explain decentralization entail different philosophical and methodological outlooks regarding what the future holds for manufacturing activity in the urban core, and, consequently, on what can be done to improve the employment situation and to redevelop derelict industrial properties (see Box 10.4 for a summary of five main schools of thought related to the study of IL). Theorists like Scott, Chapman, and Walker see little future for industries in city cores. As Scott (1980, p. 58) put it over two decades ago, any attempt to revitalize the economy of central city areas is fraught with a basic dilemma: "since the geography of enterprise in the modern metropolis is rooted in the dynamics of capitalist commodity production, any growth of new production at the core of the city immediately establishes the foundations of its own eventual dissipation in the form of new rounds of decentralization of economic activity." This would imply that the only option available to a city core is to encourage alternative forms of employment and alternative land uses on old industrial properties. Chapman and Walker (1991) see some hope in the core's ability to maintain some of its industrial vitality by proposing that economic development efforts that encourage local entrepreneurship can be successful with the aid of government. However, they emphasize the futility of attracting large firms to the core for the same reason put forward by Scott — namely that the gradual replacement of human labor by technological processes has reduced the need for such firms to stay close to a large labor force in city cores. Norcliffe, Goldrick, and Muszynski (1986) also see a bleak future for manufacturing within the city core, mainly because they see industry as seeking greater profits through decreased overhead costs by locating outside of expensive city cores. They, therefore, suggest local governments should abandon making policies designed to attract IL within the core to policies that would focus instead on retraining the workforce to meet new labor demands.

A more optimistic view vis-à-vis the role of city cores in the future is espoused by Gertler and Berridge Lewinberg Greenberg Dark Gabor Ltd (1995, p. 55), who emphasize that "falling scales of production, vertical disintegration, smaller establishments, the network enterprise, clustering, closer integration with markets, time-based competition — all of these are forces which are favorable to the central city." The authors point out that these factors will coalesce to make the city core attractive to industry, and that the coalescence process can be enhanced by diminishing the influence of "push and pull" forces — obstructive planning and development controls, high industrial taxation in comparison to suburbs, stringent decommissioning guidelines regulating the remediation of contaminated property, etc. — through appropriate political and legislative measures. Fitzgerald and Leigh (2002) also see "Just-In-Time" production as another solution for many of the smaller industrial buildings and land-plots in brownfield jurisdictions. However, they also note the other limitations of urban industrial space, such as outdated/poor infrastructure, higher land costs, traffic congestion, quality-of-life issues, and regulatory problems.

Box 10.4: Overview of Theories of Industrial Location

According to Chapman and Walker (1991), there are five main schools of thought related to the study of IL: (i) *normative industrial location theory*; (ii) the *behavioral approach*; (iii) the *geography of enterprise*; (iv) *manufacturing in redevelopment theory and planning*; and (v) the *structural approach*. To this typology, the more recent movement, which can be designated a *technology-based (post-Fordist) approach*, should be added, since it is the focus of much discussion in the industrial geography literature.

Most analytical work on IL prior to the 1960s adopted *normative industrial locational* theory. Normative theorists tended to explain the decision to locate in a specific area as the result of rational decision-making at the executive level. The two main versions of normative theory, according to Chapman and Walker (1991), have come to be known as *least cost location theory* and *market area approach*. Based on the work of the economic theorist Max Weber, the former espouses the point-of-view that the best location for a firm is the one where the costs of transporting raw material and manufactured products in and out of the location are minimal; the latter sees the best location as the one that allows for the greatest access to the marketplace. Chapman and Walker (1991, p. 19) remark that while normative theory is, by and large, a valid one, its main weakness is the assumption that "the decision maker has the single-mindedness of profit maximization and the possession of complete knowledge of all relevant economic information," which, clearly, is difficult, given the complexity of actual decision-making.

The *behavioral approach* came onto the scene in the early 1960s, stressing the importance that the entrepreneur's intuitive and emotional responses to a location play in its ultimate selection, rather than purely normative considerations. Behavioral theorists emphasize that location decisions are made, more often than not, by individuals and organizations virtually on "gut feelings," and not necessarily by rationally considering the situation in its entirety, as the normativists assumed. As Chapman and Walker (1991, p. 24) state, these two theories are clearly not mutually exclusive, since the normative approach seems to explain the decision-making process associated with larger firms, and the behavioral approach the decision-making process associated with smaller businesses: "Studies tend to emphasize the significance of firm size as a variable influencing the nature of the location decision-making process, and to provide some evidence in support of the proposition that the kind of rational behavior upon which normative theory is based is more frequently associated with large organizations than with small businesses."

The *geography of enterprise approach* explains location as a consequence of the power and economic clout of large industrial enterprises to influence the allocation and management of space within urban centers, regions, and even nations. This influence is manifest especially when a change in some manufacturing process is sufficient to bring about changes in the spatial configuration of the location in which the industry and its subsidiaries are located. As Chapman and Walker (1991, p. 25) put it, this approach reveals "a significant shift in emphasis away from a concern, exemplified by normative locational theory, with the influence of the spatial dimension of the economic environment upon industrial location (i.e., proximity to raw materials, market, etc.) towards an interest in the impact of the activities of industrial enterprises upon the environment."

The *manufacturing in regional development and planning approach* has recently become a major focus of work on IL, and it is the one adopted as a primary framework by several of the authors consulted here (Norcliffe et al., 1986; Gertler & Berridge Lewinberg Greenberg Dark Gabor Ltd, 1995). Unlike the other approaches, which focused directly on the location of industries, this approach takes a broader, more interdisciplinary perspective of IL theory, highlighting how historical linkages forged between different types of industry play a significant role in locational decisions (Chapman & Walker, 1991, pp. 26–27).

The *structural approach* came to the forefront in the early 1980s when industrial decline was felt by many to be a signal of the inevitable decline of the capitalist system in developed countries. Unlike other IL theories, structuralists utilize Marxist concepts to explain decline in terms of social forces and, especially, the struggle between capital and labor interests (Chapman & Walker, 1991, pp. 29–30).

The *technology-based (post-Fordist) approach* assesses locational tendencies in terms of the broader movement of industrial systems away from "Fordist" mass-production processes to "post-Fordist" (non-mass-production) ones (Gertler & Berridge Lewinberg Greenberg Dark Gabor Ltd, 1995). In a post-Fordist scenario, industry is seen to be evolving toward smaller plant sites, more specialized production, and more flexible production strategies. This radical shift entails changes in location configurations, since it makes necessary more collaborative inter-firm relations, causing firms to locate in districts where interaction and cooperation is more realizable.

As this overview of explanatory frameworks for decentralization has attempted to show, there is little consensus on the reason why there has been an extensive migration of industry from the city core to peripheral areas. In the absence of strong empirical proof to support any one theory over another, it would appear judicious to posit that the truth lies partially in all of them. Indeed, decentralization reflects a trend tied to social and technological changes that can be understood only in the light of broader sociohistorical forces. If city cores are to maintain their manufacturing roles, then we should seek to understand these forces, looking critically at policy-making processes and tailoring them to meet the demands of an increasingly globalized industrial world.

Bringing Work Back to the City

There has been considerable effort and debate regarding how to bring investment back into inner cities affected by deindustrialization and disinvestment. In his extremely influential work, Michael Porter (1995) argues for a radically new approach to revitalizing inner cities. Porter points out that

> a sustainable economic base can be created in the inner city, but only as it has been created elsewhere: through private, for-profit initiatives and investment based on economic self-interest and genuine competitive advantage — not through artificial inducements, charity, or government mandates.

Porter argues that cities should stop trying to cure the problems of their inner cores by perpetually increasing social investment and hoping for economic activity to follow and, instead, should start taking into consideration the competitive advantages associated with their inner cores and to harness those advantages in order to stimulate economic development. The competitive advantages of which he speaks includes many of the factors discussed by Gertler and Scott, that is:

- *Strategic location*: Inner cities can offer a competitive edge to companies that benefit from proximity to downtown business districts, logistical infrastructure, entertainment or tourist centers, and concentrations of companies;
- *Local market demand*: Many inner-city markets remain poorly served (by retailing, financial services, and personal services) and even though incomes are low, high population density translates into a large market with substantial purchasing power; furthermore, the inner-city market has a unique character that is often not served by products and services that are designed for wealthy customers and businesses;
- *Integration with regional clusters*: Inner-city areas can capitalize on nearby regional clusters, those unique-to-a-region collections of related companies that are competitive nationally and even globally (financial-services, health care);
- *Human resources*: Access to a loyal labor pool that will work for a moderate wage.

Porter indicates, however, several disadvantages of locating businesses in the inner city that need to be addressed include: the likelihood of businesses facing an inadequate supply of developable land; high building costs (due largely to bureaucracy), high costs for water, utilities, and workers' compensation; along with a host of related problems, attitudes, and the like (health care, insurance, permitting, and security, disrepair of the road infrastructure, limited employee and management skills, limited access to capital, and a sense of anti-business attitudes).

While many cities have since aimed to measure and publicize the competitive advantage of their inner cores and to deal with any relevant disadvantages, many critics argue that such communities continue nevertheless to spiral into decline. In his study of Milwaukee, Levine (2002) found that "declining real income coupled with demographic 'hollowing out' since the late 1970s has meant that real aggregate income and real aggregate purchasing power *have declined precipitously* over the past twenty years in the inner city." Thus, the "competitive advantage" argument is conceptually flawed — aggregate purchasing power in the inner city was substantially higher in the 1970s than it is today, and population density was significantly greater, yet disinvestment, retail decline, and commercial abandonment all *accelerated* in the 1970s and 1980s (Levine, 2002). If aggregate purchasing power were a crucial factor in investment or development decisions, the inner city should have been a much more "competitive" place in 1979 than it is today, and would have had even greater advantages over suburbs than it does presently. Levine goes on to note that advantages in density and aggregate purchasing power did not generate a surge in inner-city economic development in the 1970s nor in the 1980s, so why should those factors, all greatly reduced since the 1970s, result in a "competitive advantage" today? As Goozner (1998, p. 60) puts it in his trenchant critique of "market-driven" inner-city economic development: "If cities do have latent competitive advantages ... the market has spectacularly failed to grasp them in recent years."

The above debate and the history of decline show that urban brownfields redevelopment for industrial and employment-based activities faces considerable challenges, particularly in those inner-city areas where disinvestment has been particularly strong. The objective here is not to promote one form of economic development over the other, but to show how some cities have used brownfields as spaces for reindustrialization and re-employment despite the daunting obstacles faced. It also alludes to the barriers associated with raising the bar in terms of trying to promote more sustainable industrial development, even when traditional development seems hardly to be viable.

A Sustainable Vision for Industry

Devising a more sustainable vision for industry is particularly relevant given that it involves not only reusing and reindustrializing brownfield sites, but more importantly, ensuring that industrial practice is more environmentally sensitive and that it does not generate future brownfields. A basic sustainability goal is clearly the reuse of building and land resources for industrial purposes. Many of the benefits associated with such reuse have already been outlined in Chapters 2 and 3.

The more difficult problem consists in making industry more "environmentally friendly." Indeed, a theme surfacing continually in the field of environment and resource management is that industrial and environmental processes are basically incompatible. The debate between industrialists and environmentalists has often reached fever pitch levels, as logging industry lobbyists cry out for more liberal access to old-growth forests and manufacturing companies criticize the need for more stringent air pollution standards, among other similarly based complaints. Attempts to reconcile the two camps have resulted in the construction of various strategies. One of the more sustainability-oriented visions has been *industrial ecology* (IE), which gained momentum in the 1990s, but seems to have waned slightly over the last few years. Put simply, IE is an approach to investigating ways in which industrial systems can be made to operate more like natural ecosystem (i.e., how products, manufacturing processes, and industrial infrastructures can be designed to simulate natural processes) (Côté, 1996). Among its areas of interest are the processes underlying the production of raw materials, the management of air, liquid, and solid wastes, and the recycling of manufactured products (Graedel, 1994). Although many in the literature have reacted to IE as no more than yet another "environmentally friendly concept" that is bound to be "here today and gone tomorrow," it has nevertheless been receiving more attention, as both industrialists and environmentalists seek creative alternatives to the current status quo.

Since the early 1970s, more and more pressure has been placed on the entire industrial complex by governments and the general public alike to make the production of material goods less destructive to the natural environment. Large-scale environmental disasters in the 1980s — such as the Bhopal gas leak tragedy and the Chernobyl reactor meltdown — engendered in society an "apocalyptic" vision of the kinds of health and environmental impacts industry can have on the world if left unchecked. It has therefore become clear that both the emission of pollutants and the consumption of energy need to be reduced. It is not possible to go into an in-depth discussion here of all the impacts industry has had on the environment. Suffice it to say that three destructive global impacts have been amply documented over the last century. These are (Fischer & Schot, 1993, p. 4):

- An exponential increase in air, water, and soil pollution (e.g., between 1900 and 1980 sulfur oxides increased by 446% and nitrogen oxides by 900%).
- The release of deleterious organic compounds and production of radioactive materials that are highly toxic even in minute quantities and that persist in biological systems or in the atmosphere for many years.
- A gradual spreading of the impacts, from local contexts to the entire globe (e.g., global warming, acid rain, ozone depletion, etc.).

Given this predicament, it is not surprising that pressure on industry to become more ecologically sensitive has intensified. Moreover, this pressure is not only coming from the traditional sources (government, environmentalists, etc.), but also from within industry itself, as more and more manufacturers not only recognize the importance of preserving the environment, but also of becoming more efficient and cost-effective, so as to remain competitive with more environmentally sensitive companies (Porter & van der Linde, 1995; Williams, Medherst, & Drew, 1993).

Biological ecosystems are codependency systems within which different species coexist and cooperate for the benefit of all (Jelenski, Graedel, Laudise, McCall, & Patel, 1992, p. 793). So, by analogy, an *industrial ecosystem* is envisaged as being an industrial system within which different industries must learn to operate codependently to everyone's mutual benefit. Frosch and Gallopoulos (1989, p. 144) characterize such systems as follows:

> In a biological ecosystem, some of the organisms use sunlight, water, and minerals to grow, while others consume the first, alive or dead, along with the minerals and gases, and produce wastes of their own. These wastes are in turn food for other organisms, some of which may convert wastes into the minerals used by the primary producers, and some of which consume each other in a complex network of processes in which everything produced is used by some organism for its own metabolism. Similarly, in the industrial ecosystem, each process and network of processes must be viewed as a dependent and interrelated part of the larger whole.

Clearly, industrial ecosystems will work in ways that parallel biological ones only if they operate in a cyclical fashion, whereby one industry utilizes the waste materials, products, etc. of another as resource inputs, and then its own waste outputs are used subsequently as resource inputs by another industry, and so on. At present, industrial systems are hardly codependent. On the contrary, they tend to be isolated units whereby the flow of materials (energy, waste, etc.) from one stage of the cycle (i.e., harvester, manufacturer, consumer, waste processor) to the next is independent of other flows. Jelenski et al. (1992, p. 793) and Graedel (1994, p. 24) refer to this traditional form of manufacturing as a Type I industrial system. In concrete terms, a Type I company would typically take in a large supply of energy and raw material, and then use it to generate products along with extensive amounts of waste, oblivious to its effects on the ecosystem and without envisaging its use by other industrial units.

An IE system, however, would entail what Graedel (1994, p.25) refers to as either a more efficient Type II re-utilization system whereby energy and limited material inputs are repeatedly cycled within the "industrial ecosystem" by its members with much more limited amounts of waste being generated, or a fully integrated Type III system in which materials are recycled efficiently among the industrial components in the system. The ultimate goal of an IE system is to encourage flows both within the individual sectors themselves (i.e., the raw material extractors, the manufacturers, the consumers, and the waste processors) and among sectors within the entire IE system, in order to ensure that industrial operations are maximized and waste products reduced to a minimum.

The widespread installation of IEs throughout the world will require different levels of industry to become more codependent. Specifically, this implies that (i) at the intra-firm level, improvements in manufacturing processes must be envisaged within each firm; (ii) at the intra-sector level, companies within a sector must become more cooperative and interdependent; and (iii) at the inter-sector level, companies across the industrial spectrum must become more cooperative.

The first step toward implementing an IE system is to start at the "grass roots" by getting individual companies to improve their own production and recycling processes (intra-firm strategies). One way in which this can be achieved is to get a firm to follow more stringent environmental management standards. Perhaps the most well-known and widely adopted quality management standards are those created by the International Standards Organization — the ISO 14000. Engineering and management standards that any manufacturing company can adopt to make its own production processes more environmentally sensitive, these are based on the technique known as Total Quality Environmental Management (TQEM), a method for involving production workers in the improvement of product quality through incremental improvements in both products and processes. Quality management systems have been adopted by individual firms extensively in the past (to foster improvements in safety, to ensure product interchangeability, etc.), but only recently have these been used to promote environmental sensitivity.

Another intra-firm strategy often discussed in the literature is getting employees directly involved in converting their own company's production and technological processes into more environmentally friendly ones without compromising the company's economics. One employee-incentive program that has been reported as being extremely effective is the one initiated by Dow Chemical at its Louisiana division in 1981 (Hileman, 1992; Nelson, 1994). This program started by challenging employees to come up with ways for improving energy efficiency, and soon became so successful that it was expanded to include waste reduction. Indeed, soon after its initiation, the employee-devised projects were saving Dow Chemical over $110 million per year and having a significant impact on the company's overall energy use and waste production.

There is a difference, however, between the greening of industrial practice, which is the topic of discussion here, and green industries, which offer products, processes, and/or services aimed at preventing pollution and cleaning the environment. Given the demolition and cleanup actions taken at many brownfields districts, and the need for numerous environmental management services in cities, some have also proposed that firms possessing specialized scientific and technical expertise in the areas of water and wastewater treatment, solid and hazardous waste management, site remediation, energy conservation, air pollution control, recycling, and/or environmental monitoring are a good fit for brownfields. The rapid growth of this industry is a result of the growing market for green products and services both nationally and internationally (e.g., according to Industry Canada, 2004, the green industry market is valued at $29 billion in Canada with exports of $1.4 billion per year, the global market is valued at $800 billion).

The next step in getting an IE system into place is to encourage companies within an industrial sector to become more interdependent, seeking ways to collectively improve the production and recycling processes of the entire sector (intra-sector strategies). One intra-sector strategy that has become a central focus of the theoretical literature is the so-called Design for Environment (DFE). According to the DFE approach, a large firm within a sector is normally expected to be the one responsible for establishing an interdependence network among its suppliers. It is thus meant to entreat large manufacturing industries to re-examine their current approaches in terms of the environmental consequences associated with the lifecycle of their products, from the raw material stage to the final disposal one. Paton (1994, pp. 354–357) usefully summarizes the ways in which the different business processes can be made more environmentally friendly:

• Product design — reduced material storage, reuse, recyclability, better product definition, and product design reviews.
• Manufacturing process — selection of new process technology, selection of new equipment.
• Materials management — material selection (i.e., easier to recycle, contains recycled content, etc.), hazardous material elimination, and chemical use evaluation.
• Supplier management — technology partnerships (to exchange information on new products and/or technology), reuse or recycling relationships, and evaluation of suppliers.
• Order fulfillment — packaging, forecasting and inventory management, and distribution practices.
• Service and support — material sourcing for maintenance and repair, collection/ recycle/disposal systems.

Perhaps the best-known example of a DFE strategy in the US is the one adopted by the automobile industry. A classic DFE partnership, called the Vehicle Recycling Partnership, is the one established among Ford, Chrysler, and General Motors. These three companies agree, for example, to identify the plastic products they use by type (in order to facilitate their separation and recycling), to reduce the number of resins they use, to develop environmentally appropriate attachment and detachment techniques, and to improve the compatibility of auto parts (Klimisch, 1994). Many European automobile companies, such as Volvo, Volkswagen, BMW, and Mercedes Benz, have also introduced similar intra-sector programs with comparable success. Volvo, for instance, has adopted a life cycle analysis (LCA) strategy to determine the impacts of the different components and parts it uses to manufacture its vehicles from the initial raw material to the final disposal stages of a vehicle's life cycle.

The IE movement's ultimate goal, and the most relevant in terms of redeveloping industrial brownfield districts in a sustainable manner, is the creation of industrial systems whereby industries from different sectors enter into an integrated network of a *Type II* or *III* kind, often called an *industrial park*. As Ayres and Ayres (1996, p. 279) point out, "the industrialized analog of an ecosystem is an industrial park (or some larger region) which captures and recycles all physical materials internally, consuming only energy from outside the system, and producing only non material services for sale to consumers." But the barriers toward achieving inter-sector cooperation are immense. Indeed, such complex integrated systems are rare even in nature. Indeed, if total ecosystem integration had developed within the natural world, such things as fossil fuels, which are the waste products of animals and plant life from millions of years ago, would not have been possible. These waste remnants are proof that the natural ecological system is not totally integrated. Nevertheless, a more modest form of inter-sector cooperation is foreseeable, whereby the firms in different sectors can share input and output materials through the coordination efforts of a single raw materials processor, through the use of a waste recycler, etc. (Ayres & Ayres, 1996).

The most cited prototype of a successful inter-sector system is the one established by the Danish town of Kalundborg in the mid-1960s (Ayres & Ayres, 1996; Côté, 1996; Frosch & Gallopoulos, 1989). Industrialists and the town's municipal leaders devised a cooperative system, whereby industries across sectors use residual materials and energy in a cyclical regenerative fashion. The process was set in motion when the electric power plant of the town was modified so that it could provide heat energy to the local refiner. The plant was then modified further to deliver process steam to a pharmaceutical plant, heat to local greenhouses, and hot water to a fish farm and local homes. This created sufficient conditions for an inter-sector system of cooperation. Indeed, shortly thereafter sulfur gas removed from the refinery was re-routed to the power plant to reduce coal use; gypsum removed from the power plant by scrubbers was redirected to a gyproc plant to offset its need to import raw gypsum; and sludge from the pharmaceutical plant's operations, as well as the waste from the fish farm, were re-routed to the farmers in the region to be used as fertilizer supplements. Given its success, municipal officials in Kalundborg are currently seeking other ways to internalize the energy and waste flows of the area more efficiently.

In the late 1990s, eco-industrial parks (EIPs) emerged as an answer to the environmental problems generated by industry, given that they could be modeled in terms of "real world parks," attracting a significant amount of attention from policy-makers across the US and Canada. Moreover, answering the question of where to put EIPs in the US appeared obvious — EIPs would be plausible and sustainable ways to revitalize industrial brownfields districts. However, could such a model provide a sustainable "fix" to address deindustrialization and the various social, environmental, and economic problems associated with it? West (2007) identified 13 conceptual or functional EIPs proposed in the late 1990s in the US that matched the situation of urban brownfield redevelopment under IE tenets. These included projects in the following communities:

1. Londonderry, New Hampshire
2. Fairfield/Baltimore, Maryland
3. Alameda, California
4. Anacostia, Maryland

5. Berks County, Pennsylvania
6. Brownsville, Texas
7. Cape Charles, Virginia
8. Chattanooga (Smart Park), Tennessee
9. Intervale (Food Center), Vermont
10. Plattsburg (Plattsburg Airbase Redevelopment Corporation, PARC), New York
11. Red Hills (Eco-Plex), Mississippi
12. St. Croix (Renaissance), Virgin Islands
13. Trenton, New Jersey.

Unfortunately, as West (2007) found out, most of these projects failed to materialize — only the first three continue to pursue an eco-industrial mission, and even those involve watered-down versions. West suggests this outcome was not due to the presence of brownfield conditions at these sites, whose presence was actually beneficial because it made governments become more involved politically and financially in the projects. While in theory eco-industrial development maintains the potential to revitalize urban industrial areas in a manner most consistent with environmental, economic, and social sustainability, West (2007) notes that it remains to be seen whether its goals can be practically achieved in the US, since it cannot be demonstrated that the EIPs constitute a viable solution without garnering a verifiable commitment to the principles of IE from all stakeholders, a degree of flexibility among regulatory agencies, and an infinite supply of patience.

Despite its appeal, four key barriers have to be overcome to make the implementation of an EIP realizable:

- *Technical/economic barriers*: Namely, the high costs and technological difficulties involved in setting up the appropriate systems for the collection, transportation, and separation of materials over a wide network, particularly when they currently have access to relatively cheap raw materials and waste disposal facilities.
- *Information barriers*: At present, there is scarce information on the long-term costs associated with recycling certain materials, on what long-term financial implications are involved in adopting one material or other as the basic one, and on who is producing the materials.
- *Regulatory and liability barriers*: Many regulations are incompatible with the implementation of processes to recycle waste and energy that would be required by IE systems; for instance it is often in the best interest of the original producers of toxic material to dispose of it themselves rather than offer it as a raw material, simply because current laws make them liable for that material throughout its lifecycle, even if it is reused by other firms (although government agencies are seeking to change these laws).
- *Organizational and coordination barriers*: A major difficulty concerns the balancing of environmental and industrial factors in an integrated, efficient, and cost-effective manner; at the intra- and inter-sector levels the problem is even greater since it involves amalgamating separate, self-sufficient, units into an integrated cooperative network.

While the desirability of IE systems is evident, the challenges posed in implementing them are significant. It certainly would help if government and/or larger firms took the lead in implementing and then coordinating the IE system. It seems, clearly, that people are unwilling to allow for the necessary amount of time required for these systems to mature. However, the IE movement is far from dead. Indeed, as the global environment continues to deteriorate, it continues to present itself as a reasonable solution. The cases-in-point discussed here suggest, moreover, that the concept of IE can be made to be more attractive to industry and society at large, and that it can become an effective contributor to long-term sustainable development.

Office and Commercial Revitalization and Sustainability

Despite the decline in manufacturing in many urban centers, there is hope that retail and office development can make use of the vast supply of brownfields in a way that brings jobs and taxes back to the city. In addition to hiring local residents and increasing local income levels, other benefits associated with retail development include increasing proximity to goods and services, environmental and health benefits from being able to walk to these locations, and safety benefits from the increased presence of secure and legitimate business activity. Fitzgerald and Leigh (2002) point out that as the suburban retail market shows signs of being "tapped out," central cities and older suburbs may be the last frontier for big box and other retail development given the arguments put forward by Porter:

> The untapped potential of urban markets has begun to draw the attention of Big Box and other retailers to inner cities and inner ring suburbs. The US Department of Housing and Urban Development (1999) has identified large retail gaps existing in the nation's cities whereby cities do not capture adequate proportions of their own residents' buying power or that of visitors to them. This gap has developed because of the decades-long commercial and retail investment in suburban greenfields. As a consequence, inner cities and inner-ring suburbs are "understored."

The main challenge, however, is to ensure that the retail establishments are a good fit with the scale and design of the existing neighborhoods in which they locate and that environmental impacts (brought about by new acres of impervious parking) are also mitigated. Many central cities have the power to limit the square footage of such buildings and to employ design standards that promote more efficient buildings and more "pedestrian friendly" experiences. In addition to large-scale big-box stores (e.g., Home Depot, Wal-Mart) that can reuse large agglomerations of brownfield space, chain drugstores and other smaller retailers are also interested in central city locales, having reused smaller brownfields that were previously street corner gas stations or automotive repair shops.

Offices present another opportunity for brownfields redevelopment, both in terms of reusing industrial buildings and creating new space. Although the advance of telecommunications has reduced the need for businesses to remain in central districts and congested urban locales, there are still many attractions to being in or near the central city, given the psychological importance of face-to-face contact in the routines of a business and the agglomeration of built space. Brownfield rehab projects often make for fashionable spaces that attract architectural, advertising, and many other service firms. Furthermore, companies that want their own office building within or near the CBD will often construct a building "to-suit" on vacant brownfields property (see the Sigma Environmental case in Chapter 11). The problem, however, is how to attract such projects away from being located in greenfield areas and to ensure they are sustainable in their design.

A Sustainability Vision for Office and Retail Environments

Efforts to forge the link between sustainability and employment in both the US and Canada have focused largely on the buildings in which people work. The construction and operation of these buildings consumes tremendous amounts of natural resources while producing wastes and pollutants that contribute to environmental damage and may compromise the health and productivity of building occupants. In response, green buildings are being designed, constructed, and operated to boost environmental, economic, health, and productivity performance over that of conventional building. As discussed, the most widely accepted standard for green building in the US, and increasingly in Canada, is the voluntary Leadership in Energy and Environmental Design (LEED) rating system developed by the US Green Building Council (USGBC), which is a nonprofit organization that was incorporated in 1993 with the primary goal of creating a sustainability rating system. After a sequence of starts and stops, the USGBC membership approved LEED Version 1.0 in late 1998. As discussed in Chapter 2, LEED promotes a whole-building approach to sustainability by assessing performance in five key areas: (i) sustainable site development; (ii) water savings; (iii) energy efficiency; (iv) materials selection; and (v) indoor environmental quality. Although the initial program focused on the new construction of commercial buildings, numerous programs have since been developed, including:

- New Commercial Construction and Major Renovation projects;
- Existing Building Operations and Maintenance;
- Commercial Interiors projects;
- Core and Shell Development projects;
- Homes;
- Neighborhood Development; and
- Guidelines for Multiple Buildings and On-Campus Building projects.

The USGBC is also developing LEED for Schools, LEED Retail for New Construction, LEED for Commercial Interiors, and LEED for Health care. The promotion of green building by the USGBC and other related programs is based on the extensive sustainability benefits such programs can bring about. The USGBC (2005a) summarizes the main benefits:

- Environmental benefits — reduce the impacts of natural resource consumption.
- Economic benefits — improve the bottom line.
- Health and safety benefits — enhance occupant comfort and health.
- Community benefits — minimize strain on local infrastructures and improve quality of life.

The economic benefits are particularly significant, given that green buildings are often perceived as costing more than conventional structures. The USGBC (2003) reports that while many green buildings can be constructed at comparable or lower cost than conventional buildings, integration of high-performance features can increase initial costs from an average of 2–7% depending on the design and extent of added features. Although some of these features can be recouped in a relatively short period, decision-makers rarely use life cycle cost analysis to account for reduced operating expenses or other economic benefits. Green building can lower infrastructure and materials costs, more energy-efficient building envelopes can reduce equipment needs (e.g., chillers, HVAC), using pervious pavement can limit stormwater management costs, and energy and water efficiency can lower utility costs. In addition, green building can increase the value of buildings themselves, as well as decrease vacancy, improve retention, enhance marketing, and reduce liability.

While benefits to buildings are important, those related to improved occupant performance are often considered to be even more valuable to corporations since workers constitute by far the largest expense for most companies (for offices, salaries are 72 times higher than energy costs, and they account for 92% of the life cycle cost of a building). Studies have shown that students perform better in green school buildings and that employees in buildings with healthy interiors have less absenteeism and tend to stay in their jobs (USGBC, 2005a). The ING Bank headquarters in Amsterdam, for instance, uses only 10% of the energy levels of its predecessor, cutting worker absenteeism by 15%, with a savings of US $3.4 million per year (Roodman & Lenssen, 1995).

Brownfields-to-Industrial-and-Commercial Reuse

The focus of brownfields research since the mid-1990s has concentrated on a range of issues and measures aimed at the economic development of these sites. In general, this has included envisioning approaches for identifying the scale of the problem (Colten, 1990; Simons, 1999), identifying barriers to redevelopment and devising and testing policies aimed at reducing them (Meyer, Williams, & Yount, 1995; Page, 1997; Rogoff, 1997; De Sousa, 2001; Leigh, 1994; Bartsch & Dorfman, 2000;

Simons & El Jaouhari, 2001); understanding private sector redevelopment efforts (Meyer & Lyons, 2000; Howland, 2003); and formulating optimal practices for guiding economic development (Iannone, 1996; Bartsch, 1996; Simons, 1998; De Sousa, 2000; Fitzgerald & Leigh, 2002). While the results of this research have already informed much of the discussion throughout this book, it is useful to briefly highlight and restate some key research themes and contributions, particularly as they relate to industrial and commercial reuse.

Economic development research has always been concerned with why such development is necessary. The main arguments for "putting brownfields back to work" relate to the need for a healthy, multi-sector economy that provides living-wage employment for members of society in a manner that promotes long-term sustainability. The author's own research and that by Persky and Wiewel (1996) point to a broad array of public-oriented benefits associated with keeping jobs on brownfields, as opposed to greenfields (see Chapter 3). It would also be remiss not to note that in analyzing the impacts of land uses, the notion that some types of land use are better fiscally than others has become widely accepted. Indeed, Burchell's (1998, p. 56) well-known table illustrating the hierarchy of land uses based on fiscal impacts (i.e., service-costs versus tax-revenues) clearly reveals that non-residential land uses, for the most part, have been shown to be more profitable, and thus more desirable, than residential ones (Table 10.1).

Much of the early literature on the economic development of brownfields focused on the barriers to redevelopment and how these could be overcome. Various early

Table 10.1: A hierarchy of land uses and fiscal impacts.

(+) Municipal break-even	• Research office parks • Office parks • Industrial development • High-rise/garden apartments (studio/1 bedroom) • Age-restricted housing • Garden condominiums (1–2 bedrooms) • Open space
(+) School district break-even	• Retail facilities • Townhouses (2–3 bedrooms) • Expensive single-family homes (3–4 bedrooms)
(−)	• Townhouses (3–4 bedrooms) • Inexpensive single-family homes (3–4 bedrooms) • Garden apartments (3+ bedrooms) • Mobile homes

Source: Adapted from Burchell et al. (1998).

publications, such as those by Bartsch (1996) and Simons (1998), found that despite their strategic location, brownfields were not being developed due to difficulties in site assembly, inadequate transportation access, negative perceptions of the area related to crime, a poor labor force, uncertainty over demand, liability, and the relative costs of brownfields versus greenfields projects. These and other works of the same period (Leigh, 1994; Meyer et al., 1995; Iannone, 1996; Page, 1997; Pepper, 1997) put forward an agenda aiming to overcome these barriers that has guided regulatory and financing efforts ever since. It is important to note that at this time, the prospects for brownfield redevelopment seemed grim. In her important early work comparing brownfield case studies, Pepper (1997, pp. 33–34) summed up the difficult, but hopeful, situation as follows:

> Although the projects profiled in Lessons from the Field differ markedly, several overarching conclusions have emerged. The most important finding is that brownfield cleanup and redevelopment often are not viable without public-sector intervention to alleviate conditions of "uncertainty" surrounding liability, cleanup standards, or regulatory requirements. The case studies reveal that, where government agencies have made a concerted effort to reduce grey areas through legislation or issuance of guidance, more projects are moving forward with fewer complications. Equally important is the public sector's role in bridging financing gaps — a need stemming from the fact that private-sector entities often do not view brownfield initiatives as attractive or viable investments .... Also key are institutional or organizational factors — such as the presence of a local government agency dedicated to brownfield reuse, strong project leadership, or coordination among different government agencies — that ensure brownfield redevelopment occurs in a timely and cost-effective manner. These "soft factors," which can be difficult to pinpoint, frequently make or break a project.

As described throughout this book, the implementation of regulatory policies and financing mechanisms proposed by Pepper and others to deal with the costs and risks facing brownfields have resulted in a rapid increase in brownfields redevelopment for employment-based uses. More recent research has found that industrial and commercial redevelopment is also being undertaken via the market in the absence of financial support from government, and that the market is adjusting to costs and risks accordingly. Indeed, Howland (2000) found that in Baltimore, documented land contamination did not deter buyers from purchasing land and that land purchases and redevelopment were occurring on larger parcels, where sellers were willing to lower their price to compensate for costs associated with the site. In her 2004 study, Howland also found that parcels with known contamination were being discounted compared to clean properties and suggested that more significant barriers to the revitalization included incompatible land uses, obsolete roads, inadequate infrastructure, and obsolete buildings. Furthermore, Meyer and Lyons (2000) documented the emergence of firms operating throughout the US that are redeveloping brownfields without public intervention, and not just for housing as discussed in Chapter 5.

Conclusion

The forces of deindustrialization and the urban problems it has left in its wake have challenged efforts to put brownfields back to work. That said, manufacturing, in particular, is still considered by many to be the hub of an economy and an optimal use for brownfields because it generates jobs, taxes, and is often the land use already zoned in place. The first part of this chapter described the causes and consequences of deindustrialization according to different schools of thought to stress the obstacles that reindustrialization efforts are up against. Indeed, many offer little hope for reindustrializing the urban core. Some, however, see competitive advantages in inner cities and opportunities for growth in the shift of manufacturing to more streamlined, connected, and time-based models. It is also felt that governments can also pave the way by improving infrastructure, streamlining planning and development, supporting entrepreneurship, reducing industrial taxes, managing traffic congestion, and making industrial brownfield districts more attractive.

To add to the challenge, the chapter also explains how industry can become more sustainable through intra-firm, intra-sector, and inter-sector strategies that incorporate best management practices, as well as location and design features. The ultimate goal would be the creation of industrial parks on brownfields that act as ecosystems whereby the firms in the park share input and output materials to minimize raw materials coming in and waste going out. Early efforts to replicate the success achieved in Kalundborg, Denmark in both the US and Canada have, unfortunately, met with limited success; although many intra-firm and inter-sector ventures seem to be gaining ground. Forging the link between sustainability and employment is also starting to focus on the buildings in which people work in an effort to boost environmental, economic, health, and productivity performance over that of conventional building.

The need for a healthy, multi-sector economy that provides living-wage employment for members of society in a manner that promotes long-term economic sustainability is essential. Research has revealed that brownfield cleanup and redevelopment are often not viable without public-sector intervention to alleviate conditions of uncertainty surrounding liability, cleanup standards, or regulatory requirements. While the re-orientation of the market to deal with industrial brownfields in some places is positive, it has brought with it another quandary facing many brownfield districts — namely, how do we enhance and retain industrial and other employment-uses versus allowing the market to operate freely and redevelop brownfields to their "highest-and-best" use (i.e., the most profitable according to the market). Accordingly, it is argued in the next chapter that public intervention in the market continues to be needed to support the retention and expansion of these employment-oriented uses on brownfields (particularly in a sustainability-oriented fashion) if we wish to balance the live, work, and play requirements of the sustainable city.

Chapter 11

Brownfields to Work: Trends, Efforts, and Case Studies

While early brownfields redevelopment efforts focused primarily on bringing industry back to affected areas, the industrial reuse of brownfields as a percentage of total brownfields redevelopment is small. Indeed the survey of 244 cities by the United States Conference of Mayors (2003) locates light manufacturing in the miscellaneous category along with green space, schools, parking, and transportation. Commercial (25%) and retail (23%) uses, on the other hand, make up primary end uses in those US cities. In communities with a strong manufacturing tradition, such as Milwaukee County, the reindustrialization of brownfileds still constitutes a popular end use (19%), while office (31%) and retail (12%) projects are also significant.

Industrial redevelopment on brownfields has been rather paltry in Canadian cities, where a review of seven large cities shows that it only accounted for 2% of redevelopment activity. While residential was the primary reuse (47%), this was followed by retail (20%) and commercial/office (16%) activity. In the City of Toronto, the author's own research shows that commercial floor space development in the 1990s represented 31% of the total floor space change on brownfields, well behind residential statistics (De Sousa, 2002a, 2002b). Larger commercial projects in that city were concentrated closer to the central business district in the southwestern part of the city, while smaller commercial projects were scattered throughout the city.

As discussed in the previous chapter, there has been a good deal of research on reindustrialization and bringing employment back to brownfield areas conducted by professional and scholarly researchers. While much of the author's own research has focused on other alternative uses, reindustrialization and other employment-oriented efforts are strongly supported because of the extensive public benefits that a healthy and multi-sector economy brings about. The programs and case studies described below not only bring jobs back to brownfields, but do so in a manner that seeks to contribute to sustainable urban development. This chapter examines efforts being undertaken in Chicago, Illinois, Hamilton, Ontario, Minneapolis, Minnesota, and Milwaukee, Wisconsin to bring manufacturing and other employment uses back to brownfields, and to move these projects toward sustainability.

Chicago's Reindustrialization Efforts

With just under 100,000 manufacturing employees, the City of Chicago is the nation's number one manufacturing center in terms of employment and gross regional product (City of Chicago, 2003; City of Chicago, 2006a). The city has an extensive inventory of industrial space (192 million square feet, $17,837,000 \, m^2$) located throughout the urban area (City of Chicago, 2006b). In an effort to create and retain industrial jobs, the city has developed and implemented an array of strategies. Fitzgerald and Leigh (2002) summarize these as follows:

(i) *Brownfields initiative*: City initiative to address physical, legal, and other impediments to assembling and improving brownfield property for redevelopment.
(ii) *Planned manufacturing districts*: Areas delineated by the city with strict manufacturing zoning that prevents encroachment of competing uses.
(iii) *Tax increment financing districts*: Designated blighted areas to which the city seeks to attract investment by returning tax revenue generated through development above the original assessed value for improvements in the area.
(iv) *Local industrial retention initiative*: Areas in which community organizations are designated to act as liaisons between firms and city.
(v) *Industrial corridors*: Currently 24 industrial corridors with defined geographic boundaries and unique identities.
(vi) *Industrial parks*: Industrial parks developed by the city with updated services and infrastructure, as well as subsidies.

The first three of these are discussed here because they have proven to be very effective for redeveloping brownfields districts — Fitzgerald and Leigh (2002) provide a more comprehensive discussion of all strategies.

The Brownfields Initiative was initially developed to focus on industrial and economic redevelopment, job creation, and tax revenues while addressing environmental problems throughout the city. An interdepartmental team of project managers from the Mayor's Office and the city departments of Environment, Planning and Development, Law, and the Office of Management and Budget guided the initiative. Given a broadening of its mission to include housing, open space, and other urban issues, this has since expanded to include other departments. The initiative's basic aim has been to level the playing field between the development of brownfields and clean space in the city, as well as greenfields in the periphery. The program commenced in the early 1990s by investing US$2 million from General Obligation Bonds to redevelop five brownfield properties. Considered a quick success, creating 239 jobs, retaining another 950 jobs and producing over US$337,000 in annual tax revenues, this "Brownfields Pilot" raised interest in redeveloping brownfields generally and helped leverage funds from federal agencies to continue to support the brownfields programs.

An important component of the initiative early on was the Chicago Brownfields Forum, a brainstorming event that the city hosted in 1994. This forum allowed representatives from government, business, finance, environment, community, academic, and civic organizations to discuss legal, financial, and ethical issues related to urban disinvestments. The Forum generated a list of recommended actions to facilitate brownfields cleanup and redevelopment that both formed a model for Chicago and was also replicated by other cities in the US and Canada (Chicago Brownfield's Forum, 1995). The Chicago program provides another example of how multi-departmental planning and the multi-stakeholder interaction was necessary early on to get a grasp of the problems posed by urban brownfields and the measures needed to address it.

As part of the Chicago initiative, brownfields are assessed on the basis of accessibility, cleanup costs, and development value. If a brownfield is deemed to have industrial, commercial, or residential development potential, the city can acquire the site through negotiated purchase, lien foreclosure, or tax reactivation on property. Once the site is assessed, the city may choose to add the property to its "investment portfolio" of acquired sites. After the initial review, a risk assessment is performed if warranted, and cleanup strategies and cost estimates are determined. The city devotes most of its funds to assessing sites so that those not requiring cleanup can be quickly put on the market. The city enrolls nearly all of its sites that require cleanup into the Illinois EPA (IEPA) Site Remediation Program, a voluntary cleanup program that sets out investigation and cleanup guidelines based on end use. On successful completion of the program, the IEPA issues a "No Further Remediation" (NFR) letter stating that cleanup is satisfactory and that the owner has no additional responsibility.

Another important program supporting brownfields redevelopment in Chicago has been its Tax Increment Financing (TIF) Program, which is considered to be the most extensive in the US. A funding tool used to promote private investment in blighted sections of the city, TIFs gained popularity in the 1980s as federal funds for urban economic development declined. TIF funds are generated by growth in the so-called Equalized Assessed Valuation (EAV) of properties within a designated district over a period of 23 years. When an area is declared a TIF district, the amount of property tax the area generates is set as a base EAV amount. As property values increase, all property tax growth above that amount can be used to fund redevelopment projects within the district. The increase, or increment, can be used to pay back bonds issued to pay for upfront costs, or it can be used on a pay-as-you-go basis for individual projects. At the conclusion of the 23-year period, the increase in revenue over the base amount is distributed annually among the seven taxing bodies in the city that are based on property values.

TIF funds are generally used to build and repair roads and infrastructure, clean polluted land, and put vacant properties back into productive use, usually in conjunction with private development projects. More recently, the TIF Works program was introduced allowing businesses located within Chicago's TIF districts to use TIF funds for workforce development activities, such as customized training, English-as-a-second-language instruction, and industry-specific instruction related to regulatory compliance. TIF assistance for eligible projects usually exceeds US$1 million.

Under Illinois state law, areas proposed for TIF designation must possess several "blighting" factors to be eligible for support. These relate to age, obsolescence, code violations, excessive vacancies, overcrowding, inadequate/dilapidated utilities and conditions, deleterious land use, or lack of physical maintenance and community planning. Those receiving TIF funds (as well as other city funds) are now also required to include various public assets in their development, such as affordable housing and green building. Industrial projects receiving TIF funds must incorporate 10% green roof or Energy Star roof and be a Local Economic and Employment Development- (LEED) certified building. Retail projects over 10,000 sq ft (930 m^2) require 75% green roof or 50% green roof and LEED-certified building, while retail under 10,000 sq ft require 25% green roof or LEED certified building. Office projects over 80 ft require 100% green roof, while office projects under 80 ft require 50% green roof or Energy Star roof and LEED-certified building.

Chicago's efforts to deal with underutilized industrial districts through its Planned Manufacturing District (PMD) program have also received considerable interest from those engaged in industrial retention. Put simply, a PMD is established to prevent competing land uses, specifically residential and commercial, from encroaching on manufacturing areas and undermining their long-term viability. Although the PMD replaces zoning on land already zoned for manufacturing, it creates an industrial area in which land use is specifically defined and uncontestable (Fitzgerald & Leigh, 2002). While zoning codes in many cities are contestable on a plot-by-plot basis, zoning within a PMD can only be changed with a majority vote by city council. This prevents "higher and better" uses from picking these areas apart site-by-site and utilizing a "death by a thousand cuts" strategy to destroy a viable manufacturing zone.

Furthermore, Fitzgerald and Leigh (2002, p. 109) note "in enacting enabling legislation for a PMD, a city makes the statement that the public benefits from manufacturing uses supersede the public benefits of competing uses." PMDs were established, in large part, to retain and create well-paying jobs for the benefit of city residents. In rapidly gentrifying areas in Chicago, such as the Clybourn Corridor and Goose Island, PMDs represented a trade-off whereby the city willingly forgoes the higher property tax revenues possible through rezoning these areas for residential or retail development in order to create and preserve industrial job opportunities. How well PMDs have performed in fostering manufacturing employment is thus an important criterion in evaluating their importance more generally (Rast, 2005).

The origins of Chicago's PMDs date back to the mid-1980s, when industrial displacement was first identified as a concern in the city's North River Industrial Corridor located along the north branch of the Chicago River (Rast, 2005). The LEED Council, a Near North Side community development corporation affiliated with the YMCA, had been working with area manufacturers to increase the hiring of local residents. Through these efforts, the council discovered that gentrification in the surrounding neighborhoods of Lincoln Park and River North was beginning to threaten the viability of the industrial area. Piecemeal zoning changes allowing residential and retail development on former industrial property began to introduce land uses incompatible with heavy industry. Real estate speculation increased and manufacturers became hesitant to invest in the area as its future viability as an industrial district was increasingly called into question (Rast, 2005).

In 1986, a PMD for the so-called "Clybourn Corridor" portion of the North River Industrial Corridor was created. In 1990, the Goose Island and Elston Corridor PMDs were established nearby. Although efforts by the city to create PMDs subsided during the 1990s, when only two additional PMDs were established, the city became proactive again and created 8 in 2004/2005, bringing the city's total to 13 (Rast, 2005).

A good example of a typical PMD story is Goose Island — the only large plot of land in the city entirely surrounded by water. While initially a dense residential area, it was the island's navigable waterways that first spurred its development as an industrial corridor in the 1920s (although its proximity and access to downtown are considered the prime assets for industry today). As with other industrial areas in the city, Goose Island was affected by industrial restructuring in the 1970s and 1980s. This was exacerbated by a rapidly changing near north side, which was experiencing significant industrial displacement due to residential and commercial reinvestment that created land use uncertainty on Goose Island (City of Chicago, 1991). Although many companies remained on the site, 37% of the land was vacant by the late 1980s and fears followed the zoning of a 3-acre (1.2 ha) property for river lofts in 1987.

The New City YMCA's LEED council pushed hard for PMD designation. It convened a task force in 1989 that comprised of industrial developers, Goose Island businesses, staff of the economic development commission, and other neighborhood groups to study the implication of changing land use. The ensuing study (LEED Council, 1990) provided a technical economic and revenue impact analysis of several different land use scenarios and demonstrated that "sustaining industrial uses on Goose Island will benefit Chicago more than any other use and that allowing infringement by residential and retail uses would cause irretrievable loss to the city's economy." Their particular concern, however, was the thousands of jobs in and near the island that were at risk.

Arguments such as these led to the area's PMD designation in 1990. A plan for industry was then developed for the 146-acre (59 ha) site that set aside $30 million for infrastructure investment. By 2002, US$76 million in public funds had been invested in the area and were responsible for leveraging US$129 million in private investments. Indeed, the LEED Council (2003) notes that in 1991, 14 companies employed 1,076 people on Goose Island and by June 2002, 36 companies employed 5,000 people. More comprehensive data compiled by Dun and Bradstreet and provided by the LEED Council (2006) shows that while the number of businesses involved in manufacturing did not increase from 1991 (7 businesses) to 2004 (7), Services and Wholesale trade industries that are compatible with manufacturing grew significantly (8 and 12 businesses in 1991 to 27 and 19 in 2004, respectively). One early industrial success story was Republic Windows and Doors, which built a US$35 million, 375,000 sq ft (34,800 m^2) manufacturing facility on 15 acres of the Island that employs approximately 700 people, 90% of whom reside in Chicago (Figure 11.1).

Recent research on Chicago's oldest PMDs (Clybourn Corridor, Goose Island, and Elston Corridor) by Rast (2005) also found that these areas have experienced impressive growth in businesses and jobs from 1988 to 2004, but that much of this

Figure 11.1: Goose Island, Republic Windows and Doors Facility (courtesy of the LEED Council, 2006).

growth came in sectors besides manufacturing. He found manufacturing represented just 29% of all employment in the three PMDs by 2004, leading him to argue that "the term Planned Manufacturing District has become something of a misnomer," and that "a worker on Goose Island today is more likely to be employed in a warehouse than in an industrial firm." The study highlights how concerns about the declining share of manufacturing jobs in the PMDs are tempered somewhat by the revival of manufacturing in those PMDs between 2000 and 2004 when both manufacturing jobs and manufacturing businesses increased, even as manufacturing in the City of Chicago as a whole declined. Further studies should examine the issue from a wage perspective given that the light assembly jobs that have replaced the heavy manufacturing jobs may not be as well paid. At the same time, research should also assess whether wages in other sectors are comparable to manufacturing.

Rast notes that a healthy PMD requires a combination of careful planning, support by stakeholders, and a strong and perceptible commitment from the city. If any one of these conditions is absent, a PMD is likely to encounter problems because the security to make long-term investments is just not there and real estate speculation will increase. He finds that the Clybourn Corridor, Goose Island, and Elston Corridor PMDs have successfully weathered opposition due, in part, to being developed through a broad-based community planning process. As the planning process moved forward, manufacturers gradually came to view the PMDs as their initiative. Indeed, for several of the companies Rast interviewed, this sense of ownership remains palpable today and while support for the PMDs among manufacturers is not unanimous, those arguing for the dismantling of the PMDs are clearly in the minority.

Chicago's Center for Green Technology

An excellent example of green brownfield redevelopment is the Center for Green Technology in Chicago. Located just two miles from Goose Island, the building was originally constructed in 1952 and since then has had a number of different owners. When it came to the attention of the city in 1995, a crushing company that owned the property had gone far beyond its permit, filling in all 17 acres of the site with illegally dumped debris that reached up to 70 ft (21 m) high. The city took the company to court, closed down their operation, and became the new owner. The cleanup took 18 months to complete and cost US$9 million dollars.

By 1999, the City of Chicago was the proud owner of a cleaned site and vacant building. Rather than simply renovating the building using traditional methods, it created an energy-efficient building using the highest standards of green technology available. Environmental features of the building include solar panels, rainwater collection for irrigation, recycled building materials, smart lighting, a green roof, and a geothermal exchange system. The building is the first municipal building in the US to receive Platinum LEED rating. A team of local architects designed the building using guidelines established by the US Green Building Council and, to match the vision of the building, the city originally selected tenants that were environmentally focused, including Greencorps Chicago, the city's community landscaping and job training program; Spire Solar, a manufacturer of photovoltaic panels; and WRD Environmental, an urban landscape design/build firm (Spire Solar recently moved its operations). The building is now one of the top-rated green buildings in the US and provides a "model" of sustainability in the center of what was considered an old, derelict brownfield district (Figure 11.2).

The Chicago Department of Environment now offers guided and self-guided tours of the building and grounds, as well as a variety of free educational programs for both professionals and the public. These programs relate to architecture, building, and construction management, do-it-yourself greening, engineering, green business, interior design, and landscape design.

Hamilton, Ontario's ERASE Program

Hamilton is one of the oldest and most heavily industrialized cities in Canada, well known for its steel industry. It is a relatively large city (population 500,000) with a moderate real estate market. The combination of structural changes and deindustrialization during the 1970s resulted in the decline of the steel industries, which have left behind numerous brownfields, particularly in the old industrial core

Figure 11.2: Students learn about the Center's green building features.

where several hundred sites lie vacant and account for over CDN$10 million in unpaid taxes (Piccioni, 2003).

In 1997, the city established a multi-stakeholder *Industrial Redevelopment Task Force* to identify barriers to brownfield redevelopment and to formulate a management plan that would promote industrial redevelopment, as well as other end uses. Research and consultation exercises resulted in the drafting of an *Environmental Remediation and Site Enhancement* (ERASE) *Community Improvement Plan* in 1999, approved by the province of Ontario in 2001 after extensive consultation. The plan was the first of its kind in Canada. To overcome the tight provincial restrictions on municipal support for private redevelopment, the city employed a rarely used section of the Ontario Planning Act allowing municipalities to financially assist those rehabilitating lands and buildings within a designated Community Improvement Area (in this case Hamilton's old industrial area).

Properties within the ERASE Community Improvement Project Area are eligible for the programs, subject to meeting the program requirements contained in the ERASE Plan and all other requirements of the city. The programs include:

(i) *The ERASE Redevelopment Grant Program* provides annual grants to the owner for up to 10 years to pay for remediation and other eligible costs (e.g., demolition, site preparation); using a tax-increment financing approach, the grant equals 80% of the municipal portion of the increase in property taxes that result after redevelopment takes place.

(ii) *The ERASE Study Grant Program* provides matching grants from the city to landowners or purchasers to pay for up to one-half the cost of a Phase II and/or a Phase III Environmental Site Assessments; the maximum city contribution per study is $15,000 to a maximum of two studies and $20,000 per property.

(iii) *ERASE Development Charge Reduction Program*, a planning and development fees program that provides a rebate on planning and development fees.

(iv) *A Redevelopment Opportunities Marketing/Database Program*, whereby city staff inform, educate, and market the ERASE program.

(v) *ERASE Municipal Acquisition and Partnership Program* provides a *Brownfield Reserve Fund* (using a 20% portion of municipal taxes leveraged by the ERASE Grant program) to promote public/private partnerships for pilot projects that can showcase the use of innovative tools such as new environmental remediation technologies.

(vi) *ERASE Tax Assistance Program* provides a financial incentive in the form of a freeze or cancellation of part of the educational tax portion on a brownfield property; the Province of Ontario may match the municipal tax treatment for the education portion of the property tax that results from remediation and rehabilitation of the property and is paid on annual basis for up to three years, commencing once the redevelopment is complete (City of Hamilton, 2006).

Hamilton's economic development-oriented approach is similar to that employed by many US cities, but without the financial support from upper levels of government. It focuses primarily on industrial reuse aimed at bringing employment back into its older industrial areas; at facilitating this process by providing information on the condition of sites and on financial options available to developers; and by actively acquiring, investing, and partnering with brownfield projects. As of 2003, the ERASE program had resulted in the cleanup of 11.3 acres of land, the construction/refurbishing of 228,000 sq ft (21,200 m^2) of building space, and six major redevelopment projects (one industrial, two commercial, one residential, one institutional, and one open space). The city's investment of approximately CDN$1 million had leveraged $15 million in private sector investment and $400,000 in increased property taxes, although it had limited success in fostering reindustrialization (Piccioni, 2003).

An early example of an industrial warehouse project in Hamilton is the construction of a 186,000 sq ft (17,300 m^2) building that is home to Zyplex (a subsidiary of the Defasco steel company) which makes lightweight steel skin composites used primarily as a liner for the inside of trucks. The project developed by JNE Consulting replaced a vacant and obsolete industrial building with a state of the art industrial warehouse with high ceilings and modern crane bays to be used primarily for steel storage. Cleanup involved the demolition of the old building and infrastructure. Under the ERASE Program, the city provided a CDN$1 million Redevelopment Grant over 10 years. This grant leveraged a CDN$14 million project and increased fivefold the site's assessed value. The grant covered the costs of demolishing the old industrial building and replacing old sewer and water lines. The grant will be paid by the City of Hamilton to the owner from the increase in taxes on the site.

The Green Institute, Minneapolis

Founded in 1993, The Green Institute (2006) was created by the residents of the Phillips neighborhood of Minneapolis, Minnesota. The group formed in response to a proposed garbage transfer station, which was to be built in the middle of their community. After 12 years of community activism, the group finally won their battle and defeated plans for the station. After this victory, members of the neighborhood opposition group organized in order to ensure the rights of other communities in opposition to unwanted operations. This local battle for environmental justice spawned the group that today works toward creating sustainable and green developments. The Green Institute is a nonprofit organization that continues to lead communities toward their goal of environmental justice through community activism, with a commitment to community rights continuing to be of top priority for the group.

One high priority goal of The Green Institute is the reduction of waste. The Project's programs include economic development opportunities, such as The ReUse Center, founded in 1995 in order to sell salvaged, reusable materials for new building projects. A related business, Deconstruction Services, was established in 1997 to supply the ReUse Center with salvaged building materials. Together, these two businesses generate in excess of US$1 million dollars per year and employ local residents for their operations. The efforts of The Green Institute and its operations have also reduced the amount of waste going into landfills.

Another example of The Green Institute's commitment to sustainable development is The Phillips Eco-Enterprise Center. Constructed using ReUse products, this building features many aspects of The Green Institute's vision for future development. The high-tech building measures 64,000 sq ft (5,900 m^2), and is home to 14 energy and environmental sector nonprofit tenants. The green building design combines the Project's vision of occupant health, green building materials, green space, water conservation, energy efficiency, and the use of renewable energy. The Project also used Innovative Power Systems to design and install one of the largest solar electric systems in the Midwest.

The Green Institute sees the challenges faced in constructing this building as a learning experience that will allow them to better advise developers looking for green building opportunities. The project's greatest challenges were scheduling the installation of salvaged materials and receiving approval on innovative products and systems. By setting precedent in the movement toward sustainable green development, The Green Institute has paved the way for future projects that involve green methods in Minneapolis.

Another project of interest is the Community Energy Program — a program committed to developing distributed clean and local energy systems. Using the supply side of the energy delivery system, the group works toward the generation of solar energy as well as biomass heat and power. This project also works on the demand side of the energy delivery system by establishing conservation and efficient means of energy use. This concerted effort in both conservation and supply has resulted in the sustainability of the Phillips Eco Enterprise Center and the possibility of making the transition from brownfield to green much smoother.

Milwaukee's Menomonee Valley Redevelopment

As an urban area in the "Rustbelt," the City of Milwaukee has an extensive brownfields inventory resulting from its industrial past. To attract investment, the city and other levels of government in Wisconsin have been very active since the mid-1990s in implementing a variety of policies and programs designed to lessen the costs and risks associated with brownfield redevelopment. Many of these have garnered widespread support from both public and private sector stakeholders.

Of particular interest has been the redevelopment of Milwaukee's Menomonee Valley, once the heart of the state's economy and now the state's largest brownfields district. The Menomonee Valley, located southwest of Downtown Milwaukee, has always had an important influence on the social and economic life of the Milwaukee region. Its trails, fish, and waterfowl provided the necessities of daily life to the indigenous Potawatomi tribe. As European settlement increased in the late 1800s, the Valley's accessibility to railways, Lake Michigan, and local river systems made it a prime location for industrial activity. In 1869, a group of business leaders supported by local authorities planned a network of canals and slips in the Valley surrounded by parcels of land for industrial use. The project took barely a decade to complete, even though it required vast quantities of material to fill the marsh, including dredge spoil, gravel, and municipal and industrial wastes. As the noted Milwaukee historian John Gurda (1999, p. 126) aptly observed, "lumber yards, coal yards and sash, and door factories sprouted in the eastern end of the Valley even before the muck was dry."

Larger industrial complexes, including tanneries, breweries, stockyards, and railroad shops dotted the entire Valley by the late 1800s (Figure 11.3). The transformation of the Valley from a natural ecological system to an industrialized one is the feature that has most epitomized Milwaukee's evolution. To quote an 1882 newspaper article (Sentinel, August 18, 1882, cited in Gurda, 1999, p. 128):

> Nothing, perhaps, more strikingly exhibits the rapidity and solidarity of Milwaukee's growth than the march of improvement in the Menomonee Valley. The bogs and marshes in that locality are being converted into firm ground, and the waters which formerly spread themselves thinly over a large surface are being confined to

Figure 11.3: Menomonee Valley Shops Property over time (Photos courtesy of Menomonee Valley Partners).

an artificial channel and made navigable for great ships. The vast tract, which but a few years ago was the home of the wild duck and the resort of the sportsman with his gun, is now partially converted, and soon will be entirely so, to the seat of manufacturing and commercial enterprises, which take rank among the first of their kind in the entire Northwest.

By the end of the nineteenth century, residential communities had spread extensively along the Valley's bluffs, producing some of the most densely populated neighborhoods in the State of Wisconsin. Industry prospered and expanded well into the 1920s, despite problematic labor movements and prohibition. Only the Great Depression of the 1930s was able to curtail the Valley's industrial growth, but growth picked up dramatically with the onset of World War II in response to wartime needs.

Menomonee Valley's industrial growth, and its crucial role in Milwaukee's economy, began to decline in the decades following World War II. Construction of interstate highways made it possible for people to live further away from their place of work and for industry to ship goods via highway, leading to a reduction in use of the Valley's railways and waterways. By the 1970s, the Valley suffered the same fate as other urban industrial centers in the so-called rustbelt — it saw an exodus of industry to the suburbs and to other countries in search of more space, less regulation, and lower wages (McMahon, Moots, & White, 1992). According to White, Zipp, Reynolds, and Paetsch (1988, p. 6), Milwaukee experienced a net loss of over 50,000 manufacturing jobs (23% of its manufacturing employment) between 1979 and 1986. The Valley witnessed employment drop from over 50,000 jobs in the 1920s, to approximately 20,000 jobs in the mid-1970s, to barely 7,095 jobs by 1997 (City of Milwaukee, 1975). While a recent economic boom has generated more economic activity within Milwaukee's urban landscape, such activity tends to occur at the edges of the metropolitan area, not in the Valley or in the city itself, where one-third of the metropolitan area's population resides and most of its poverty and un(der)employment is concentrated (McMahon et al., 1992; Levine & Callaghan, 1998; Wood, Whitford, & Rogers, 2000).

With economic decline, a host of problems followed. A "spatial mismatch" between people in the city and jobs in the suburbs limits the access of Valley dwellers to employment opportunities that were once a short walk away. The flight of industry and wealth from the city, combined with the flight of the middle and upper classes to the suburbs, meant a diminished city tax base and, thus, a diminished ability to deal with social problems.

In addition to social problems, over 100 years of industry left a legacy of environmental pollution in the Valley. Some have even referred to it colloquially as "one large landfill site." Many old buildings stand vacant and empty lots fill up with scrap. The Valley's location at the confluence of major city and state highways also results in traffic congestion and extensive vehicle pollution emissions.

In the last few decades, several public and private sector organizations have developed various proposals and plans aimed at renewing the Valley. The most comprehensive one was put forward in 1998 by the City of Milwaukee itself. Titled *Market Study, Engineering, and Land Use Plan for the Menomonee Valley*, it recommended that the Valley be upgraded and revitalized as an urban industrial and mixed-use district that will be able to provide sites for a broad range of uses, particularly industrial on the western and central portions, and commercial, residential and public open space usage on the eastern parts. An action agenda for implementing the plan established mechanisms for (i) public/private partnerships; (ii) zoning amendments; (iii) environmental analysis; (iv) financing remediation and site improvements; (v) promoting redevelopment; (vi) eliminating blight and "unpleasant" industrial uses; (vii) reconstructing roads; and (viii) enhancing the appearance of the Valley through green space and other visual amenities. The Menomonee Valley Partners (MVP), a public–private partnership bringing together members of the business world, community organizations, and government agencies, was established to facilitate the implementation of the city's Land Use Plan. On the whole, the MVP (2006a) have put forward a sustainability oriented vision that sees:

a redeveloped Valley that is as central to the city as it was in the past:

- economically with strong companies and jobs near workers, homes;
- ecologically, with healthy waterways and green space;
- geographically, with renewed tie to the surrounding city; and
- culturally, with firm roots in its past and a role in histories to come.

Other levels of government together with private sector agencies and nonprofit organizations have also been actively involved in planning and implementing initiatives aimed at breathing new life into the Valley. Federal Agencies, such as Housing and Urban Development (HUD) and the Environmental Protection Agency (EPA), provided funds and technical expertise to deal with contaminated properties and their redevelopment. The Wisconsin Departments of Natural Resources, Commerce, and Transportation have all been involved in project implementation and support. Various nonprofit groups and neighborhood associations, such as the Sixteenth Street Community Health Center and Esperanza Unida, have also been actively involved in projects aimed at revitalizing the Valley and its surrounding neighborhoods.

Over the next decade, the City of Milwaukee and the MVP project three million square feet (278,710 m²) of new construction in the Valley. A primary goal of the MVP (2006a) is that the Valley be recognized as a national model for sustainable redevelopment in 2010. To achieve this goal several considerations related to the environment, development, and business have been identified and addressed. These will now be discussed.

Environmental Considerations

Early on, those interested in Valley redevelopment knew that it was necessary to address the negative environmental stigma associated with the area. So, to provide information on environmental conditions, the MVP, City of Milwaukee, the Wisconsin Department of Natural Resources, the US EPA and the US Geologic Survey conducted scientific investigations of the Valley's soils and groundwater. Of particular concern were initial indications that groundwater flow might be moving between parcels, which meant that contamination could be spreading and that the cleanup of one property might not improve groundwater conditions adequately.

The City of Milwaukee received a Brownfields Redevelopment Pilot Grant in 1998 from the US EPA to conduct the environmental investigation. The initial Cooperative Agreement was awarded in 1998 and provided US$200,000 in federal assistance for site assessment work. A study group of scientists, lawyers, environmentalists, real estate professionals, and state agency representatives were asked to assist in the direction of the study. Their first recommendation was that an area-wide approach to groundwater investigation and management be taken rather than a site-specific approach. They also recommended that the study be divided into two parts: a physical characterization of the groundwater (location, flow, etc.) and a chemical sampling to determine the nature of area-wide contamination. Modeling for the physical characterization revealed that the two major receptors for shallow groundwater were Milwaukee's Deep Tunnel System and Lake Michigan. Fortunately, the travel time to these receptors was also very slow, which would allow for the natural attenuation of many dissolved contaminants.

To complete the physical characterization and begin chemical sampling, the City of Milwaukee received an additional US$150,000 from the EPA. Chemical sampling showed that groundwater impacts greater than background levels or Department of Natural Resources (DNR) regulatory standards were not present on a Valley-wide basis, and that groundwater quality at any point in the Valley was reflective of its relative location. Thus, properties with no soil contamination are unlikely to find groundwater contamination. Furthermore, subsurface conditions were found to be conducive to biodegradation, making natural attenuation a viable remedial option for groundwater contamination related to specific sites. Overall, the study concluded that there was minimal risk from existing groundwater contamination, which alleviated many area-wide concerns. While individual properties may have site-specific concerns, their respective landowners and purchasers can manage these.

Sustainable Development Visions and Tools

Sustainable development principles were embraced early on in 1999 when a Community Visioning Workshop (or Sustainable Design Charrette) resulted in designs that gave form and substance to the community's vision for sustainability. Teams of design professionals, public, private, and nonprofit sector stakeholders, students, and community members participated in a two-day charrette to consider the challenge for sustainable development in the Valley. The teams identified seven "Keys for Sustainability," including (i) transportation and circulation, access and linkage; (ii) mixed use and density; (iii) bundling utilities in a single corridor; (iv) cost-effective environmental remediation through site-specific, engineered solutions; (v) green building; (vi) open space and habitat restoration; and (vii) using the river as an amenity. These ideas were published in a comprehensive report entitled *Vision for Smart Growth*.

In 2002, the Sixteenth Street Community Health Center, together with the City of Milwaukee and other sponsors, organized a national design competition referred to as *Natural Landscapes for Living Communities* to plan the redevelopment and greening of a 140-acre (57 ha) former Milwaukee Railroad Shops property in the western end of the Menomonee Valley. The acquisition and preparation of this site was an extensive challenge. Once home to a cluster of railroad-related manufacturing plants, the site had been vacant since the late 1970s when The Milwaukee Road went bankrupt. The site later became the subject of Milwaukee's largest eminent domain action and the city finally acquired the land from Chicago-based CMC Heartland for US$3.55 million in August 2003. The site required massive cleanup, demolition, removal, and management of six miles of brick sewers, asbestos, over a million square feet (93,000 m^2) of old building foundations, as well as the trucking of half a million cubic yards of fill to create an environmental cap to protect human health and the environment and to raise the site out of the flood plain. The City of Milwaukee aggressively raised funds for the remediation project, winning more than 15 individual state and federal grants, totaling over US$3.5 million dollars.

The aims of the design competition for the site were implicit in the criteria presented to the four finalist design teams:

- To design an industrial park accommodating at least 1.2 million square feet of development (proposed by the city);
- To extend Canal Street (a major connection road within the Valley);
- To expand the Hank Aaron State Trail;
- To interconnect the railroad property to Mitchell Park and neighborhoods to the north and south of the Valley;
- To devise site-specific storm and flood water management techniques;
- To resolve site-specific environmental and geo-technical issues;
- To landscape the area; and
- To establish community connections to the site by means of open space planning, educational opportunities, and signage (Sixteenth Street Community Health Center, 2002).

The preliminary vision for the site put forward by Wenk Associates of Denver Colorado, selected in the summer of 2002, incorporates the full range of criteria listed above. Their design includes an industrial park surrounded by a variety of natural and open space features, including a "storm water" park, trails, a community green space, and a re-naturalized Menomonee River (Wenk Associates, 2002). In all, the 140-acres site is slated to encompass 70 acres of light industry, a mile segment of the Hank Aaron State Trail, and 70 acres of streets, parks, and natural areas along the banks of the Menomonee River (Figure 11.4).

The city is virtually finished with remediating and preparing the site for redevelopment and looks forward to the estimated US$6 million it should generate in the first year, and then the millions of tax dollars per year thereafter, according to

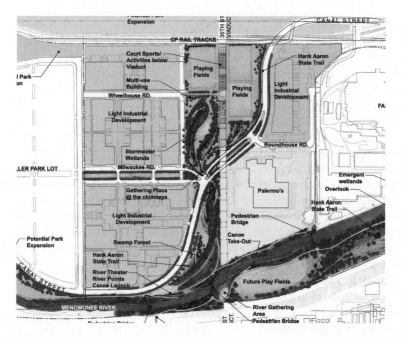

Figure 11.4: Menomonee Valley Industrial Center and Community Park (City of Milwaukee, 2006, printed with permission from the MVP).

estimates in the plan for the Tax Incremental District for the park (the Milwaukee Common Council has approved the $16 million dollar TID).

The Menomonee Valley Sustainable Design Guidelines use the principles outlined above to provide specific steps by which new buildings should be designed to achieve high performance. Specifically, the Guidelines (MVP, 2006b) are intended to:

- Simplify and demystify sustainable design throughout the redevelopment process, in part by sharing lessons learned from other projects;
- Provide a predictable climate for future investment;
- Help Valley businesses stay competitive by improving the performance of their facilities;
- Improve the aesthetic quality and environmental performance of the Valley; and
- Expedite the municipal and state permitting/approval process.

Recommendations in the guidelines were evaluated on the basis of their potential benefits, practicality, and cost-effectiveness. Many of the strategies proposed may also earn credits under the LEED green building rating system:

- Site design
  - o Site analysis and planning
  - o Storm water management

- o Natural landscape
- o Parking and transportation
- o Exterior site lighting.
- Building design and energy use
  - o Building design
  - o Energy efficiency
  - o Daylighting and internal lighting
  - o Alternative energy
  - o Building commissioning.
- Materials and resources
  - o Exterior and interior materials
  - o Water conservation.
- Construction and demolition
  - o Waste and recycling
  - o Erosion and dust control
  - o Pre-occupancy controls for indoor air quality.
- Indoor environmental quality
  - o Indoor air quality
  - o Acoustic quality.
- Operations and maintenance
  - o Operations manual and monitoring
  - o Facility maintenance
  - o Maintenance and stewardship of site and landscape elements (MVP, 2006b).

Following the success of the West End's conceptual design, Wenk and Associates worked with MVP and the city to develop a vision for the Central and Eastern Valley. Much of the plan dealt with creating a "spine" for the Valley — that is, connecting it via a new roadway (Canal Street) and a pedestrian trail (Hank Aaron State Trail). The latter was initiated in 1992 and officially opened in 2000 on the Valley's west side. The Department of Natural Resources of Wisconsin is the lead agency in planning, implementing, and managing the trail project. The City of Milwaukee is involved primarily in raising funds, releasing land, and maintaining the trail itself. Various federal agencies have provided financial support for accessories such as signage and art works. Local community groups and neighborhood associations such as the Friends of the Hank Aaron State Trail have helped to raise awareness and funds, while assisting with special events. Private landowners are being contacted by the state to donate easements for the trail and help finance development and re-naturalization activities (e.g., Miller Park Stadium Corporation, The Sigma Group). The Department of Natural Resources estimates that the open space cost approximately US$450,000 and site assessment and cleanup US$500,000. The Canal Street Reconstruction completed in 2006 was estimated to cost over US$40 million dollars, with approximately US$2.5 million for demolition and site remediation.

Employment and Business Development

One key goal of the Menomonee Valley redevelopment is to promote new business and to ensure that employment results in living-wage jobs for residents in the surrounding community. In 2002, MVP convened a workgroup of business and community representatives to decide upon a family-sustaining living wage for the Valley. From that, the MVP now recommends that employers moving into the Valley pay a wage of US$12 per hour. Employers are also encouraged to provide health insurance in addition to that wage. Employers who do not offer the Family-Sustaining Wage for all employees are asked to prepare a "Sustainable Wage Plan" summarizing the steps they will take to meet the family-sustaining wage in the medium term (1–3 years). MVP also recommends that employers recruit a workforce reflective of the population of Milwaukee and recruit workers via several local nonprofit organizations. Given that the Menomonee Valley is in a federal Renewal Community, employers can also qualify for significant tax credits ($1,500 per person) if they hire workers who live in the renewal community.

To support development, the Partners also provide an up-to-date list of the parcels available for redevelopment, a list of assistance providers, and a database of other sources of financial assistance (i.e., government grants, loans, incentives, tax credits and deductions, which include information on the incentive program, as well as its uses, amounts available, requirements, contacts, and application deadlines).

Overall, the sustainability approach to economic development has already resulted in many positive economic benefits for the Valley and the surrounding community. As discussed in Chapter 2, the Menomonee Valley Benchmarking Initiative (2006) has already tracked positive performance on several key benchmarks:

- Employment in the Valley and in the manufacturing sector declined slightly between 2002 and 2005, while service employment grew (the decline was due primarily to the loss of a single large company that was forced to move out of the Valley due to a multi-million dollar highway project).
- The number of jobs per acre increased slightly from 25.4 in 2002 to 25.5 in 2005.
- The average salary reported in 2005 was almost 2.7% higher than in 2002 with the highest average salary reported by the Wholesale Trade sector (interestingly, manufacturing income was at the lower end).
- Total annual sales rose for companies in the Valley.
- One-fourth of Valley employees now live in closely surrounding areas.
- The assessed value of commercial property in the Valley has risen faster than the average city value.
- Businesses agree on several key advantages to locating in the Valley, particularly its central location, freeway access, proximity to downtown, access to workforce, availability of parking, access to customers, and its improving reputation.

Response to the Valley's renewal has been positive among business. Indeed, as recently as August 2006, several companies have planned and constructed new facilities in the Valley, including:

- *Calleffi Hydraulic Solutions* is building a 35,000 sq ft manufacturing facility for hydraulic heating and cooling systems that intends to employ 28 people over the next three years.
- *Badger Railing* is building a 21,000 sq ft facility for manufacturing custom metal railings that will employ 27 people, and over 40 within the next three years.
- *Proven Direct Inc.*, a direct mail marketing firm, will move into 56,000 of a 143,000 sq ft light industrial building being constructed by a local developer on the former stockyards property.
- *Palermo Villa* has constructed a 147,000 sq ft manufacturing and distribution facility for its frozen pizza business that employs 270 people.
- *Harley Davidson* is building a new 130,000 sq ft museum and convention center that will employ 70 people and attract an estimated 350,000 visitors each year.

The development of the new headquarters for The Sigma Group provides an optimal example of efforts in the Valley to develop businesses and to assess their impacts in a manner that conforms with sustainability goals. The Sigma Group is a collection of three separate entities (Sigma Environmental Services, Inc., Sigma Development, Inc., and Sigma Leasing, Inc.) engaged primarily in environmental engineering and environmental services.

The Sigma property was originally a shallow marsh, which over time was filled with a variety of materials and adapted for industrial use. Historic records indicated coal and lumber companies utilized the site for box making, storage, and warehousing. The site also had storefronts, railroad sidings, and several variations of dock walls constructed of timber planks and piles anchored with buried tieback rods and stakes. More recently, the city used the land as a staging area for the construction of a drawbridge.

Prior to acquisition, Sigma completed an environmental site assessment that involved the review of historical records and regulatory documents, local area geology and hydrogeology information, and a site inspection. The Phase I assessment showed that environmental problems may be present from the release of hazardous and petroleum hydrocarbon substances. A soil, groundwater, methane, and geotechnical investigation revealed several challenges that needed to be addressed in planning and design as well as integrated with the construction process. Generally, these involved poor soil conditions requiring a series of piles to support the building, the management of contaminated soils, and a means to control the methane that was being generated by the decay of both naturally occurring and land-filled organic materials (Sigma Group, 2007).

For site grading, a soil management plan allowed for excavated materials to remain on site and be utilized for non-structural berms and fill. The swampy soil conditions required a foundation design consisting of a network of piles driven to between 50 and 90 ft (15–27 m) and linked by pile caps and grade beams. To prevent the possibility of methane exhaust accumulating under the building, the plan called for a network of slotted pipes embedded in a beneficial reuse product called Minergies produced by Wisconsin We Energies, a mixture of fly ash and lightweight concrete. The building's footprint was also reoriented to minimize site costs and enhance cleanup efforts. The site also accommodates public access to the Menomonee River with a walkway that will border the site's river edge and link up with the Hank Aaron Trail.

Both the building and site incorporate several aspects of a "green building," including natural day lighting, storm water management, beneficial reuse of materials for constructing the floor slab, and a high-efficiency HVAC system. A prominent building element is the use of bow truss structure for the main roof, which combined with the brick color and other building materials complement the neighboring drawbridge and blend with the industrial look of the Valley. The Sigma Group was honored with the 2003 Mayor's Design Award that recognizes design excellence throughout Milwaukee.

Sigma purchased the vacant brownfield parcel from the City of Milwaukee and started construction in March 2003. Upon completion in December 2003, Sigma worked with the Sixteenth Street Community Health Center to evaluate the impact of the project on its own and in relation to their former offices. The project objectives were to answer the following:

(i) What is the impact of Sigma's development to the Valley?

(ii) What impact has occurred to Sigma as a result of relocating to the Valley?

(iii) What is the impact of the relocation and development to other stakeholder groups?

The intent of this study was to provide measurable impacts on several dozen short- and long-term benchmarks based on Sigma's experience. The study is also intended to be part of the broader efforts of the Menomonee Valley Benchmarking Initiative (see Chapter 2). The results of the report are summarized here (for the complete report see Gramling & Kaszubowski, 2004) in point form because they represent the type of considerations required to move projects toward sustainability and to think of project outcomes as more than just adding to tax assessment value and employment:

1. Environmental impact
   - Direct contact risk associated with impacted soil: Prior to construction, the 2.79-acre (1.13 ha) site contained shallow polynuclear aromatic hydrocarbons (PAH) impacted soil that posed a direct contact risk. Remediation was accomplished by capping the affected soils with the building, parking lots, a geotextile membrane and at least 6 in of clean soil.
   - Minimization of off-site impacted soil disposal: The on-site management of approximately 9,720 t of PAH impacted soil excavated during site development resulted in only 250 t (or 2.5%) of soil requiring off-site transportation and landfill disposal. The 9,720 t of impacted soil was reused on-site as

non-structural fill and within landscaping berms. Most of the material removed
from the site actually consisted of debris unusable as fill material.

- The relocation of Sigma's headquarters from a suburb south of Milwaukee and
  the cleanup of the site have also lead to a 20% reduction in employee commute-
  related air emissions and improvement in the quantity and quality of storm
  water discharged to the Menomonee River and Lake Michigan (e.g., a 14%
  volume reduction and 80% reduction in total suspended solids). Water efficient
  design has also reduced the company's annual consumption of water by 83%
  compared to their previous facility.

2. Economic/business impact
   - Annual tax revenue: The development has created $78,000 in annual property
     tax revenue for the City of Milwaukee.
   - Security: Addition of the facility and its employees creates a stronger presence
     of security in the Valley. The new building includes exterior lighting pro-
     grammed to be illuminated every day from dusk until dawn.
   - Aesthetic Value: The company was honored with the 2003 Mayor's Design
     Award that recognizes design excellence throughout the City of Milwaukee.
     Recipients of the award "have added value to their neighborhoods by restoring,
     constructing, or enhancing their properties in a way that respects the urban
     fabric and contributes to the character of their surroundings."

The second phase of the study included an analysis of environmental, economic, and
employment-oriented parameters over a longer-term period of approximately six
months.

3. Environmental impact
   - Resource utilization: A resource-utilization comparison between the former
     facility and the new location revealed that total water consumption, pesticide/
     fertilizer use, salt application, and fuel consumption for lawn mowing were
     reduced. In addition, natural gas usage normalized on a square foot basis
     declined by approximately 20%. Interestingly, electrical usage turned out to be
     150% higher in the new facility, despite the lower level of artificial lighting
     supplied. Further investigation revealed that the electric baseboard-heating
     units used in the new facility below windows were not being properly operated
     and controlled; the problem has since been addressed.
   - One lesson learned from the study was the value of a formal baseline and
     building commissioning study. As noted in the study, "the thrill of completion
     of the project takes center stage and the formal commissioning, benchmarking,
     and measurement of the building's performance against expectations
     becomes a potentially forgotten element." Such information is essential,
     however, as part of an overall continuous improvement plan for the building
     and operations.
   - Company employees also recorded local sightings of wildlife. Fox and
     raccoons were observed as well as numerous species of birds and ducks. Prior
     to development, there was no vegetation on the site and native wildflowers,

grasses, and other species were introduced. An education and action program was established with the Wisconsin DNR to improve the success rate of these plants and to train employees to perform future assessments.

4. Economic and business impact
   - A mail survey was conducted in an effort to understand the impact of the new facility on surrounding businesses and neighbors. Responses from the survey were favorable:
     o New neighbors strongly approve of Sigma's relocation to the Menomonee River Valley (MRV) site.
     o There is no real impact to Sigma's potential business from their new neighbors as a result of the relocation as most businesses responded that business opportunities are evaluated on a case-by-case basis.
     o Awareness of the potential to develop additional properties in the Valley has increased as a result of Sigma's relocation.
     o In general, there exists a belief that Sigma's relocation to the Valley will be a catalyst for future development in the Valley, has enhanced the image of the Valley, and will help improve the local economy in the Valley.
     o Existing valley businesses are more likely to consider expanding their business in the Valley as a result of Sigma's relocation to the Valley.
   - Sigma has also started to purchase goods and services from businesses located in the Valley, such as a local printer and landscaping firm. The company has also teamed up with a mechanical contractor from the Valley to pursue industrial design/build work.
   - Sigma employees have also indicated that they are more likely to get involved with community organizations and other local philanthropic groups due to the move to the Valley. Several of Sigma's employees are currently involved with the Menomonee Valley Business Association. A survey of approximately 100 customers was also very positive, with comments as follows:
     o Sigma's relocation to the Valley site has made doing business with Sigma more convenient for most clients.
     o Sigma's new phone system of individual direct lines has made it more convenient for clients to contact Sigma employees.
     o In general, clients believe Sigma's image has been enhanced due to the Valley relocation.
     o Sigma's clients' awareness of the physical and environmental conditions in the Valley has generally increased since Sigma's relocation.
     o Due to Sigma's relocation, clients are more likely to utilize the downtown area for dinner, entertainment, and shopping while they are in the area.
     o In general, clients believe Sigma's responsiveness to their needs has improved due to the relocation to the Valley.

5. Employment and social benefits
   - An employee survey on commuting habits and attitudes also revealed the following:
     o Relocating to the Valley has tripled the number of times employees expect to bike to work.

o Commuting to the Sigma location in the Valley is preferred by employees over the suburban Oak Creek location.
o Sigma employees are more likely to work more hours per week and/or weekends at the Canal Street office than at the former Oak Creek location.
o In general, Sigma employees feel more productive at the Canal Street office compared to the former Oak Creek office.

Overall, the concerted efforts of stakeholders to reindustrialize the Valley in a sustainable manner are already paying off. As the MVP recently highlighted (2007), since 1998 the US$148 million in public investment has already attracted some US$541 million private investment and created more than 2,100 new jobs (with another 2,000 expected to be created by the end of 2008). In addition, over 557,000 sq ft of green buildings have been developed along with 60 acres of new park land and 7 miles of trails.

Conclusions

While efforts to bring work back to brownfield sites have faced continued challenges from globalization, deindustrialization, and decentralization trends, many cities continue to press on in an effort to reap the substantial benefits that employment-oriented redevelopment brings about. In addition, many of these communities are trying to "gently" raise the bar in terms of creating and implanting a vision for sustainability that incorporates family-supporting wages, sound design, ecological restoration, and connections to the community. Although the vision of district-wide, multi-firm industrial ecosystems on brownfields seems to be out of reach at the moment, a more cautious incremental approach toward the sustainable development of employment zones may be the proper way to move forward.

Discussions with those involved in industrial development often reveal that brownfields redevelopment continues to be perceived as being less cost-effective and more risky than greenfield development for developers, landowners, and other private sector stakeholders. Industrial projects on brownfields are typically challenged by higher costs associated with site preparation (demolition, site assessment, and remediation), lower lease rates, complex regulatory environments, and longer project timelines than those in the periphery, in addition to being located in more blighted districts and/or feeling pushed out by other land uses. As such, these projects require a more vigorous management approach incorporating a variety of policy and funding mechanisms in order to make them attractive to potential investors and developers; and more marketable for landowners. Cost/risk sharing mechanisms related to financing site cleanup and preparation, reducing project timelines, and limiting liability, must be implemented along with schemes to improve basic infrastructure, the physical environment, and the local workforce through training. Another possibility would be to rezone industrial sites to more profitable land uses, which raises the question of whether the government should use the development of other types of projects as a cure for brownfield sites, or whether it should involve itself more directly in preserving industrial lands for the economic and social benefits manufacturing entails.

The case studies examined here show that there is hope for bringing work back to brownfields, particularly in the form of office and retail employment. While industrial projects typically require considerably more effort and public funding than those uses (per dollar of private investment), the benefits of such jobs are still an important component for a healthy multi-sector economy. As with other land uses discussed in previous chapters, however, manufacturing projects will also need to be visioned, planned, and evaluated using a range of environmental, social, and economic indicators to move them toward sustainability. While this is starting to come about in several of the cities examined in this chapter, moving industry and other employment-oriented activities toward sustainability and doing so in areas that many vacated in the last half-century will require a concerted effort from multiple stakeholders in all sectors, as well as support from consumers.

Chapter 12

Towards the Sustainability Promise of Brownfields Redevelopment: A Synthesis

Since the latter part of the twentieth century, researchers, policy-makers, and planners in Canada and the US have become extremely worried about the serious problem of urban brownfield sites, given that such sites may contain hazardous pollutants that pose risks to human health and the environment and constitute a detriment to the appeal of neighborhoods. Interest on the part of developers and lending institutions in redeveloping contaminated and derelict sites tended to be minimal because these stakeholders faced high cleanup costs and potential future liability for any negative environmental effects that could be traced to redeveloped brownfield properties. On the other hand, brownfields are valuable sites for the simple reason that they are found typically in urban cores and are, thus, prime candidates for urban regeneration projects. The brownfields issue is hardly a trivial one and constitutes a major area of concern in urban development.

The research presented and examined in this book was motivated by a desire to ascertain how brownfield redevelopment contributes to *sustainable development* as applied to the urban context. Since the mid-1980s, sustainable development has become a widely discussed approach for integrating environmental needs with economic and social ones in human development. As discussed previously, the World Commission on Environment and Development (1987, p. 3) characterizes the goal of SD as: "development that meets the needs of the present without compromising the ability of future generations to meet their own needs."

The crux of the sustainable development approach is to be found in the concept that sustainable development can be attained without compromising the environment, suggesting ways in which a balance and interconnectedness can be maintained among the environmental, social, and economic requirements of human societies (Haughton & Hunter, 1994). In effect, sustainable development entails that development must attempt to coordinate the protection of ecosystems with a guarantee of basic social rights (from health care to cultural expression) and with the provision of an economic system that will have a limited impact on the natural and social spheres.

Sustainable development constitutes a model with a high degree of elasticity and broad applicability. It is, in fact, at the urban level where the environmental, social, and economic dimensions of development often collide and vie for predominance.

Moreover, as cities continue to expand topographically, demographically, and economically, it is becoming clear that a sustainable development approach can help deal with poverty, social inequality, and environmental degradation.

The dominant finding of the sustainability literature is that the preservation and reuse of the city's built environment and the proper management of its urban form is a necessary step towards achieving sustainable development. For these reasons policy-makers, planners, and environmentalists have turned their attention to the role of urban redevelopment in breaking the destructive pattern of urban sprawl in North American cities, which has often led to a serious under-use of city lands, buildings, and infrastructures.

Given the brownfield situation in the US and Canada, this book's principal objective has been to examine more closely the barriers to brownfield redevelopment, the benefits it entails to both the public and private sectors, and the appropriate strategies available for solving the problem in relation to redeveloping brownfields into places to live, work, and play. While the quest for more sustainable urban development faces numerous critiques and challenges, ranging from its definition to its implementation and assessment, not trying to balance economic, social, and environmental needs would constitute a true failure.

The goal of this book's first part was to set the stage by discussing the brownfields problem in the US and Canada. As outlined in Chapter 1, the relevant point-of-departure to studying the brownfield problem consists of examining the scale of the problem, the types of policies adopted historically for addressing it, and the objectives and style of policy-making employed in the two countries. The chapter argues that both countries have already come a long way and that brownfields-related policies and programs employed to overcome obstacles to remediation and redevelopment are converging as governments are sharing similar types of costs and risks with the private sector in the hope of solving the brownfields problem. The conceptual stage model outlined demonstrates how this convergence seems to be unfolding in more or less predictable stages. The argument made is that given the rising interest in sustainable urban development in both the US and Canada, future policy will continue to demand and move incrementally towards cost/risk sharing that seeks to address sustainability goals more broadly, as opposed to contamination and economic development issues specifically. While sustainability arguments already have been used to lend support to implementing policies for stimulating brownfields redevelopment, this next phase will "raise the bar" on brownfields redevelopment at both site-specific and regional scales by tying policy, programming, and funding more closely with marked sustainability objectives and outcomes.

The second chapter elaborated upon sustainable development and linked it to brownfields redevelopment in terms of its challenges, opportunities, and stake-holders. The end of that chapter argued that developing benchmarks to monitor the scale of the brownfields problem and the effectiveness of policies and programs at managing it, and linking these to sustainability outcomes, is essential not only to justify government spending, but also to systematically and directly track real progress in economic, social, and environmental terms. As the third chapter highlighted, development of brownfields is largely market driven and involves real costs and risks. While a more sustainable development framework may raise these, the public benefits ensuing from such redevelopment are already high and a more sustainable approach could raise these further. The achievement of both of these private and public objectives can increase considerably via good planning and supportive policies and programs, but the justification for these will come from achievements measured in concrete terms via case study examples and benchmarking.

The book's central part discussed brownfields redevelopment for housing, green space, and employment. While these were examined separately in order to better assess issues, trends, and cases, moving towards sustainability will require working on all three in an integrated fashion. While this book has focused primarily on the efforts of a handful of cities in the US and Canada, the range of cities examined make it evident that such redevelopment is possible regardless of the number of brownfields a city possesses, its real estate conditions, or other socioeconomic factors.

There are many lessons and broad themes that emerge from the cities and cases examined that researchers, planners, and public officials should take into consideration when dealing with their brownfields. These lessons include the following:

Brownfields Redevelopment and More Sustainable Models of Brownfields Redevelopment Exist

Perhaps the most obvious lesson to be gleaned from the programs, projects, and case studies examined here is that brownfields redevelopment activity contributes to more compact sustainable urban development and that more and more communities are enhancing the sustainability features of their redevelopment projects on an area-wide and site-specific basis. While many brownfields projects are achieving these goals by default, in terms of cleaning up land and erasing blight on spaces that have been vacant and underutilized for years, others are enhancing sustainability by design, in terms of creating new urban spaces that are compact, green, and efficient. These initiatives, while clearly not perfect and confronting a host of common urban problems, show that redevelopment is possible and more sustainable urban paths do exist. Moreover, collectively the cases provide guidance about the tools, techniques, methods and strategies that can be employed in the pursuit of brownfields redevelopment and more sustainable urban development.

The book provides many tangible examples of the benefits and promise of brownfields redevelopment and of creating urban environments that are environmentally sustainable, exhibit a high quality of life, and display a high degree of attractiveness to residents and employers. This has been done by strategically "filling in the missing teeth" in some neighborhoods through site-specific redevelopment, and by developing area-wide plans for other districts affected by deindustrialization and blight. This has not been a simple task, but the willingness of diverse stakeholders to meet the brownfields challenge has succeeded and given many of them the skills and confidence to move onto new challenges.

Strong Leadership (Public, Private, Nonprofit)

A second lesson that emerges clearly from the development of many of these policies, projects, and cases is that they have been successful because of key individuals and groups who possess strong leadership, persistence, and creativity. This leadership can come from any sector and can have many motivations, including profit, pride, and survival. For example, it can come from the public sector in the form of a mayor interested in revitalizing and/or greening their city, a developer in the form of wanting to be the first to build and market a green building, or a faith-based nonprofit interested in the future of their parish community. Regardless of the source, numerous individuals that the author has interviewed over the last decade indicate that behind every successful brownfield project is a person or small group of people responsible for triggering action and pushing the process forward.

Critical to both triggering and supporting the success of proposed brownfields projects is the presence of a strong local government entity that can push projects forward and find ways to support them. In instances where profit potential is low or uncertain, such local entities are critical for acquiring land, conducting or aiding with site assessment, preparing properties for redevelopment (demolition, infrastructure), marketing, and, in some cases, development. Where profit potential is higher, these entities are the main ones that can seek sustainability-oriented gains. These entities are particularly effective when they act as a one-stop-shop for redevelopment, but, at the same time, bring together representatives from multiple city agencies through an ongoing coordinated effort.

Strong Public, Private, and Nonprofit Partnerships

At the same time, strong partnerships between the public and private sectors, and increasingly the nonprofit sector, are essential for moving brownfields redevelopment forward. This is particularly true for large area-wide projects seeking to incorporate sustainability features. As discussed, alliances between business interests and public sector objectives have seen significant results in housing (e.g., Milwaukee's Beerline B), alliances between nonprofits, community groups, and the public sector are particularly effective for green space development (e.g., Toronto's Don River revitalization), and alliances between business, government, nonprofits, and the community has been essential for employment-based efforts (e.g., Chicago's Planned Manufacturing Districts (PMDs), and the Menomonee Valley Redevelopment) and for comprehensive large-scale redevelopment projects such as False Creek in Vancouver. In all, a spirit of collaboration has often developed among the disparate stakeholders involved in these projects resulting in less divisiveness and a greater sense of the mutuality of their agendas and objectives that often carry to other issues and affected parts of the city. Working together on issues, such as green building design or living wage goals, can be mutually beneficial for all sectors.

Consolidated and Coordinated Institutional Capacity within and between Local, State/Provincial, and Federal Governments

Governments are most effective when they work together to solve the brownfields problem and promote more sustainable development. When representatives from multiple city agencies (e.g., planning, economic development, public health, housing, public works, social planning) are regularly brought together to discuss brownfield projects specifically, and urban development and renewal generally, their diverse interests and concerns are dealt with on an equal plane that aligns with the objectives of sustainability. Working to promote sustainability requires efforts to break down the administrative and disciplinary boundaries of different city departments and agencies.

In addition, coordination among multiple levels of government is also essential for supporting such projects and has been a fundamental difference between the US and Canada, except in the case of Vancouver's False Creek where federal and provincial government involvement was necessitated by the World's Fair and now the Winter Olympics. Federal and state governments in the US have been responsible for many important policy initiatives (i.e., liability protection) and for extensive funding of everything from policy development, program implementation, to supporting individual projects via direct funding, loans, and tax breaks. This coordinated effort has made more challenging forms of redevelopment, such as reindustrialization, possible.

Know Where you are and Where you Want to Go

The location and character of brownfields redevelopment activity is better coordinated and has a more measurable impact when governments and communities understand their present situation and develop a clear vision for the future. Simply put, when brownfield redevelopment is part of a broader revitalization initiative or redevelopment project, it stands a better chance of being supported and funded. Brownfield-to-green space projects in the US provide a good example of projects that require being part of a larger initiative. Having brownfields considered in a citywide sustainability initiative, as well as site-specific plans would be the optimal approach.

Having a vision also helps promote a more holistic and integrated approach that embraces many places and sectors. Knowing what the city's goals are in terms of green space provision, transportation linkages, employment, affordable housing, and the like can help maximize the benefits ensuing from brownfields projects and expand the range of potential end-uses considered.

A community's desires and a region's visions, policies, and activities should reinforce each other at different geographic scales and jurisdictional levels. Attention to each of these scales is important for creating sustainable districts and for enhancing connections and linkages among neighboring locales. Many of the developments examined in this book have become important "connecting places," connecting people with each other, connecting locations, connecting people to their natural environment, and connecting visions of a more sustainable urban future. Planning for these connections, especially in underserved neighborhoods, seems to be an important element in attracting use and, ultimately, in enhancing quality of life for all citizens.

Be Aware of the Market and Work with it to Maximize Public and Private Benefits

In a few of the cases examined in this book, the quest for public benefits has trumped the market and private profit potential in a city's decision about what should be done with a brownfield area (e.g., industrial versus retail/residential use in Chicago's PMDs). In most cases, however, the city must be acutely aware of market conditions in an area in order to determine the best course of action. Knowledge of an area's market will help government determine what level of support is required to get a project moving and, on the flip-side, help government figure out how much public benefit (i.e., green building, parks, local employment) it can "squeeze" from a project that has stronger market viability. The planning department in the city of Vancouver, for instance, has an extremely detailed knowledge of the viability and profit potential of its real estate market, which they have used strategically to secure extensive public services and amenities from developers who wish to build on them.

Incentives and Mechanisms to Make Sustainable Brownfields Redevelopment Profitable and Elicit Public Benefits

Brownfields redevelopment has become successful over the last half-decade because governments have stimulated investment through the implementation of policies and programs that reduce the costs and risks associated with remediation and redevelopment for the private sector. As developers become more familiar with these costs and risks, and with the marketplace generally, they will continue to operate via state Voluntary Cleanup Programs, but not seek private financing if the market driven conditions are right. However, these government incentives and programs provide a mechanism for continuing to advance more sustainable forms of brownfields redevelopment that aims to maximize public benefits. For instance, access to public brownfield land and financial assistance in Chicago now requires that developers build green, include affordable housing, hire locally, and construct green roofs. As brownfields redevelopment advances, cities should do more to use the tools at their disposal as positive incentives to enhance such public benefits and continue to advance ecological and social features in a way that make sustainability profitable for developers.

Support, Publicize, and Market Success in Brownfields Redevelopment

Another factor that has supported brownfields redevelop in the US and Canada, and can push it further towards greater sustainability, has been the existence of a number of supportive networks, associations, and government agencies that help publicize and market its success. These organizations serve a number of useful functions, including lobbying, education, and publication and dissemination of information related to what different communities are doing. In the US, the EPA has taken the lead in spreading the brownfields word via its annual conferences, research, and publications. Other organizations such as the Northeast-Midwest Institute, the International City/County Management Association, the International Economic Development Council, The US Conference of Mayors, and the National Brownfields Association have taken a leading role in supporting and celebrating success. In Canada, marketing of brownfields potential has come more recently from the National Round Table for the Environment and the Economy, the Canadian Mortgage and Housing Corporation, the Canadian Urban Institute, and the Canadian Brownfields Network. While many of these groups have promoted brownfields redevelopment generally, more needs to be done to strengthen the link to sustainability.

At the same time, municipal governments must celebrate their own achievements and make them known to residents. Nonprofits and other groups involved in housing, employment, and other issues also need to promote brownfields redevelopment, as has been the case to some extent with green space. It is important that these groups push to raise the bar on incorporating sustainability features into brownfields redevelopment.

If you Build it, they will Come; if you Build it Better, Even More will Come

Brownfields projects are catalytic projects. Time and time again, soon after one developer builds a successful brownfields project, others quickly follow. Whether following market signals or simply acting like "kids following the soccer ball," the fact is that a domino effect most often follows a successful brownfields project. The benefits of remediation, demolition, and redevelopment are also felt off-site in terms of raising the value of surrounding property and sparking renovation and neighborhood repair. This renewal is intensified when projects are built in a way that contributes to the economic, ecological, and social aspects of the community by bringing to it jobs, recreational space, amenities, good design, and the like. As mentioned, the complete willingness of business leaders, government officials, community residents and others involved in these projects to speak with the author on hundreds of occasions is often motivated by the remarkable transformation that these sites have had on their communities and their sincere hope that this transformation can occur elsewhere.

Overall, people choose to live and businesses choose to invest in attractive communities that have a high quality of life. They want neighborhoods that are safe, abound in cultural amenities, support family life, celebrate the past, nurture creativity and an entrepreneurial spirit, and bring people together in a pleasant local environment. Given that many of these considerations are typically associated with suburban life, those redeveloping urban brownfields must think beyond narrow site remediation and economic-oriented goals and integrate them with community revitalization and sustainability-oriented objectives. While these broaden the land-uses to be considered and may require an additional layer of planning, the end result will be worthwhile as the projects examined in this book demonstrate. While the redevelopment of brownfields contributes to this sustainable vision by default, we have the tools to realize urban renewal and growth on a higher plane. Simultaneously, the demand is growing to move brownfields away from being considered simply in terms of economic development, and towards considering them in terms of a more economically, socially, and environmentally sustainable future.

References

Abercrombie, C., Abercrombie, S., Dees, J., Ford, E., & Runnells, J. (2003). Brownfields 2003: Browing a Greener America news and information. *Environmental Practice, 6*(1), 19–22.

aboutremediation.com (2006). *Government initiatives page.* Mississauga, Ontario: Ontario Centre for Environmental Technology Advancement (OCETA). http://www.aboutremediation.com/default.asp

Adams, D. (2004). The changing regulatory environment for speculative house building and the construction of core competencies for brownfield development. *Environment and Planning A, 36,* 601–624.

Adams, D., Hutchison, N., & Munjoma, T. (2001). Ownership constraints to brownfield redevelopment. *Environment and Planning A, 33,* 453–477.

Adams, D., & Watkins, C. (2002). *Greenfields, brownfields and housing development.* Oxford: Blackwell.

Agyeman, J. (2005). *Sustainable communities and the challenge of environmental justice.* New York: New York University Press.

Alexander, C. (1977). *A pattern language: Towns, buildings, construction.* Oxford: Oxford University Press., Unpublished draft circulated in 1971 as Cells for Subcultures

Alker, S. J., Roberts, P., & Smith, N. (2000). The definition of brownfield. *Journal of Environmental Planning and Management, 43,* 49–69.

AMEC Earth and Environmental. (2004). *Remediation of the Sydney Tar Ponds and Coke Ovens sites.* Sydney, Nova Scotia: Report Prepared for the Province of Nova Scotia, Sydney Tar Ponds Agency.

American Institute of Architects. (1999). *Survey of state and local officials on livable communities.* Washington, DC: Fredrick Schneiders Research.

Arendt, R. (1996). *Conservation design for subdivisions: A practical guide to creating open space networks.* Washington, DC: Island Press.

Auditor General of Canada. (1995). Environment Canada: Managing the legacy of hazardous wastes. In: Auditor General of Canada (Ed.), *1995 Report of the Auditor General of Canada.* Chapter 2. Ottawa: Queen's Printer. http://www.oag-bvg.gc.ca

Austin, M. (2004). Resident perspectives of the open space conservation subdivision in Hamburg Township, Michigan. *Landscape and Urban Planning, 69,* 245–253.

Ayres, R., & Ayres, C. (1996). *Industrial ecology: Towards closing the materials cycle.* Brookfield: Edward Elgar.

Barnett, J. (1995). *The fractured metropolis — improving the new city, restoring the old city, reshaping the region.* New York: Harper Collins.

Bartsch, C. (1996). Paying for our industrial past. *Commentary,* (Winter), 14–24.

Bartsch, C., Collaton, E., & Pepper, E. (1997). *Coming clean for economic development: A resource book on environmental cleanup and economic development opportunities.* Washington, DC: Northeast-Midwest Institute.

Bartsch, C., & Deane, R. (2002). *Brownfields state of the states: An end-of-session review of initiatives and program impacts in the 50 states.* Washington, DC: Northeast-Midwest Institute.

Bartsch, C., & Dorfman, B. (2000). *Brownfields and housing: How are state VCPs encouraging residential development?* Washington, DC: Northeast-Midwest Institute.

Bayer, M. (2005). Housing sprouts in downtown Milwaukee. *WAPA* May. http:// wisconsinplanners.org/wapanews/downtown.html.

Beatley, T. (2000). *Green urbanism: Learning from European cities.* Washington, DC: Island Press.

Beck, E. (1979). The love canal tragedy. *EPA Journal* (January), 1 (see http://www.epa.gov/ history/topics/lovecanal/01.htm).

Benazon, N. (1995). Soil remediation: A practical overview of Canadian cleanup strategies and commercially available technology. *Hazardous Materials Management, 7*(5), 10–26.

Berke, P. R., MacDonald, J., White, N., & Holmes, M. (2003). Greening development to protect watersheds: Does new urbanism makes a difference. *Journal of the American Planning Association, 69*(4), 397–413.

Besleme, K., & Muffin, M. (1997). Community indicators and healthy communities. *National Civic Review, 86*(1), 43–52.

Bibby, P., & Shepherd, J. (1999). Refocusing national brownfield housing targets. *Town and Country Planning, 68*(10), 302–305.

Bjelland, M. (2004). Reclaiming brownfields sites: From toxic legacies to sustainable communities. In: D.G. Jannelle, B. Warf & K. Hansen (Eds), *Worldminds: Geographical perspectives on 100 problems.* London: Kluwer Academic Publishers.

Blais, P., & Berridge Lewinberg Dark Gabor Ltd. (1995). *The economics of urban form.* Toronto: Report prepared for the Greater Toronto Area Task Force.

Bolitzer, B., & Netusil, N. (2000). The impact of open spaces on property values in Portland, Oregon. *Journal of Environmental Management, 59*(2000), 185–193.

Bond, S. (2001). Stigma assessment: The case of a remediated contaminated site. *Journal of Property Investment and Finance, 19*(2), 188–210.

Bourne, L. S. (1995). *Reurbanization and urban land development: US cities in comparative context.* Washington, DC: Office of Technology Assessment, Congress of the United States.

Bourne, L. S. (1996). Reurbanization, uneven urban development, and the debate on new urban forms. *Urban Geography, 17*(8), 690–713.

Box, J., & Shirley, P. (1999). Biodiversity, brownfield sites and housing. *Town and Country Planning, 68*(10), 306–309.

Bradshaw, A. (2000). The use of natural processes in reclamation-advantages and difficulties. *Landscape and Urban Planning, 51*(2–4), 89–100.

Braswell, B. (1999). Brownfields and bikeways: Making a clean start. *Public Roads, 62*(5), 32–39.

Bullard, R. (1990). *Dumping in dixie: Race, class and environmental quality.* Boulder: Westview Press.

Bunster-Ossa Ignacio, F. (2001). Landscape urbanism. *Urban Land,* (July), 37–47.

Burchell, R., Shad, N., Listoken, D., & Phillips, H. (Center for Urban Policy Research, Rutgers University), Downs, A. (The Brookins Institution), Seskin, S., & Davis, J. (Parsons Brinckeroff Quade and Douglas, Inc.), Moor, T., Helton, D., & Gall, M.

(ECONorthwest). (1998). *The Costs of Sprawl-Revisited*. Washington, DC: National Academy Press, Report Prepared for the Transportation Research Board, National Research Council.

Burger, J. (2000). Environmental restoration and ecological restoration: Long-term stewardship at the department of energy. *Environmental Management, 26,* 469–478.

Burger, J., Carletta, M. A., Lowrie, K., Miller, K. T., & Greenberg, M. (2004a). Assessing ecological resources for remediation and future land uses on contaminated lands. *Environmental Management, 34*(1), 1–10.

Burger, J., Powers, C., Greenberg, M., & Gochfeld, M. (2004b). The role of risk and future land use in cleanup decisions at the department of energy. *Risk Analysis, 24,* 1539–1549.

Cairns, J. (1995). Ecosystem restoration: Reestablishing humanity's relationship with natural systems. *Environment, 37,* 4–9.

Calthorpe, P. (1993). *The next American metropolis — ecology, community, and the American dream*. New York: Princeton Architectural Press.

Canada Mortgage and Housing Corporation (CMHC). (1997a). *Conventional and alternative development patterns — phase 1: Infrastructure costs*. Ottawa: Canada Mortgage and Housing Corporation report prepared by Essiambre-Phillips-Desjardins Associates.

Canada Mortgage and Housing Corporation (CMHC). (1997b). *Conventional and alternative development patterns — phase 2: Municipal revenues*. Ottawa: Canada Mortgage and Housing Corporation report prepared by Hemson Consulting.

Canada Mortgage and Housing Corporation (CMHC). (2001). Southeast false creek design charrette: Exploring high density, sustainable urban development. *Research Highlights, 81,* 1–7.

Canada Mortgage and Housing Corporation (CMHC). (2004). *Brownfield redevelopment for housing: Literature review and analysis*. Ottawa: CMHC, Report prepared by RCI Consulting and Regional Analytics.

Canada Mortgage and Housing Corporation (CMHC). (2005). Brownfield redevelopment for housing: Literature review and analysis. *Research Highlight, 05013,* 1–4.

Carroll, B. W., & Jones, R. (2000). The road to innovation, convergence or inertia: Devolution in housing policy in Canada. *Canadian Public Policy, 26*(3), 277–293.

CCME. (1991). *Interim Canadian environmental quality criteria for contaminated sites*. Winnipeg: Canadian Council of Ministers of the Environment.

CCME. (1993). *Contaminated site liability report: Recommended principles for a consistent approach across Canada*. Winnipeg: Canadian Council of Ministers of the Environment, Core Group on Contaminated Site Liability.

CCME. (1996). *Guidance manual for developing site-specific soil quality remediation objectives for contaminated sites in Canada*. Winnipeg: Canadian Council of Ministers of the Environment.

CCME. (1997). *Recommended Canadian soil quality guidelines*. Winnipeg: Canadian Council of Ministers of the Environment.

Center for City Park Excellence. (2006). *2006 City park facts*. Washington, DC: The Trust For Public Land (see http://www.tpl.org/tier3_cd.cfm?content_item_id = 20531andfolder_id = 3208).

Chapman, K., & Walker, D. (1991). *Industrial location*. London: Basil Blackwell.

Chemistry and Industry News. (1996). Cleanup reform bill to limit litigation. *Chemistry and Industry*. http://ci.mond.org/9703/970307.html.

Chicago Brownfield's Forum. (1995). *Chicago brownfield's forum final report and action plan*. Chicago: City of Chicago.

Chicago Department of Housing. (2004). *Build, preserve, lead: A housing agenda for Chicago's neighborhoods, affordable housing plan 2004–2008*. Chicago: City of Chicago Department of Housing.

Chiesura, A. (2004). The role of urban parks for the sustainable city. *Landscape and Urban Planning, 68*, 129–138.

City of Brampton. (1999). *City of Brampton budget summary 1998 and 1999*. Brampton, ON: City of Brampton, Office of Financial Reporting.

City of Chicago. (1991). *A plan for industry on goose Island*. Chicago: City of Chicago, Department of Planning.

City of Chicago. (2003). *Chicago brownfields initiative: Recycling our past, investing in our future*. Chicago: City of Chicago, Department's of Environment and Planning.

City of Chicago. (2006a). *Chicago manufacturing employment*. Chicago Fact Book, Manufacturing, data from the Illinois Department of Employment Security 2005, figures are through March 2004. Chicago: City of Chicago, website www.cityofchicago.org

City of Chicago. (2006b). *Chicago industrial market*. Chicago Fact Book, Industrial Space, data from Colliers, Bennett and Kahnweiler Inc. Chicago: City of Chicago, website www.cityofchicago.org

City of Hamilton. (2006). *Brownfields ERASE program*. Hamilton, Ontario: City of Hamilton, Planning and Economic Development.

City of Milwaukee. (1975). *Menomonee valley 1975 business needs and attitudes survey*. Milwaukee: Report prepared for the City of Milwaukee Department of City Planning by Dun and Bradstreet Inc.

City of Milwaukee. (1998). *Market study, engineering, and land use plan for the Menomonee valley*. Milwaukee: Report prepared for the Department of City Development, City of Milwaukee, by Lockwood Greene Consulting, Fluor Daniel Consulting, Trkla, Pettigrew, Allen, and Payne, Inc., and Edwards and Associates.

City of Milwaukee. (2002a). *Milwaukee's housing stock*. Milwaukee: City of Milwaukee Report.

City of Milwaukee. (2002b). *City of Milwaukee housing strategy: Goal to create diverse housing choices*. Milwaukee, WI: City of Milwaukee.

City of Milwaukee. (2006). *Menomonee valley industrial center and community park: Master land use plan*. Milwaukee: Prepared by the Department of City Development for the Redevelopment Authority of Milwaukee.

City of Milwaukee, Department of City Development. (2004). *Housing: Downtown Milwaukee*. Milwaukee: City of Milwaukee, Department of City Development.

City of Toronto. (1993). *Outdoor air quality in Toronto: Issues and concerns*. Toronto: City of Toronto, Department of Public Health, Environmental Protection Office.

City of Toronto. (1998). *Brownfields profiles for Village of Yorkville, Sorauren, Woodbine Park, and Parliament Square*. Toronto: Parks and Recreation Division, Economic Development, Culture and Tourism.

City of Toronto. (1999). *Toronto Parkland naturalization update*. Natural environment and horticulture section, parks and recreation division, Economic Development, Culture and Tourism, Toronto.

City of Toronto. (1999a). *City of Toronto 1998 current budget summary of gross expenditures and gross revenues* (http://www.city.toronto.on.ca/ourcity).

City of Toronto. (1999b). *City-wide development charge by-law — Appendix B: fiscal impact of residential development in the city of Toronto*. Toronto, ON: City of Toronto, Chief Financial Officer and Treasurer.

City of Toronto. (1999c). *City-wide development charge by-law*. Toronto, ON: City of Toronto, Chief Financial Officer and Treasurer.

City of Vancouver. (2004). *False creek north official development plan*. Vancouver: City of Vancouver, adopted 1990.

City of Vancouver. (2006). *South east false creek official development plan*. Vancouver: City of Vancouver, adopted 2005.

CMHC. (2006). *Comparing neighbourhoods — Ottawa*. Ottawa: CMHC comparing neighbourhoods for sustainable features, Ottawa page (see http://www.cmhc-schl.gc.ca/en/co/buho/sune/sune_005.cfm).

Coder, K. D. (1996). Identified benefits of community trees and forests. *Citizens for a scenic Florida* (see http://www.scenicflorida.org/lsctreebenefits.html).

Coffin, S. (2002). Establishing the brownfields-housing connection: Modeling the effects of brownfields on section 8 households in Cleveland, Ohio. Paper presented at the 44th annual conference of the association of collegiate schools of planning, November 21–24, 2002, Baltimore.

Coley, R., Kuo, F., & Sullivan, W. (1997). Where does community grow? The social context created by nature in urban public housing. *Environmental Behavior, 29*, 468–494.

Colliers International. (2000). *Greater Toronto industrial report – spring 2000*. Toronto: Colliers Macaulay Nicolls Inc.

Colten, C. (1990). Historical hazards: The geography of relict industrial wastes. *The Professional Geographer, 42*, 143–156.

Colton, K. (2003). *Housing in the twenty-first century*. Cambridge, MA: Harvard University Wertheim Publications Committee.

Colton, K. W. (2003). *Housing in the twenty-first century: Achieving common ground*. Cambridge, MA: Harvard University Press.

Congress for the New Urbanism. (2006). *CNU history*. Chicago: Congress for the New Urbanism, Website downloaded December 2006, http://www.cnu.org/history

Consumer Renaissance Development Corporation. (1998). *National comparative analysis of Brownfield redevelopment programs*. Washington, DC: Consumer Renaissance Development Corporation.

Contaminated Sites Management Working Group, (1997). *Annual report 1996–1997*. Ottawa: Contaminated Sites Management Working Group.

Côté, R. (1996). Industrial ecosystems: An oxymoron? *Ecocycle: Environment Canada*, Issue 4 (see http://www.ec.gc.ca/ecocycle/issue4/en/index.cfm).

Council for Urban Economic Development (CUED). (1999). *Brownfields redevelopment: Performance evaluation*. Washington, DC: Council for Urban Economic Development.

Cozens, P., Hillier, D., & Prescott, G. (1999). The sustainable and criminogenic: The case of new-build housing projects in Britain. *Property Management, 17*(3), 252–261.

Cranz, G. (1982). *Politics of park design*. Cambridge, MA: The MIT Press.

Cranz, G., & Boland, M. (2004). Defining the sustainable park: A fifth model for urban parks. *Landscape Journal, 23*, 102–120.

Crompton, J. (2001). *Parks and economic development*. Washington, DC: American Planning Association Advisory Service Report 502.

Crompton, J., Love, L., & Moore, T. (1997). Characteristics of companies that considered recreation/parks/open space to be important in (re)location decisions. *Journal of Park and Recreation Administration, 15*(1), 37–58.

Cullen, G. (1961). *Townscape*. London: Architectural Press.

Cybriwsky, R. A., Ley, D., & Western, J. (1986). The political and social construction of rental neighborhoods: Society Hill, Philadelphia, and False Creek Vancouver. In: N. Smith & P. Williams (Eds), *Gentrification of the city* (pp. 92–120). Boston, MA: Allenand Unwin.

Dair, C., & Williams, K. (2001). Sustainable Brownfield re-use — who should be involved, and what should they be doing? *Town and Country Planning, 70*(6), 180–182.

Dale, L., Murdoch, C., Thayer, M., & Waddell, P. A. (1999). Do property values rebound from environmental stigmas? Evidence from Dallas. *Land Economics, 75(2)*, 311–326.

Deason, J., Sherk, G. W., & Carrol, G. (2001). *Public policies and private decisions affecting the redevelopment of brownfields: An analysis of critical factors, relative weights and areal differentials.* Washington, DC: Environmental and Energy Management Program, The George Washington University, Project funded by the Office of Solid Waste and Emergency Response and the US EPA.

Department for Communities and Local Government. (2006). *Housing quality indicators.* London: Program developed by the former Department for Environment, Transport and the Regions (DETR) (see http://www.communities.gov.uk/index.asp?id = 1155832 downloaded).

Derus, M. (2000). City development takes a step back with an eye to the future. *Milwaukee Journal Sentinel*, January 23, p. 1. F.

Design Center for Sustainability at UBC. (2006). *Greater Vancouver green guide: Seeding sustainability.* Vancouver: Design Center for Sustainability at UBC.

De Sousa, C. (2000). Brownfield redevelopment versus Greenfield development: A private sector perspective on the costs and risks associated with brownfield redevelopment in the greater Toronto area. *Journal of Environmental Planning and Management, 43*(6), 831–853.

De Sousa, C. (2001). Contaminated sites management: The Canadian situation in international context. *Journal of Environmental Management, 62*(2), 131–154.

De Sousa, C. (2002a). Measuring the public costs and benefits of Brownfield versus Greenfield development in the greater Toronto area. *Environment and Planning B, 29*(2), 251–280.

De Sousa, C. (2002b). Brownfield redevelopment in Toronto: An examination of past trends and future prospects. *Land Use Policy, 19*(4), 297–309.

De Sousa, C. (2003). Turning brownfields into green space in the city of Toronto. *Landscape and Urban Planning, 62*(4), 181–198.

De Sousa, C. (2004). The greening of brownfields in American cities. *Journal of Environmental Planning and Management, 47*(4), 579–600.

De Sousa, C. (2005). Policy performance and Brownfield redevelopment in Milwaukee, Wisconsin. *The Professional Geographer, 57*(2), 312–327.

De Sousa, C. (2006a). Urban brownfields redevelopment in Canada: The role of local government. *The Canadian Geographer, 50*(3), 392–407.

De Sousa, C. (2006b). Green futures for industrial brownfields. In: R. Platt (Ed.), *The humane metropolis: People and nature in the 21st-century city* (pp. 154–168). Amherst, MA: University of Massachusetts Press in association with the Lincoln Institute of Land Policy.

De Sousa, C. (2006c). Unearthing the benefits of Brownfield to green space projects: An examination of project use and quality of life impacts. *Local Environment, 11*(5), 577–600.

De Sousa, C., Gramling, B., & Lemoine, K. (2006). *2005 State of the valley: Evaluating change in Milwaukee's menomonee valley.* Milwaukee: Report prepared for Menomonee Valley Benchmarking Initiative, UW-Milwaukee Center for Urban Initiatives and Research and the Sixteenth Street Community Health Center.

DETR (Department for Environment, Transport and the Regions). (1998). *Derelict land surveys in 1988 and 1993.* London: Department for Environment, Transport and the Regions.

DETR (Department for Environment, Transport and the Regions). (1999a). *A better quality of life: A strategy for sustainable development for the UK.* London: The Stationary Office.

DETR (Department for Environment, Transport and the Regions). (1999b). *Quality of life counts.* London: Department of Environment, http://www.sustainable-development.gov.uk/sustainable/quality99/index.htm.

Dewar, M., & Deitrick, S. (2004). The role of community development corporations in Brownfield redevelopment. In: R. Greenstein & Y. Sungu-Eryilmaz (Eds), *Recycling the city: The use and reuse of urban land* (pp. 159–174). Cambridge, MA: Lincoln Institute of Land Policy.

Dickinson, N. M. (2000). Strategies for sustainable Woodland on contaminated soils. *Chemosphere, 41,* 259–263.

Dion, K. (2001). Immigrants' perceptions of housing discrimination in Toronto: The housing new Canadians project. *The Journal of Social Issues, 53*(3), 523–539.

Edwards, B. (2000). Sustainable housing: Architecture, society, and professionalism. In: B. Edwards & D. Turrent (Eds), *Sustainable housing principles and practice* (pp. 12–35). London: E and FN Spon.

Eisen, J. B. (1999). Brownfields policies for sustainable cities. *Duke Environmental Law and Policy Forum, 9*(2), 187–229.

Ermann, L. (2003). On top of Mt. Slag, homes sprout. *New York Times,* March 6, 2003. Retrieved 5/14/2004 from http://www.nyt.com

European Commission. (1996). *Report of the expert group on the urban environment.* Brussels: European Commission.

Evergreen Foundation. (2004). *Green space acquisition ad stewardship in Canada's urban municipalities.* Toronto: Evergreen Foundation.

Ewing, R. (1997). Is Los Angeles-style sprawl desirable? *Journal of the American Planning Association, 63*(1), 107–126.

Faber, T., Kuo, F., & Sullivan, W. (2001). Coping with ADD: The surprising connection to green play settings. *Environment and Behavior, 33,* 54–77.

Faber, T., Kuo, F., & Sullivan, W. (2002). Views of nature and self discipline: Evidence from inner-city children. *Journal of Environmental Psychology, 22,* 49–64.

Fischer, K., & Schot, J. (1993). *Environmental strategies for industry: International perspectives on research needs and policy implications.* Washington, DC: Island Press.

Fitzgerald, J., & Leigh, N. G. (2002). *Economic revitalization: Cases and strategies for city and suburb.* London: Sage Publications.

Foster, J. (1997). Introduction: Environmental value and the scope of economics. In: J. Foster (Ed.), *Valuing nature: Economics, ethics and the environment* (pp. 1–19). London: Rutledge.

Francis, M. (2003). *Urban open space: Designing for user needs.* Washington, DC: Island Press.

Frank, J. (1989). *The costs of alternative development patterns.* Washington, DC: Urban Land Institute.

Frosch, R., & Gallopolous, N. (1989). Strategies for manufacturing. *Scientific American, 260,* 144–152.

Fulford, C. (1998). The costs of reclaiming derelict sites. *Town and Country Planning, 67*(1), 21–23.

Fung, A. S., Aydinalp, M., Ugursal, V. I., & Farahbakhsh, H. (1998). A residential end-use energy consumption model for Canada. *International Journal of Energy Research, 22*(13), 1133–1143.

Galbraith, C., & DeNoble, A. (1988). Location decisions by high technology firms: A comparison of firm size, industry type and industrial form. *Entrepreneurship: Theory and Practice, 13*, 31–47.

Gans, H. (1962). *The urban villagers: Group and class life in the life of Italian Americans.* Glencoe, NY: Free Press.

Gans, H. (1968). *People and plans: Essay urban problems and solutions.* New York: Basic.

Garczynski, L. (2000). The brownfields economic redevelopment program. *Renewable Resources Journal, 18*(2), 15–18.

Garvin, A., & Berens, G. (1997). *Urban parks and open space.* Washington, DC: Urban Land Institute and the Trust for Public Land.

Gertler, M. Berridge Lewinberg Greenberg Dark Gabor Ltd. (1995). *Adapting to the new realities: Industrial land outlook for metropolitan Toronto, Durham, York, Halton, Peel, Hamilton-Wentworth and Waterloo.* Toronto: Municipality of Metropolitan Toronto.

Gobster, P. (1992). *Managing urban and high-use recreation settings.* St. Paul, Minnesota: US Forest Service.

Gobster, P. (1995). Perception and use of a metropolitan greenway system for recreation. *Landscape and Urban Planning, 33*, 401–413.

Gobster, P., & Delgado, A. (1992). Ethnicity and recreation use in Chicago's Lincoln park: In-park user survey findings. In: P. Gobster (Ed.), *Managing urban and high-use recreation settings.* St. Paul, MN: US Forest Service.

Godbey, G., Grafe, A., & James, W. (1992). *The benefits of local recreation and park services. A nationwide study of the perceptions of the American public.* Pennsylvania, PA: Pennsylvania State University.

Goozner, M. (1998). The porter prescription. *The American Prospect, 9, 38*, 60.

Gordon, P., & Richardson, H. W. (1996). Beyond polycentricity: The dispersed metropolis, Los Angeles, 1970–1990. *Journal of the American Planning Association, 62*(3), 289–295.

Graedel, T. (1994). Industrial ecology: Theory and implementation. In: R. Socolow, C. Andrews, F. Berkhout & V. Thomas (Eds), *Industrial ecology and global change* (pp. 23–42). Cambridge: Cambridge University Press.

Gramling, B., & Kaszubowski, K. (2004). *Locating in Milwaukee's menomonee river valley.* Milwaukee: Study prepared by the Sixteenth Street Community Health Center and the Sigma Group in conjunction with the Menomonee Valley Benchmarking Initiative.

Great Lakes Commission. (2001). *Linking brownfields redevelopment and Greenfields protection for sustainable development.* Ann Arbor, MI: Report sponsored by the Great Lakes Commission, the National Wildlife Federation, and the Council for Great Lakes Industries.

Green Institute. (2006). Official website of the Green Institute. http://www.greeninstitute.org

Greenberg, M. (1999). Improving neighborhood quality: A hierarchy of needs. *Housing Policy Debate, 1*, 3601–3624.

Greenberg, M. (2002). Should housing be built on former brownfields sites? *American Journal of Public Health, 92*(5), 703–705.

Greenberg, M., Craighill, P., Mayer, H., Zukin, C., & Wells, J. (2001b). Brownfield redevelopment and affordable housing: A case study of New Jersey. *Housing Policy Debate, 12*(3), 515–540.

Greenberg, M., & Lewis, M. J. (2000). Brownfields redevelopment, preferences, and public involvement: A case of an ethnically mixed neighborhood. *Urban Studies, 37*, 2501–2514.

Greenberg, M., Lowrie, K., Mayer, H., & Miller, K. T. (2001a). Brownfield redevelopment as a smart growth option for the United States. *The Environmentalist, 21*(2), 129–143.

Greenberg, M., Schneider, D., & Martell, J. (1994). Hazardous waste sites, stress, and neighborhood quality in USA. *The Environmentalist, 14*(2), 93–105.

Groeneveld, T. (2002). *Navigating the waters: Coordination of waterfront brownfields redevelopment.* Washington, DC: International City/County Management Association.

Ground-Water Remediation Technologies Analysis Center (GWRTAC). Accessed December 2005. http://www.gwrtac.org/html/techs.html

GTA (Greater Toronto Area) Task Force. (1996). *Greater Toronto: Report of the GTA task force.* Toronto: Queens Printers of Ontario.

Guntermann, K. (1995). Sanitary landfills, stigma and industrial land values. *Journal of Real Estate Research, 10,* 531–542.

Gurda, J. (1999). *The making of Milwaukee.* Milwaukee: Milwaukee County Historical Society.

Hanley, N. D., & Spash, C. L. (1993). *Cost-benefit analysis and the environment.* Aldershot, UK: Edward Elgar.

Hara Associates. (2003). *Market failures and the optimal use of Brownfield redevelopment policy instrument.* Ottawa: Report prepared for the National Round Table on the Environment and the Economy.

Harnik, P. (2000). *Inside city parks.* Washington, DC: Urban Land Institute and The Trust for Public Land.

Harnik, P. (2006). *The excellent city park system.* Washington, DC: The Trust for Public Land.

Harrison, B. (1992). Industrial districts: Old wine in new bottles? *Regional Studies, 26,* 469–483.

Harrison, C., & Davies, G. (2002). Conserving biodiversity that matters: Practitioners' perspectives on brownfield development and urban nature conservation in London. *Journal of Environmental Management, 65,* 95–108.

Harrison, K. (1996). *Passing the buck: Federalism and Canadian environmental policy.* Vancouver: University of British Columbia Press.

Haughton, G., & Hunter, C. (1994). *Sustainable cities.* London: Jessica Kingsley Publishers.

Hayes, M. (1992). *Incrementalism and public policy.* New York: Longman.

Hemphill, L., Berry, J., & McGreal, S. (2004). An indicator-based approach to measuring sustainable urban regeneration performance: Part 1, conceptual foundations and methodological framework. *Urban Studies, 41*(4), 725–755.

Hemson Consulting. (1998a). *Retaining employment lands – morningside heights: A report to the city of Toronto economic development, tourism and culture.* Toronto: Hemson Consulting.

Hemson Consulting. (1998b). *The need for new residential density and mix policies.* Brampton: Hemson Consulting.

Hemson Consulting. (2000). *The port area of Toronto: Maintaining a valuable asset.* Toronto: Report prepared for Lafarge Canada Inc.

Hileman, B. (1992). Industrial ecology route to slow global change proposed. *Chemistry and Engineering, 24,* 7–14.

Hird, J. A. (1994). *Superfund: The political economy of environmental risk.* Baltimore: John's Hopkins University Press.

Hough, M. (1994). *Cities and natural process.* London: Rutledge.

Hough, M., Benson, B., & Evenson, J. (1997). *Greening the Toronto port lands.* Toronto: Waterfront Regeneration Trust.

Hough, Stansbury, & Woodland, (1990). *Don Valley Brickworks Master Plan.* Toronto: Metropolitan Toronto Parks and Property Department.

Howland, M. (2000). The impact of contamination on the Canton/Baltimore land market. *Journal of the American Planning Association, 66*(4), 411–420.

Howland, M. (2003). Private initiative and public responsibility for the redevelopment of industrial brownfields: Three Baltimore case studies. *Economic Development Quarterly, 17*(4), 367–381.

Hulchanski, J. D. (2002). *Housing policy for tomorrow's cities.* Discussion paper F/27. Ottawa: Canadian Policy Research Networks Inc.

Huther, A. (1997). *Brownfields and urban development — the reuse of industrial sites for residential use in the City of Toronto.* Unpublished Master of Arts research paper, Department of Geography, University of Toronto, Toronto, ON.

Iannone, D. (1996). Sparking investment in Brownfield sites. *Urban Land,* 43–45.

IBI Group. (1995a). *The GTA urban structure concepts study revisited: Broad revisions of selected cost estimates.* Toronto: Report Prepared for the GTA Task Force.

IBI Group. (1995b). *Full cost transportation and cost-based pricing strategies.* Toronto: Prepared for the Canadian Global Change Program, Canadian National, Environment Canada, National Round Table on the Environment and the Economy, and the Ontario Round Table on Environment and the Economy.

ICF Consulting. (2003). *Study of HUD's site contamination policies.* Washington, DC: Report Prepared for the US Department of Housing and Urban Development, Office of Policy Development and Research.

ICMA (International City/County Management Association). (2002a). *Growing greener: Revitalizing brownfields into green space.* Washington, DC: International City/County Management Association.

ICMA. (2002b). *Measuring success in brownfields redevelopment programs.* Washington, DC: International City/County Management Association.

ICMA. (2003). *Coordinating brownfields redevelopment and local housing initiatives.* Washington, DC: International City/County Management Association.

Ihlanfeldt, K., & Taylor, L. (2002). *Assessing the impacts of environmental contamination on commercial and industrial properties.* UC San Diego Division of Social Sciences Working Paper.

Industry Canada. (2004). *Canada's environmental industry: An overview.* Ottawa: Sustainable Technologies and Service Industries Branch, Industry Canada.

Industry Canada. (2005) *Digging in the dirt: A profile of Canada's "Soil Remediation" subsector.* Ottawa: Industry Canada Website, Section 3 (http://strategis.ic.gc.ca/epic/internet/inea-ae.nsf/en/ea02206e.html).

Institute for Responsible Management. (1998). *The pilots' own database: Our innovations and discoveries.* New Brunswick, NJ: Institute for Responsible Management http://www.instrm.org/piltdata/piltdata.html

International Economic Development Council. (2001). *Converting brownfields to green space.* Washington, DC: International Economic Development Council.

Isin, E., & Tomalty, R. (1993). *Resettling cities: Canadian residential intensification initiatives.* Ottawa: Canadian Mortgage and Housing Corporation.

Jacobs, J. (1961). *The death and life of great American cities.* New York: Vintage.

Jacobs, P. (1983). Frederick G. Todd and the creation of Canada's urban landscape. *Bulletin of the Association for Preservation Technology, 15*(4), 27–34.

Jelenski, L., Graedel, T., Laudise, R., McCall, D., & Patel, C. (1992). Industrial ecology: Concepts and approaches. *Proceedings of the National Academy of Sciences, 89,* 739–797.

Jenkins-Smith, H., Silva, C., Berrens, R., & Bohara, A. (2002). Information disclosure requirements and the effect of soil contamination on property values. *Journal of Environmental Planning and Management, 45*(3), 323–339.

Jenner and Block.Roy F. Weston Inc. (1997). *The brownfields book*. Chicago: Jenner, Block and Roy F. Weston Inc.

Joint Program in Transportation. (1996). *The transportation tomorrow survey*. Toronto: Joint Program in Transportation, University of Toronto (http://www.jpint.utoronto.ca/travcon. htm).

Jones, R. E., & Rainey, S. (2006). Examining linkages between race, environmental concern, health, and justice in a highly polluted community of color. *Journal of Black Studies, 36*(4), 473–496.

Kaplan, R. (1993). The role of nature in the context of the workplace. *Landscape and Urban Planning, 26*, 193–201.

Kaplan, R. (2001). The nature of the view from home. *Environment and Behavior, 33*(4), 507–542.

Kaufman, D., & Cloutier, N. (2006). The impact of small brownfields and greenspaces on residential property values. *Journal of Real Estate Finance and Economics, 33*, 19–30.

Kellert, S. (2002). Experiencing nature: Affective, cognitive, and evaluative development in children. In: P. Kahn & S. Kellert (Eds), *Children and nature: Psychological, sociocultural, and evolutionary investigations* (pp. 117–151). Cambridge, MA: MIT Press.

Kent, T. (2002). For affordable housing: Have Ottawa pay the rent. *Policy Options, March*, 6–9.

Ketkar, K. (1992). Hazardous waste sites and property values in the state of New Jersey. *Applied Economics, 24*, 647–659.

Kirkwood, N. (2001a). *Why is there so little residential redevelopment of brownfields? Framing issues for discussion*. Cambridge: Joint Center for Housing Studies, Harvard University.

Kirkwood, N. (2001b). *Manufactured sites*. London: E and F Spon.

Klimisch, R. (1994). Designing the modern automobile for recycling. In: B. Allenby & D. Richards (Eds), *The greening of industrial ecosystems* (pp. 137–148). Washington, DC: National Academy Press.

Kolluru, R. (1995). Minimizing EHS risks and improve the bottom line. *Chemical Engineering Progress*, 44–52.

Kuo, F. (1998). Fertile ground for community: Inner-city neighborhood common spaces. *American Journal of Community Psychology, 26*(6), 823–851.

Kuo, F., Bacaicoa, M., & Sullivan, W. C. (1998). Transforming inner-city landscapes: Trees, sense of safety, and preference. *Environment and Behavior, 30*(1), 28–59.

Kuo, F., & Sullivan, W. C. (2001). Environment and crime in the inner city. Does vegetation reduce crime? *Environmental Behavior, 3*(33), 343–367.

Lange, D., & McNeil, S. (2004). Brownfield development: Tools for stewardship. *Journal for Urban Planning and Development, 130*(2), 109–116.

Leechman, M., & Nyden, P. (2000). *Housing discrimination and economic opportunity in the Chicago region: A report for the human relations foundation of Chicago*. Chicago: Center for Urban Research and Learning, Loyola University Chicago.

LEED Council, New City YMCA. (1990). *Keeping jobs for Chicago's future: A development impact assessment of Goose Island*. Chicago: Report prepared by the New City YMCA LEED Council Goose Island Task Force.

LEED Council, New City YMCA. (2003). *Private investment on Goose Island since the establishment of the Goose Island planned manufacturing district in 1991: As of June 2002*. Chicago: Data provided by the LEED Council, October 2003.

LEED Council, New City YMCA. (2006). *Goose Island industrial corridor*. Chicago: Power-Point presentation provided by the LEED Council, November 2006.

Leigh, N. G. (1994). Environmental constraints to Brownfield redevelopment. *Economic Development Quarterly, 8*, 325–328.

Leigh, N. G., & Coffin, S. L. (2000). How many brownfields are there? Building an industrial legacy database. *Journal of Urban Technology, 7*(3), 1–18.

Leitmann, J. (1999). Can city QOL indicators be objective and relevant? Towards a participatory tool for sustainable urban development. *Local Environment, 4*(2), 169–180.

Lerner, S., & Poole, W. (1999). *The economic benefits of parks and open space.* Washington, DC: The Trust for Public Land.

Levine, M. (2002). *The economic state of Milwaukee's inner city: 1970–2000.* Milwaukee: Report prepared by The University of Wisconsin-Milwaukee Center for Economic Development.

Levine, M. (2006). *The economic state of Milwaukee's inner city: 2006.* Milwaukee: Center for Economic Development Policy Research Report.

Levine, M. V., & Callaghan, S. J. (1998). *The economic state of Milwaukee: The city and the region.* Milwaukee: Center for Economic Development Policy Research Report.

Lindblom, C. (1959). The science of muddling through. *Public Administration Review, 19,* 79–88.

Lindblom, C. (1980). *The policy-making process* 2nd ed. Englewood Cliffs, NJ: Prentice-Hall.

Longo, A., & Alberini, A. (2006). What are the effects of contamination risks on commercial and industrial properties? Evidence from Baltimore, Maryland. *Journal of Environmental Planning and Management, 49*(5), 713–737.

Lowrie, K., Greenberg, M., & Knee, D. (2002). Turning brownfields into ballfields, open space and parks. *New Jersey Municipalities,* 6–8.

Lubowski, R. N., Vesterby, M., Bucholtz, S., Baez, A., & Roberts, M. J. (2006). *Major uses of land in the United States, 2002.* Washington, DC: US Department of Agriculture, Economic Information Bulletin No. (EIB-14).

Lynch, K. (1960). *Image of the city.* Cambridge: MIT Press.

Maclaren, V. W. (1996). Urban sustainability reporting. *Journal of the American Planning Association, 62*(2), 184–202.

Maclaren, V. W. (2001). Blighted or booming? An evaluation of community indicators and their creation. *Canadian Journal of Urban Research, 10*(2), 275–291.

Maillat, D., Lecoq, B., Nemeti, F., & Pfister, M. (1995). Technology district and innovation: The case of Swiss Jura Arc. *Regional Studies, 29,* 251–263.

May, J. H., & Scheuernstuhl, G. J. (1991). Land use, transportation and air quality analysis. In Transportation Research Board, 70th Annual Meeting, January.

McAliney, M. (1993). *Arguments for land conservation: Documentation and information sources for land resources protection.* Sacramento, CA: The Trust for Public Land.

McCarthy, L. (2006). In the dark about brownfields. *Papers of the Applied Geography Conferences, 29,* 292–301.

McCarthy, L. (2007). Off the mark? Economic efficiency in targeting the most marketable sites rather than spatial and social equity in public assistance for Brownfield redevelopment. Paper presented at the 2007 association of American geographers annual meeting, San Francisco, CA.

McCluskey, J. J., & Rausser, G. C. (1999). *Stigmatized asset value: Is it temporary or permanent?* Discussion paper. UC Berkeley College of Natural Resources http://www.cnr.berkeley.edu/pdf/dean_rausser/stigmatized_asset_values.pdf

McElwaine, A. S. (2003). Slag in the park. In: J. Tarr (Ed.), *Devastation and renewal: An environmental history of Pittsburgh and its region* (pp. 174–192). Pittsburgh, PA: University of Pittsburgh Press.

McHarg, I. (1969). *Design with nature.* New York: Natural History Press.

McMahon, W., Moots, G., & White, S. (1992). *Restructuring of the Milwaukee economy, 1979–1989*. Milwaukee: Urban Research Center, University of Wisconsin-Milwaukee.

McNeil, S., & Lange, D. (2001). Engineering urban Brownfield development: Examples from Pittsburgh. In: N. Kirkwood (Ed.), *Manufactured sites*. New York: Spoon Press.

Menomonee Valley Partners (MVP). (2006a). *A vision for the Menomonee valley*. Milwaukee: Menomonee Valley Partners, http://www.renewthevalley.org/archives

Menomonee Valley Partners (MVP). (2006b). *Sustainability design guidelines for the Menomonee valley*. Milwaukee: Menomonee Valley Partners, http://design.renewthevalley.org

Menomonee Valley Partners (MVP). (2007). *Menomonee valley Milwaukee, Wisconsin*. Milwaukee: Presentation by L. Bray, Association of Collegiate Schools of Planning Conference, Milwaukee WI, October 19, 2007, mobile workshop on Rethinking Industrial Land Use: Milwaukee's Menomonee Valley.

Metropolitan Toronto Planning. (1988). *Metropolitan plan review: Parks and open space*. Toronto: Metropolitan Toronto Planning Department, Policy Development Division.

Metropolitan Toronto Planning Department. (1997). *State of the land information system project*. Toronto: Metropolitan Toronto Planning Department, Research and Information Services Division.

Metropolitan Toronto Roads and Traffic Department. (1987). *Metropolitan Toronto goods and movement study*. Toronto: The Municipality of Metropolitan Toronto.

Meyer, P., & Lyons, T. (2000). Lessons from private sector Brownfield redevelopers: Planning public support for urban regeneration. *APA Journal, 66*(1), 46–57.

Meyer, P. B., & Reaves, C. W. (1998). Accounting for stigma on contaminated lands. *Center for environmental policy and management*. Louisville: Kentucky Institute for the Environment and Sustainable Development, http://www.cepm.louisville.edu

Meyer, P., Wernstedt, K., & Alberini, A. (2004). All incentives for infill development on contaminated land are not equal: Developers' ratings of different forms of support. *Urban Land*, 28–31.

Meyer, P., Williams, R., & Yount, K. (1995). *Contaminated land: Reclamation, redevelopment reuse in the United States and European union*. Aldershot, UK: Edward Elgar.

Minneapolis Park and Recreation Board. (2004). Personal communication with Rachel Ramadhyani, project manager for mill ruins park.

Minnesota Pollution Control Agency. (2001). Brownfields to green space. *MPCA Magazine*, (Fall), 1–2.

Misky, D. (2005). *City of Milwaukee waterfront initiative*. Presentation at the Wisconsin waterfront revitalization conference organized by the Great lakes commission and held on April 13, 2005 in Sheboygan, Wisconsin (http://www.glc.org/wiconference/).

Moore, E. (1981/1982). A prison environment's effect on health care service demands. *Journal of Environmental Systems, 11*, 17–34.

National Center for Housing and the Environment. (2003). *Redeveloping Brownfield for residential use, a resource for builders and developers*. Washington, DC: National Center for Housing and the Environment.

National Environmental Justice Advisory Council (NEJAC). (1996). *Environmental justice, urban revitalization, and brownfields: The search for authentic signs of hope*. A report on the public dialogues on urban revitalization and brownfields: Envisioning healthy and sustainable communities. EPA Report 500-R-96-002.

National Round Table on the Environment and the Economy (NRTEE). (1997). *Removing barriers: Redeveloping contaminated lands for housing*. Ottawa: National Round

Table on the Environment and the Economy, Canadian Mortgage and Housing Corporation. Report prepared by Delcan Corporation, Golder Associates Ltd., and McCarthy-Tetrault.

National Round Table on the Environment and the Economy (NRTEE). (1998a). *State of the debate: Greening Canada's Brownfield sites*. Ottawa: National Round Table on the Environment and the Economy.

National Round Table on Environment and Economy (NRTEE) (1998b). *Greenhouse gas emissions from urban transportation*. Ottawa: National Round Table on the Environment and the Economy.

Nelson, K. (1994). Finding and implementing projects that reduce waste. In: R. Socolow, C. Andrews, F. Berkhout & V. Thomas (Eds), *Industrial ecology and global change* (pp. 371–376). Cambridge: Cambridge University Press.

Netherlands Ministry of Housing, Spatial Planning and Environmental Affairs. (2004). Personal correspondence with Meich de Steenwinkel, March 31, 2004.

Neuman, M. (2005). The compact city fallacy. *Journal of Planning Education and Research, 25*, 11–26.

Newman, P., & Kenworthy, J. (1989). *Cities and automobile dependence: An international sourcebook*. Aldershot, UK: Gower.

Norcliffe, G., Goldrick, M., & Muszynski, L. (1986). Cyclical factors, technological change, capital mobility, and deindustrialization in metropolitan Toronto. *Urban Geography, 7*, 413–436.

Novac, S., Darden, J., Hulchanski, D., & Seguin, A. (2002). *Housing discrimination in Canada: The state of knowledge*. Ottawa: Canada Mortgage and Housing Corporation.

NRTEE. (1996a). *Contaminated sites issues in Canada*. Ottawa: National Round Table on the Environment and the Economy, Financial Services Task Force. Report prepared by Slmcleod consulting.

NRTEE. (1996b). *The financial services sector and Brownfield redevelopment*. Ottawa, Ontario: National Round Table on the Environment and the Economy, Financial Services Task Force. Report prepared by M.M. Dillon Limited, Global Risk Management Corporation, and Tecsult. (for information see http://www.nrtee-trnee.ca/).

NRTEE. (2003). *Cleaning up the past, building the future: A national brownfield redevelopment strategy for Canada*. Ottawa, Ontario: NRTEE.

Office of the Deputy Prime Minister. (2005). *Housing policy: An overview*. London: Her Majesty's Stationery Office (HMSO).

Olds, K. (1995). Globalization and the production of new urban spaces: Pacific Rim mega-projects in the late 20th century. *Environment and Planning A: International Journal of Urban and Regional Research, 27*, 1713–1743.

O'Neill, B. (1996). Life on the Banks Herrs Island is luring suburban dwellers into the city. *Pittsburgh Post-Gazette*. Section C, March 10, p.1.

Ontario Ministry of the Environment. (1997). *1995 Pollution emissions for the greater Toronto area*. Personal Communication, Environmental Monitoring and Reporting Branch, Toronto, ON.

Ontario Ministry of Transportation. (1995). *Ontario commercial vehicle survey*. Toronto: Ontario Ministry of Transportation.

Organisation for Economic Co-operation and Development (OECD). (2000). *OECD proceedings towards sustainable development: Indicators to measure progress (proceedings of the Rome conference)*. Paris: OECD – Organisation for Economic Co-operation and Development.

Otto, B., McCormick, K., & Leccese, M. (2004). *Ecological riverfront design: Restoring rivers, connecting communities*. Washington, DC: American Planning Association Planning Advisory Service Report Number 518–519.

Page, W. (1997). *Contaminated sites and environmental cleanup: International approaches to prevention, remediation, and reuse.* San Diego: Academic Press.

Page, G. W., & Rabinowitz, H. (1993). Groundwater contamination: Its effects on property values and cities. *Journal of the American Planning Association, 59*(4), 473–481.

Paton, B. (1994). Design for environment: A management perspective. In: R. Socolow, C. Andrews, F. Berkhout & V. Thomas (Eds), *Industrial ecology and global change* (pp. 349–358). Cambridge: Cambridge University Press.

Pearce, F. (1998). A real waste: Focus bulldozing disused city land to meet housing needs could be far worse for conservation then using open countryside. *New Scientist, 11*, 20–21.

Pearce, D. (2000). Cost-benefit analysis and environmental policy. In: J.D. Helm (Ed.), *Environmental policy: Objectives, instruments and implementation.* New York: Oxford University Press.

Pennsylvania DEP (Department of Environmental Protection). (1999). *Green opportunities for Brownfield.* Harrisburg, PA: State of Pennsylvania, Department of Environmental Protection, Land Recycling and Cleanup Program.

Pepper, E. (1997). *Lessons from the field — unlocking the economic potential with an environmental key.* Washington, DC: Northeast-Midwest Institute.

Persky, J., & Wiewel, W. (1996). *Central city and suburban development: Who pays and who benefits?* Chicago: Great Cities Institute, University of Illinois at Chicago.

Piccioni, L. (2003). The 'erasing' of brownfields in Hamilton, Ontario, Canada. In: E. Tiezzi & C. Brebbia (Eds), *Ecosystems and sustainable development IV.* Southampton: WIT Press.

Platt, R. (1998). Recycling brownfields. *Urban Land, 57*, 30–35, 96.

Platt, R. (2006). *The humane metropolis: People and nature in the 21st-century city.* Amherst, MA: University of Massachusetts Press in association with the Lincoln Institute of Land Policy.

Porter, M. (1995). The competitive advantage of the inner city. *Harvard Business Review, 73*, 55–71.

Porter, M., & Van der Linde, C. (1995). Green and competitive. *Harvard Business Review, 73*(5), 120–134.

Public Policy Forum. (2003). *Vital Issues for Milwaukee: Issue #1 property values.* Milwaukee: Public Policy Forum, Deborah Curtisand Emily Van Dunk, sponsored by the Helen Bader Foundation.

Punter, J. (2003). *The Vancouver achievement.* Vancouver: UBC Press.

Putaro, S., & Weisbrod, K. (1999). Web pages for the Washington's landing site. Pittsburgh: Carnegie Mellon University http://www.ce.cmu.edu/Brownfields/NSF/sites/Washland/index.htm

Rast, J. (2005). *Curbing industrial decline or thwarting redevelopment? An evaluation of Chicago's Clybourn Corridor, Goose Island, and Elston Corridor planned manufacturing districts.* Milwaukee: University of Wisconsin-Milwaukee, Center for Economic Development, Policy Research Publication.

RECS (US Department of Energy, Energy Information Administration Residential Energy Consumption Survey). (2001). *Residential energy consumption survey.* Washington, DC: US Department of Energy (see http://www.eia.doe.gov/emeu/recs/contents.html).

Regional Municipality of Peel. (1999). *Regional municipality of peel 1999 current and capital budget.* Brampton, ON: Regional Municipality of Peel, Finance Department.

Richardson, H., & Gordon, P. (2004). US population and employment trends and sprawl issues. In: H. Richardson & C. Bae (Eds), *Urban sprawl in Western Europe and the United States* (pp. 217–235). Hants: Ashgate.

Rogoff, M. J. (1997). *Status of state Brownfield programs — a comparison of enabling legislation*. Paper presented at the 90th annual meeting and exhibition air and waste management association Toronto, Ontario, Canada.

Roodman, D. M., & Lenssen, N. (1995). *A building revolution: How ecology and health concerns are transforming construction*. Washington, DC: Worldwatch Paper 124, Worldwatch Institute.

Rybczynski, W. (1999). *A clearing in the distance: Frederick law Olmsted and North America in the nineteenth century*. New York: Touchstone.

Sagoff, M. (1988). *The economy of the earth: Philosophy, law and the environment*. Cambridge, CN: Cambridge University Press.

Scanlon, J. (1984). Site selection and design for growth industries. *Industrial Development, 153,* 26–29.

Schopp, D. (2003). *From brownfields to housing: Opportunities, issues, and answers*. Washington, DC: Northeast-Midwest Institute.

Schuyler, D. (1986). *The new urban landscape*. Baltimore, MD: The Johns Hopkins University Press.

Scott, A. (1980). *Locational patterns and dynamics of industrial activity in the modern metropolis: A review essay*. Discussion paper No. 27. Toronto: University of Toronto, Department of Geography

Scottish Executive. (2003). *Scottish Vacant and Derelict Land Survey 2002 — Statistical Bulletin ENV/2003/1*. Glasgow: Scottish Executive. http://www.scotland.gov.uk/stats/bulletins/00241-10.asp

Shafer, C. S., Lee, B. K., & Turner, S. (2000). A tale of three greenway grails: User perceptions related to quality of life. *Landscape and Urban Planning, 49,* 163–178.

Sharkey, W. (2005). *What's green in brown? A literature review of "Green" language in Brownfield research*. Milwaukee: Graduate research paper, University of Wisconsin-Milwaukee, Department of Geography.

Shuman, D. (2002). *Developing successful infill housing*. Washington, DC: Urban Land Institute.

Sigma Group. (2007). *The sigma group building menomonee river valley brownfield redevelopment*. Milwaukee: The Sigma Group website, Portfolio, http://www.thesigmagroup.com/port_sigma.html

Simons, R. (1998). *Turning brownfields into greenbacks*. Washington, DC: Urban Land Institute.

Simons, R. (1999). How many brownfields are out there? An economic base contraction analysis of 31 US cities. *Public Works Management and Policy, 2*(3), 267–273.

Simons, R., Bowen, W., & Sementelli, A. (1997). The effect of leaking underground storage tanks on residential sales prices. *Journal of Real Estate Research, 14*(2), 29–42.

Simons, R., & El Jaouhari, A. (2001). Local government intervention in the brownfields arena. *Commentary,* 12–18.

Simons, R., Pendergrass, J., & Winson-Geideman, K. (2003). Quantifying long-term environmental regulatory risk of brownfields: Are reopeners really an issue? *Journal of Environmental Planning and Management, 46*(2), 257–269.

Sisson, K. (1989). *Toxic real estate manual*. Toronto: Wilms and Shier.

Sixteenth Street Community Health Center. (2002). *Menomonee river valley national design competition, executive summary*. Milwaukee: Competition Sponsored by the Sixteenth Street Community Health Center, Menomonee Valley Partners Inc., the City of Milwaukee, the Milwaukee Metropolitan Sewerage District, Wisconsin Department of Natural Resources and Milwaukee County.

Snepenger, D., Johnson, J., & Rasker, R. (1995). Travel-stimulated entrepreneurial migration. *Journal of Travel Research, 24*(1), 40–44.

Solitare, L. (2001). *Public participation in brownfields redevelopments located in residential neighborhoods.* Unpublished Doctoral Dissertation. New Brunswick, NJ: Rutgers, the State University of New Jersey.

Solitare, L., & Greenberg, M. (2002). Is the US environmental protection agency brownfields assessment pilot program environmentally just? *Environmental Health Perspectives, 110*(2), 249–257.

Sprigg, G. (2003). The choice is yours. *Industrial Environmental Management, 14*(2), 27.

State of Illinois. (2003). *Executive order to establish comprehensive housing initiative.* Springfield, IL: State of Illinois Executive Department.

Statistics Canada. (1996). *Agricultural profile of Ontario.* Ottawa: Queen's Printer.

Stren, R., White, R., & Whitney, J. (1992). *Cities: Urbanization and the environment in international perspective.* Boulder: Westview Press.

Stroup, R. L. (1997). Superfund: The shortcut that failed. In: T.L. Anderson (Ed.), *Breaking the environmental policy Gridlock* (pp. 115–139). Stanford: Hoover Institution Press.

Sustainable Measures. (2006). *Housing indicators* (See http://www.sustainablemeasures.com/Database/Housing.html).

Sydney Tar Ponds Official Site of Clean Up Effort. (2006). Accessed October 14, 2006. http://www.tarpondscleanup.ca

Takano, T., Nakamura, K., & Watanabe, M. (2002). Urban residential environments and senior citizens' longevity in megacity areas: The importance of walkable green spaces. *Journal of Epidemiology and Community Health, 56*, 913–918.

Task Force to Bring Back the Don. (2004). Chester springs marsh east community stewardship program: 2003 report. Toronto: Task Force to Bring Back the Don, City of Toronto. Report prepared by S. Gillis.

Taylor, D. E. (1999). Central park as a model for social control: Urban parks, social class and leisure behavior in nineteenth-century America. *Journal of Leisure Research, 31*, 420–477.

The Trust for Public Land. (2004). *No place to play: A comparative analysis of park access in seven major cities.* Washington, DC: The Trust for Public Land.

Thompson, J. W., & Sorvig, K. (2000). *Sustainable landscape construction.* Washington, DC: Island Press.

Tiesdell, S., & Adams, D. (2004). Design matters: Major house builders and the design challenge of Brownfield development contexts'. *Journal of Urban Design, 9*(1), 23–45.

Till, K. (2001). New urbanism and nature: Green marketing and the neotraditional community. *Urban Geography, 22*, 220–268.

Toronto Mayor's Homelessness Action Task Force. (1999). *Taking responsibility for homelessness: An action plan for Toronto.* Toronto: City of Toronto.

Toronto Planning. (2000). *Toronto at the crossroads.* Toronto: City of Toronto report.

Toronto Waterfront Revitalization Corporation (WRC). (2002). *Making waves: Principles for building Toronto's waterfront.* Toronto: Waterfront Revitalization Corporation.

Turner, R., Pearce, D., & Bateman, I. (1993). *Environmental economics: An elementary introduction.* Baltimore, MD: Johns Hopkins University Press.

Tyler Norris Associates. (1997). *Redefining progress, and sustainable Seattle. The community indicators handbook: Measuring progress toward healthy and sustainable communities.* San Francisco: Redefining Progress.

Tyrvainen, L. (2001). Economic valuation of urban forest benefits in Finland. *Journal of Environmental Management, 62,* 75–92.

United Church of Christ. (1987). *Toxic waste and race in the United States: A national report on the racial and socio-economic characteristics of communities with hazardous waste sites.* New York: United Church of Christ.

United States Census Bureau. (2000). *Construction spending statistics.* Washington, DC: The United States Census Bureau. http://www.census.gov/const/www/Sitemap.html

United States (US) Conference of Mayors. (2000). *Recycling America's land: A national report on brownfields redevelopment* (Vol. III). Washington, DC: United States Conference of Mayors.

United States (US) Conference of Mayors. (2003). *Recycling America's land: A national report on brownfields redevelopment* (Vol. IV). Washington, DC: United States Conference of Mayors.

United States (US) Conference of Mayors. (2006). *Recycling America's land: A national report on brownfields redevelopment* (Vol. VI). Washington, DC: The United States Conference of Mayors.

United States Department of the Interior, Office of Surface Mining. (2003). *25th Anniversary of the surface mining law. Surface coal mining reclamation: 25 years of progress, 1977-2002.* A report on the protection an restoration of the nation's land and water resources under the Surface Mining Law, Washington, DC, 20240.

URA (Urban Redevelopment Authority of Pittsburgh). (2006a). Before and after photo presentation of brownfields Projects.

URA (Urban Redevelopment Authority of Pittsburgh). (2006b). *Showcase projects: Washington's landing.* Pittsburgh: Urban Redevelopment Authority of Pittsburgh http://www.ura.org/showcaseProjects_washLanding2.html

Urban Land Institute. (2001). *Urban infill housing: Myth and fact.* Washington, DC: Urban Land Institute.

US Department of Transportation. (1995). USDOT/FHWA Visual database of transportation enhancements, Stone Arch Bridge, http://ntl.bts.gov/lib/1000/1700/1728/mnf01.html.

US EPA. (1980). EPA, New York State announce temporary relocation of Love Canal residents. *US EPA Press Release, May 21, 1980* (see http://www.epa.gov/history/topics/lovecanal/03.htm).

US EPA. (1998). *Characteristics of sustainable brownfields projects.* Washington, DC: US EPA, Office of Solid Waste and Emergency Response, EPA-R-98-001.

US EPA. (1999). *A sustainable brownfields model framework.* Washington, DC: US EPA, Office of Solid Waste and Emergency Response, Report # EPA500-R-99-001.

US EPA. (2000a). *Introduction to phytoremediation: Fact sheet and order information.* Solid Waste and Emergency Response (5102G), EPA 542-00-007 March, Washington, DC, 20460.

US EPA. (2000b). Announcement by the US Environmental Protection Agency's administrator Carol Browner. May, 2000.

US EPA. (2001). *Reusing superfund sites: Recreational use of land above hazardous waste containment areas.* Washington, DC: Office of Emergency and Remedial Response.

US EPA. (2002). *Observations on EPA's plans for implementing brownfields performance measures.* Washington, DC: US EPA, Office of Inspector General, Final Memorandum Report, Report Number 2002-M-00016.

US EPA. (2003). *Choosing green space as a brownfields reuse. Brownfields success story series.* Washington, DC: US EPA Solid Waste and Emergency Response. (5105) EPA-500-F-03-248.

US EPA. (2004). *FY 2004 superfund annual report.* Washington, DC: US EPA Superfund Office.

US EPA. (2006). *Love Canal superfund cleanup history.* http://www.epa.gov/history/topics/lovecanal.

US EPA. (2006a). *State brownfields and voluntary response programs — updated in August 2006.* Washington, DC: Report by SRA International, Inc., Arlington, Virginia (see http://www.epa.gov/brownfields/pubs/st_res_prog_report.htm).

US EPA. (2006b). *Bioremediation of chlorinated solvents.* Washington, DC: US EPA Technology Innovation Program (see http://clu-in.org/techfocus/default.focus/sec/Bioremediation%5Fof%5FChlorinated%5FSolvents/cat/Overview/).

US EPA. (2007) *About brownfields.* http://www.epa.gov/brownfields/about.htm

US General Accounting Office. (2000). *Brownfields: Information on the programs of EPA and selected states.* GAO-01-52, December 15, 2000.

USGBC (US Green Building Council). (2003). *Building momentum: National trends and prospects for high-performance green buildings.* Washington, DC: US Green Building Council, Prepared by ICF Consulting.

USGBC (US Green Building Council). (2005a). *An introduction to the US Green Building Council and the LEED Green Building Rating System.* Washington, DC: Power Point presentation US Green Building Council.

USGBC (US Green Building Council). (2005b). LEED for homes project checklist with resource categories and credit types. Version 1.72, August. Washington, DC.

USGBC (US Green Building Council). (2005c). *Rating system for pilot demonstration of LEED® for homes program.* Washington, DC: US Green Building Council.

Von Baeyer, E. (2006). Parks, City. In: J. Marsh (Ed.), *The Canadian encyclopedia.* Toronto: The Historical Foundation of Canada, Geography.

Wali Mohan, K. (1999). Ecological succession and the rehabilitation of disturbed terrestrial ecosystems. *Plant and Soil, 213,* 195–220.

Walton, W. (2000). Windfall sites for housing: An underestimated resource. *Urban Studies, 37*(2), 391–409.

Warson, A. (1998). Toronto's waterfront revival. *Urban Land,* 50–59.

Wegler, E. (2000). Condo market explosion fueled by many sources. *The Toronto Star,* June 24, Section N6.

Wenk Associates. (2002). *A vision for the Menomonee River Valley.* Denver: Prepared for the Menomonee River Valley National Design Competition, Milwaukee, Wisconsin, sponsored by the City of Milwaukee Department of Environmental Health, the Sixteenth Street Community Health Center, and other stakeholders.

Wernstedt, K., Crooks, L., & Hersh, R. (2003) *Brownfields redevelopment in Wisconsin: A survey of the field.* Discussion paper 03–54. Washington, DC: Resources for the Future.

Wernstedt, K., & Hersh, R. (2003). *Brownfields redevelopment in Wisconsin: Program, citywide, and site-level studies.* Discussion paper 03–53. Washington, DC: Resources for the Future.

Wernstedt, K., Meyer, P., Alberini, A., & Heberle, L. (2006). Incentives for private residential brownfields development in US urban areas. *Journal of Environmental Planning and Management, 49,* 101–119.

West, K. (2007). *Eco-industrial parks in the United States: Do practical examples exist and can they serve as models for brownfields redevelopment?* Unpublished Doctoral, University of Wisconsin-Milwaukee, Milwaukee.

Wexler, M. E. (1996). A comparison of Canadian and American housing policies. *Urban Studies, 33,* 1909–1921.

White, R. (1994). *Urban environmental management.* Chichester: Wiley.

White, S., Zipp, J., Reynolds, P., & Paetsch, J. (1988). *The changing milwaukee industrial structure, 1979–1988*. Milwaukee: The Urban Research Center, University of Wisconsin-Milwaukee.

Williams, H., Medherst, J., & Drew, K. (1993). Corporate strategies for a sustainable future. In: K. Fischer & J. Schot (Eds), *Environmental strategies for industry: International perspectives on research needs and policy implications* (pp. 117–146). Washington, DC: Island Press.

Williams, K. (2004). Reducing sprawl and delivering an urban renaissance in England: Are these aims possible given current attitudes of urban living? In: H. Richardon & C. Chang-Hee (Eds), *Urban sprawl in Western Europe and the United States*. Aldershot: Ashgate.

Williamson, K. (2003). *Growing with green infrastructure*. Doylestown, PA: Heritage Conservancy.

Wisconsin Brownfields Study Group. (2000). *Brownfields study group final report*. Madison, WI: Wisconsin Department of Natural Resources.

Wisconsin DNR. (2002). *Wisconsin green space and public facilities grant program — 2002*. Wisconsin Department of Natural Resources. http://www.dnr.state.wi.us/org/aw/rr/rbrownfields/greenspace_grant.htm

Wong, E. (2000). *Ping Tom memorial park*. ASLA Illinois Chapter. http://www.il-asla.org/Awards/2000winners/Ping.htm

Wood, D., Whitford, J., & Rogers, J. (2000). *At the center of it all: The high-road strategy for Milwaukee's Menomonee Valley*. Milwaukee: Report prepared for the Menomonee Valley Partners by the Center on Wisconsin Strategy.

World Commission on Environment and Development. (1987). *Our common future*. New York: Oxford University Press.

Yount, K. (2003). What are brownfields? Finding a conceptual definition. *Environmental Practice*, 5, 25–33.

Zimmerman, J. (2001). The "nature" of urbanism on the new urbanist frontier: Sustainable development, or defense of the suburban dream? *Urban Geography*, 22(3), 249–267.